RUHLEBEN | A PRISON CAMP SOCIETY

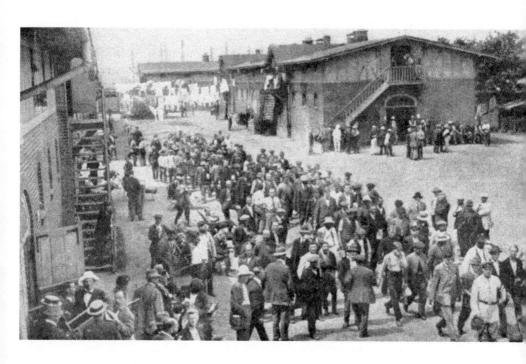

"Die Engländer holen ihr Mittagessen"—*Die Woche*, Berlin, September 11, 1915. Ruhleben prisoners on their way to a mid-day meal.

Ruhleben

A PRISON CAMP SOCIETY

J. DAVIDSON KETCHUM

With a Foreword
and Postscript
by ROBERT B. MacLEOD

University of Toronto Press
London: Oxford University Press
1965

© University of Toronto Press 1965
Toronto Buffalo London
utorontopress.com

Reprinted in paperback 2020

Also published by Oxford University Press 1965

ISBN 978-0-8020-5150-9 (cloth)   ISBN 978-1-4875-2575-0 (paper)

Library and Archives Canada Cataloguing in Publication

Title: Ruhleben : a prison camp society / J. Davidson Ketchum ; with a
  foreword and postscript by Robert B. MacLeod.

Names: Ketchum, John Davidson, 1893–1962, author.

Description: Reprint. Originally published: Toronto: University of Toronto
  Press, 1965. | Includes bibliographical references and index.

Identifiers: Canadiana 20190237465 | ISBN 9781487525750 (softcover)

Subjects: LCSH: Ruhleben (Concentration camp) | LCSH: World War, 1914–
  1918 – Prisoners and prisons, German. | LCSH: Social groups – Case studies.
  | LCSH: Prisoners of war – Psychology. | LCGFT: Case studies.

Classification: LCC D627.G3 K55 2020 | DDC 940.4/72–dc23

University of Toronto Press acknowledges the financial assistance to its publishing program of the Canada Council for the Arts and the Ontario Arts Council,
an agency of the Government of Ontario.

Canada Council   Conseil des Arts
for the Arts   du Canada

ONTARIO ARTS COUNCIL
CONSEIL DES ARTS DE L'ONTARIO
an Ontario government agency
un organisme du gouvernement de l'Ontario

Funded by the   Financé par le
Government   gouvernement
of Canada   du Canada

Canada

To my fellow-prisoners

FOREWORD

Robert B. MacLeod

JOHN DAVIDSON KETCHUM, Professor of Psychology in the University of Toronto, known to hosts of friends and students as "Dave" and to innumerable others as "J.D.K.," died on April 24, 1962. He left the memory of a buoyant personality, a scintillating wit which could mercilessly parody anything sacred, an amazing capacity for translating obfuscated jargon into simple English, a genius for stimulating young minds, a fund of love which could immediately infect anyone who had even remote contact with him. Ketchum was a great teacher and a great human being. Something more of his life and career is given in the biographical tribute by Professor D. O. Hebb, printed below.

Ketchum also left an incomplete manuscript. For more than thirty years, and through a variety of demanding professional activities, he had nursed and coddled the story of his experience as a prisoner in Ruhleben during the World War of 1914–18. Anyone who had heard him talk of Ruhleben at any time looked forward to the book with undiminished anticipation. As a teenager with great musical promise he had gone to Germany to study music. He was caught by the war, was interned for more than four years in the prison camp, and was later returned to his native Canada. His experience had not diminished his passion for music, but it had generated an interest in human problems which led him first to religion and then to psychology. This book was written by Ketchum the reflective social scientist, but one readily recognizes too the humanist, the artist, the man of deep religious concern. Ketchum was never a wild-eyed evangelist, but there was always more than a little of the missionary in him, even in his teaching, and for him the Ruhleben story contained a message to which he hoped his students would hearken.

It was with great humility and a feeling of utter inadequacy that in his last illness I agreed to round out the manuscript for publication. In many hours of conversation over the years I think I had come to understand something of what Ketchum learned from Ruhleben, but I am sure that

I have not been able to interpret it adequately. Since he was a perfectionist in his writing, who could never proceed to the next chapter without having satisfied himself that the previous one was complete, the seventeen chapters of manuscript he left have required almost no editorial modification. They leave us at New Year's of 1918, a date which marked the beginning of a slow transformation of Ruhleben into what Ketchum called "an aging society." Several more chapters were projected, but for these there are only the scantiest of notes. One has the feeling that the author could not quite face the task of bringing the story to an end. Rather than try to re-create the final chapters, which only Ketchum could write, I decided merely to complete the narrative and to systematize a few of the main themes that keep recurring in the book. These I have presented as a Postscript. The narrative is, I hope, faithful to the notes; for the inadequacies of the final interpretation I must bear the responsibility. Ketchum would have done a far better job.

The primary sources of this book are, of course, Ketchum's memories of his four years in Ruhleben, supported by a meticulously kept diary and the somewhat disguised reports included in his letters. He first began to think of his material as a book while he was working on a dissertation at the University of Chicago. The dissertation, as it happened, never materialized, but the notes he was assembling proceeded to expand as he established contact through correspondence with more and more of his former fellow-prisoners who had also kept records. From these, from official sources, and from the growing library of published reminiscences and interpretations, he gradually filled out the picture. In 1933 he mailed a questionnaire to the dwindling number of Ruhlebenites for whom addresses could be found, many of whom were generously co-operative during the succeeding years. Ketchum's last trip to England in the autumn of 1961 was to interview as many as possible of the survivors to make sure that no remaining source of information remained untapped and that no person was quoted in the text even though under a pseudonym without authorization. This final task was halted by his illness. He was deeply concerned that no one be quoted without explicit permission, and after his death his colleague, Professor C. Roger Myers, undertook the tedious task of tracking down individuals who might conceivably have been missed. Because of Ketchum's ingenious system of concealing identities, which we never fully solved, we cannot be absolutely certain that someone has not been overlooked. We can assure readers, however, that every effort was made by Ketchum to preserve the anonymity of the individuals who appear in the text. With the exception of those who are quoted from published sources, the authors of all quotations were given fictitious names or some other disguise. In the very unlikely circumstance that an unwarned reader will recognize himself in print, we humbly ask his forgiveness.

Ketchum himself may be identified as Denton. The part which he played in the life of Ruhleben cannot be deduced from his formal report, and it would be disloyal to him to add items which he did not see fit to include. Those who knew him, however, will realize at once that the modest "Denton" who crops up here and there in the story was more than an inconspicuous observer. He was very much involved in the religious, the musical, the theatrical, and the educational activities of the camp; he enjoyed sports but was not an outstanding athlete; he had little of the drive for power that makes men jostle for position in an administrative hierarchy. This pattern of interests and values undoubtedly influenced his observation and his subsequent account of Ruhleben life. Another observer might have dwelt at greater length on the seamier side of the story, on crime and perversion, on the moral collapse of individuals, on the despair that pushed some of the prisoners to insanity and suicide. There was probably a good deal that Ketchum did not see. Such is my respect for his integrity as a social scientist, however, that I am willing to accept his account as substantially correct. Ruhleben society was certainly not normal in the conventional sense of the word, but it was astonishingly viable. This is what makes it so interesting.

As I have saturated myself with the Ruhleben story, I have come to feel that this book may rank in a modest way as one of the classics of modern social science, a book to which we shall keep returning as we do to *Middletown* or to Malinowski's descriptions of life in the Trobriand Islands. The fact that the setting is World War I gives it a date in history, but it is not "dated" in the other sense of the term; the story of a society that was suddenly forced into being, that grew, matured in its own peculiar way, and then ceased to exist, is a story which in a different setting and with different characters might have been written at many other times and places in history. It just happened that in Ruhleben there was an alert observer who kept careful notes and who was to spend his spare hours during the better part of a lifetime thinking about the meaning of it all. It can be read, of course, as a contribution to the history of World War I, but it should also be read as a basic study of the dynamics of individual and group behaviour.

Ketchum's book naturally invites comparison with the books that have come out of the Nazi concentration camps, but it should not be placed in the same category. Ruhleben was not like a Nazi concentration camp. Life was rough, it is true, but the Germans of 1914–18 were not the

Nazis of 1933–45. The Germans with whom the Ruhlebenites had to deal were stern, often stupid and uncomprehending, but on the whole relatively decent. There were sadists among them, but there was nothing like the organized brutality which in the Nazi camps reduced both the perpetrator and the victim to a level lower than that of the beasts. Social scientists who contemplate the horrors of the Nazi period find themselves concentrating on the lurid extremes, and the best of the books that have emerged tend to be clinical studies of social pathology. From these we can learn a great deal, just as we can gain insight into the normal personality from the study of neurosis and psychosis, but there is always the danger of the psychiatrist's bias. Ruhleben society is still recognizably a society, a strange one it is true, but still not so far removed from the societies we know as to be obscured by a film of unreality. Here are ordinary people, humdrum Britishers of all sorts, suddenly thrown together in a disorderly mass and forced to find in themselves and in their own tradition a basis for individual and group living. There is a great deal in the story to make the sociologist and the psychologist think.

Ithaca, New York
April, 1964

CONTENTS

PREFACE

THIS BOOK might be called an excursion into social psychology through the gates of a prison camp. It traces the social and psychological history of four thousand British men and boys, interned at Ruhleben, near Berlin, Germany, throughout the First World War. I have long wanted to write it, for I was interned among them myself; to recall four such stimulating years could be only a labour of love.

Even if I had never seen Ruhleben, however, I would still have wished to write about it, not as an ex-prisoner but as a social scientist. For this camp provides the fullest picture known to me of the actual growth of a human society, from its origin in a miscellaneous collection of individuals to its culmination in a complex social order. The dynamics of social growth are familiar in theory, and their operation has been studied in social movements, institutions, and small experimental groups. But only Ruhleben, to my knowledge, shows them in action from their very beginnings, over a period of years, and in a large, isolated, and markedly heterogeneous population. That makes its story well worth telling.

The possibility of telling it at this date depends of course on the availability of source material, and material on Ruhleben is fortunately abundant. Many of its inhabitants were highly articulate; they never stopped talking while they were in the camp, and they put on paper, then and later, much that they noticed, felt, and thought. None of it represented systematic social observation—1914 was a little early for such studies to be thought of—and there are certain gaps that cannot now be filled. On the other hand, what the men wrote down at the time, in their own way and for their own purposes, has a freshness and concreteness that research data often lack. The gravest defect of these incidental records is one with which every student of a vanished society must contend: that they come almost entirely from the more literate section of the population. I have done my best to correct the resulting bias, but it could not be completely removed.

A summary of the materials may be helpful here. First comes a mass of contemporary documents: 379 letters and postcards and 10 diaries, all written in Ruhleben; 21 issues of magazines published in the camp, comprising 700 pages of print and drawings; a larger number of mimeographed news sheets and special journals; the minutes, announcements, and reports of camp societies and institutions; and a vast quantity of other material, largely mimeographed—military and civil regulations, programmes, posters, catalogues, notices, songs, poems, and all the miscellaneous paper that a busy society churns out. Some of this I already had, much more was loaned me by fellow-prisoners, and an almost complete collection (apart from personal documents) is in the library of the Harvard University Law School at Cambridge, Massachusetts. The sheer bulk of the Harvard collection is astonishing; when I first saw it in 1933 I exclaimed, "How could we ever have turned out so much?"

After these primary sources come the books and articles dealing with Ruhleben, of which I have found almost fifty, exclusive of contemporary news stories. Added to these is the score of official "White Papers" on Ruhleben published by the British Foreign Office. That so much was written about a single camp was partly because the mass internment of civilians, let alone under such circumstances as obtained at Ruhleben, was without precedent in 1914 and aroused intense indignation in Britain. This was followed by widespread interest in the social developments in the camp, so that Ruhleben received more publicity than any other of the 150 British prison camps in Germany. Interned writers, therefore, found a market waiting for them on their release. Some of the stories were, naturally, sensational or propagandist, but others were excellent and have been freely drawn upon here. A bibliography is given following this Preface.

Finally there are the materials that I myself collected. When I first envisaged this book in 1933 my main object was to secure contemporary diaries and letters. But I also persuaded 116 ex-prisoners to fill out a detailed questionnaire on their camp experience, interviewed a considerable number of others, and received letters and statements from many more. These documents, written fifteen years after release, required cautious treatment, but they provided some statistical data and scores of illustrative quotations.

The book I have drawn from these sources is primarily a social history, concerned with the movements and changes through which four thousand detached individuals became a close-knit society, and with the functioning of that society during its four years of life. As a social psychologist, however, I have also tried to relate the social changes to the state of mind of the prisoners: the emotional turmoil aroused by internment, the mental deprivations that drove them into society-building, and the striking effects of social organization on their conduct and outlook. I have thus attempted to explore, in this miniature setting, the central problem area of social psychology—the complex, reciprocal relationships between the experience and behaviour of the human being and the social milieu in which he finds himself. This is an area in which precise theoretical formulations are lacking, and the analysis is therefore descriptive rather than explanatory. It provides, I believe, some fresh insights into large-scale social dynamics, but the value of these still requires experimental testing.

The background of the study is provided by a running account of the camp itself and what happened in it; most of this has been highly condensed, but I have left a good deal of concrete detail, described some incidents rather fully, and used more quotations from the prisoners than were strictly necessary. Apart from the intrinsic interest of the material, I felt that the social developments would be best understood by those who had some knowledge of Ruhleben as a place and its inhabitants as people.

Except for references to a few contemporary internment camps, all the comparative material I had collected before the Second World War has been omitted. That war produced many hundred additional camps, of widely different kinds, which I could not attempt to survey. A comparative study of prison camp societies should some day be made, for social growth under restricting conditions has considerable theoretical interest. I have yet to read of any developments as complete as those at Ruhleben, but this is not surprising in view of our remarkable population and the unusual freedom we enjoyed.

A word about the use of names. All those who sent me personal documents were promised that their identities would not be disclosed; though some no longer insist on anonymity, it seemed best to treat all alike and assign them pseudonyms or numbers. These are explained on a later page. As for other prisoners, I have used their names wherever it seemed necessary or natural, but have not made any attempt to do justice to all who would deserve mention in an official history. No Ruhleben *Who's Who* was ever published, and I am certainly not competent to compile one. At this date it also seemed most fitting to write chiefly as an outsider, referring to the prisoners as "they" rather than "we," and treating my own letters from the camp no differently from others. My role there was a restricted one, and to write in the first person about events in which I had no share would be misleading.

My experience of Ruhleben was of course indispensable in interpreting and relating the contemporary documents; whether it has also coloured my judgment is not for me to say, but I do not think it has done so. My memories of events were so often contradicted by the records that I was in no danger of mistaking them for facts, and my general view of the camp derives almost exclusively from the materials I have worked with.

Since the book is in no way a personal narrative, a brief account of my own connection with Ruhleben may be permissible here. When war began in August 1914 I was a naive youth of 21, studying piano in Berlin under Josef Lhevinne, and hoping to return to Canada in 1915 as a fully fledged pianist. Two years of political science at the University of Toronto had not made much impression on me, and my chief interest outside music was in the rites of the Anglican church, of which I was a devout adherent.

Like most British subjects in Berlin I was arrested as soon as England declared war on August 4, and then set free to continue my studies until the supposed repatriation of civilians was arranged. I had to report regularly to the police and could not change my lodgings, but otherwise I resumed my usual routine of piano practice and recreation. The diary I kept at this time shows that I fully accepted the German version of the war; Britain's intervention is described as "a terrible mistake." And I had no hesitation in attending concerts, going to service at the English church, and swimming with German acquaintances at a nearby pool. This humdrum existence, however, seemed unbearably tame in comparison with what was happening in Europe, and I secretly resolved to have at least one exciting war experience before I was sent home. By "forgetting" to carry my police pass I succeeded in being re-arrested on August 28, but instead of being quickly released again, like the Berlin friend I was emulating, I remained in custody for the rest of the war.

I was first housed in the Berlin jail or *Stadtvogtei* with a couple of hundred other suspects, among them forty British; then, on September 9, we were all transferred to stables on the suburban racecourse at Ruhleben, where twelve hundred Russian labourers were already concentrated. They were removed in October, but the *Stadtvogtei* party remained, and were joined by the crews of three small English vessels. Finally, on November 6, 1914, a mass internment of male British civilians brought more than four thousand fellow-countrymen to share our stableyard. In this community of exiles I lived until November 24, 1918, when the last of us were shipped back to England under the terms of the armistice.

The intense activity that arose in the camp stimulated me as it did others, and I played games, studied languages, and took some part in musical affairs. But most of my interest was gradually funnelled into religious channels—church services and Y.M.C.A. work—and these pursuits, though deeply absorbing, lay somewhat outside the main stream of camp life. Now that I have learned how much Ruhleben had to offer in science, literature, and the arts, I look back on these religious pre-occupations with a certain regret. It is no use quarrelling with one's past, however, and in spite of my narrow sphere Ruhleben did more for me than I can measure. Merely to be one of that varied and wonderful crowd was an education in itself, and awakened in me a life-long interest in the human being and his potentialities. This drew me after the war into school teaching, then back to the university for a degree in English and History, and finally into a satisfying career in psychology.

The interest which Ruhleben might have for social scientists was first brought home to me in 1932 by Professor Robert E. Park of the University of Chicago, and in the following summer I secured most of my material during a visit to England. I worked at it sporadically for some years, and in 1938 wrote a paper that sketched some of the ideas in the present book. The book itself, however, suffered endless delays, through external interruptions as well as my own inertia. The outbreak of the Second World War, besides taking me for three years into government service, almost discouraged me from further work, for who would ever again read anything about the *first* great war? Not until 1948 was I persuaded that the value of the study was still unimpaired, and then heavy teaching loads and the editing of a psychological journal left me little time. Only now, at the end of my academic career, have I been able to concentrate upon the writing, and so repay in part the great debt I owe to Ruhleben and its indomitable inhabitants. The book is un-doubtedly the better for its long incubation, but many of the friends who provided material for it are now, unhappily, not here to read it.

I have dedicated the book to my fellow-prisoners, in admiring recog-nition of their courage and comradeship during four trying years. They will be my sharpest critics, however, for their memories of Ruhleben are dangerously vivid and detailed. Errors of fact will certainly be found, and for these I apologize in advance, but I do not think they will invali-date the more significant portions of the book. For I have used the history of Ruhleben only as the framework for a reconstruction and interpretation of the social and psychological changes that took place; this is my own contribution and must stand on its merits. Like all interpretations, it goes somewhat beyond the facts, but it is at least consistent with much that we already know about human nature and human society.

The mass internment of aliens in wartime seems today to be taken for granted, but I cannot close this Preface without a protest against the practice and what it signifies. Ruhleben was the first instance of it in modern history, but it was far from being the last; during the Second World War countless thousands were similarly punished for their nationality, race, or religion. Internment, indeed, was the least that many of them suffered, but it typifies a trend that I find intolerable—the increasing use of human beings as mere implements of state policy.

Why were the pioneer internees at Ruhleben condemned without trial to four years' imprisonment? Not for anything they had done or even thought of doing, but as an "act of reprisal" by one government against another. And a few months later, in a counter-reprisal, 20,000 further unfortunates were put behind barbed wire in Britain. Trifling hardships, these, in comparison with the cruelties of the last war and the worse ones now being sedulously prepared. But the same ominous facts underlie them all: the ruthless inhumanity of the modern armed state, and the readiness of millions to acquiesce in it. It is this passive acquiescence that is so frightening, for it means that we are losing the most human of all our capacities—the power of imagination, the ability to feel with and for our fellow-men. If this is the price we must pay for "national security" its cost will be disastrous.

Not much is said in the following pages about the sufferings of the Ruhleben prisoners, but they were genuine and severe. And the worst of them, to some men at least, was the knowledge that their sufferings were utterly useless, accomplishing nothing whatever but the infliction of like sufferings on others in Britain. The statesmen were absorbed in a game and gave no thought to the feelings of the pawns they were playing with. It so happened that these particular internees were able, through their own creative efforts, to find meaning and purpose in their caged existence. The credit for that, however, is theirs alone; the governments that kept them confined so long can claim no part of it.

J. D. K.

Toronto
November, 1961

REFERENCES AND ABBREVIATIONS
IN THE TEXT

A. UNPUBLISHED MATERIAL

1. *Contemporary Diaries and Letters.* The thirteen prisoners whose diaries and letters are most quoted are referred to by pseudonyms. These follow, with a few personal data on each man.

"Abbot"   Age 23 when interned, single. Export trade, Germany, since 1911.
            Interned: Nov. 7, 1914; repatriated: Nov. 22, 1918.
"Burton"   Age 34, married. Marine engineer, ship interned at Hamburg.
            Interned: Nov. 6, 1914; repatriated: Nov. 22, 1918.
"Chapman"   Age 34, married. Mining engineer, Canadian. Visiting relatives.
            Interned: Mar. 13, 1915; repatriated: Nov. 22, 1918.
"Denton"   (The author). Age 21, single. Piano student in Berlin.
            Interned: Sept. 9, 1914; repatriated: Nov. 24, 1918.
"Ewing"   Age 20, single. Undergraduate, Bristol (?). Walking tour.
            Interned: Nov. 6, 1914; repatriated: Nov. 24, 1918.
"Farwell"   Age 27, single. Graduate student, Berlin University.
            Interned: Nov. 6, 1914; repatriated: Nov. 24, 1918.
"Graham"   Age 42, married. Manager, German branch of British firm.
            Interned: Nov. 6, 1914; repatriated (over 45) Jan. 2, 1918.
"Henley"   Age 38, married. Engineer, German staff of British firm.
            Interned: Nov. 7, 1914; sent to Holland (invalid): Apr. 25, 1918.
"Irwin"   Age 24, single. Electrical engineer, employed in Germany.
            Interned: Nov. 1914; repatriated: Nov. 1918.
"Jarvis"   Age 20 (?), single. Student (engineering?).
            Interned: Nov. 28, 1914; repatriated: Nov. 24, 1918.
"Kendall"   Age 30, single. Railway engineer. On holiday, Black Forest.
            Interned: Nov. 28, 1914; repatriated: Nov. 22, 1918.
"Leslie"   Age 20, single. Undergraduate, Oxford. Travelling in Germany.
            Interned: Nov. 1914 (?); repatriated; Nov. 24, 1918 (?)
            (The letters here attributed to "Leslie" were published anonymously in *In Ruhleben*, ed. D. Sladen.) See Bibliography, item 43.
"Merton"   Age 28, single. Metal merchant. Visiting friends on holiday.
            Interned: Nov. 28, 1914; repatriated, Nov. 24, 1918.

2. *Retrospective Material.* The 152 prisoners with whom I was in touch in 1933 or later are referred to by numbers. These are used as follows:

L 65   refers to a letter from Informant 65.
M 65   refers to material supplied by him in writing or interview.
Q 65   refers to material from his completed questionnaire.

3. *Collections, Minutes, etc.*

H   refers to material in the Ruhleben Collection in the library of Harvard University Law School, Cambridge, Mass.
S   refers to material in the collection of William Stern, Esq.
CC refers to the "Reports of Business Conducted by the Captains' Committee," first issued at Ruhleben in March, 1916.

Minutes of societies and circles are not abbreviated.

B. PUBLISHED MATERIAL

1. *Contemporary Camp Publications*

IRC   refers to *In Ruhleben Camp* (10 issues, June to December, 1915).
RCM   refers to *The Ruhleben Camp Magazine* (6 issues, March 1916 to June 1917).
RBE   refers to *The Ruhleben Bye-Election*, published July 1915.
PP   refers to *Prisoners' Pie*, published January 1916.

Other camp publications, printed and mimeographed, are not abbreviated.

2. *Later Publications.* Books and articles dealing with Ruhleben, and with certain other camps, are listed in the List of References and referred to in the text by number and page (in brackets).

Other works referred to are identified in footnotes.

C. CAMP SOCIETIES AND SERVICES

A.S.U.   refers to the Arts and Science Union.
M.E.A.   refers to the Marine Engineers' Association (Ruhleben Branch).
R.D.S.   refers to the Ruhleben Dramatic Society.
R.X.D.   refers to the Ruhleben Express Delivery, an intra-camp postal service.

BOOKS AND ARTICLES DEALING
WITH RUHLEBEN

1. An interesting reminiscence (lathe made of scrap in Ruhleben). *Our Journal* (Mather & Platt, Ltd.), vol. 3, no. 4, October, 1922. (E. W. Scholis)
2. Art at Ruhleben. *Musical Standard*, Oct. 14, 1916, pp. 275–276, and Oct. 21, 1916, pp. 293–294. (Based on material sent by Leigh Henry)
3. Brooks, Cyrus Harry. Inside the wire. (Newspaper clipping in possession of Mr. W. Eric Swale; paper unidentifiable, date January 18, 19 . .)
4. Bury, Rt. Rev. Herbert. Concerning prisoners of war. *Nineteenth Century*, April, 1916, pp. 800–812.
5. Bury, Rt. Rev. Herbert. *Here and there in the war area.* London: A. R. Mowbray & Co., 1916.
6. Bury, Rt. Rev. Herbert. *My visit to Ruhleben.* London: A. R. Mowbray & Co., 1917.
7. Cimino, Hugh. *Behind the prison bars in Germany.* London: George Newnes, Ltd., 1915.
8. Cohen, Israel. *The Ruhleben prison camp.* London: Methuen & Co., Ltd., 1917.
9. Cohen–Portheim, Paul. *Time stood still: my internment in England, 1914–1918.* N.Y.: E. P. Dutton & Co. Inc., 1932.
10. Davies, Alfred T. *Student Captives*, No. II (pamphlet). London: British Prisoners of War Book Scheme (educational), no date (1917?).
11. Ellison, Wallace. Escaped! *Blackwood's Magazine*, May-September, 1918.
12. Ellison, Wallace. *Escapes and Adventures.*
13. Farmer, Eric. The psychology of an internment camp. *Quarterly Review*, April, 1919, pp. 396–408.
14. Flint, E. J. Ruhleben: a civilian prison in Germany. *Canadian Magazine*, July, 1916, pp. 235–237.
15. Fuchs, Carl. *Erinnerungen eines Offenbacher Cellisten.* Druckerei der Anstalt Bethel bei Bielefeld, Germany, 1933 (?)
16. Gerard, Ambassador James W. *My four years in Germany.* New York: George H. Doran & Co., 1917.
17. Govett, Tom. Social, mental and moral effects of internment. *Chambers' Journal*, July, 1919, pp. 235–237.
18. Gribble, Francis. Germany seen from an internment camp. *Nineteenth Century*, Dec., 1915, pp. 1272–1286.

19. Gribble, Francis. Leaves from a Ruhleben note-book. *Fortnightly Review*, Jan., 1916, pp. 60–70.
20. Gribble, Francis. The treatment of prisoners in Germany. *Nineteenth Century*, July, 1916, pp. 73–87.
21. Gribble, Francis. The medical history of Ruhleben. *Edinburgh Review*, April, 1919, pp. 290–309.
22. Gribble, Francis. *Seen in passing*. London: Ernest Benn, Ltd., 1929.
23. Hoffmann, Conrad. *The prison camps of Germany*. New York: Association Press, 1920.
24. Hopford, Wim. Twice interned. *Cornhill Magazine*, Feb., 1919, pp. 211–224.
25. Hughes, A. M. D. Ruhleben. *Cornhill Magazine*, Nov., 1915, pp. 662–672.
26. *In the hands of the Huns: an account of 15 months' imprisonment at Ruhleben* [anon.]. London: Simpkin, Marshall, Hamilton, Kent & Co., 1915.
27. Jungmann, Nico. My life at Ruhleben. *International Studio*, 1918, vol. 64, pp. 90–99.
28. Ketchum, J. D. Social behaviour during four years' internment. *Civil Service News* (Ottawa, Can.), 1938, vol. 16, pp. 225–233.
29. Legge, Robin. Musicians at Ruhleben. *Musical Opinion*, Jan. 1916, p. 252. (Based on article by Legge in "recent issue" of the *Daily Telegraph*)
30. Mackness, G. M. Religion at Ruhleben. *Vernon Baptist Chapel Magazine*, June, 1918.
31. Mahoney, H. C. *Sixteen months in four German prisons*. London: Sampson, Low, Marston & Co., Ltd., 1917.
32. Mahoney, H. C. *Interned in Germany*. New York: Robert M. McBride & Co., 1918.
33. McCarthy, D. J. *The prisoner of war in Germany*. New York: Moffatt, Yard & Co., 1918.
34. McLaren, A. D. Berlin and Ruhleben during war. *Contemporary Review*, Feb., 1916, pp. 214–222.
35. McLaren, A. D. *Germanism from within*. London.
36. Michelson, Peter. In Ruhleben prison camp. *Century Magazine*, July 1917, pp. 364–375.
37. Molony, W. O'Sullivan. *Prisoners and Captives*. London: Macmillan & Co., 1933.
37a. Philip, Terence. Poems written at Ruhleben. London: Grant Richards Ltd., 1920.
38. Powell, Joseph, and Gribble, Francis. *The history of Ruhleben*. London: Collins Sons & Co., 1919.
39. Pyke, Ernest L. *Desperate Germany*. London: Hodder & Stoughton, 1918.
40. Pyke, Geoffrey. *To Ruhleben and back*. Boston: Houghton, Mifflin Co., 1916.
41. Ruhleben Camp School. *The Times Educational Supplement*, July 24, 1919, p. 376.

42. Ruhleben Prisoners Release Committee. *The Ruhleben Prisoners: the case for their release* (pamphlet). London: Pen Corner House, Kingsway, 1917.

43. Sladen, Douglas (Ed.). *In Ruhleben: letters from a prisoner to his mother.* London: Hurst & Blackett, Ltd., 1917.

44. Study in Internment. *The Times Educational Supplement,* Nov. 23, 1916, p. 217.

45. Taylor, Alonzo E. *Report by Dr. A. E. Taylor on the conditions of diet and nutrition in the internment camp at Ruhleben.* H.M. Stationery Office, Harrison & Sons, London, 1916.

46. Vischer, Dr. A. L. *Die Stacheldraht-Krankheit: Beiträge zur Psychologie des Kriegsgefangenen.* Zürich: Rascher & Cie, 1918.

47. Welland, Archibald. Impressionism at Ruhleben. *English Review,* Jan., 1919, pp. 19–25.

48. Williams, Rev. H. M. Prison Camps in Germany. *Church Times,* June 27, 1919.

49. Willmot, F. Handicrafts Department of the Camp School. In *Catalogue of Exhibits,* Ruhleben Exhibition, Central Hall, Westminster, 1919.

PART I | Introduction

INTRODUCTION

THIS IS THE story of four thousand British men and boys in a First World War internment camp—of their four years' life together, and of the strange city they built in the heart of wartime Germany. All were civilians, caught in enemy territory by the outbreak of the war, and interned for its duration on the Ruhleben racecourse, just outside Berlin. The many hardships they suffered were borne stoutly and cheerfully, but it is not for its hardships that Ruhleben is remembered today. It is rather for the unique social world that the men created for themselves—a world so complete and many-sided that its existence in a prison camp is almost unbelievable.

For this social achievement two factors were mainly responsible: the extraordinary nature of Ruhleben's population, and the challenging conditions of their internment. The prisoners were almost a cross-section of British society, from the manor house to the slum; scarcely a trade or profession was unrepresented. All were jammed together in a small stableyard—company directors and seamen, concert musicians and factory workers, science professors and jockeys. Few had ever met previously; their only common bond was their British citizenship. The Germans, for their part, merely penned them up and left them to their own resources; no work was required of them, no recreation provided, no social structure imposed. As long as order was maintained they were free to pass the time as they wished, mingle together as they chose, and work out, if they could, a collective way of life that would make four years' confinement bearable. The whole picture suggests an elaborate social experiment—callous, but undeniably intriguing. How it turned out is the subject of this book.

What were four thousand Britishers doing in Germany when their country declared war? The answer—that none of them had the faintest idea of what was coming—is almost incomprehensible today. After a quarter of a century of war and preparation for it, we can hardly imagine a time when people travelled all over Europe without passports, and when the very thought of war between civilized nations seemed absurd.

Yet that was the situation in 1914, and particularly among the English. Except for the long struggle in South Africa and other colonial affrays, Britain had been at peace for almost sixty years, and peace had brought her unexampled wealth. France and Germany, too, had kept the peace since 1870, and were similarly prospering. It seemed obvious that a new epoch had begun, that industry and commerce, rather than conquest, were now the road to national greatness. And the view had learned support; in 1910 the economist Norman Angell had demonstrated, in *The Great Illusion*, that war could no longer be profitable even to the victor. His arguments seemed unanswerable and the enormous sales of his book, in eleven different languages, proved that the world was finally ready for them. No nation in its senses would start another war.

Other ideas were certainly held in military and political circles, but hardly a whisper of them reached the general public. The few alarmists in Britain were dismissed as crack-pots; the only sources of public anxiety in 1914 were the mad antics of the suffragettes and the possibility of a rising in Ulster against Irish Home Rule. As that sun-filled summer began, business had never been better, steamships were booked to capacity, and a record number of tourists were confidently planning to visit Bavaria, the Black Forest, and other German resorts.

And on June 27, with the same sense of perfect security, I returned from a visit in England to continue my musical studies in Berlin. Next evening the German papers headlined the assassination of the Austrian Crown Prince in Sarajevo, but neither this nor Austria's ultimatum to Serbia on July 23 disturbed me in the least. All my English friends in Berlin were unanimous in their views: these Balkan flare-ups were chronic, the Serbs would give in, everything would blow over. Even when ominous rumblings came from Russia we felt only pleasurable excitement; perhaps there would really *be* a war, and we would have ring-side seats. No doubt it would be localized, but if Russia came in, Germany might too, and wouldn't that be something to see! Whatever happened, everyone knew that England could not possibly be involved; this was one quarrel in which she had no interest whatever.

We were young, and we were naive, but not more so than many of our elders. Israel Cohen, a respected journalist, had for three years represented several London papers in Berlin; his days were spent in studying the German press, listening to speeches in the Reichstag, and gossiping with fellow-journalists. Although Austria declared war on Serbia on July 28, all these newsmen were convinced that the conflict would be brief and local, and next day Cohen left for a long-planned vacation near Dresden. He ended up in Ruhleben, and wrote one of the best books on the camp. Even more remarkable, on Friday, July 31, a sizable party of British tourists, including several honeymoon couples, actually arrived in Germany to begin their holidays.

A few panicky souls, it is true, were heading for home; on the same Friday evening a party of us from the English church went to the Berlin station to see some acquaintances off. Their train, as it turned out, was the last to run; by next morning Germany was mobilized and all remaining foreigners were trapped. The army took over the railways, and civilians were left with only a handful of local trains. The weekend that followed was exciting, and I and my friends, still confident of British neutrality, cheered with the crowds in *Unter den Linden.* Then on Tuesday, August 4, the incredible blow fell. England declared war on Germany, and British subjects in Germany became "enemy aliens." All British diplomatic representatives left the country, and the United States Embassy took over protection of British nationals.

How many there were can only be guessed at; 5,500 males of military age were at some time in Ruhleben, and women and children would bring the total to at least 7,000. Residents of Germany, permanent and temporary, were the largest group; they included businessmen of all categories, from proprietors to agents, clerks, and foreign correspondents; professors and teachers of English; students at German universities, technical schools and musical academies; engineers in the great German electrical, dyeing, and mining industries; skilled workers and apprentices in many trades; golf and football professionals (sport was booming in Germany); most of the leading jockeys and trainers; and an assortment of music-hall artists, circus performers, hairdressers, waiters, valets, coachmen, grooms, stablehands, race-track touts, and those resourceful vagabonds known as "continental stiffs."

Among the long-term residents were a surprising number who were British in only a technical sense. German citizenship was easy to lose and hard to acquire; children born to German parents temporarily in England or the colonies were British subjects until they were naturalized, and so were the German-born children of British citizens who had married and settled in Germany. Naturalization was a complicated process, and there was little inclination to seek it, for foreign nationals were exempt from three years of military service. Many of these "British" had never spoken English in their lives and were purely German in outlook and sentiment; some did not realize their status until they were herded into Ruhleben in November 1914. The more influential quickly gained their release, but six or seven hundred were still there in January 1915, and a dwindling number remained until the end of the war.

In sharp contrast to the residents of Germany were the officers and crews of merchant vessels, over twelve hundred of whom were caught in Hamburg, Bremen, and other German ports. There was no ambiguity about their status; they were British to the core, and few of them knew a word of German. The large number was partly due to the fact that no ships were allowed to leave German harbours after July 31, and it was swelled during the war by the crews of further vessels, captured by raiders and submarines.

Finally there were the hundreds of visitors who were on walking tours, mountain-climbing, attending music festivals, "taking the cure" at German spas, or simply holidaying and sight-seeing. The bulk were professional people—dons and undergraduates, public school masters and boys, scientists, musicians, and so on—but they also included many in business and other occupations. And a good number of German settlers in Canada and South Africa had chosen this summer to revisit their homeland; they too found their holiday a protracted one.

Britain's declaration of war was a stunning surprise to most Germans as well as British, and no plans had been made to deal with the horde of enemy aliens. Public bitterness against "perfidious Albion" resulted in some rough handling of individuals, especially during the hysterical spy-hunts that marked the first week of war. The government, however, quickly suppressed any violence, chiefly to avoid antagonizing the United States. For several thousand Americans were also stranded in Germany, without transportation and almost without funds, since no foreign cheques were being cashed. They too spoke English and were sometimes mistaken for British; even the Ambassador, James W. Gerard, was spat upon in the street. The Americans finally got away on special trains at the end of August, but by that time feelings were more subdued and the British could move about without fear of molestation.

The official attitude was that Germany had no quarrel with civilians; they would presumably be shipped home, but not until mobilization was complete. Meanwhile the British were variously dealt with, depending on local conditions and sentiments. Women and children suffered little inconvenience, and those who wished to return to England were ultimately able to do so by way of neutral Holland. A good many residents, however, preferred to remain, some until the end of the war. The harshest treatment was meted out to the seafaring men; in the early months of the war they were gradually concentrated on abandoned hulks in the Hamburg harbour, and kept there under miserable conditions until November. Of the remainder, various "suspects" were arrested the day after war broke out and never set free again; most others, after arrest and investigation, were released under police supervision; a few were left undisturbed save for a courteous visit from a police inspector. The majority seem to have passed August, September, and October in relative freedom—a freedom qualified by regular reporting to the police, punctuated by occasional unpleasantness with officious citizens, and sustained by the slowly fading hope that some day, somehow, they would get away.

Hope gave place to alarm at the end of October, when an inspired press campaign demanded retaliation for the alleged internment of German civilians in England. It is true that two shiploads of military reservists had been prevented from sailing for Germany at the outbreak of war, and that increasing numbers of penniless Germans, thrown out of their jobs for "patriotic" reasons, were being placed in improvised camps. But no general internment took place in Britain until May 13, 1915, after the sinking of the *Lusitania* had inflamed public opinion. The German authorities, however, were in bellicose mood, and on October 31 an ultimatum to Britain was published, stating that unless all German civilians were released by November 5 every Englishman in Germany would be interned.

The ultimatum was ignored, the orders went forth, and on November 6 every male British subject between the ages of 17 and 55 was placed under arrest. The only exceptions were men from dominions and colonies where no Germans were yet interned; they were not gathered in until January 1915. As all still at liberty were under police supervision, the round-up took place promptly and smoothly. In police vans, by taxi, and on foot, the *Engländer* were collected and lodged in the nearest jails; from these they were transferred in batches to the place assigned to them —a deserted race-track on the western outskirts of Berlin. There, in the stables once tenanted by racehorses, most of them were kept for the next four years.

PART II | Crisis and Solidarity

1

IT IS LATE AFTERNOON on Friday, November 6, 1914. Over the North German plain heavy clouds have lain all day. The stripped fields below them, settling down for the winter, stretch in sober browns and greys as far as the eye can see. The war, too, is settling down. The massed German attacks on Ypres that followed the "race to the sea" are in their final phase; the rest of the western front is already locked in the stalemate of the trenches. The Russian armies, swept out of East Prussia and Galicia, have withdrawn behind the Vistula, and the German and Austrian commanders, abandoning their thrust towards Warsaw, have broken off the battle. Hopes of a German victory before Christmas have vanished, and the early enthusiasm has changed into grim resolution.

On the racecourse at Ruhleben twilight is falling. There is no wind, and the air is misty and raw. The three large grandstands stare vacantly across a deserted track, for there has been no racing since the Kaiser's armies marched. The public enclosures have been surrounded with high barbed wire, and grey-coated sentries, pacing methodically, only emphasize their emptiness. In the stableyard, however, there is an air of expectation. German soldiers move briskly between the main gates and the weighing-office, now a guardroom; two officers are waiting near the administration building, and in the centre of the open square an excited *Feldwebel* is waving his arms at a slow-witted private.

In the shadows of the long stables stand little groups of men, dressed in shabby civilian clothes, their eyes turned towards the closed gates and the sentry who guards them. Others are moving aimlessly about the compound, glancing often in the same direction. There is some desultory talking in low voices, and the language is English. For about eighty British are already housed in the Ruhleben stables, half of them "suspects" transferred here from Berlin on September 9, the remainder the crews of three small vessels, brought in on October 6. An official German statement, issued two days ago, read: "British subjects in Germany, with very few exceptions, are being treated with every politeness and consideration, and enjoy comparatively great freedom."[1] These men are presumably among the "exceptions." And they are not the only ones; the rat-ridden hulks at Hamburg have been crammed with seafarers since mid-October, and all over the Reich there are men who have spent weeks and months in prison. In addition to the British, some sixty Russian, French, and Belgian civilians have also been at Ruhleben since September.

At five o'clock a report from outside the main entrance sends a stir through the compound. The gates are thrown open, the guards stand back with their rifles ready, and in comes the head of a long column of men. They walk wearily in uneven fours, and their harmless appearance makes the bristling demeanour of their police escorts slightly ludicrous. All are in civilian dress—business suits and overcoats for the most part, with a sprinkling of work clothes and sweaters. Their arms are laden with bags and parcels, and their felt hats look pathetically out of place between the rows of spiked helmets. Several hundred of these incongruous war-prisoners straggle in, the gates are shut behind them, and harsh voices order them to line up, stand still, and not to talk. They are little inclined to conversation; dropping their heavy luggage they stand meekly in two long lines. The German commandant, attended by a group of officers, approaches; he makes a short speech to which the prisoners listen gravely, though many of them cannot understand German. Then the soldiers burst into activity, searching luggage, asking questions, and entering names, ages, and occupations on long lists. Some of the shadowy figures in the background take the opportunity to draw nearer and peer at their new companions. It is too dark for easy recognition, but here and there a man picks out an old acquaintance from Berlin. In any case, the large contingent tells its own tale. The threatened mass internment of British has begun, and Ruhleben is entering on a new phase of its history.

The proceedings at the gate are long drawn out, and there is much counting and re-counting. But at last the Berlin police are given receipts for so many "head" of English and the prisoners, now in military hands, pick up their luggage and are marched off towards the stables. A little later another convoy arrives to be given the same treatment. The "installation" of the British is without ceremony. As the head of each column enters the long, dimly lit stable corridor, a German sergeant, shouting "The first six in here!" thrusts open the sliding door of a horse-box and six bewildered men shuffle in. One after another the 27 boxes are filled and 200 left-overs are turned into the haylofts above. From five o'clock

1. *Berliner Tageblatt,* morning edition, Nov. 4, 1914.

until after midnight the influx continues, men pouring in at the gates and being herded in columns into the stables. There they find, many of them, only a thin layer of straw on the cement and one horse-blanket each; some of the boxes are still littered with manure. Other men have straw-sacks to lie on, and a few of the luckiest iron military bunks. The early detachments are given a tin bowl of cocoa and a piece of blood sausage —the first meal of the day for many; later arrivals get nothing. There is no attempt to sort the crowds out, and wealthy businessmen, invalids from the spas, sailors, workmen, and students are thrown indiscriminately together.

The scene that night is vividly recalled by all who were present. Here and there among the three hundred in each stable someone could be heard bitterly cursing the Germans; others tried to treat the whole affair as a ridiculous practical joke. Most of the men, however, were quiet and apprehensive. All were tired, hungry, and dazed by their sudden arrest and the strangeness of their surroundings; a few were close to tears. Up and down the corridors ranged the three German guards assigned to each building, noisily demanding silence, suspiciously questioning any-one who left his place, angrily repeating that there was no more straw, no straw-sacks, blankets, towels, or bowls. The night was chilly, the stables unheated, but the military order was *"Schlafen gehen!"* and the men did their best to follow it. It was one in the morning, however, before the last seaman from Hamburg found a corner to stretch out in, and few prisoners slept more than fitfully on their cold, hard beds. Then, at half past six, the guards tramped again through the stables bellowing *"Aufstehen!"* and the weary men opened their eyes on the strange world in which they were to spend the next four years.

The suburb called Ruhleben ("peaceful life") lies about two miles west of the boundaries of Berlin as they were in 1914, and a mile east of the important industrial suburb of Spandau. The racecourse, now demolished,[2] was situated on low, flat land reclaimed from the marshes of the Spree; the canalized river ran just north of it. In summer, when Berlin crowds flocked to bet on the trotting races, the site was not un-attractive, but in winter it was damp, dreary, and windswept. The soil was a loose, dirty sand; in the public enclosures it was covered with lawns and shrubberies, but in the stableyard every shower turned it into a sea of mud, dotted with pools and lakes. When these dried up, any gust of wind raised clouds of choking dust.

A plan of Ruhleben as it was in 1915 will be found in Figure 1. Only the cross-hatched buildings existed when the prisoners arrived; Barracks

2. It was torn down in 1958 to provide space for a new Berlin sewage plant.

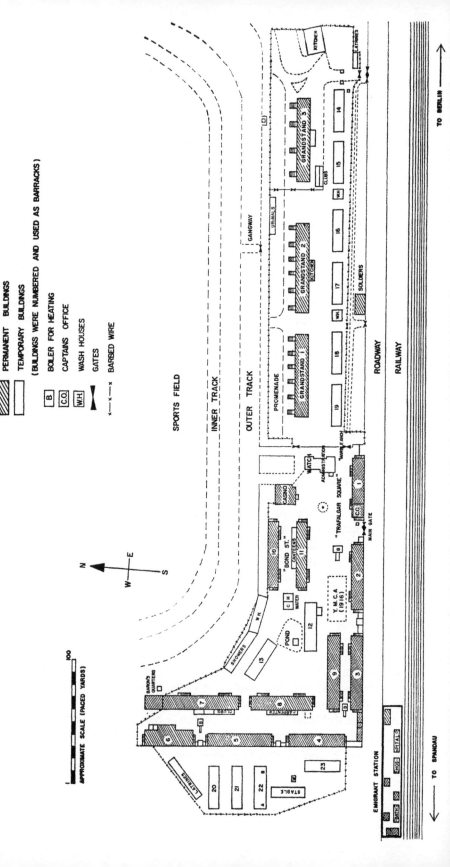

12 to 23 were army huts, added in 1915 to relieve the congestion. As will be seen, the property stretched along a roadway, parallel to a railway embankment carrying the main lines from Berlin. On the opposite side of the race-track (not shown in the plan) were some smaller stands for spectators, and then the river. Part of the centre of the race-track was rented as a sports field for the camp in 1915; until then the prisoners were confined to the areas shown, the stableyard and the adjoining grandstand area. There was a large restaurant under the second grandstand, and an ornate Tea House at the east end; from their kitchens, now equipped with huge soup-boilers, the men fetched their meals. The total area available to them was just under ten acres, inclusive of buildings; actually it was considerably less, since the administration building, the "casino" or staff restaurant, and much of the space under the grandstands were occupied by the military, and the use of the lawns behind the grandstands was for some months forbidden.

Into these ten acres were poured in November 1914 some 4,000 men and boys; by the following March they numbered 4,400. Most of them were packed into the eleven stables, but the Tea House, cleared of tables and chairs, housed about 100 throughout the internment, and 300 more slept for a fortnight on the floor of the main restaurant. Ten of the stables were substantial buildings of brick and stucco, about 160 feet long by 30 feet wide; No. 6, later occupied by the orthodox Jews, was smaller, older, and constructed of wood. All became "barracks"[3] on November 6, 1914, and it was imprudent to call them stables within the hearing of the military. Through each ran a wide cement corridor, on which opened the 27 horse-boxes and two stableboys' rooms, now used by the guards. The six prisoners allotted to each box had to fit themselves and all their belongings into a space 10 feet square, with cement floor, whitewashed walls, and one small window close to the high ceiling. The only equipment at first was an earthenware manger fixed in one corner and a layer of straw on the floor; straw-sacks, military bunks, small tables, stools, and floor boards were gradually issued. There was never any space in which to hang or store clothing, and the men had to live permanently in their suitcases. The inner walls of the boxes ended three feet below the ceiling; they were thus always open to the noise and draughts of the corridor.

The upper storeys of the stables were partitioned into two haylofts. These were reached by outside stairways—so steep that there were many falls in snowy weather, two of them fatal. In the lofts it was always dark, for the windows were small, low, and overhung by deep eaves. Heavy

3. Following German rather than British usage, the prisoners used "barrack," not "barracks," as the singular form.

beams and struts cut the space into sections that the seamen called "bays," and only in the centre was there height enough to stand upright. Here the men slept in one row along each wall and a double row down the middle, with only two narrow gangways; there was not an inch of free space.

The congestion in the stables was almost intolerable. It was bad enough in the boxes, where six men lived, ate, dressed, and slept amid constant jostling for elbow-room. But in each of the lofts a hundred men lay side by side, their luggage piled on their feet or above their heads, their bodies touching at every movement. H. C. Mahoney arrived in Ruhleben on November 13; his description, in *Interned in Germany*, of his introduction to Barrack 5's loft is scarcely overdrawn:

> We wound our way up a creaking, ramshackle staircase which threatened to give way under our weight. We blundered through a narrow door and then pulled up dead. The interior was as black and forbidding as a coal-hole. It was some minutes before our eyes grew accustomed to the darkness, and then we descried upon the floor a seething, misshapen mass of humanity, tumbling and jostling restlessly for elbow-room in which to settle down. (P. 23)

When Geoffrey Pyke was turned into another loft late in January 1915 conditions were no better:

> We were so closely packed that it was impossible to put one's arms above one's head. I could not sleep. It was intensely cold. All night long the doors at the end banged with people going out to the latrines. So close were we all that there was hardly any gangway, and curse and prayer accompanied any riser making his way to the door. "Damn your bloody soul, why the hell can't you look where you're going?" or, "Oh, for God's sake don't knock all my rugs off!" (Pp. 123 ff., condensed)

Henley, a civil engineer, was one of 280 men quartered in the grand-stand restaurant until the last horses were removed from Stable 7. His diary for November 12 reads:

> Our chief inconvenience is lack of space. We have only one bed and one chair. Daytime we roll our mattress up and put the chair in the space thus gained. No hooks, shelves, boxes. My portmanteau is a mix-up of soap, sugar, cheese, bread, pots, and linen. Our soup bowls are kept in bed and under the pillow at night.

The crowding was somewhat relieved later, but Ruhleben was still a congested community, and the impossibility of ever being alone was for some men a continuous trial.

The water supply for the three hundred men in each stable consisted of two taps in the ground floor corridor. Here the prisoners had to line up between six and seven on cold mornings to fill their soup-bowls for a hasty wash, line up again to rinse them before fetching their coffee, again to wash them out, and so .on through the day. The water was icy cold, and it.fell three feet into a shallow gutter, soaking the legs of all who approached it and keeping the corridor permanently wet. This, with the ceaseless drip of the taps all night, was one of the minor discomforts of stable life. Those who insisted on bathing poured bowls of water over themselves in the passage; from December onwards each barrack got a fortnightly warm shower at the Emigrant Control Station by the railway.

Horses do not read or write, and the Ruhleben stables had little lighting. Two electric bulbs in the downstairs corridor—nothing at all in the boxes—and two in each loft were all the men had to see by, and all winter it was pitch dark when they were roused in the morning and again from mid-afternoon on. Even in full daylight the boxes were far from bright, while the lofts were always too dark for reading except immediately against a window. The twilight in which much of life had to be lived was so depressing in itself, and such a hindrance to any effort to pass the time constructively, that a real "light-hunger" resulted. Every evening a score of men crowded under each lamp in the corridors, huddled together on stools and suitcases, poring over books, playing checkers, mending their clothes, or trying to write home. Every inch on which a beam fell was occupied in spite of the freezing draughts that swept the passage, and exasperated groans arose as someone's shadow fell for the twentieth time across the page. Some gave up the struggle and sought their beds in the darkness, but others could be seen, even on the coldest nights, reading under the arc lamps that always burned in the compound.

The situation in the stables would have been more bearable had there been any other shelter during the day, but for the first month there was nothing but the open air. In reasonably dry weather the men walked up and down continually, especially on the well-drained "enclosure" in front of the grandstands—soon dubbed the *Promenade des Anglais*. Walking kept them warm and provided exercise; the scenery, however, was hardly inspiring. On the south the horizon was bounded by the railway embankment with its endless troop trains, on the north by three small grandstands across the race-track. To the northwest and west the sky was broken by a great arc of smoking chimneys above the munitions works at Spandau. Only to the east, beyond the Tea House, was there any relief from drabness—a ridge and a patch of woodland, always alluring to those who could gaze but not enter. It rained a great deal in the late fall of 1914, and in wet weather no one went out unnecessarily, for the stableyard reverted to its origins and became a semi-liquid morass. Three times a day, however, it had to be waded through on the long trek to the kitchens, and more often than this to reach the two crude latrines. There was of course no way of drying anything, and the men's clothes and footwear were chronically damp.

To call the latrines unsatisfactory is too mild; they were inadequate in size, hopelessly inefficient in operation, and so far from some barracks as to make night visits an exploit for heroes. They were early condemned by the American Ambassador as "a danger not only to the camp but to Berlin" (Gerard, p. 5), and new ones were finally opened in June 1915. The difficulties of drainage on the low ground were insuperable, however, and the offensive odours were a permanent feature of camp life.

"The cold was perhaps the worst of our discomforts," said Gribble in *Seen in Passing*; "it is certainly the one which I find it hardest to forget" (p. 293). And several of those who answered the 1933 questionnaire replied to the query, "What was the greatest single hardship you had to endure at Ruhleben?" with the one word, "Cold." No heating whatever was provided until November 18—a week later in some barracks—and then it was an improvised system of pipes, connected to a traction engine which could raise steam for only a few hours a day on the fuel provided. Often coal failed to arrive, and the boiler was shut down for a week at a time. The climate on the North German plain is severe, and most of the landsmen had only city clothes. Until sweaters and other heavy garments could be secured from England or Germany they were perpetually cold, in or out of doors.

There was of course no hot water for washing or shaving, let alone for brewing a cup of tea. But ingenious prisoners soon learned to warm a cupful of water by letting steam from the exhaust valves of the heating system run through it. It took time, but it worked. A very early pencil notice shows an engineer's concern about the health of his fellows: "DON'T DRINK IT! Exhaust water from steam heating system is not fit to drink. Don't use it for making tea, coffee or cocoa" (S). In cold weather the end boxes were made almost uninhabitable by condensing steam from the valves; a typical complaint from Kendall's diary reads: "Steam in box appalling. Walls streaming with moisture."

Two extracts from Henley's diary will make the picture more concrete:

Nov. 19. Moved from grandstand to stable number seven. O Lord, what a mess and rough and tumble. Frost set in to make matters worse. We had a terrible scrap for places and got in the loft. Dark and damp, no lighting or heating. A miserable day and night. All papers stopped today.

Nov. 25. At last we have got heating; that makes 19 days and 18 nights without heating, all of which have been raining, stormy, wet, damp or frosty. This diary for the past 18 days has been so scanty because I simply couldn't keep my hands warm enough to write more than a few words at once. Still our position is both degrading and demoralizing. We are badly housed and badly fed, and I don't know how those without money keep body and soul together. It costs me about two marks per day to live decently, including tobacco. Our crowd, about three hundred, have been treated worse than anyone. First we were housed in the grandstand—damp, lofty, cold, all on the floor, and some of us lay seven nights on the stone floor without boards, most had straw-sacks but some had loose straw. In Barrack 7 we were up to today without heating, and even now we have no bedsteads as in other barracks, and we are more crowded.

All these hardships, and particularly the cold, could have been more easily borne if the men had been decently fed, but the food was as wretched as the accommodation. Catering was in the hands of a German named Griese, who had contracted to feed the prisoners for 66 pfennigs each per day. The allowance was meagre at best, and Griese's profiteering efforts did not help matters. The military authorities passed the daily bill of fare in advance but took no steps to discover whether it was adhered to, and many of the carcases displayed outside the kitchens during the day were calmly resold by the contractor and removed at night. Thus the dinner, "Beef, cabbage, and potatoes"—to quote the Berlin press—took form as a watery soup, with a few potatoes but hardly a trace of meat in it, while "Mutton and carrots, boiled together" appeared as an almost identical solution. Breakfast consisted of a bowl of *ersatz* coffee, without milk but sometimes faintly sweetened; supper of weak skilly, watery cocoa, or a small piece of blood sausage. One two-pound loaf of dark and unpalatable war-bread was supplied to each man every other day.

Those who had money could supplement this thin diet with rolls, butter, and other foodstuffs from a little canteen for which a German woman held the concession; but the two thousand destitute men, among them nearly all the seamen, had no such luxuries. Except for an occasional five marks from charitable funds and the generosity of fellow-prisoners, they had to exist on the German rations until February 1915, when weekly relief payments of four marks from a British Government fund started. In the meantime they were chronically underfed. On November 27 the "skilly riot" occurred—a spontaneous demonstration by hungry sailors against a supper of repulsive gruel. Henley described it in his diary:

Strike against skilly. There was a terrible row in the kitchen and we all turned up and boycotted the skilly. I expected a riot but things went off better than anticipated. We were all put to bed earlier than usual by the simple method of sounding "Fire," and once we were in our places we were kept there.

The incident did draw the attention of the military, and contributed to the contractor's removal some months later. Until then, however, things remained much the same, and the brief sentence, "Sold my banjoline to buy bread," in Burton's diary for December 18, tells the story in six words.

Much might be added to this rapid survey, but the reader can at least picture Ruhleben in its first months. The prisoners are crowded almost beyond endurance, their quarters are cold, damp, and dark, and the nights are filled with the sound of coughing. Their food is scanty and distasteful, and they are forbidden to smoke anywhere in the stables. Many of them are past middle age, many are chronic invalids, but all have to tramp to the kitchens for food, and medical attention is worse than perfunctory. There was to be marked improvement in all these conditions, but Ruhleben was never a desirable residence even in the summers. As for the winters, the men looked forward to them with a dread that appears in their letters every August. Nothing, moreover, has been said of the mental hardships—long confinement, separation from homes and families, complete uncertainty about the future, and a gnawing sense of injustice. These were for many the real sufferings of internment, and in them time could bring no improvement.

The picture is a pitiful one, but it is not presented to arouse pity. It is meant to give point to three extracts from former prisoners' letters, the first two received in 1933 from men of whom I had heard nothing for fifteen years. One of them, an artist, after describing his life in the camp, added: "I repeat, I enjoyed every day of my stay in Ruhleben" (L 106). It sounds absurd, but that is how he put it. The second, a university professor, wrote:

For me the word "Ruhleben" connotes just four amazingly interesting and stimulating years which I would not have missed for anything, spent among people who are still a good deal more real to me than most of the people I have met either before or since. (L 58)

The third was written in 1949 by a seafaring friend, now a dock worker in England:

I went to Ruhleben 17, a boy, and came out 21, a man, and yet to my mind those four years are more vivid and real than the years of World War II. . . . We did not realize what lay before us, but I think we were a fine crowd, and now I know we were happy although we did not know it. (L 49)

These tributes, though certainly not typical, are far from being the only ones of their kind; my own view would be quite similar. Whatever may be thought of them, they at least suggest that something remarkable must have happened at Ruhleben.

2 NOVEMBER 1914: THE FIRST THREE WEEKS

THE QUOTATIONS that closed the previous chapter provide the key-note of this book. The Germans had turned a racecourse into a cage for prisoners; what these quotations imply is that the cage was somehow changed into a place where life could be stimulating and even happy. It is this second transformation that makes Ruhleben worth writing about.

It was of course an inner transformation. The earmarks of a prison, as Lovelace perceived, are not stone walls and iron bars, but prisoners. And Ruhleben ceased to be one, not through the removal of barbed wire and sentries, but because its inhabitants ceased to think and behave like prisoners. Going into prison, like going into politics or the church, means playing a prescribed part in a kind of social drama, and the interned men played theirs well enough for a time. But the German prompters were inefficient; the prisoners took liberties with their lines, began to improvise, and finally constructed a completely fresh play, with an intriguing role in it for everyone who desired one. In other words, they built their own society on the racecourse.

Although the new society grew with extraordinary rapidity, it still required about a year for its full development, and Parts II to IV of this book are devoted to the formative twelve months. They deal in turn with the social and mental turmoil of the first three weeks and the emergence of solidarity and high morale; with the men's gradual adaptation to Ruhleben during the ensuing winter and the growth of an ordered community; and with the great expansion in the spring and summer of 1915, when a prolific outburst of activity and organization turned the community into a complex society. The new play was complete and had settled down for a long run. The three years that followed saw relative stability through 1916 and 1917, then the decline of the society in 1918 and its dissolution at the end of the war. The time divisions are of course arbitrary, but give the story a convenient pattern. The relevant dates and periods can be summarized as follows:

August 4, 1914   *England declares war on Germany*
November 6, 1914   *General internment at Ruhleben*

November 6 to 30, 1914   Period I: Crisis and Solidarity
December 1914 to March 1915   Period II: Settlement and
                                   Community Formation
April to October, 1915   Period III: Expansion and Full
                                   Organization
November 1915 to end of 1917   Period IV: Stability
January to November, 1918   Period V: Decline
November 11, 1918   *Germany signs armistice*
November 24, 1918   *Last prisoners leave Ruhleben*

A varying number of chapters is devoted to each period, the first usually containing a narrative of events and a general description of social and mental conditions. Succeeding chapters deal in more detail with social changes during the period, their effects on the men, and related topics. The scheme involves considering some periods more than once, but at different levels of analysis.

We left the prisoners on the morning of November 7, getting their first real view of themselves and their new surroundings. Several thousand men in a small stableyard look like a multitude, and the Ruhlebenite's initial feelings were of astonishment that there could be so many British in Germany. And more kept coming; these are Geoffrey Pyke's impressions when he arrived in January 1915:

> I found myself in a square. In the centre of the square was an electric light standard with an arc light which flickered. Beneath this arc light walked up and down hundreds of couples. Then a soldier took me. We went down alleys, through doors. Everywhere there were people. The place was crowded with them. A great noise of chatter filled the air. I felt rather dazed by it all. (Pp. 120 ff., condensed)

Even more striking than the size of the population was its variety. On November 8 Henley noted: "We are very mixed up—cobbler and banker, cook and engineer, high and low, poor and rich, healthy and unhealthy, old and young, all in one mass." A. M. D. Hughes, released after three weeks, wrote on his return to England:

> One saw with surprise how many of the British of all classes earn their living in this country—jockeys and trainers, golf and tennis professionals, foremen and workers from factories, seamen and ships' stewards. . . . There were many merchants and business men, some in a big way; artists and musicians from the schools and centres of art, and the first-fruits of the holiday traffic from England, which had just arrived on August 4, and in which the most conspicuous elements were undergrads, public school masters and invalids for the Spas. (P. 666)

In the same article Hughes listed as sleeping beside him in his loft a German millionaire's coachman, a steward from an Atlantic liner, an estate agent from the north of England, a Canadian trapper, and a musician of European distinction. This was not exceptional.

The actual population of the camp, excluding the handful of other nationalities, is shown in percentages in Figure 2. In round numbers, the

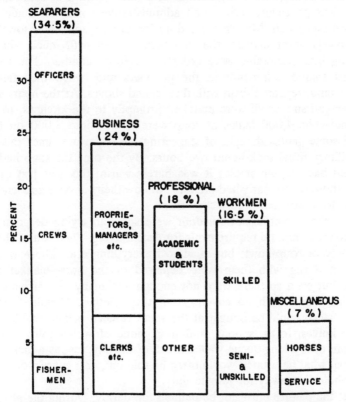

FIGURE 2. Occupational categories, in percentages, of 4,098 "permanent" prisoners in Ruhleben on March 11, 1915. Some 300 others, released that year into Germany, were excluded from the breakdown. (From the "Ruhleben Book," British Prisoners of War Records.)

largest occupational group were the 1,400 seafaring men of all ranks, who gave the land-locked racecourse the air of a busy seaport. Next came almost 1,000 businessmen; then 750 from the professions—a significantly high proportion. About 700 were skilled and semi-skilled workmen, while jockeys, waiters, and other miscellaneous occupations made up the remainder. This explains the Ruhlebenite's surprise at the first sight of his fellow-prisoners—what a mob, and what a mixture!

After a breakfast of cold coffee and black bread on November 7 the prisoners were drafted in parties for fatigue work. Hundreds of straw-sacks had to be drawn from stores, filled with straw, and carried into the barracks; military bunks, fitting one above another, had to be placed in the horse-boxes, and many similar tasks undertaken. For some men the work was physically trying, and administrative confusion made it exasperating as well. Men were lined up for an hour to receive towels, but the towels never arrived; the iron beds carried with much whispered cursing into one stable were ordered moved to another. The German guards roared commands at the prisoners and, when they failed to understand, repeated them with threats and shoves. At the hours set for dinner and supper all were marched promptly to the kitchens, to stand in line while 4,000 ladles of soup were poured into 4,000 tin bowls. Until some genius thought of staggering the departure times this piece of military ritual took about two hours. By the time the soup had been carried back to the stables it was barely warm; this was just as well, since those served early had often to swallow theirs at once and lend their bowls to newcomers who lacked them.

The short intervals of freedom were spent in trying desperately to secure the minimum requirements for decent living. There was a shortage not only of soup-bowls but of almost everything else. Those who had brought a rug with them were deprived of the horse-blanket issued them, but even so there were not enough and many late arrivals spent freezing nights with no covering but their clothes. Certain foodstuffs and tobacco could be bought at the small canteen behind Stable 11, as could knives, forks, spoons, and soap, none of which were provided. In front of it a long queue waited much of the day; just as a man neared his goal what he wanted would often be sold out, or a guard would order the whole line away for fatigue duty.

Yet the picture must not be painted too darkly. During the afternoon improvised football matches were going on in the square, surrounded by excited spectators (Burton); after lights out at nine there were "singing and funny stories" in at least one loft (Farwell). Shouting and cheering were frequent, and a certain boisterous elation was much in evidence. This did not mean that the prisoners accepted what had been done to them, for resentment was strong and vigorously expressed. But the deficiencies of Ruhleben were so glaring as to be actually reassuring; interment under such conditions could be nothing but a German bluff, and one that would be called in a week. Meanwhile one had to make the best of it.

Another uncomfortable night passed and Sunday, November 8,

brought little change. The day was cold and damp, the men were turned out at six, fetched their coffee from the kitchens, drank it cold in their boxes and lofts, and then at nine were lined up in front of their respective stables, counted, and addressed by the *Lageroffizier*, Baron von Taube. Before each of his little speeches on prison decorum the Baron asked for an interpreter, and from each stable-company someone who spoke German either volunteered or was pushed forward by others. This was the modest beginning of the Captains' Committee, which became in a year the all-powerful government of the camp. During the day several hundred new arrivals made further fatigue work necessary; there was a better dinner—pea soup with bits of fat pork in it—but no supper, since the cooks had the afternoon off. Pastimes were more conspicuous; two scratch football matches were played in the afternoon, games of "horse and rider" amused the crowds in the evening, and at bedtime there were extempore concerts in several stables and in the grandstand dormitory. And at every hour, today and every day, there were rumours of impending release to be listened to, chewed over, and passed on to others.

How the next four days impressed Burton, a ship's engineer, may be gathered from his diary:

Mon., Nov. 9. Long march round this morning—three quarters of an hour getting bread and coffee. Several hundred Hamburg residents arrived during the night, having been quartered on the hulks since we left. Dinner today cabbage soup flavoured with carroway seed—most horrible mess; meat, as generally, a minus quantity. Am writing to B. to send me a sweater as the weather is very cold. Had a job this evening in the rain, carrying bales of straw from outside. Guess these are beds for new chums. Shifted my quarters to first class—on the floor.

Tues., Nov. 10. Weather cold and raw. 160 new arrivals today. Report that bags are being sent up from the hulks.

Wed., Nov. 11. Weather cold but fine, getting settled down to new quarters. Very little news how war is progressing, suppose for us no news is good news. Raining tonight, turned in at 8 P.M., three quarters of an hour before bedtime. Got the pip.

Thurs., Nov. 12. Bitter cold. Lined up twice today. I collared a side pallet vacated by a Russian Jew, but was nearly turned out by Unterofficier for newcomers. Won the day, and new chums got first class on the floor. Turned in at 7. Bed the best place.

Then November 13 comes, and the men have been interned a full week. To some it seems more like a month, but at least release is one week nearer. And the rumours are as encouraging as ever: the United States is officially protesting the internment, all arrangements for exchange are complete, the prisoners are leaving on Monday—on Wednesday—on the 22nd. Everyone is betting on the precise day: "Even money we're not here a week from today!"; "The best dinner you can order in London, with wine, if we get there later than December 1!" Someone raises a howl by offering to bet that they will spend Christmas in Ruhleben—but that is so far only a joke. It is a good-humoured, talkative crowd that mills around between the barracks, though the good humour is only that of men making the best of a few unpleasant days. "The *Stimmung* is excellent," Henley notes on November 12, "and the whole day a series of jokes and chaff." And Hughes writes after his brief stay, "We were a medley of people passing the time together, so that good humour was a common advantage and a common need and the only business of the day" (p. 668). This buoyant atmosphere will concern us later.

During the week some order has been imposed on the initial confusion. The barrack interpreters of November 8—now mysteriously styled "captains"—are ignoring rumours and working long hours. Whether release comes this week or next there are urgent problems to be dealt with, and for lack of anyone else these dozen men are acting to represent the prisoners. Already, since their first meeting on November 9, they have obtained permission to telephone the United States Embassy in Berlin, and have urged the necessity of hospital treatment, clothing, and money for those in greatest need. Officials have been appointed in each barrack to collect and deliver mail, guard against fire, and perform other duties; a fund has been raised to have the noisome latrines cleaned out, and a list of sailors under or over military age—17 to 55—has been compiled and handed to the German officers. Today, November 13, has seen the organization of a small civilian police force to control queues, handle lost property, and try to maintain order without the intervention of the guards. Few know the new officials by sight, so improvised arm-bands have been made, and the prisoners are already treating their wearers with a certain puzzled respect.

These beginnings of communal organization were of some social importance, for they represented the first distinctions among the prisoners to be formally recognized, the first departures from complete equality. They arose, however, from purely practical considerations, in contrast to the spontaneous social organization that will be our chief interest. Some administrative machinery was essential, but it would have made little difference if it had been run by Germans instead of British—save that the latter were more efficient. Its scope was limited to the external aspects of life, the securing of order and physical improvements; the prisoners had to deal with their social needs themselves.

Further developments of this first week are recorded in the small, condensed diary of a young businessman, here called Abbot:

Tues., Nov. 10. Got a table. Write twice a week, short cards. All sorts and conditions of men. Allowed to go all over the camp. Football match. Settling down.

Wed., Nov. 11. "Boots and skivvy" men to clean up. The lazy Russians. Englishmen make the best of a bad job. The interrupted concert in 11. The concert on the grandstand. The valets: 1/– a week for looking after a gent. The tea-party.

On November 13 Abbot notes the appearance of shoeblacks[1] in the compound and of a shoemaker in Barrack 4, and on the same day J. H. Platford, a London chartered accountant, opened a lending library in his box in Barrack 1, with 83 books donated by the American Ambassador and various prisoners. Abbot's brief notes are very suggestive of the social ferment that has started. There is the highly stimulating situation —"all sorts and conditions of men" crowded together, free to communicate as they choose and to go all over the camp. There are the beginnings of commercial enterprise and of such group activities as concerts, games, and tea-parties. And there is the significant remark, "Englishmen make the best of a bad job"—an instance of the national pride that shaped much of Ruhleben's character.

The rest of November passed more quickly than the first week. Looking at the camp again as the month ends we find conditions little improved. The population has increased and the crowding is worse. The first snow-flurries came on November 20, the 22nd brought hard frost with a "biting east wind," and the wintry weather has continued ever since. The men have wrapped themselves in every warm garment they can find, and there is much swinging of arms and stamping of feet. The makeshift heating arrangements are functioning for a few hours daily, but do little more than take the chill off; there is no spot in the camp where the men can sit still without shivering.

The food is no better than it was, perhaps worse. "Think grub is going off," writes Burton on November 13; "soup ghastly," says Farwell on the 15th; "grub beastly," echoes Henley on the 23rd. Hot drinks, however, are being peddled through the stables at a penny (10 pf.) a cup, for the Germans have permitted small entrepreneurs with Berlin connections to

---

1. Shoe shining was the first "service" obtainable after internment, and for a few weeks the many shoeblacks prospered. If this seems strange under Ruhleben conditions, it is partly because we no longer regard the task as fit only for menials. In 1914, however, no Englishman above the working class ever cleaned his own shoes, and even in North America there was a shoeshine parlour on every busy street.

order supplies delivered to the gate. Cocoa-men are reported on November 23, and tea, coffee, and Oxo salesmen are now noisily competing with them. The milk purveyor with his startling sign, "Mother's Milk," is temporarily out of business, the sentries having discovered bottles of *Schnapps* in the incoming milk-can. The many penniless prisoners are trying to earn money for such luxuries as the canteen and peddlers provide, and the supply of stewards, launderers, and shoeblacks far exceeds the demand.

The administrative structure is growing, and officials are increasingly busy. The Captains' Committee is under the chairmanship of E. M. Trinks, now designated "Captain of the Camp," and is coming to regard itself as representing all the interned. Its efforts to secure physical improvements have not been very productive, but the authorities have made some tentative promises. And Trinks has recently persuaded the American Embassy to advance 2,000 marks for distribution among the destitute—the first of several such sums charged to the British Government.

Pastimes are becoming better organized, though some are running into German opposition. Football, played in the compound with improvised goal-posts, is immensely popular, but a pencilled notice shows that it was early threatened:

FIRST RUHLEBEN FOOTBALL COMPETITION
Nov. 16th, 1914, at 1.45 P.M.
FINAL MATCH: Oldham (Public Schools XI) vs. Tottenham (Scratch XI)
PLEASE (in your own interest) keep fairly quiet.   (H)

The warning failed, and on November 25 football was strictly forbidden. The men turned to "rounders" with a home-made ball, but two days later all ball games were banned as too exciting. There are still amusements in the compound, however; circus acrobats are practising, two music-hall performers are displaying their skill at Diabolo, and "Bicycle Billy," a tough customer who was pedalling his way across Europe, is renting out his decorated machine at a penny a ride and getting plenty of patrons. Some who find the spectator's role too chilly have reverted to childhood and are playing prisoners' base and leapfrog, while hundreds of others, alone or in couples, are walking up and down with the purposeful and preoccupied air that was always characteristic of Ruhleben. Indoors there is a great deal of chess and checkers, and cards have been found for whist, bridge, and euchre, not to mention more hazardous games such as poker. The latter are doubly hazardous, for since November 27 gambling has been forbidden under penalty of seventy-two hours' cells. This was the first of many German efforts to curb gambling; they were, of course, never successful.

Religious services have been held since early in the month when Father Schmidt, a South African priest caught on holiday in Germany, began celebrating mass in his box in Barrack 1.[2] On November 15 the largest grandstand was almost filled for two open-air Protestant services conducted by laymen, one of them the professor of English at Berlin University. These were repeated on the following Sunday, and on November 29 the Rev. H. M. Williams,[3] Anglican chaplain in Berlin, was allowed to come in and take a service. To his surprise it was fully choral—a large choir leading the hymns and performing an original anthem, without accompaniment, hymn-books, or other music. There were several church organists in the camp, and every note of the music had been written from memory and transcribed by patient copyists, while the congregation sang from manuscript hymn-sheets similarly prepared. This laborious method was soon being used for more ambitious musical productions.

Altogether, the accomplishments of November have been considerable, and the 240 men brought in on the 28th found a camp very different from that of November 6. It is still a wretched place to live in, and everyone's hope is to leave it soon. But the daily routines of meal fetching, fatigue work, and roll calls are running smoothly, and the free hours are filled with a surprising variety of activities. Nor is the atmosphere that of a prison camp; the men are not silent and depressed but noisy and almost aggressively cheerful. German soldiers are still in control, but their manner is less hostile and some prisoners do not hesitate to argue with them. And Britishers with arm-bands are playing a noticeable role. The new arrival will be assigned his place by his barrack captain; a civilian policeman will warn him about smoking, direct him to the postman's box, and keep him in line at the canteen. And at the daily roll call the efforts of the barrack sergeant to count his 300 charges would often fail without the arithmetical skill of the captain.

It was these early developments that provoked the exclamation of a German-reared internee, reported by Gribble: "You English seem to set

2. Ministers of religion were exempt from internment, but the Germans had questioned Father Schmidt's credentials. By the time his status was established he had resolved to stay with his flock in Ruhleben, where he ministered to them until the end.
3. Mr. Williams refused a place on the British Ambassador's train out of Berlin on August 6, and devoted himself throughout the war to the British nationals in Germany, particularly the prisoners of war. In spite of great privation and difficulty he kept the Berlin church open, and also travelled regularly to camps and hospitals all over the country. Ruhleben usually saw him once a fortnight.

to work as if you were founding a new colony!" (19, p. 63). This is the first recorded comment on the Ruhlebenites' refusal to play their allotted role, but it was not the last. The German officers, besieged with requests for improvements and privileges, often remonstrated: "*Aber, meine Herren*, you are forgetting that you are prisoners." The men accepted the reminders politely, but promptly began to forget again. Forgetting that they were interned came naturally to these Britishers—they were, after all, not professional prisoners but rank amateurs—and it proved in the end to be their most precious accomplishment.

This brief summary of Ruhleben's first three weeks reveals some significant social beginnings. Most obvious is the growth of a second, civilian organization alongside the military one; though it was the product only of stark necessity, it resulted finally in the prisoners taking over the internal administration of the camp. Necessity was also behind the economic activity that had sprung up; shortages of many kinds had opened a market for everything that dealers could order from outside, and for whatever goods or services the prisoners had to sell.

More interesting, because at first sight less necessary, is what the men were doing in their spare hours: reading, playing games, arranging sing-songs and religious services. More food, warmth, and comfort were not all they craved for; they were also seeking mental stimulation and dis-traction, the pleasure of group games and singing, and the satisfaction of achieving something as a team or a choir. These intellectual and social needs are sometimes treated as secondary, but they are as intrinsic to the human being as hunger or other appetites. And they were of the first importance in Ruhleben; the mental health of the prisoners depended on how well they could be met, and the chief institutions of camp society grew up around them.

Another development not mentioned previously began as soon as the camp opened: the growth of social ties between men thrown together in the same box or loft section. Henley wrote on November 12: "We five have stuck together, still on the cold stone floor"—and "we" is the word to notice. The intimate groupings that resulted were of such importance that a later chapter is devoted to them; here it need only be said that by the end of November almost every prisoner was living, not "on his own," but in close relationship with a few others—eating and sleeping with them, and sharing with them his hopes, problems, and anxieties.

This brings us to the mental state of the prisoners, which has scarcely been touched upon. The narrative so far might suggest merely a resource-ful body of men, adapting themselves surprisingly quickly to an un-pleasant situation. Some readers, however, will have noted other features;

on the one hand the continual rumours, the shouting and singing, the exaggerated cheerfulness; on the other the crowds flocking to church services, and the fits of depression recorded in Burton's diary. These reflect uncertainty, suggestibility, emotional tension—all signs of some disturbance of normal mental processes. The disturbance went deep and we must examine it rather closely. For what happened to the prisoners psychologically during their first days together had decisive effects on their later experience.

The mental effects of what may be called the "crisis" of internment are not well documented. No letters could be written from the camp until March 1915, and the postcards and diary entries are too brief to contain much introspection. They are mainly records of concrete events, with the postcards adding a few reassuring words to those at home. And later accounts of Ruhleben refer only in passing to the "chaos and confusion" of its opening days; memories of so disorganized a period were inevitably vague and quickly effaced by what followed. There is, however, enough incidental evidence to provide a convincing picture.

The men and boys herded into Ruhleben were normal human beings, but they were in a highly abnormal situation. Each of them had been plucked up by the roots, torn from his accustomed setting, and plunged into a totally strange one. Such an uprooting is deeply disturbing, for the human being depends on his familiar social context for most of his psychological needs. He is seldom aware of these needs; like the body's need for oxygen, they are too regularly satisfied to become conscious. But when oxygen is lacking the body makes immediate, automatic efforts to secure it, and the Ruhleben prisoners struggled similarly to meet the needs that internment had blocked. They could not have put them into words, but the directions their efforts took were enough indication.[4]

What specifically did the men need beyond food, water, and shelter? Perhaps first of all to know what was going to happen to them—whether they would be released again, sent to England, kept in Ruhleben, or perhaps even shot, as some pessimists maintained. This need to know one's future is seldom listed in text-books, for it is a purely intellectual need, found only in man, and apparently illogical—since the future is strictly unknowable. We humans, however, are habit-forming creatures whose behaviour is highly repetitive, and we live in societies where day-to-day conformity is ensured by a variety of controls. In such societies

4. The concept "need" is not an explanatory one; nothing is gained by asserting, for example, that the fish which lives in water has a "need" for water. The term is used here and elsewhere only as a shorthand method of stating an observable fact: that, when certain psychological and social conditions are lacking, the human being (like the fish out of water) ceases to function normally.

we can and do count upon the future; we assume, and with good reason, that our business will still operate and our family still put up with us next year, that we can safely plan a convention or a holiday months ahead, and that we ourselves are unlikely to be murdered tomorrow—unless by a drunken motorist. Thousands of years of such settled, predictable existence have made the future an integral part of our make-up; life appears to us an unbroken stream, the remembered past blending into the experienced present, and the present merging smoothly into a confidently expected future. And such a future is indispensable to our mental functioning, for without it we could form no plans or purposes, and existence would be aimless and meaningless.

Internment made a sharp break in this mental continuity. The past was left intact, but it was so different from the alarming present, so hard to relate to it, that the two could not co-exist in the mind. In the first shock it was often the present that was rejected; "The day seemed a dream," was how Henley, a hard-headed engineer, described it in his diary on November 7. Then, as Ruhleben asserted its undeniable reality, it was the past that tended to become remote and unreal. Not for several weeks was it possible to knit the two together intelligibly, and meanwhile the prisoner found his conception of himself strangely shaken. Which was he—the respected solicitor and suburban householder, or the unshaven, straw-splattered outcast, picking the last scrap of potato out of a rusty tin bowl? That he could be *both* was for a time incredible.

A worse shock, however, was the wiping out of the future; for the first time since early childhood the men could not see even one day ahead. As a result, all the purposes around which their lives had been organized were nullified, and no new ones could be formed. This gap in the mental world was acutely disturbing; one ex-prisoner wrote feelingly of the emotional tension caused by "trying to find your feet in a totally new environment with the immediate future an absolute blank" (L 58). But the men's pressing need for a predictable future is shown most clearly by their prompt though unconscious efforts to create one. The first method, illusory but momentarily satisfying, was the spawning of countless rumours of release. The second, which finally replaced it, was to build within the camp the only context in which long-range purposes can be formed—a stable social order. The two methods of recapturing a future were of course incompatible, for rumours of release militated against every effort at social organization, and much of the camp's history was woven around the conflict between them.

A whole set of further needs was revealed by the snapping of the prisoner's social ties, his abrupt removal from his place in the social world. The needs regularly satisfied by society as a whole, and in family, friendship, and other groups are of course innumerable, but those of greatest psychological importance are generally agreed on.[5] First is the primitive need simply to belong, to be accepted, to identify oneself with some social body; on this depends any security we feel in the world. Then there is the complementary need to feel oneself a unique individual, with a role and group position that are distinctively one's own. These two aspects of group attachment are basic to the existence of a self, for we cannot picture ourselves at all except as belonging to a given nation, class, family, and so on, and possessing defined status within them.

Society also supplies, directly and through various groupings, the system of values by which we judge the aims and conduct of others and ourselves, labelling them right or wrong, praiseworthy or ignoble. These "social norms" are instilled into us in childhood and enforced through life by a variety of controls; they largely determine both our aspirations and our actual behaviour. Without them, if such a thing were conceivable, we would be adrift, rudderless, lacking any goals or standards save those of immediate bodily pleasure.

Internment, of course, did not cut the prisoner off completely from these vital necessities; he knew that he still belonged to his old groups and that his status in them was unchanged, and he brought his code of conduct with him. But knowledge of who and what he was gave little reassurance among a mob of strangers who did not share it, and his self-picture was often badly shaken. Similarly, he felt no certainty as to what standards would apply in a situation so unlike anything he had known before. And his only remaining goal, to get out of Ruhleben, was one he could do nothing to attain—except by filling out fruitless petitions for release. It is not surprising if he felt deeply uncertain of himself and of how to behave.

Not all were equally affected; the seafarer still belonged with his interned crew, and those with friends or relatives had at least some continuing attachments. But the crisis had its effects here too, for such groupings derived from the past, and the past no longer counted. Ship's crews lacked any further function and broke up fairly quickly; kinship was similarly affected except where it had been transformed into friendship; and, though many pre-war friendships survived internment, a surprising number disintegrated.

5. The following summary is largely derived from M. Sherif (*An Outline of Social Psychology*; New York: Harper & Brothers, 1948), and is elaborated in my article, "Meaning, Motives, and Social Organization" (*Canadian Journal of Psychology*, 1949, *3*, 218–25).

In the first hectic days, however, every established relationship was a precious source of security, and those who lacked ties in the camp sought eagerly for them. Crew members stuck closely together until they formed new attachments, and so did relatives and groups of friends. Anyone who ran across a previous acquaintance hailed him with the absurd warmth shown at chance meetings in a foreign city. Even encounters with an unknown fellow-townsman were regularly noted in diaries and postcards; Ewing wrote home in December: "There is a Dawlish sailor here and we often talk about the dear place." And the efforts of some prisoners to re-establish their shaken self-pictures led to behaviour that several writers make fun of: that of expatiating to anyone who would listen on the importance of their outside positions. It was pathetic rather than amusing, for the past could not be reinstated; new roles had to be found in the present.

And some men were already finding them, for if social uprooting was disturbing, it was also exciting and liberating. No one knew what norms should apply, no one expected the prisoner to play his previous role; he was therefore free to conduct himself almost as he chose. To a few elderly men this was no boon; all they wanted was to get back to their normal lives. But the footloose youngster exulted in his freedom, and most of the prisoners were markedly affected by it. Through the shock of internment they were in some measure reborn; their set habits were broken down and their behaviour became fluid and plastic. They were thus able to act in new ways in the new situation, to assume new roles and develop somewhat different selves, and this was the very making of Ruhleben. The next two chapters will tell how the making began.

3 | THE ACHIEVEMENT OF SOLIDARITY

THE GENERAL EFFECTS of such an uprooting as the Ruhleben prisoners had experienced are well known. The removal of all a person's familiar guide-posts disturbs him emotionally; his behaviour is largely determined by the impulse of the moment and may appear bizarre and disorganized; and his pressing need for some cues to action makes him abnormally responsive to the words and deeds of others, that is "suggestible."

Effects of this sort may be seen in the peasant set down in a great metropolis or the refugee transplanted to a strange soil. Unlike them, however, the early arrival in Ruhleben was not placed in an established social order, where acceptable conduct was clearly defined and his role largely prescribed for him. Instead he found himself one of an unorganized mass of individuals, all uprooted like himself, and all forced, for lack of a definite future, to live in and for the present. The results were predictable; the prisoners were highly excitable, and their collective behaviour was often that of a crowd—impulsive, emotional, and markedly contagious.

Few writers on Ruhleben do more than mention the excitement and suggestibility of the opening days, but their results were so important that I am devoting two chapters to them. For it was the emotional shock of internment and the collective behaviour it unleashed that fused these four thousand individuals into one body, creating a solidarity that conditioned all subsequent social development. No society can come into existence unless its components feel that they are in some way akin and belong together.[1] And in Ruhleben this necessary minimum of mutual acceptance was far exceeded.

Some degree of solidarity would be expected, even in a heterogeneous population, after years of shared confinement, but the solidarity of Ruhleben was different in two crucial respects. It appeared at the very outset of internment, creating an esprit de corps that carried the men on

1. For the early sociologist Franklin H. Giddings, this awareness of likeness or "consciousness of kind" was the subjective basis of all society (*Principles of Sociology*, New York: The Macmillan Co., 1926).

to great social accomplishments; and it was an emotional experience of such intensity that it coloured their mutual relationships for years to come. No comparable unity could have been achieved later; men of such widely different backgrounds could only coalesce while they were still uprooted and seeking new attachments, still plastic and suggestible, and still stirred by powerful emotions. These were the conditions during the November days that I have called the Period of Crisis, and it was then that the prisoners took their first step towards building an all-inclusive society.

Solidarity was primarily a response to pressing emotional needs, for the men brought to Ruhleben in the week of November 6 were more deeply shaken by their experience than appeared on the surface. They were civilians, not fighting men, and civilians to whom "war" had meant chiefly the romantic adventure stories of G. A. Henty. Except for the seafarers, who played a special role, all had been living or travelling in Germany; their contacts with the people had been friendly, and most of them, restricted to local news sources, had tended to sympathize with German views of the war. An unmailed letter that Denton wrote in Berlin on August 24 remarks: "English cavalry have come into collision with the Germans already, and have been defeated apparently. I am very sorry for the poor devils, but what *are* they doing here in Europe?" And for three months they had been completely out of touch with Britain; not a word of patriotic propaganda had reached them. They knew that Britons were being killed in Belgium and France, and grieved for it, but the idea of active enmity between Germans and themselves had little reality except to those who had been imprisoned or otherwise maltreated.

To men so devoid of hostile sentiments November 6 came as a devastating shock. Not the fact of internment—the papers had prepared them for that—but the experience of being handled like dangerous criminals, herded through the streets by armed police, shouted at and struck for imaginary offences, locked in small cells without food or toilet facilities, and finally, after painful hours of travel, plunged into a situation that was to many of them frankly terrifying. To be marched into Ruhleben late at night, searched by enemy soldiers, and then bedded down on straw among hundreds of strangers brought an overwhelming sense of helplessness, of exposure to unknown perils. One man who arrived on November 6 wrote years later: "I shall never forget the atmosphere of semi-hysteria in my loft during the first night" (L 58); and Powell, in *The History of Ruhleben*, graphically describes the scene as another barrack was filled:

I pulled back the heavy sliding iron door of one of the horse-boxes, to see whether any one had taken possession of it. There were revealed . . . two silent men standing in two of the corners, each with a suit-case at his feet, and a look of despondent perplexity on his face. I closed the door and withdrew. Half an hour later, I returned, bringing four other men to share their shelter. The two original occupants were still standing there, in the same attitude, and in the same dazed bewilderment. (P. 9)

If little is said about panic and despondency in the Ruhleben literature it is simply because they were almost immediately dispelled. The "semi-hysteria" in that stable loft gave place next evening to "singing and funny stories," and all later arrivals were greeted with cheers of enthusiasm. Few will need to be told the source of the sudden cheerfulness, for the change is as familiar as it is wonderful; it was the merging of frightened individuals into a social unity too strong to feel fear. Whenever men are shaken by events they cannot control we find them turning spontaneously toward one another, forgetting their terror in mutual support and sympathy. And the immediate effect of the shock of internment was to draw the Ruhleben prisoners together in a stirring experience of unity.

Although this laid a firm basis for the new society, it was markedly different from the slower process of community building which began almost as soon. That was a matter of individuals gradually forming specific social relationships, whereas the sense of general solidarity arose, not piecemeal, but immediately and in everyone. Urgently needed though it was, it could not have appeared without two related conditions: the men had to perceive themselves as sharing a common definition, belonging in the same category; and they had to perceive this with such dazzling clarity that the wide differences among them were for the time invisible.

The common definition was of course at hand; strangers to one another, separated by great differences of background and education, they were yet one and all *British subjects*. Most of them had simply taken it for granted before August 1914, and some had almost forgotten it during long years on the Continent.[2] By the act of internment, however, the Germans had defined them all as a single group, and had done so on the sole basis of their nationality. The solidarity that resulted was therefore a national solidarity, deeply infused with patriotism. C. H. Brooks (3) wrote, in a sensitive description of his internment:

Patriotism was a thing mentioned rarely and shamefacedly before the war. . . . But, like all profound things, it was present silently, waiting in the hinterland of memory, ready to stir under the shock of catastrophe to a real

___

2. The role of these Germanized prisoners during the crisis period is obscure, and my discussion applies primarily to the "genuine" British. Certain allusions, however, suggest that at least some men were caught up in the crowd excitement and did their best to be "Britishers" until subjected to derisive criticism.

and poignant thing. The name of England . . . became suddenly like a red streak in the evening sky—bright with deep meaning, lurid with mysterious auguries.

The prisoners' fresh awareness of themselves as *British* was heightened by every circumstance of internment. They were sharply defined spatially —a tiny island in a German ocean. On that island they were marked off from the aliens, not only by uniforms and by language, but by the jarring spectacle of German dominance and British submission. Obeying orders given by Germans, enduring hardships inflicted by Germans, turned an abstract self-definition into a vivid personal experience. There was further needed only a glance at their companions, a flashing realization that they too were suffering in the same cause, to make each man feel himself part of a single body, united by a common allegiance and a common fate. This was the basis of the original solidarity of Ruhleben, a solidarity by its nature short-lived, but one that for a time transcended all differences and made internment a memorable experience of "belonging." The experience is remarkably reflected in a letter written at Christmas 1950 by my seafaring friend, interned at age 17:

If we could only have in the world of today the same spirit that I think we all shared in the old days in Germany. We were prisoners of war but we were all pals, and I feel that all our minds were alike regarding each other. An argument was friendly and no matter who one met in the camp all was pleasant, yet we had all been drawn from different planes, our education, our work, our homes, our lives had all been different, yet in a few days we were one hard hit family facing up, not knowing what was going to happen, or coming, but just sticking together solid. (L 49)

Belonging, however, is a reciprocal matter. The individual escapes from isolation and fear not merely by identifying himself with his fellows, but by the knowledge that identification is mutual. Thus Ruhleben's solidarity, like that of any other body, had to be achieved and expressed through communication. A great hum of talk filled the compound from the day of internment onwards; as Cohen says: "Although my fellow-prisoners had been talking with one another the whole day long, they no sooner got into bed than the floodgates of conversation were let loose as though they had been held in check for the last twelve hours" (p. 200). Conversation sprang up wherever men found themselves together, start-ing most often with the stereotyped question, "Where did they get *you*?" The story of each man's arrest was recounted scores of times, views on the war and the prospects of release were endlessly exchanged. The talk was banal and repetitious and the talkers had no notion what drove them to it, but its functions were vital ones. "Men build their cultures," wrote Kenneth Burke, "by huddling together, nervously loquacious, at the edge of an abyss."³ And the lavish sharing of his experiences with others did more than reduce the prisoner's anxiety; it united him to his fellows in a sense of identity that made a camp society possible.

Simple conversation, however, was not enough to establish solidarity among so many men; that required a more dramatic form of communication in which hundreds could share at once—the mass shouting and singing that broke out irrepressibly during the first days together. The barracks would be lined up in fours to march to the kitchens; as each moved off, those awaiting their turn would burst into deafening cheers, and these were repeated as barrack met barrack, coming and going, throughout the day. Sometimes a marching song would start in spite of the guards' angry shouts, and the old British catchword, "Are we down-hearted?"—quickly shortened to "*Are* we?"—brought again and again its thundering "NO!" There was no logic in this behaviour—the men had nothing to cheer about—but it met strong, unconscious needs. In part it was a gesture of defiance, for the soldiers objected to it fiercely; but the greatest need was to do something—anything—*together* and thus make solidarity concretely evident.

Similar demonstrations welcomed every new contingent of prisoners. "We were greeted with shouts of encouragement," says Molony, who arrived in a small convoy (p. 16); Cohen says of a body of sailors, "We cheered these men as they sturdily marched into the Camp" (p. 36); Mahoney, arriving on November 13, says, "A large crowd of the prisoners . . . gave a lusty cheer when they caught sight of us and pressed forward eagerly" (p. 18); and Cimino, three days later, reports the stock greeting, "Halloa, boys! Are we down-hearted?" (p. 86). Nor was it all to reassure the newcomers; the cheerers too were gaining courage from Ruhleben's growing strength.

The new prisoner might still spend a desolate night, but next morning his spirits rose unaccountably. The mere sight of so many Britishers was a tonic, and when he was physically joined to them in marching and shouting his quickened step and animated face reflected his changed outlook. On November 19 daily marches around the race-track were ordered for exercise, and the whole body of men was simultaneously in view. Its size was impressive; Burton wrote that evening, "We look a rare big crowd when in procession." The hour of tramping around the track soon grew boring, but the marching songs—"John Brown's Body," "Tipperary," "Men of Harlech"—must have been heard in Spandau.

Nor was singing confined to the march; as Mahoney says: "Whenever we had the opportunity to sing we did so with gusto" (p. 52). Diarists report it in the lofts as early as November 7, and there were constant

3. *Permanence and Change* (New York: New Republic Inc., 1935), p. 351.

singsongs, especially in the little sheds between the barracks where men gathered to smoke. Topical verses quickly appeared—true folk-songs, anonymous, and growing directly out of shared experiences. In *The History of Ruhleben* Gribble quotes the chorus of the "Ruhleben Alphabet," several versions of which are preserved:

> Merry, oh merry, oh merry are we,
> And Ruhleben Camp is the one place for me.
> There's soup and there's skilly, and coffee and bread,
> And a nice German coffin as soon as you're dead.

He first heard it from one of the sheds, and adds: "For hours, as it seemed to me, the melodious men droned and re-droned that melancholy ditty. The effect, on a night so dark that one could not see their faces . . . was very strange and weird" (38, p. 200). There was grim pleasure in singing satirically of the discomforts of the camp and (*pianissimo*) of the impending fate of the Kaiser, but the content mattered little—the singing was the important thing. It was an activity in which everyone could join, and from which each gathered again the assurance that he was not alone in his plight. As Mahoney says later, "The words were immaterial; indeed some of the songs were the most inane ever sung or heard, but they went down like good red wine" (p. 218).

Inside the barracks, however, when little groups of men ate their miserable suppers or prepared for bed in the dark, courage was harder to sustain. Supper time and bedtime are closely associated with home, and in the relative quiet loneliness and dejection often returned. It was on their bunks that the men wrote their diaries, and the early diaries have much more to say of hardship and anxiety than of exuberance. But the barracks developed their own form of crowd behaviour—the loud, ironical cheer whenever someone dropped his soup-bowl or made some other audible disturbance. Cohen says: "It was a strange sense of humour that made us roar with laughter or shout 'Hurrah!' whenever a fellow-prisoner smashed his dinner-bowl" (p. 76), and the practice, by then a recognized custom, is mentioned ten months later in one of Tom Govett's "Phoebe" dialogues in a camp magazine:

"People have a curious habit of shouting here in the barrack. You will perhaps be happily dozing or smoking—no, not smoking, amusing yourself —when someone will start to sing, or just talk a little loudly, whereupon throughout the whole barrack yell upon yell will ascend to the heavens. . . . And it's the same when anything is smashed. What would happen outside?"
"Curses, bright and beautiful," I suggested.
"Exactly, but here they cheer like mad." (*IRC* 8, p. 4)

The yells had various functions, but the principal one, at least in the early days, was to remind insecure men of the many unseen comrades about them.

All these assertions of solidarity had their effect. As the prisoner joined with so many others in the same cheers, slogans, and rhythmic singing, he became less a separate individual and more a member of the new collectivity. And with the change came a warm feeling of security, unjustified by any improvement in his situation, but welling up from the source always available to the human being—the sense of belonging to a social unity greater and more powerful than himself.

Crowd behaviour was most characteristic of November 1914, when hopes of quick release were still so strong that no real "settling down" could occur. As hope dwindled and a new social world took shape, the need for collective reassurance grew less insistent. Cheering for broken crockery was preserved as a folkway, and singing on the route-marches would also have become a matter of habit if it had not been strictly forbidden on December 10. No other prohibitions are recorded; there are only the significant facts that in time barrack passed barrack at mealtime with no sign of recognition, and that spontaneous group singing became as rare as in any outside community. The change was gradual and no date can be assigned to it, but its meaning is obvious. It showed that the prisoners were no longer uprooted but had established stable relationships within the camp; emotional solidarity, therefore, was no longer so necessary.

What were the Germans doing during all this excited behaviour? A united crowd of four thousand, resentful of their treatment, might easily have become a rebellious mob. The Germans knew this, and in the lack of any inner, stabilizing organization did their utmost to enforce external discipline. For a frantic day or two the guards even attempted to break up all groups of more than three persons in the compound, and every outburst of cheering brought furious demands for silence. Elaborate regulations covering the most minute details of life were posted in bewildering succession; this is an early example:

Until 6.00 A.M.	Absolute quiet
6.30	General waking-up
6.40	Opening of windows
7.00	Fetching of coffee
7.30–8.00	Cleaning the barracks
8.00	Carrying out paper
8.30	Carrying out tins, etc.
9.00	Bread distribution
10.30–1.00	Dinner—see special notice

Dinner till 3.00	Quiet in barracks
5.00	Supper—see special notice
6.30–7.00	Cleaning the barracks
8.45	Go to bed. *Everyone must be in his place*
9.00	Lights out. *Absolute quiet* (H)

Enforcement was left to the guards, who were kept understandably busy, especially since new rules were constantly being made. Henley writes on November 25: "Every day new and more stringent regulations come out. Breach of rules is punished severely, and there are always several sitting in the cells."

Many of the regulations were so absurd and vexatious that the prisoners consistently ignored them, and full enforcement would have required far more soldiers than the authorities possessed. During the first weeks, however, their mere existence and the soldiers' efforts to enforce them provided enough external pressure to head off any open resistance. The seamen were often angry and rebellious, and their "skilly riot" on November 27 was potentially dangerous, but the guards were able to suppress it promptly. The Germans thus kept the initiative during the critical period when an uprising was conceivable; later on, when they had largely lost it, the prisoners themselves were too stably organized to be carried away by emotion.

Meanwhile a good deal of resentment was discharged through the milder forms of collective behaviour, for cheering, shouting, and singing on the march were all offensive to the Germans. Their function was thus a double one; while creating and affirming the prisoners' solidarity they also proclaimed that it was in part a reaction to hostility from without, and therefore directed against the Germans. In this way the first, crude pattern of organization was imposed on the men's new social world; they perceived it as sharply divided into a British in-group and a German out-group. These broad simple categories were mutually exclusive, and those who identified with the in-group soon lost any remaining sympathy with the government that had interned them.

The Ruhleben prisoners were always suggestible, for their situation was always an unstable one. Even when social organization had given them a protective shell of extraordinary toughness they were still vulnerable, for they never knew when their internment might end. The more conspicuous forms of crowd behaviour rapidly subsided, but they were never far below the surface. Whenever something occurred to remind the men that they were prisoners, to recall the basic distinction between British and Germans, the old feelings stirred again and the barracks began once more to cheer.

Solidarity, of course, does not consist in cheering or singing together but in the actual identification of each individual with his fellows, severally and collectively. That most men were strongly identified with the camp as a whole was shown in numberless ways during internment, and is still evident at the annual gatherings of the Ruhleben Association in London. And during the first tumultuous days there was also a remarkable sense of comradeship among all the individuals in the compound. It was not mere recognition of the need to stand together, but rather the stirring discovery by each prisoner that all his companions, of whatever class or kind, were wonderful people, whom it was a privilege to know. The veneer, it seemed, had been stripped away and men were seen for the first time as they really were—friendly, kind, and full of good humour and courage. The experience was a brief one, but it was never forgotten. Cohen writes:

The men who arrived in the course of that first afternoon quickly made friends with one another, abandoning all conventionality and freely exchanging experiences, sentiments, and hopes. If there is anything that mitigates the hardship of internment it is certainly the comradeship that is quickly established. (P. 31)

And Hughes, interned from November 6 to 27, writes on release: "The pleasantest and, I hope, the longest [memories] belong to the chapter of comradeship. It was the opportunity of a life-time for making friends." (P. 669)

References in contemporary diaries and postcards are scanty, since concrete events demanded all the space. Abbot's sentence on November 12, "Have met a lot of very nice fellows," is typical, and does poor justice to the warmth that pervaded the compound. Some of that warmth, however, is still apparent in the letters permitted from March 1915 onwards, though by then personal contacts were more selective:

Mar. 6, 1915. There are many fine and interesting men here, and I have made numerous friends. (Ewing)

Mar. 15, 1915. My life here has been made very agreeable on account of the men I have had an opportunity of meeting. It is of intense interest to talk with men whose outlook on life is far removed from your own. On the other hand, you get to know men really well in a very short space of time. (Leslie, pp. 48–9)

Apr. 5, 1915. We have a *wonderful* crowd here, everything from peers of the realm to cabin boys, and all ages from twelve to nearly seventy. There are many extremely fine fellows; I shall never regret my time here, that is if it doesn't last *too* long! (Denton)

Moreover, not one negative comment on other prisoners can be found in letters or diaries before mid-1915.

An earlier quotation showed how vividly a seafarer recalled the universal friendliness even in 1950, and the same theme was constantly heard in the 1933 questionnaires. More than 40 per cent of the "compensations" of internment listed had to do with comradeship and friendship. A few samples follow:[4]

Comradeship, and association with kindred spirits.   (Bank clerk)
The lasting comradeships that I made there, and the appreciation of others' position with the consequent withholding of adverse judgments.   (Student)
Personal friendships, and the spirit of good fellowship prevailing in general.   (Student architect)
The companionship of other men of all types.   (Businessman)
The extraordinarily large number of pleasant and interesting people I was fortunate enough to get to know.   (Student)

Such statements, written fifteen years after release, show the deep impression left by Ruhleben's brotherly spirit, and the spirit was at first practically all-inclusive.

Its most concrete expression was in the universal kindness shown to fellow-prisoners. Food supplies were shared as a matter of course, clothing given to any who needed it, money lent to chance acquaintances. In the generous atmosphere of the time such actions were seldom recorded, but there are a few early allusions. Henley's diary for November 12 reads:

The sailors are a fine lot and keep the spirit of the whole camp up. They are mostly without money. Stokers, seamen, etc. do manual work, but the officers are hard hit as they cannot lower their stand. We have four officers within two yards and find them decent chaps—we give them a lift with luxuries.

And Ewing writes in a postcard on January 8, 1915: "Have had first parcel, many thanks. Am now well equipped with clothes, but many are not, so nothing will go begging." Later references are numerous; Cohen mentions "the copious outpouring of sympathy in the early months" (p. 110), an ex-prisoner writes, "I have the happiest recollections of my fellow-prisoners, of their kindnesses, unselfishness and sportsmanship" (L 89), and the questionnaires list among the compensations of intern-

4. Since I frequently use questionnaire replies as illustrations, it should be noted that the respondents were far from being a representative sample. The 500 names circularized were secured from the Ruhleben Association, to which relatively few sailors and workingmen belonged. Of the 116 who completed the questionnaire, 54 per cent were professional men, 34 per cent in business, and 6 per cent workingmen; there were only three seafarers, two waiters, and one stableman.

ment: "The general good humour and kindness," and "Opportunity of helping others worse off than oneself."

Generosity was particularly in evidence towards newcomers. Geoffrey Pyke has much to say about his reception when he arrived from prison in January 1915:

> I still had nothing but a thin summer suit and a perfectly diaphanous shirt, the soles of my boots were worn away, and I had worn my one collar for sixteen weeks. My friends swept me away and clad me from head to foot in clothes that made my body glow with warmth. My friends, and their friends, not merely clothed me, but fed me for the first few days, gave me stores and books, bored themselves with my company, and left not a stone unturned to bring me back to life. It was not merely my friends. People I had never seen before were continually doing things for me, men whose purse was short, and who had a limited amount of parcels sent them from home. (P. 131)

Such responsiveness to any special need was always typical of Ruhleben, and particularly in the first few weeks. The Samaritan Fund for the sick and destitute was the earliest voluntary organization formed, and was seeking out and helping the most needy cases long before the captains secured financial relief from outside. The fund was started by a few well-to-do prisoners, but frequent contributions were made at concerts, services, and privately by all who had even a mark to spare. There was little sense of duty about it; everyone *wanted* to help if he could.

This mutual identification, however, was most complete in November, when no one expected internment to last more than a few weeks. Like the communism of the early Christian church, which endured only while Christ's second coming was momentarily awaited, the semi-communism of Ruhleben was greatly modified as the prisoners settled down for a long stay. Comradeship and kindness continued to characterize the camp, but they were no longer extended indiscriminately. As the individual became integrated into smaller groups he no longer needed his four thousand brothers, and in time he regarded most of them with apparent indifference, and some with active dislike. Only the sentimentalist will regret this, for it meant that social growth was occurring; men were perceiving differences among their fellows and no longer lumping them all into one category. Total, emotional solidarity had been the only type that could be achieved quickly, when it was most needed; it was actually self-limiting, however, for by uniting the prisoners and assuaging their fears it opened the way for constructive tasks that no undifferentiated body could handle. Organization was required, and organization is incompatible with mass solidarity.[5]

5. A valuable analysis of the inherent opposition between solidarity and organization is given by R. F. Bales in his *Interaction Process Analysis* (Cambridge, Mass.: Addison-Wesley Press, 1950).

The experience of solidarity, however, had gone too deep to be obliterated; in spite of countless later divisions it remained the unchanging substratum of Ruhleben life. The artist Nico Jungmann, captured at sea, never saw the camp until the end of 1916, but described himself as "filled with admiration for the spirit of patriotism and comradeship" (p. 93). Patriotism and comradeship had been the twin foundations of Ruhleben's original unity; though sometimes denied in practice, they continued to be men's supreme values, sacred and never to be questioned.

Comradeship implies perfect equality, whereas the prisoners were as unequal as they well could be in birth, education, and social position. These wide differences were ignored at the start of internment and greatly minimized thereafter, and how this was managed is of considerable social interest. For a day or two the emotional state of the men was probably the chief factor, for strong feeling is a powerful equalizer. Duke and ditch-digger may behave very differently under normal circumstances, but frighten or excite them sufficiently and their reactions become almost identical. Thus the shock of internment was in most cases enough to blind the Ruhlebenite to everything about his companions except the single fact that they, like himself, were Britons in distress. And throughout the winter feelings often rose high enough to revive this broad definition.

As the weeks wore on, however, more and more time was spent in routine activities that aroused no emotion, and simple blindness to social differences became impossible. Their influence was still negligible, however, because of other mental and behavioural adjustments—some forced by circumstances, some seemingly voluntary, but all making unconsciously for continued solidarity. The adjustments affected three areas: the individual's own awareness of his social position; his unwitting disclosure of it through a variety of external signs; and the recognition of these distinguishing marks by others. In each area changes occurred that tended to lessen awareness of social differences.

To take the last one first, the visibility of status marks was much reduced by the indiscriminate mixing of the population and the uniform conditions under which all had to live. It was not easy to pick out the titled aristocrat in a soup line—especially when frost had forced him to wear every garment he possessed. More significant, however, was the fact that no one was interested in picking him out, for social distinctions had lost their felt importance. Everything tended to shift the prisoners' attention away from extraneous differences and focus it on more essential ones; the vital question in a congested barrack was not whether a man had been to Eton but whether he was a good sort to live with. The two did not necessarily go together.

The individual's own consciousness of his status was also much attenuated. One factor has already been suggested: the temporal dislocation of internment, which made his previous existence seem dim and remote. And this was intensified by the fact that he could play none of his accustomed roles, since the groups to which they were relevant were missing. Here lay the cardinal difference between civilian and military camps; civilians began internment as individuals removed from their settings, whereas soldiers were still members of an existing social structure with built-in differences of status. For this reason, as Dr. A. L. Vischer implied in his 1918 study of war prisoners, only civilian camps were capable of such solidarity as Ruhleben evinced:

[Mental] unity is particularly characteristic of the civilian camps; in military camps, especially among the officers, the differences in rank create artificial divisions. But the civilian camp is a unit, representing as it does a varied mixture of chance acquaintances, who have no real mental or social ties with one another, but who are united by one longing and one hope. (P. 19, translated)

Social differences among the Ruhlebenites were wider than any found in military camps, but much of their reality was lost when the individual was cut off from the groups that recognized them.

A further agent in diminishing subjective distinctions was the early collective behaviour. The respectable bankers and scholars who cheered with the crowd and shouted its hackneyed slogans were inevitably changed in the process; they lost what remained of their dignity, they felt strangely irresponsible, they became years younger. Age differences, indeed, almost vanished in the crisis period; all the prisoners seemed equally juvenile. It was another aspect of the levelling, "homogenizing" process that made solidarity possible.[6]

Finally there was the problem of distinctive behaviour. Almost everything that a prisoner said or did reflected the norms he had learned in his home and thus revealed his general social background. Little could be done about such indelible stigmata as an "Oxford accent," but significant modifications were made in a wide range of customs and conventions. Their net result was a convergence of norms towards a common level, so that the everyday behaviour of seamen and "swells" was no longer easily distinguishable. The modifications were of course unplanned—those concerned felt they were merely behaving "naturally"

6. Cohen-Portheim noted the same phenomenon at the start of his internment in England: "The great secret of masculine psychology is that all men of all ages act and behave like re-become schoolboys as soon as their individualities are merged in a crowd" (*Time Stood Still*, p. 30).

—but they were highly conducive to solidarity, and this seems to have been their chief function. For they occurred during the crisis period and remained in force only as long as solidarity was needed; once the men had settled down, the conventions in which they had been reared were gradually re-established. The incidence of change was also significant. Norms that were fairly uniform throughout British society—those relating to property, decency, and bodily cleanliness, for example—were altered only slightly and for a short period, whereas those peculiar to certain groups, particularly the upper and middle classes, were more drastically affected. The latter are of course ways of marking and preserving social distinctions, so that their immediate suspension and later reinstatement are useful indicators of changes in the camp.

Accurate description of the shifts in convention is hampered by the fact that the information and comments come almost entirely from middle-class people. Their impressions were all alike: of a "breakdown" of customary behaviour, followed by a gradual return to more conventional living. In a clever parody of *The Mikado* a new arrival was instructed as follows:

> You had best forget
> Rules of etiquette;
> Vain indeed are manners formal
> Circumstances so abnormal
> Make us all forget
> Rules of etiquette.[7]
> (*RCM* 5, p. 16)

This is a middle-class view; the "forgetting" would certainly have been less apparent to members of lower occupational groups. For in the convergence upon common standards it was the upper and middle classes that did most of the shifting; the new norms were closest to those of seamen and workingmen. For this there were obvious reasons; for one, the white collar classes were in a numerical minority. Stable life was also a more drastic change for them than for those accustomed, say, to the forecastle; they were therefore more prepared for concomitant changes in custom. And conditions did more than make refinements of conduct seem out of place; in November they rendered many of them quite impracticable. Daily shaving, hand washing before each meal, separate spoons for soup and coffee, the use of table napkins—all these inevitably went by the board. And there was the further fact that many

---

7. Although camp life was always unconventional, the verse is much more applicable to the first winter than to 1916, when it appeared. By that date a good deal of social etiquette had re-appeared.

bourgeois conventions are notoriously burdensome to the male; thus their temporary abandonment was a kind of holiday. In small groups, however, there must have been a good deal of levelling up as well as levelling down, particularly after the first winter, and it is a pity that there are no detailed accounts from men who messed with groups a step or two above them socially.

The most striking change in convention affected every social class; this was the immediate, spontaneous removal of all restrictions on social intercourse. The change was essential, for solidarity required complete freedom of communication. We have seen how quickly conversations sprang up in the opening days; no one hesitated to join a chatting group of strangers, for there were no real strangers in the compound. Men who met at the canteen or in the latrines were most often entirely unknown to one another, but talking was as natural in Ruhleben as silent reticence would be elsewhere. Farwell might be described as a fairly conventional person, but during the first two months his many conversations are recorded simply as "talked to a young Boer," "talked to a man who had been in Moabit prison," and "talked to a young sailor from our loft." Not until January 15, 1915, does he record for the first time an "introduction" to a Shetland Islander.

All this may seem too natural to deserve mention, but it underlines the complete freedom of Ruhleben's early days and distinguishes them from the months that followed, when much of this freedom was lost. Cohen says, for instance:

> We dispensed with introductions during the first few months, and started a conversation with anybody we met. . . . But the innate reserve of the Englishman soon manifested itself even in captivity, and we felt in time we must not address a fellow-prisoner without an introduction, lest we should be snubbed. (P. 111)

"Innate reserve," however, explains nothing, for the usual sequence had been completely reversed. The four thousand did not start as strangers and gradually get to know one another; instead, they began as comrades and in time got *not* to know one another. A young business-man tells a similar story:

> At first in our barrack we used to barge into any box and pass the time of day, or see if someone had some tea. But soon we began knocking, and of course later on I never thought of going into a strange box unless I had some special reason, like arranging a rugby practice. (L 47)

The meaning of these changes is obvious. The men came into internment so insecure that they could tolerate no obstacles to the mutual contacts they needed, while the later social growth entailed the appearance of barriers between groups and of an etiquette for crossing them.

Uniformity in dress was of course impossible and costume was brought to a common level only by the rigours of the winter. In the early days the variety of the population and the caprice of some individuals made the scene a colourful one. Henley writes on November 12:

> Costumes are amusing—riding, ski-ing, motoring, sailors', officers', jockey's, sailing suits, caps and hats of all descriptions. One chap with white duck trousers has drawn large broad arrows on them and looks a fair sight. Kindersley looks very smart in knee breeches, sweater, coat, gloves and so on.

The majority of course wore whatever they had, with a diminishing care for appearances, but for a time certain men made a point of dressing well and kept the shoeblacks busy, while others, as Henley notes, were already emphasizing their abandonment of convention. The approach of winter, however, forced everyone into a drab uniformity. Cohen writes:

> We soon shed the hats and coats of civilization and donned cloth or woollen caps, which we pulled over our ears, and huge woollen mufflers which we wrapped around us; and then we put aside our box-calf boots and put on huge clogs or Wellington boots, which made a fearful clattering on the stone floors of the stable passage. (P. 73)

From now until spring appearances ceased to matter; collars and ties gave place to sweaters, the shoeblacks vanished, and numbers of men let their beards grow or shaved only on Sundays.

It might be thought that freedom from any compulsion to dress respectably would be one of the few compensations of internment, but the growth of a society in 1915 reinstated many conventions, and dress was not exempted. Of course the men had to replace worn garments; clothes were shipped from England, two tailors are regular advertisers in the early magazines, and in later years the official canteens had a tailoring department. Laundries and cleaners were also available. It is still surprising, however, to see the collars and ties in group photographs, and most prisoners also "dressed up" regularly for church, concerts, and the theatre. Denton writes home in June 1915: "I have had quite a nice suit made here, as I was very ragged and had to have something for Sundays, concerts, etc."

Denton, however, was the Anglican choirmaster, and those in public positions were the first to feel that appearances must be maintained.[8]

8. The stricter conformity to group norms expected of leaders than of followers is remarkably shown in W. F. Whyte's *Street Corner Society* (Chicago: University of Chicago Press, 1943).

Barrack captains were rarely seen except in business suits, and A. C. Ford, chairman of Ruhleben's remarkable Camp School, gives this account of his first public lecture in 1915:

> I was asked to speak in the grandstand, on Bernard Shaw, I think. Until then I had been wearing a full beard, but I felt that if I were going to be called upon to do the kind of work I did in the outside world it would not do to get too unconventional, so before the lecture I shaved the beard off. When I arrived no one recognized me, and when I stood up on the platform there was a titter which grew into a loud roar of laughter, and the whole audience laughed steadily for about five minutes. (M 29)

This suggests the intimate connection between playing a specified social role and conforming to the norms that govern it. In 1914 these norms were suspended; Flint describes a well-known violinist, caught on tour, playing at an early concert "oblivious of his short running trunks, soiled shirt and bare legs" (p. 237). But a few months later, when serious lectures were organized, Ford felt that even a beard "would not do."

Except on formal occasions, class distinctions in dress were readily recognizable; perhaps the way in which the ship's officers stuck to their uniforms gave a lead to middle-class landsmen. In any case, collars and ties were always more numerous than would be likely today. Hot weather as well as cold, however, brought a general relaxation, and the prisoners themselves considered that they dressed very informally. Jarvis gives a first-hand view from the grandstand on a warm, cloudy Sunday at the end of May 1915:

> You'd be amused at the peculiar garb worn by the people passing, and incidentally at mine. Coloured handkerchiefs are the most popular head-gear, worn pirate fashion. Collars are noticeably more plentiful because it is Sunday, but still they are comparatively scarce. A number of sailors are in uniform, some with white-topped caps. College and school blazers are also popular. One man has a Tirolese peasant costume. There are more beards than usual, and some freaks have let their hair grow unusually long. I'm wearing no socks, flannel bags, khaki shirt with a khaki handkerchief in place of a collar, and a month's growth of hair.

The styles would hardly be "peculiar" in a holiday resort today, but standards were then very different; not until August 1915, for instance, did Ewing ask his mother to send him soft collars instead of stiff ones, because of laundering difficulties and because "they are not necessary here."

If norms of dress were little altered, manners were drastically affected; customary courtesies seemed out of place, meals were eaten in the atmosphere of the forecastle, and in Denton's box, at least, it was months before "please" and "thank you" were heard at table. Middle-class prisoners often wondered how they would again adapt to society; Abbot notes in his diary in November 1914: "Rules for men leaving Ruhleben: When getting refreshments for lady at dance don't call 'Line up!' to those in front. Don't stick your spoon in your button-hole and go to the kitchen with your plate at a restaurant." Ewing writes in June 1915, "I fear my manners when I get home will be awful," and a mock advertisement in a 1916 magazine reads:

TO FORTY-FIVERS[9]: The Rules of Polite Society explained in Simple Language. Sample Chapters:
"When to use a pocket-handkerchief"
"What to do upon seeing a female for the first time"
"When not to use a knife at table"

(*RCM* 5, p. 63)

After the first winter, however, many small groups established at least some of the amenities to which their members were accustomed. Abbot writes home in October 1915: "Yesterday our tea-service arrived and we had our first drink out of a cup and saucer for nearly twelve months —we were like children with new toys." And a schoolmaster reports on his box: "We didn't bother about words, but kept up a high standard of behaviour to each other, and we always laid our meals decently and kept the box clean and tidy" (Q 31). Class differences, of course, largely determined how much loss and recovery of such niceties would occur.

Not much can be said of the conventions concerned with decency; contemporary references are lacking, and little is known about class norms in 1914 except that the upper classes were less prudish about bodily exposure than the lower. Some relaxation was forced by the necessity of bathing in the open corridor in the early weeks; young and better educated men appeared less sensitive about this than elderly seamen and workingmen, who could often be found bathing in mid-afternoon when few people were about. Codes of decency, however, are complex and somewhat puzzling; though drilled in far more rigorously than, say, table manners, they also alter markedly with the situation. They are immediately modified, of course, when the sexes are segregated, and they apply, not to bodily exposure itself, but to *unnecessary* exposure, which may be variously defined. The same prisoners who crowded together under the showers in the Emigrant station often took great pains to avoid exposing themselves when undressing for bed. And in May 1915 two Catholic missionaries in Barrack 1 complained to the Com-

---

9. "Forty-fivers" (men over 45) became eligible for exchange under an agreement made in 1916, but not implemented until January 1918.

mandant about men bathing in the corridor, with the result that the practice was forbidden in that barrack. In general, group norms in this field were probably little altered.

A real shifting of standards, however, was forced by the open latrines, which provided not even a screen between the seats; some men must have suffered as acutely as did Cohen-Portheim, a German citizen interned in England, who says feelingly, "One could not get used to it ever" (p. 36). For a few days there were huge line-ups at the small pay-toilet under the first grandstand, but nearly all Ruhlebenites, unlike Portheim, soon got used to the facilities described by Henley: "There are batteries of open closets in the stableyard, one is 48 plus 36 seats long, and it is a funny sight to see so much 'business' being attended to at once, and in one line." Here, certainly, social differences were thoroughly erased.

The most conspicuous levelling occurred in the prisoners' speech habits, and was signalized by a flood of profanity that engulfed every section of the camp. Again the middle class wondered how they would fit in at home, and released men were advised to go into quarantine until the effects of Ruhleben had worn off. Jarvis and Graham make identical comments in 1915 and 1916 respectively:

> I'm beginning to wonder whether I'll understand conversation which leaves out half a dozen "choice" epithets. I've got so used to the sailors' lingo.

> I wonder how much bad language I shall use when I leave this place. The Ruhleben talk is shocking and is bound to leave a stain.

Cohen has no doubt about the source of contagion:

> Coarse and filthy vituperations came first from the lips of the lower stratum of our community, to which they were native, but they gradually and imperceptibly percolated through the higher strata, until even the university graduate would unblushingly utter them. (P. 194)

And Govett points out the subsequent reaction, though it began much earlier than he suggests:

> The speech of the better classes rapidly degenerated till in many cases it became as bad as (or worse than) that of the sailors, whose coarseness is proverbial. This lasted for three years, when, curiously enough, there came a reaction, and many attempted to drop the vile vocabulary they had acquired. (P. 457)

Two of those quoted (both landsmen) suggest that it was the sailors who set the common standard, but such experts as the race-track employees gave able assistance, and even the university men may not have been so immaculate as Cohen believed. However, the reputation of the seamen, firemen, and fishermen was at least well maintained, as many magazine references imply:

> The Mariner next comes upon our view;
> His uniform and language both are blue.
> A British sailor, broad of beam and bearing,
> Full of strange oaths that seamen call endearing.
> Ye landsmen pause, ye innocents be chary,
> Lest ye provoke his rich vocabulary!
>
> (*IRC* 1, p. 7)

September 23: Hied me to ye Kitchenne, or Gallie, for Soupe. Upon the Roade back I did by mischance drop some of the hot fluid upon a Maryner's smallclothes, upon which he addressed me in such scurvie language as I never heard the like of. (*PP*)

The chief interest of Ruhleben's profanity lies in the prompt reduction of behavioural differences in still another area, and in the fact that it was again the "better classes," as Govett calls them, who made the most marked change. This is regularly the case in such circumstances, chiefly because swearing, until it becomes automatic and meaningless, can relieve emotional tension. There were plenty of tensions in Ruhleben that could not be vented on those responsible, and swearing gave them at least partial release. Suggestibility was also involved, for the men who swore were defining the situation in a crude but positive way, while the negative act of refraining from profanity had no suggestive effect. And behind it all, of course, lay the initial need for solidarity; some men had to assimilate to others if distinctions were to be erased, and the more fastidious prisoners had as yet no social prestige to balance their smaller numbers.

Once an organized life was established differences in speech reappeared. Every close-knit circle, particularly those in which the men slept and ate, developed its own norms in this and other matters, and the cruder forms of profanity were often frowned upon and sometimes penalized. The "swear-book" of Denton's box, dated September 1915, lists almost every profane and obscene term in the language, along with the prescribed fine—10, 15, or 20 pfennigs, according to the violence of the expression. A clause inserted later to meet serious emergencies reads: "For the lump sum of ONE MARK, payable in advance, a member may have free use of any or all of the expressions listed for the space of five minutes." The proceeds went to provide a box feed. Control elsewhere was equally lenient, so that Ruhleben's language never lost its robust flavour. In 1916 the magazine editor is still referring to it:

"A leader of Camp thought has lately read a French drama to a select audience in order to accustom students to modern French. We are by this time all accustomed to Ruhleben English" (*RCM* 4, p. 23). Here, however, as in the previous quotations, the implied criticism shows that more than one standard existed; this was the case at least after the first winter.

A similar evolution took place in what the British delicately call "smokeroom topics." Obscenity was flagrant in the community singing of the early weeks, the "Derby Ram" and far less reputable ballads being constantly sung to delighted applause. Stories and jokes were predominantly sexual, smutty limericks and obscene photographs were produced with no trace of furtiveness. This was a level on which all but the most repressed could meet. A gradual change occurred, however. The sheets of "latrine poetry" that circulated during the first winter vanished after the spring, and the bawdy songs were no longer heard in public. They too had aided solidarity and were dropped when it was less needed. The first few issues of *In Ruhleben Camp* contain a few mildly improper allusions, but the later magazines are as pure as *Punch*. The same trend was apparent in the theatre, the frankly sexual appeal of the first "girl" shows giving way to Gilbert and Sullivan and drawing-room comedy. Sex never became taboo except in certain puritanical circles, but the proprieties of 1914 were firmly reinstated in public.

The unconventionality of Ruhleben's early days was more significant than it appeared at the time. Distinctive modes of speech and conduct are ways of asserting group differences, and so had to be modified. Common norms were reached in the only way possible—by the suspension of many middle-class standards—and the prisoners thus began their common life with the assertion, not of differences, but of identity. This was both essential to them at the time and also an inspiration for later achievements.

More was involved than this, however. Those who yielded to the demands of solidarity, abandoning old habits and acting in unfamiliar ways, were actually preparing themselves to be members of a new society. Only if they were in some degree "reborn," as suggested earlier—made plastic, malleable, flexible—could their behaviour be shaped by new forces in the camp rather than by standards from the past. And if, as seems evident, it was the middle class of whom solidarity required the most drastic changes, they would also be most responsive to the possibilities of Ruhleben. They did, it is true, recover many of their old customs, but not until the society was well established, and then in very modified form. This may partly explain why Ruhleben's creative leadership came almost entirely from a minority of educated men. It also helps to account for the contrast between Ruhleben and certain officers' camps, similar to it in size and conditions, but with no comparable social growth. For captured officers brought with them a code of conduct which they preserved almost intact during imprisonment, and this, while it immunized them against anything like crowd behaviour, also limited their spontaneity and hampered the development of new social forms.

The norms of a social group are thus conservative forces, tending to preserve it against disruption. That is why political revolutions are less important than social or industrial ones; unless a revolution changes the ways in which people lead their everyday lives, it really changes nothing. Genuine social change always involves the disruption and realignment of existing classes; hence it invariably brings a breakdown in previous standards of conduct. The moral disorder that follows is usually deplored, but it is actually an essential part of the change—both a sign that people are ready for new patterns of living, and also a powerful factor in making them so.

Before ending this chapter a paradoxical fact should be noted: that the first result of internment for many Ruhlebenites was an astonishing sense of freedom. Conventional schoolmasters, strait-laced churchgoers, dutiful sons, henpecked husbands—all found themselves suddenly free to behave, talk, and think almost as they chose. Govett says of the freedom of thought: "There was, to all intents and purposes, no 'public opinion' on any subject whatever that might tend to impose conventional standards on thought. I am convinced that we were far more free in this respect than any country on the face of the earth." (P. 458.) And an interned waiter reports, as the "one thing" that did most to make life enjoyable, "the freedom to do almost as one wished, mixing with people, doing and seeing everything different" (Q 113). Although conventional control had been largely replaced by suggestibility, the feeling of freedom was real and memorable.

All men, however, do not welcome a holiday from convention; while some "go native" in the jungle others dress for dinner. The difference lies of course in the degree to which certain customs have been absorbed as parts of the self. To Cohen-Portheim, interned in England, adherence to convention meant preserving his integrity as an individual:

I can imagine no circumstances where it is more necessary to stick strictly to the outward decencies and conventions of life. They cease to be taken for granted, they become an effort, but also they become a symbol of resistance to outward circumstances; they come to mean that one will not give in, that one remains oneself in no matter what company or place, they become a strong and most necessary moral support. (P. 39)

To remain unaltered by a social crisis, however, results in isolation from the developments that follow it, and Portheim's accounts of both Knockaloe and Wakefield camps are those of a detached spectator. Ruhleben had its detached observers in later days, but they had also been part of the crowd and had shared its solidarity and elation. That meant that they did not "remain themselves," in Portheim's phrase, but were drawn into the current of change and emerged with new standards and somewhat new selves. No book as penetrating as *Time Stood Still* came out of Ruhleben, but there was a ring of reality about the life of the camp itself for which one listens in vain in Portheim's narrative. The spectator, it is true, sees most of the game, but the typical Ruhlebenite was a player.

4 RUMOURS AND MORALE

THE BEHAVIOUR of a population reflects the degree of social organization existing in it, and the simple, undifferentiated unity of Ruhleben's opening weeks, though so exhilarating to the prisoners, could do little or nothing to settle them down. Only a more complex social structure could bring that about—one in which the individual, instead of floating in a warm sea of solidarity, would be anchored and controlled by a variety of specific group attachments. The setting apart of officials and the growth of informal ties among messmates were the beginnings of such a differentiated structure, but only the beginnings; it was six months before organization was advanced enough to have obvious stabilizing effects. In the meantime, and particularly during the three weeks of the crisis period, there were many signs of continuing social unrest. The mass cheering ceased quickly, but suggestibility and emotional tension remained, and one of their most striking manifestations was the prevalence of rumours.

Rumours occur wherever a sizable number of people are communicating freely, are deeply concerned about some issue, but lack any reliable information about it. And the talkative Ruhlebenites, burning with unanswered questions about their own fate and that of their country, inevitably became wholesale rumour manufacturers. Every account of the camp gives space to the subject; the following excerpts, from Hughes's article and the anonymous *In the Hands of the Huns* (26), are brief and typical. The first refers to the earliest outbreaks, Hughes having been released on medical grounds on November 27, 1914:

We just walked and talked, and watched for omens of release and bamboozled ourselves with rumours; and the price of any solid news was above rubies. (P. 669)

Day after day brought its crop of rumours, and hardly a day passed without the invention of some impossible story regarding the release of prisoners by a certain date. There seemed to be a section of rumour-mongers in our midst who took a delight in inventing "authentic" reports. (P. 75)

The rumours did not have to be "invented," however; they arose spontaneously from the men's common needs and the uncertainty of their situation. Man's primary intellectual need is to live in an organized mental world, one where his present and future are known and predictable. Lacking such a world he is driven to construct one, using the two kinds of material available to him: his own wishes, fears, and guesses, and the suggestions he gathers from others. Both operate in everyday life—in wishful thinking, for instance, and in the acceptance of hearsay and gossip; but these seldom monopolize our thinking because they are quickly corrected by hard facts and better information. In Ruhleben's first weeks, however, no such checks existed; everyone was equally in the dark and all were moved by the same powerful wishes. Wishful thinking, therefore, instead of being corrected by communication with others, was progressively reinforced, and the result was a rumour epidemic of tremendous proportions.

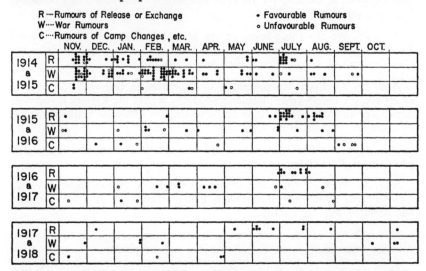

FIGURE 3. Incidence of rumours of release, war events, and administrative changes recorded in diaries and letters of thirteen prisoners. Each vertical column represents a three-day period. The bottom line is extended to show November 1918.

Since rumours directly reflect current tension and uncertainty they supply valuable insights into the mental state of a given population, as was demonstrated during the Second World War.[1] And the Ruhleben diaries and letters provide a record of their nature and incidence in the

1. See especially G. W. Allport, and L. J. Postman, *The Psychology of Rumor* (New York: Henry Holt & Co., Inc., 1947).

camp that is, though inevitably incomplete, quite unique. Figure 3 shows the total distribution of rumours, and will be referred to at several points. The matter of immediate interest is the heavy concentration during November 1914; though the month was half over before any rumours could be specifically dated, its total is the second largest in the whole four years. This is sure evidence of the emotional tension existing.

Farwell's diary is particularly valuable for its regular record of rumours, and the following are those he heard in the last two weeks of November. To read them is to breathe the very atmosphere of the period.

Nov. 17. We are all to be sent to Frankfurt an der Oder on the 25th instant.

Nov. 19. 250,000 Germans drowned at Dixmuiden. Russians have taken Breslau. Germans admit the loss of 24 guns in France. One of the 42cm. guns captured at Verdun. We are to be exchanged at the rate 5 to 1. Russians have got far into East Prussia.

Nov. 20. We are going home on the 26th. Lille has been retaken by the French. Naval engagement in the North Sea, we took two cruisers from the Germans and turned their own guns onto them.

Nov. 22. Kitchener has presented an ultimatum to Germany that he will arrest every German (man, woman and child) within the Empire if she does not accept an exchange of 10 to 1. Three English first-class battleships sunk by German submarines off Dover.

Nov. 27. Ireland has declared war on England. The Germans admit 50,000 prisoners at Dixmuiden.

Nov. 28. Portugal has declared war on Germany. *Planmässiger Rückzug* from Ypern. Thousands of Germans being arrested in England. Bulgaria has declared war on Turkey.

Nov. 29. We are to be deported to a German colony or to England. Another attempt made on Friedrichshafen by our airmen.

Nov. 30. Russians in Breslau. Conference of eight meeting at the Hague to decide about us. Colonials among us to be released.

Dec. 2. "Derfflinger" sunk by Queen Mary in 6 minutes. Ostende occupied by British troops. We are all to go out by the 14th.

Just as a prisoner's diary or letter reflects his state of mind when he wrote it, so these rumours reflect the beliefs, perceptions, hopes, and fears common to most of the population. Not completely, of course, since matters of certainty were never projected as rumours, but fully enough to be very revealing.

It is obvious that the prisoners were incessantly occupied with two unresolved issues: their own future and the progress of the war. The two were of course related, for everyone knew that a quick British victory would also mean release. About both issues the men's wishes were intensely strong, but frustrated by almost complete lack of knowledge. No newspapers were allowed at the time of these extracts, so that even German war news was unavailable, while the future of the prisoners was known to literally no one. For there were no precedents for such an internment; its outcome depended on agreement between the two warring governments. The German authorities had no desire to perpetuate Ruhleben, for they hoped with their 4,000 internees to buy the return of 26,000 German civilians from England. They were accordingly in favour of total exchange, all for all. The attitude of the British, however, was coldly realistic; they were in favour of exchange, certainly, but on the basis of man for man. The two standpoints were equally logical but quite irreconcilable, and they remained so throughout the war.[2] Since neither government thought it necessary to give the victims any information, the Ruhleben prisoners spent four years of nagging uncertainty.

Most of the rumours listed reflect wishful thinking, but not all: the prisoners are going to a German colony (by what route, one wonders!), the British have lost three capital ships. Pessimistic rumours of this sort were common during the earlier stages of the Second World War, and may serve, as Allport and Postman suggest,[3] to rationalize and "explain" the anxiety of people who know they are not being told everything and who have, at the back of their minds, fears too dreadful to be put into words. This might account for some early camp rumours, when the German press announced almost daily that Britain was clearly losing the war. Later, however, most of the stories of Allied defeats were probably due to the poorly concealed pleasure that we take in any disaster that does not directly affect us, and particularly in being the first to startle others with the news. In any case, as Figure 3 shows, "wish" rumours greatly outnumbered "fear" rumours throughout Ruhleben's history.

Another mental characteristic revealed by Farwell's rumours is a naive self-importance that is both amusing and pathetic in retrospect. Kitchener is making extravagant threats, conferences are being sum-

---

2. British Government White Papers, Miscellaneous, No. 25 (1916), "Further Correspondence Respecting . . . the Proposed Release of Interned Civilians," July 1916 (Cd. 8296). A summary of the negotiations to the end of 1916 is contained in *The Ruhleben Prisoners: The Case for their Release* (42).

3. See *The Psychology of Rumor*, ch. 1.

moned—all on behalf of the handful of civilians at Ruhleben. To the prisoners their internment is a matter of immense consequence, which must naturally be of central concern to their government; not for many months was this warped perspective corrected. And it may not be fanciful to see these rumours, not only as wish-projections, but also as unconscious defences against the bitter knowledge that slowly penetrated the camp—that the fate of its inmates was, to a government at war, of no importance whatever.

All the rumours listed are short and definite, without qualifying phrases; they are also highly specific, bristling with names, numbers, places, and dates. Here we are on surer ground, for experiments on the verbal transmission of stories regularly show a tendency to "sharpen" the material by heightening its central features, adding circumstantial detail, and omitting irrelevancies and implied limitations. However a rumour starts, it soon becomes a clear, unqualified statement of fact; human beings have a deep-rooted dislike of uncertainty and vagueness.

Finally, this batch of rumours neatly illustrates the role of information. When the camp opened Berlin daily papers were sold in it; they contained the official war reports but nothing about interned civilians. The many rumours referred to before mid-November cannot be traced, but all seem to have focussed on release. On November 17, however, newspapers were banned, and none came in until December 3, when the sensational *Berliner Zeitung am Mittag* was admitted. This is the fortnight covered by Farwell's entries, and it will be noted that war rumours outnumber all others. In contrast, during the fortnight *following* December 3 not a single war rumour is recorded. This seems conclusive, but it is not; the men's need for cheering news was often strong enough to create optimistic war rumours in spite of the German papers —whose credibility, of course, was widely questioned. A similar break in release rumours early in December may be attributed to another form of "news"—the erection of two new barracks in the compound. Again, however, the interruption was only a brief one.

How did all these rumours originate? Some represent valid information that had leaked to the prisoners from guards or captains: Portugal did announce her intended military participation on November 23, five days before Farwell heard of a "declaration of war"; certain colonials were released before Christmas, only to be interned again a few weeks later; destitute Germans were being interned in England, though the policy was neither new nor so drastic as the rumour implied. Even false rumours may have had remote factual sources; the naval disaster recorded on November 21 suggests the "resurrection" and heightening of an actual occurrence of two months earlier—the sinking of three British cruisers (not battleships) by a single submarine on September 17. And the Russian armies in Poland had appeared to threaten Breslau, though not since early November; by the 30th, when rumour put them in the city, there was not an armed Russian on German soil.

The last two examples illustrate how the rumour-making process operated. Some prisoner communicated, intentionally or otherwise, a fact, supposition, or wish to the first of a long series of others, each of them eager to "know" about the war and his own fate, and particularly eager for knowledge that would satisfy his present needs, whether for hope and encouragement or for a dramatic disaster to talk about. During its passage through so many similarly oriented minds the report suffered small, cumulative alterations, usually unconscious, but all fitting it more closely to the prevailing mood of the camp. Details were omitted, added, or distorted, time and place appropriately shifted, until the original report became a piece of collective fiction for which no individual was responsible. Thus, as long as the men were preoccupied with their two great questions, any reference to them, no matter how guarded, was enough to produce rumours; if it could boast an outside source, so much the better, but at this tense period every prisoner was a potential rumour-starter. His most careless utterance might be overheard and sweep through the camp, gathering authority and detail in its progress, and be repeated to him later in unrecognizable form.

The ceaseless flow of rumours was not only a sign that the prisoners were unsettled but also an obvious factor in keeping them so, and on December 15 Burton records an official effort to suppress them: "Lined up this afternoon for fresh regulations. Commandant gave out that any-one circulating rumours would be punished with 72 hours' cells. He also informed us that we were here until the end of the war!" In the next eight days there are no rumours of release in any diary—not, of course, because of the Commandant's unenforceable threat, but because he had stated that Ruhleben was a permanency. This was only an inspired guess—negotiations for total exchange continued at least until 1916—but it was precisely what was needed if the prisoners were to sober up and settle down. At this time, however, no single statement could dam the flood for long; on December 23 rumours of exchange were again recorded, and on the 29th the prisoners heard, on mysterious authority, that the first batch of exchanged Germans had left Tilbury for Rotterdam.

Effective control of rumours had to await the appearance of new needs and interests as the camp became organized; in the meantime, however, the disease itself produced a partial immunity. The constant raising of illusory hopes became so intolerable that many men protected their feelings by deliberate scepticism. "Most cheerful rumours going about," Henley wrote as early as November 19, "but as Ruhleben is noted for rumours I don't believe much." And by 1915 a deep-grained scepticism was as characteristic of most Ruhlebenites as was their early credulity. Denton and Graham wrote as follows, in April and September respectively:

There are always rumours of exchange floating about, but I stop my ears to them. We have had too many.

When we first came we thought it was a question of days or weeks. Now we talk of longer periods quite seriously, and take not the slightest interest in camp rumours of "getting out soon"—this month, next month, and so on.

These letters were written when organization had rendered the camp relatively stable—only relatively, of course, since rumours were still circulating. Indeed, though the disease was often arrested for long periods, it could never be cured, for the prisoners' future was never clarified. Whenever the universal wish for release was intensified, as it was most notably by the first hint of each further winter, new large-scale outbreaks regularly occurred.

Almost every important trend in Ruhleben's later history had its roots in the critical opening weeks, and this is especially true of the "morale" of the prisoners—of how they bore themselves emotionally. The previous chapter described the almost magical transformation of bewilderment and panic into something like elation, but the picture needs some qualification. For the mental climate of this period was highly changeable, with hope and dejection, anger and exuberance, rapidly succeeding one another. The man who at six in the evening was blasphemously grumbling over his miserable supper might, at seven, be joining uproariously in "Are we down-hearted? No, No, No!" (to the hymn-tune, "Sun of my Soul"), and at eight cowering on his straw-sack, homesick and depressed. C. H. Brooks is the only writer to note this mercurial tendency; "Men," he says, "who throughout a business career have been controlled and calculating become emotional. . . . A trifle is sufficient to elevate them to extravagant hopes or throw them into extravagant despondency." Equanimity is possible only in a stable social world, and that of the Ruhlebenite was still disorganized and fluctuating.

The emotional fluctuations, however, were not random, but were determined almost entirely by the setting in which the prisoner found himself. He was never alone physically, but he could be alone in his thoughts, and at such times he was often fed up and dispirited, as some diary extracts show. But when he was shouting with his barrack, singing a ribald song, or playing rounders, he was in a social world that took him out of himself and gave him cheerfulness and courage. This duality in Ruhleben life was most marked in the early weeks, but it held true also in later years, when the high or low spirits of a prisoner depended chiefly on whether he was immersing himself in organized activities or holding aloof from them. Life from the standpoint of an isolated individual was thus always different from life in its collective aspects, and this accounts for some of the sharp discrepancies in published accounts of the camp.

The quick responsiveness of the opening weeks was another aspect of solidarity, which had made emotions as "contagious" as beliefs and actions; whatever the men felt when together they tended to feel in common. They also felt it with great intensity, for when a laugh or a cheer is echoed back by others the feeling it expresses is reinforced. The mood of the crisis period was therefore seldom neutral, but swung from one extreme to the other. A new German outrage could make the men tense with indignation, patriotism had unprecedented fervour, and anything amusing seemed indescribably funny. When rumours were vivid the mood was extravagantly hopeful; on the night of the skilly riot it was thoroughly ugly. And the solemnity of the first death, as Burton's account suggests, hushed every voice in the compound:

Nov. 24, 1914. All hands mustered this morning and marched past hearse containing body of donkeyman of S.S. Sappho who died Saturday night. Very impressive sight. Poor devil, he would be proud of his funeral, could he but see it.

When the hat was passed around afterwards the prisoners filled it with money to be sent to the widow in England.

The outstanding fact about the emotions of this period, however, is that they were not being given free rein but were under effective control. Hughes's early comment suggests the deliberate suppression of gloomy feelings: "Qualms of weariness and longing must needs come, but you would never guess it from the breezy demeanour of the camp" (p. 664). And the men's aggressive high spirits when together, their jokes about hardships, the studied cheerfulness of their postcards home—all these look like morale rather than mood, like determination not to give in rather than mere light-heartedness. A nondescript collection of civilians, plunged unprepared into the backwash of war, had somehow become convinced that they must bear themselves like good soldiers and keep up a bold front. Such a collective resolve establishes a social norm—a standard to which all are expected to conform—and this is what seems to have happened in the first days of internment. The men's buoyant cheerfulness thus had two sources; though it arose naturally from the sense of solidarity, its maintenance also became obligatory upon all who wished to "belong."

Most prisoners had no sense of obligation in the matter; they merely felt cheerful when together and acted accordingly. But this is precisely what happens when individuals are fully identified with a group; its norms are "internalized" as their personal standards and need little bolstering from others. That external pressure also existed, however, is clear from the immediate appearance of the morale-raising imperatives: "Keep your pecker up!" / "Grin and bear it!" / "Never down-hearted!" / "Keep smiling!" Their incessant reiteration obviously helped to maintain conformity to the standard and ensure its acceptance by each new batch of prisoners. Compliance was at first so general and spontaneous that the norm was not consciously recognized; Denton, for instance, was merely puzzled by the behaviour of a middle-aged acquaintance: "Yes, Mr. F. is here," he wrote in January 1915, "he is an extraordinary person, always groaning about something." As time went on, however, it became evident that Ruhleben's high morale was not automatic, but was achieved by individual effort and guarded by an unwritten law. From 1915 onwards the prisoners constantly referred, somewhat nostalgically, to "the spirit of the first winter"—not "mood" or "atmosphere," but "spirit," implying active struggle against opposing forces. And in November 1915 Jarvis gave clear and unexpected testimony to the existence of a norm:

> I'd love to be able to make you and father feel less lonely than you must feel now, and I think the best way to do that is to tell you straight off that I'm as fit as a fiddle and that there's no down-heartedness allowed here. It would do you good to be able to look into this loft. In our end there are four landsmen and 73 sailors, firemen, cooks, engineers, mates, and ships' masters, and though belonging to a tribe of grumblers they're always cheery.

"No down-heartedness *allowed*" is explicit confirmation of what had happened: not just a uniform response by all to the same situation, but the emergence of a rule of conduct. It was the first restriction on the men's freedom to be imposed by themselves and not by the Germans, but it was only the first of many.

Even in November 1914 conformity was not universal, but the individual, though often tempted to bemoan his fate, no longer felt quite free to do so. To master his feelings was his first obligation as a Ruhlebenite; no one knew how it had arisen, but it was there and it was enforced. "Oh, for God's sake stop grousing," was frequently heard in the barracks; "if you can't say anything cheerful, keep your mouth shut!" And an engineer, describing his mess, wrote in 1933: "We had, however, one member (probably the brainiest) who took an unreasonably pessimistic attitude. He finally got so on the nerves of the rest that he was persuaded to leave the mess" (L 111). Men who were trying to suppress their own anxieties could not tolerate the presence of someone who made no such effort; he was too dangerous to the group's morale.

Ruhleben's original social norm never lost its force. Even in 1918, when years of internment had taken their toll, Nico Jungmann wrote after his transfer to Holland: "The splendid courage and good nature shown by the prisoners would make the gloomiest man ashamed to indulge his melancholy. . . . Indeed, it was only the concentrated determination of these men to make the best of a bad job that made existence bearable, and even cheerful" (pp. 98-9). To maintain this "concentrated determination" was the supreme moral law of Ruhleben. The camp was tolerant of much that would be disapproved elsewhere— profanity, obscenity, gambling, drunkenness—but it never tolerated self-pity or complaining of one's fate. To find any trace of these we have to look into the men's private letters, whereas the demand for a "stiff upper lip," compressed into easily memorable catchwords, was a ubiquitous feature of public life. Its clearest expression was in the "Ruhleben Song," written by C. H. Brooks for a revue in May 1915, and immediately adopted as the national anthem of Ruhleben. It had, as will be seen, a single theme: maintenance of a bold front in spite of trials and anxieties. The text follows:

> Oh, we're roused up in the morning
> When the day is gently dawning,
>   And we're put to bed before the night's begun;
> And for weeks and weeks on end
> We have never seen a friend,
>   And we've lost the job our energy had won.
> Yes, we've waited in the frost
> For a parcel that got lost,
>   Or a letter that the postmen never bring;
> And it's not all beer and skittles
> Doing work on scanty victuals,
>   Yet every man can still get up and sing. So—
>
> *Chorus*
> *Line up, boys, and sing this chorus,*
> *Shout this chorus all you can;*

We want the people there
To hear in Leicester Square
That we're the boys that never get down-hearted.
Back, back, back again in England,
  There we'll fill the flowing cup;
And tell them clear and loud
Of that Ruhleben crowd
  Who always kept their pecker up.

Oh, we send our love and kisses
To our sweetheart or the missus.
  And we say the life we lead is simply grand;
And we stroll around the Tea-'us
Where the girls can sometimes see us,
  And we say it's just as good as down the Strand.
Yet there sometimes comes a minute
When we see there's nothing in it,
  And the tale that we've been telling isn't true;
Down our spine there comes a-stealing
Just that little homesick feeling—
  Then I'll tell you, boys, the best thing you can do:

The importance of Ruhleben's first social norm needs little emphasizing. The men had to regard their internment either as a calamity to be endured or as a challenge to be met, and the turning point came very early. Had their choice been the first one they would have resigned themselves to circumstances, borne them as well as they could, and waited for release. Instead, they rose above their circumstances from the start, and the impetus carried them on to remarkable accomplishments. The choice was not a conscious one—it was too immediate for that—but it settled in broad outline the role that the prisoners were to play during the next four years. It is therefore worth inquiring how it came to be made, and what it involved psychologically.

In the first place, it *was* a choice. Captured soldiers typically entered their camps with the resolute bearing implanted by their training, and discipline by their superiors ensured its maintenance. There was nothing, however, to suggest that the Ruhleben civilians should behave similarly, and much to suggest that they might not; we have already read of "semi-hysteria" and "dazed bewilderment" among new arrivals. And secondly, it was a *collective* choice, owing nothing to leadership from above, for no such leadership existed. As such it was the emergent product of social interaction—of the myriad words and acts that give birth to all cultural forms. These are of course impossible to trace in detail, but in the case of this norm certain suggestions seem plausible.

There must obviously have been some individuals whose first reactions were not panicky but bold, and who thereby set a standard for others. And it is not hard to guess who they were: "The sailors," Henley wrote on November 12, "are a fine lot and keep the spirit of the whole camp up." Not only were they proverbially tough and intractable, but they entered the camp as bodies of men, not isolated individuals. There is thus every likelihood that Ruhleben owed its first norm and all that resulted from it to its 1,400 seafaring men. And, to judge by the 1933 questionnaires, a good many landsmen were also uncowed. While half the respondents report that they regarded their internment very seriously at first, even as "a catastrophe," the other half, including most of the younger men, say that they looked on it initially as an exciting or amusing adventure.

Given these widely differing reactions, why did the whole mass of prisoners converge on the bolder attitude and sanction it as "right"? The men themselves never had any doubt about the answer; they bore themselves as they did *because they were British*. Abbot's jottings in the first week expressed it succinctly: "The lazy Russians," he wrote; "Englishmen make the best of a bad job." An engineer was equally explicit in 1933: "There was a National Spirit among us which made us appear, if not feel, to be always cheerful and good-humoured" (L 111). Another statement may be quoted, from a letter Denton wrote on his first day in Ruhleben, when there were only forty British there among hundreds of East European land-workers:

The outlook really seemed very depressing. . . . But by the time we got out in the fresh air our spirits were steadily rising with the elasticity of youth and our British blood. I never realized before what it means to be "born free." Having the blood of freedom in one's veins had been simply a figure of speech to me until I saw the contrast between English and Russians, Serbs, etc. in captivity. They fall into it perfectly naturally, never think of resisting, or even cursing the soldiers under their breath. When we laugh at one of the big fat soldiers they shrink away with horrified looks. And if a soldier raises his voice to one of them the wretch seems absolutely to wither up![4]

"Blood," of course, had nothing to do with these contrasts; they were due to cultural, and particularly class, differences.[5] With this correction, however, the Ruhlebenites' view must be accepted: the chief source of

4. No letters were accepted for transmission at this period—which may have been fortunate for the writer, since his views on camp conditions were expressed with equal freedom.

5. These peasants, largely from Russian Poland, were little more than serfs. Hundreds of them were shipped in box-cars to Germany each summer by contractors, and hired out as harvest hands to the great landowners.

their high morale was pride in belonging to a traditionally free and indomitable nation. Conscious identification with Britain had been greatly heightened by internment, and even the most frightened prisoner could recognize the jaunty attitude of the seafarers as the only one befitting a Britisher. He was therefore compelled to try to emulate it, for the only alternative—ceasing to regard himself as British—was inconceivable. It would destroy his very identity (unless he were already pro-German). National pride, at least in 1914, was also accompanied by an unshakable sense of superiority to "foreigners," and even this ethnocentric belief was a source of courage in Ruhleben. It impelled the prisoners to differentiate themselves from the servile Russians, as the quotations suggest; it underlay their truculent attitudes towards the guards, and it also strengthened their resistance to the hardships of camp life—for nothing that any German might do could be allowed to "get a Britisher down."

It would be useful to know how other civilians behaved under similar circumstances, but specific information is very scanty. The Germans interned in England are the closest parallel, but several different camps existed there, usually divided into separate compounds, and with considerable segregation by economic status. Cohen Portheim records "vociferous cheerfulness" among a train-load of men en route to Knockaloe (p. 30) and describes the mixed and still unorganized camp as "restless, seething, and anarchical" (p. 68). Sailors filled half his compound, and one would look for a spirit like that of Ruhleben. Portheim's subsequent emphasis, however, is chiefly on hostile factions and individual "wangling"—both damaging to general morale—and he describes the "gentlemen's" camp at Wakefield, to which he was later transferred, as pervaded by mutual hatreds (p. 87). His experience was limited, however, and he insists that no generalizations can be made. Bishop Herbert Bury, who had officially visited many camps in Britain, came to Ruhleben in November 1916; his views are discussed in a letter from Abbot:

He says our Spirit is much higher than that of the people in similar camps at home. This has been my experience—at any rate it always seems that we have tried to make the best of a bad job, and in the darkest times somebody or other has struck up "Are we—?" "No, No, No!"

The bishop was, of course, far from unbiassed, and it is quite possible that some German camps and compounds attained a high level of morale. If they did not, it was probably because national consciousness was not powerful enough to submerge class differences. An effective social norm can be born only of a united body, with all its components interacting as freely as they did in the earliest days at Ruhleben. The norm that emerged there bore clear signs of its origin in a simple, undifferentiated unity; it was a broad, comprehensive prescription, covering not details of behaviour (which would differ between classes) but basic emotions and attitudes. And it faithfully reflected the one social differentiation that did exist at the time, that between the British in-group and the Germans, for what it laid down was the general nature of the prisoners' response to what their enemies had done to them. Had Ruhleben's population been segregated by classes (Wakefield even possessed a *Grafenhütte* inhabited by titled internees) norms would have arisen for these segments, but not for the population as a whole. For that, solidarity was essential.

One aspect of Ruhleben's high morale remains to be discussed: what it required of the individual. For it involved a complex and little-understood process—the conversion of fear and depression into other emotions. Many societies frown on the open expression of terror and pain, probably because of their contagious and disrupting effects on the group; but this does not mean that the emotions themselves vanish. The additional energy they release into the organism must find some outlet, and the commonest is through the expression of opposite and socially permissible feelings.

This view, familiar since Freud, throws a further light on the exaggerated cheerfulness of Ruhleben's opening days, and particularly on the men's suspiciously frequent assertion that they were *not* downhearted. Both the intensity of the behaviour and its inappropriateness to the situation suggest that it should not be taken at face value, but rather as showing the strength of the other emotions that were being repressed. The transmutation was of course unconscious, but it still demanded much of the individual, for it could occur only when fear and dejection were firmly denied expression.

Emotional conversion played its most critical role at the very beginning of internment, when mass panic could have altered the whole future of the camp. But the process operated throughout the four years, and particularly when the men's hard-won serenity was threatened, as by the exchange of a large number of their comrades. Jungmann describes the departure of 182 prisoners for Holland in April 1918:

... as we boarded the train, which drew up alongside for us, numbers of the men with no hope of release themselves clambered on the low roofs of the barracks and gave us a rousing send-off, singing "Tipperary" and "Pack up your troubles in your old kit-bag." It was heart-rending to have regained the great gift of freedom and not to be able to share it with all these fine fellows. (P. 99)

To be left behind when others started homeward was a cruel experience, making some men deeply depressed and others bitterly envious; it is clear, however, that such feelings were still being gamely repressed. And the cheering and singing that replaced them were not all for the travellers; perhaps their chief function was to bolster the courage of those who had to stay.

The disgraceful conditions of the camp during the first winter were also helpful in this respect, for they permitted the men to convert some of their dismay into anger, and anger is an outgoing emotion, incompatible with fear or self-pity. Thus even the lurid profanity evoked by the cold, the crowding, and the food was a sign of good morale.

Humour and wit, however, were the Ruhlebenites' stock outlets for emotions that had to be repressed. Nothing is more characteristic of civilized man than his treatment of danger and discomfort, when nothing can be done about them, as subjects for laughter. From the siege of Troy to the bombing of London the device has proved itself, and it was used in Ruhleben almost from the beginning. "Almost," because laughter is so essentially social that it is meaningless when it cannot be shared; whatever jests were heard as the stables were first filled must have come from those who entered them with friends or shipmates.[6] Once the men had recognized their fellow-prisoners as comrades, however, the demand for a courageous bearing made humour a constant feature of the camp. Some perception of its relation to morale is implied in Henley's diary for November 12—"the *Stimmung* is excellent, and the whole day a series of jokes and chaff"—and in a letter from Jarvis in May 1915, six hard months later:

We are all blest with good senses of humour, and so long as that is so there is no need for you to worry about our happiness. Really, considering the unusual circumstances, the people here are extraordinarily cheerful and playful. They are always more like a bank holiday crowd than prisoners.

Camp publications took a jocular line from the start; the first news sheet, in January 1915, advertised rubber stamps for signing release petitions, a boat club in the compound, and free board and lodging for the duration to anyone securing 10,000 subscribers. And a similar tone characterized all the later magazines.

Mobs seldom laugh; their emotions pass undisguised into action. But

6. This suggests why solitary confinement is so intolerable a punishment; its most trivial inconveniences are necessarily taken in deadly earnest.

where direct action is impossible aggression may be converted into ironical laughter, and Ruhleben's early crowds laughed almost as much as they cheered. Resistance to the guards was out of the question, but laughter could convey a sneer at German militarism and still be relatively safe. Not entirely, of course; more than one man was rushed to the cells for an ill-timed guffaw. But when an unpopular German sergeant came to lead his men to the kitchen and found the whole column roaring with laughter he could do little but bawl for silence. The joke might have nothing to do with him, but his flushed face and suspicious glances gave his charges deep satisfaction. Officers were not laughed at—it was too dangerous—but they were frankly puzzled by the men's frivolous reaction to a serious situation. And a German-educated prisoner, speaking to Hughes, described their early attitude as "amazingly flippant and juvenile" (p. 671). Prussians might have behaved differently, but this was Ruhleben's way, and one of obvious psychological value.

The substitute outlet supplied by humour was particularly helpful in connection with the appalling discomforts of the first winter. When cold, wet, and hunger threatened the camp's morale it was many times restored by a simple joke. Cohen's account of a high-level military inspection in March 1915 is a typical example:

A few days later we received a visit from some representatives of the Berlin *Kommandatur*. It was an ideal morning for an official inspection, as the rain had fallen throughout the night, and pools, ponds and floods had formed in various parts of the camp. The largest pond, as usual, was that around the Pond Stores. A wag had chalked upon the store: "Mixed bathing not allowed," and another prisoner fixed a pole into the muddy soil, bearing a cardboard inscription: "Good Fishing Here." And, as the military visitors passed this scene, they saw a prisoner in top boots, oilskin and sou'wester angling in the water and pulling out a dripping clog. The stern features of the military relaxed, and one of them remarked: *"Die Engländer haben Humor"* (The Englishmen have humour). (Pp. 85–6)

The jokes may have been childish but they were important, for the men's refusal to take their prison seriously was the first sign that they would ultimately transform it. Eric Farmer put it in a nutshell: "British patriotism showed itself in a determination not to bemoan our lot, but to laugh at it, and at the same time to improve it" (p. 396).

Many of the prisoners were in poor health, many were tortured by anxiety about their families and businesses in Germany, and almost all suffered from homesickness and the endless uncertainty. To demand perpetual cheerfulness from such men put a heavy strain on human nature, and the social scientist will suspect that the repressed emotions must have found some direct outlet. Such an outlet existed in the early religious services, and the great crowds that flocked to them were significant. Contemporary references are brief, as always at this period; Abbot writes on November 27: "We have two services on Sundays which are well filled. The good old hymns are sung and the whole service is very impressive." Later accounts give more detail; Mahoney writes:

The first service was one of the strangest I have attended. The wind swept the grandstand from end to end, causing teeth to chatter and feet to be numbed into nothingness. For the early services we were compelled to gather in darkness, but the hymns were led by a singer whose voice would have reflected credit on any cathedral choir. Owing to the inky blackness of the night we had to depend upon our hearing faculties entirely. Yet there was something decidedly cheering about those unconventional meetings that baffles description. (P. 60)

And another ex-prisoner writes:

I fear I was not a very regular attendant at the services. . . . But I well remember the first services on the grandstand, with about half the camp there, singing "Abide with me" and other hymns in the darkness. It was pitch dark except for the torch Professor Delmer had for reading, and the search-lights over Spandau. I found it very moving, but of course we were all upset at the time and I had my wife and children in England. (L 27)

Here at last the disturbed men had no need to make light of their anxiety; here in words familiar since childhood they could admit their fears and unashamedly ask help for themselves, their country, and those they loved. It was a great emotional release, and many wept quietly in the darkness. At the same time, as Mahoney suggests, they gained a sense of immeasurable comfort, though perhaps less from religious faith than from the solidarity expressed in the united singing and praying. Services were always crowded during the hard first winter, and on March 4, 1915, Denton wrote: "The religious work is encouraging, *everyone* feels the need for it nowadays." But once the camp was fully organized the more painful emotions subsided, the need for reassurance decreased, and religious activities became the concern only of the limited groups that kept them going.

The demand for a courageous bearing was not the only norm that crystallized in November 1914, though the others were too similar to need discussion. Patriotism, for instance, and complete loyalty to the in-group were also conditions of belonging, and their results were evident in the solid front presented to the Germans and the men's brotherly attitudes to one another. All standards at this time were similar: broad in scope, conducive to high morale, deeply tinged with emotion, and applying equally to everyone. The whole code was summed up in the significant phrase, "Be British!", and no other injunction had comparable force as long as the camp lasted.

We now leave the period of crisis, a very short one but of great importance. The prisoners, shaken from their separate backgrounds, have coalesced into a single body—a simple, homogeneous one so far, but already alive with differentiating movements. A new social entity, "Ruhleben," is taking form, and its most permanent traits—solidarity, patriotism, courage—have been defined. And the high spirits, pride, and comradeship of those first exhilarating weeks together should make the closing quotations of chapter 1 a little less puzzling.

PART III | Settlement and Community Building

5

THE WINTER OF 1914–15

THE CHOICE of November 30 for the end of the crisis period and the beginning of the period of settlement was chiefly due to one fact: that on that day workmen from Berlin began erecting two new barracks in the compound. No genuine settlement could take place until belief in immediate release was shaken, and if anything could shake it this omen of permanence should have done so. Mahoney writes dramatically: "It was not until we observed one new building after another going up that the awful truth dawned upon us. Then we realized that we were condemned to stay in this prison for an indefinite period." (3[?], p. 111). It was on November 30, too, that Burton wrote, "Everything getting very dull and stale." For him at least the early excitement was over.

In spite of these statements, however, the date was no turning point, for "settling down" was a complex process, involving many conflicting tendencies. On the one hand, the prisoners were still far from reconciled to Ruhleben; though crowd excitement had subsided, rumours of release soon reappeared and persisted all winter. On the other hand, stabilizing factors were at work long before November 30; adaptation to camp conditions had begun as soon as the men were interned, and community formation—the prime agency of settlement—had been under way almost as long. Taking this date, then, only as an arbitrary starting point, let us first get a general picture of the four months that followed, and then look at the social structures that developed.

As early as December 3 Ewing wrote on a postcard: "This is now a town the size of Dawlish, so I am very busy always. We hope to be exchanged before very long." "Town" and "city" were often used to describe Ruhleben, but this is the first record of either form. Ewing's sentences well reflect the social contradictions of the period, with a community taking shape while continued hopes of release threaten its existence. And the phrase "very busy" should be noted—an incongruous one in a camp where no regular work was required, but one that was often heard.

December, indeed, was a busy month. On the 3rd Mr. Platford announced that he now had 370 books in his lending library—and 350 borrowers. Dealers were increasing their purchases from Berlin, and on December 5 we read of a sandwich company paying a 20 per cent dividend after its first day of business. Prisoners with money had had to deposit it with the German authorities, who restricted withdrawals to ten marks a week. But even this was enough to produce a mild inflation, and traders multiplied so fast that they were shortly suppressed and all purchases channelled through the official canteens.

December 5 also saw a more significant event, a concert in the alleyway of Barrack 6, now occupied by the orthodox Jews. It was an extraordinary concert. The platform consisted of two floor boards set on benches; the conductor was a young musician, F. Charles Adler, inexperienced but ambitious. The half-dozen string players, in sweaters and clogs, looked like ragged street performers. When they began, however, the crowded passage was hushed; most of them were professionals, and the first cello was Carl Fuchs of the Manchester College of Music. They played the Golden Sonata of Purcell and a Handel Sonata for two violins and orchestra, and Fuchs gave several unaccompanied solos. This was something new in Ruhleben, something so different from the raucous life of the stables that many of the audience had tears in their eyes. Baron von Taube, *Lageroffizier*, present by invitation, gave immediate permission for concerts in the large restaurant hall under the second grandstand, opened so far only for religious services. Next day after church the hall was prepared, and the first of Ruhleben's long series of Sunday evening concerts took place. Every inch was packed, and the Commandant, Graf Schwerin, came and made a speech of thanks. Some partsongs by the Anglican choir were added to the programme, and a collection for the Samaritan Fund brought in 195 marks including a 20-mark gold piece from the Commandant.

The week of December 6 was marked by terrible weather; "miserable wet day," "very nasty day, wet and muddy," "yard like a bog," are typical diary entries. The new barracks, 12 and 13, were finished and the former was filled with arrivals from Sennelager, Brussels, and Berlin. On December 8 the captains secured a second sum of 2,000 marks from the American Embassy, but no systematic relief was yet in sight.

Thursday, December 10, saw the formation of the Ruhleben Lancastrian Society, the first and most active of the "territorial" societies, uniting prisoners from particular areas. And the 11th produced a public debate on gambling, a very topical subject. Debates had begun early in the loft of Barrack 2, but this was the first in the grandstand hall. Next day saw the organization of the Ruhleben Literary and Debating Society, under the presidency of Walter Butterworth of Manchester, to whose warm spirit Ruhleben owed much in the first winter. The question for debate was "Is life worth living?"—it is a pity there is no record of the vote. Several cheerful postcards were written this week, however, though fear of censorship and the wish to prevent distress at home must be remembered. The two quoted are from Irwin and Denton, respectively:

> We are feeling passably happy here. Have church services, chess tournaments, concerts, etc. Chummed up with a Frenchman, am working at the lingo assiduously. Cheer up, all of you, we shan't be very long. Are we? No! Never!

> Everything is going well here, we are permitted many diversions in the form of concerts, debates, etc. and with these and the church services I am always very busy.

Again the atmosphere of busyness and activity, and Irwin at least is already doing serious language study. On December 12, indeed, a "School of Languages" was announced, run single-handed by the versatile Dr. Cimino, who advertised courses in French, Italian, Dutch, Spanish, German, English, and Russian (p. 103).

At about this time, too, all university graduates were invited to the grandstand to discuss what could be done in the way of education. From this meeting arose the Arts and Science Union, of which much will be heard later. Like the Lancastrians, debaters, musicians, and singers, these university men were assembled through an announcement on the housing of the heating engine in the yard—the "boiler house" as it was called—and the boards were already covered with an astonishing variety of notices.

Sunday, December 13, with its services and concert, ushered in another week of wet and muddy weather. The orchestra had grown to nine violins and two cellos, and was assisted by a choir of Russians, singing native folk-songs in rich extemporized harmony. Most of the Russians, French, and Belgians were sent to other camps later this week, but Ruhleben still retained a slightly cosmopolitan air because of the number of British subjects who had spent their lives on the Continent. On Monday there was a meeting of Edinburgh University men, on Tuesday the first concert of the "Ruhleben Minstrels," and on Thursday eighty-six coloured men arrived and were quartered in the second new hut, Barrack 13. On Friday evening, December 18, nine newly captured fishermen were marched in, hungry and apprehensive, to find the debating society hotly arguing the question, "Should bachelors be taxed?" Their comments have not been preserved. By Sunday the 20th all hope of release

before Christmas had vanished, though the rumourists revenged themselves by sinking eleven British and twenty-six German warships in a
great sea fight. The church choir gave a carol concert in the evening,
and the orchestra, a large chorus, and a weary band of music copyists
were working feverishly for a Christmas performance of *The Messiah*.

On December 22 we read of "Swedish Drill" conducted by the
captain of Barrack 7, and next day the Lancastrians held their second
meeting and announced a membership of 222. The business discussed
is revealing. It was resolved that the question of a badge should be left
to the All-England Association, of which this is the first record. A
harmless enough topic, but six months later it aroused such a controversy as even Ruhleben seldom witnessed. The remaining business had
to do with the great dinner to be held in Manchester upon release. It
was decided to invite ladies and also the Lord Mayor of Manchester,
and to permit any garb except evening dress. After much discussion
Saturday was picked as the best day for the celebration—though *what*
Saturday even the Lancastrians failed to specify. Such preoccupation
with the details of a superlatively hypothetical occasion is evidence
enough that the prisoners were still far from settled. Few of them could
yet look at Ruhleben steadily and unblinkingly; to the majority it was still
somewhat unreal. The "real" world is apt to be that in which we wish
to believe, and no one yet wished to believe in Ruhleben.

Christmas Eve was appropriately marked by a fall of soft snow.
Great snow-ball fights started, there was a raid on the Tea House, and
some windows were broken; but the military were in lenient mood and no
trouble resulted. In the grandstand hall all afternoon an orchestra of 25,
a chorus of 100, and a group of soloists rehearsed *The Messiah* under
the indefatigable Adler. It was, as Denton puts it, a "hectic" rehearsal.
There had been a scant fortnight of practice; orchestral and vocal parts
had all been copied from one score by amateurs, working in dim light
with numb fingers, and there were frequent halts while wrong notes
were corrected and missing bars inserted. The hall was so cold that the
chorus stamped their feet on the improvised platform; it was filled with
the din of hundreds of other prisoners, scraping about in wooden clogs,
talking, and laughing; and the air was blue with smoke from the clay
pipes of seamen. Violin strings snapped and could not be replaced,
soloists broke into uncontrollable coughing, and from the cobblers'
shop in the corner came a noise of hammering so deafening and incessant
that the conductor had to be restrained from a physical assault. Somehow, with incongruous profanity, the oratorio was gone through and the
men returned to their barracks for the evening—a quiet one, save for

the singing of Christmas hymns in some lofts and minor disturbances caused by smuggled liquor. Too quiet, perhaps, for Burton, whose entry ends: "A Merry Christmas, I *don't* think!"

Christmas Day began with rain, which quickly turned the remaining snow to slush. A fuller sampling of the diaries at this point will indicate what the condensed narrative is based on. The first is that of Henley, who was married:

Christmas. Up at 6.30. Christmas card from Captains to each man. Lined up early, for bun, rolls. Paid bet. Washed after breakfast. Greetings from everyone; Christmas spirit in camp. Official greetings. Kitchen opened ten to eleven; got excellent dinner and went to grandstand for bottle of beer, cigar and toffee. Slept during afternoon. Had our own tea—4 rolls, 2 slices· of bread with margarine, jam and sausages—at 4 p.m. Did not go to the kitchen for anything. Spent most of my time thinking of former Christmases and of H. Tried to write to her but couldn't do justice to it. The Messiah was given at 4.30 in grandstand. Said to be very good.

The second, less appreciative, is that of Burton:

Fell down with my coffee this morning and hurt my knee. Had a roll presented with the coffee. Also different style of dinner—the potatoes separate from the meat. Meat a scrap you could put in your eye. Also were each given a cigar, small packet of toffee and a bottle of beer. Reminds one of a Sunday School treat. All this extra is out of the British relief fund. Evening meal was a raw salt polony, nothing else.

The third comes from Jarvis, the engineering student:

Out at 6.30 and down into the alley to wash. Snow covered landscape but slush under foot. *Antreten, Kaffee holen!* A bun six inches by three and some sugar on the top, like a bath bun. Great luxury, Christmas treat. Wouldn't touch it at home, but here it's food for the gods. Spent the morning clearing up, too muddy outside for walking. Splendid dinner, piece of smoked pork, ladleful of spuds and gravy. Ate out of my tin by fingers and spoon. Afternoon walked a bit and then prepared for tea. Put up blanket over doorway, got a candle from Mr. S's box. M. and D. came to tea. We had *Rundstücke* and white bread and a hard egg each, and some meat—how procured not divulged. Huge feed. After tea a man came from No. 1 and told us stories—the limit!—while we *smoked* and a concert proceeded further along the loft. Later we went out, and in the corner we had some good carol and hymn singing.

The three remaining diaries add little further, but Irwin and Abbott may be represented by postcards:

Xmas is over, and you will be glad to hear that we have spent it in quite jolly fashion, thinking of home, of course, a good part of the time. We had a little tree with two candles, and plenty of eatables (of a kind). I may not describe our life in detail, but don't worry, we're quite healthy and at times quite happy. The treatment is severe but humane, and the grub sufficient. Am hard at work with Russian; it is a beastly lingo but it may come in handy some day.

Xmas and New Year have passed without our realizing it fully. Xmas Day we began with the Communion Service. We had a little Xmas dinner party round an improvised table with a tree on it which I had decorated with fir, and we each contributed plum pudding and other good things to the spread. The "Messiah" was a great success.

The performance of *The Messiah* was more of a *tour de force* than an artistic triumph, for the score had not been arranged for male voices, and the effect of soprano and alto parts an octave lower than written was peculiar. But the sounds were joyful if confused, a number of men were kept busily occupied, and further possibilities of development were suggested; there were also moments, during some solos and in the Hallelujah Chorus, which stirred real emotion.

In the evening discipline was relaxed and the prisoners held their little celebrations, visited one another, smoked in the stables, and sang ribald and sacred songs until late. Much excitement was caused by a Scotsman, equipped with bagpipes and an improvised kilt, who led a large crowd through some of the barracks; but the guards were feeling convivial and even this riotous conduct was only mildly discouraged.

So the days went on to the end of the year—dark days, lightened by new rumours of victories and exchange, but "cold and pretty wearisome" (Burton). On December 30 *The Messiah* was repeated in the presence of the aged Commandant, Graf Schwerin, and after it he made a short speech with trembling voice and tears on his cheeks. Thanking the men for the music and for the good order kept over Christmas, he added that he had been touched by the way in which they bore the sad Christmas, far from home and "without a Christmas tree." He trusted that things would always run as harmoniously in the future. The speech was warmly applauded and the Graf given three cheers.

The immediate authorities, however, were less sympathetic, and New Year's Eve brought the notice: "Anyone found making a demonstration outside the barracks at midnight will be fired upon by the sentries." Parties and singsongs took place as at Christmas, but when the bagpipes appeared and the men started to form a ring in the compound they were quickly dispersed. Some went to bed and slept the New Year in, but at midnight a few bold souls emerged and sang Auld Lang Syne. Next day Henley and Burton report, "Shook hands until I was sick of it," and "Plenty of good wishes but nothing to drink." All the good wishes were of course identical: 1915 must see the end of Ruhleben.

For one group of men the holiday season must have been peculiarly trying—those whose wives and families were still in Berlin or its vicinity. Some British women had not yet been given permission to leave for Holland and England, some were delaying in the hope that their men might be released; others, especially those born or long resident in Germany, had decided to wait out the war—still expected to be a short one—in their own homes and among relatives. All lived under constant strain and difficulty. In extreme emergencies interned husbands and sons were granted a few days' leave, but no visitors whatever were allowed at Ruhleben until well on in 1916. During the first month or so of internment, and especially as Christmas approached, some of these unhappy women would come out to Ruhleben to deliver little parcels at the main gate, or walk up and down the road outside. Their men, forewarned by letter, would try desperately to exchange at least a wave with them through the open gate or from adjacent loft stairways. These fugitive glimpses were probably more tantalizing than comforting, and in any case they were soon put a stop to; delivery of parcels by hand was strictly forbidden, and the railings on the staircases were replaced by high wooden fences.

The first half of January 1915 was marked by a great deal of rain and mud, curtailing outdoor activity. The ban on ball games must have been lifted, however, for a new rounders league was organized on January 2. The second half of the month was very cold with much snow; long slides made on the frozen pools were covered with men all day. Otherwise pastimes were much what they had been: chess and checkers, now with barrack competitions and tournaments; card-playing and gambling, and an epidemic of raffles for all sorts of prizes. Further donations were swelling the library, and some diarists seem to have divided their time between walking up and down outside and reading indoors, when light permitted.

Many pastimes of this winter had the character of "crazes," spreading rapidly to large numbers and then dropping off after reaching a climax. Chess, checkers, and raffles belonged in this category, and so did two new fads precipitated by the start of a new year. The first was the engraving of pipes and soup-spoons with the owner's name, followed by "Ruhleben, 1914-15"; Mr. Mahoney, the engraver, claims to have made £150 in the next five months. As each new year came around further dates were added; by 1918 the figures could hardly be squeezed in. The other was the securing of autographs, almost everyone in the camp seeming to have an album. Both crazes were of the "souvenir" type, reflecting continued expectation of release. The first few days of

January were in fact marked by highly optimistic rumours, all focussed on January 6, when a monthly train left Berlin for Holland. It carried many British wives and children, but their men could only wave from the compound as it passed. "Explosion of all rumours," wrote Kendall tersely.

On January 10 Henley's diary contains the words, "Row about captains"—the first record of friction between them and the camp at large. They were already under attack by interned businessmen, who had been unable to make head or tail of a statement on camp finances posted a few days earlier. The present problem, however, went beyond financial matters. E. M. Trinks, Captain of the Camp, was about to be released, and was planning to forward a report to the British Government on conditions at Ruhleben. Trinks, however, was being released into Germany, which made his views highly suspect. A petition was circulated demanding that any such report be first approved by a group of barrack representatives; it received three thousand signatures and the representatives were duly elected. No report was ever submitted to them, but they formed themselves into a committee to keep tab on the captains and try to expedite the physical improvement of the camp. The "Camp Committee," as it was called, enjoyed semi-official status for a time, and in February Baron von Taube and the captains met with it to discuss drainage, leaky roofs, the food supply, and a diarrhoea epidemic (H). Two competing bodies, however, could not exist side by side, and on February 24 the Baron dissolved the committee for failure to co-operate with the captains, thus strengthening a growing feeling that the latter were too acceptable to the Germans to be entirely trustworthy.

When Trinks left camp on January 15 the following notice was posted in English and German over von Taube's signature: "Mr. E. M. Trinks, Captain of the Camp, having been released, the following Captains have been appointed: Captain of the Camp, J. Powell, Barrack 10; Vice Captain of the Camp, L. G. Beaumont, Teahouse" (S). The word "appointed" jarred on many of the prisoners, and continued to do so for years to come. But the emergence of Joseph Powell, however brought about, was an event of far-reaching importance. This strong-willed, irascible individual, who had been European manager of a film company, remained chief executive of Ruhleben until its dissolution, and played the central role in the stormy political struggle to be described later.

An important cultural move took place early in January when the Arts and Science Union called a meeting of teachers to discuss setting up a school. An organization was formed and a syllabus drawn up, but at this period lack of space crippled the movement. A few classes began to meet in boxes, however, and two engineer informants, Irwin and Kendall, were this month teaching Russian and Trigonometry respectively. *The Ruhleben Camp News* and *The Oracle*, the first camp publications, also appeared in January—both mimeographed news sheets and both short-lived. On January 13 Adler and his chorus started rehearsing *Elijah*, the copying of parts having begun much earlier, and the oratorio was presented on January 31. Preparation was not so inadequate as the dates would suggest, for at this time a full rehearsal could be held every day; conflicting engagements did not exist. It was a different matter later. Other concerts were given on the intervening Sundays, the Debating Society was meeting on Fridays, and from January 20 onwards an undenominational service on Wednesday evenings supplemented the Sunday services. There were also such events as the lecture on *Parsifal*, with musical illustrations—the first of Ruhleben's multitude of lectures— and the "Burns Nicht" concert on January 25. Abbot records this without comment, Farwell adds, "a great success," Burton says "pretty rotten," and Kendall reports: "A 'grand' concert in grandstand hall by the Scots, so 'grand' and sombre that N. and I came away thoroughly depressed." Individuals were recovering their standards and beginning to judge things differently.

After such a list of entertainments a series of extracts from Burton's diary will balance the record:

Jan. 8, 1915. Received five marks from the King Edward VII Fund. First relief I have had. Raining and blowing hard, grounds in horrible condition.

Jan. 9. Nine fresh arrivals in our loft from Saxony. White bread stopped at canteen.

Jan. 10. Hut canteen stopped today, too many "luxuries" coming into the camp. Evidently they are beginning to put the screws on.

Jan. 13. Postcard from Mr. T. who sends the cheering news that all exchange is "off."

Jan. 14. Weather muddy, murky and miserable. Mud all over the grounds, ankle deep. Lots of rain and cold.

Jan. 15. Small rolls doubled in price. Evidently getting scarce. All hands lined up this morning at 10.30 A.M. and each barrack separately harangued by the Baron, about supposed insults to Germans in the camp.

This refers to the first "pro-German" trouble, which will be described later.

Jan. 16. Weather still rotten. Started off as an autograph hunter and am tracking down the celebrities and notorieties in the camp.

Jan. 17. Sailor from S.S. Virgo or Iris died today. This is the third. Was out to tea with Mr. C., quite an event.

Jan. 20. Recommenced the tramping round the track today. Thought this was done away with, but it is not, worse luck.

Jan. 21. Lecture this evening on Wagner's "Parsifal" with musical illustrations. Was caught lighting up my pipe, just going out of the loft, and narrowly escaped cells.

Jan. 27. Kaiser's Birthday. The halyards on the flagstaff in the centre of the yard were this morning discovered to be cut. This, too, just when we wanted to hoist the flag. Owing to this outrage (!) we were all put under barrack arrest. The civil police were disbanded, and all post, both in and out, to be stopped until the culprit is discovered. Suppose it will all blow over by tomorrow.

Jan. 28. Everything as usual and post re-started. Snowing, very cold.

Jan. 29. Cabbage soup again, third time in seven days, also "tea" was a choice between "skilly" and the above-mentioned cabbage-water left over from dinner. Fire bell this afternoon and another "lecture." Someone has been sending letters out with released prisoners and these have fallen into the authorities' hands. They reckon they have some 30 letters and say that they know the writers, whom they give until tomorrow to confess. If it is not cleared up by ten in the morning the mail is to be stopped for ten days, both in and out.

Jan. 31. B.Z. am Mittag prints today new order for Berlin regarding bread, only 2 kilos to be allowed per head per week. Snowing heavy.

The Kaiser's Birthday incident, when the halyards were cut by a high-spirited sailor lad, greatly incensed the Germans, and was only smoothed over by an apology from the captains. It is minutely described in the published literature, but Jarvis's contemporary account may be of interest:

Jan. 27, 1915. Kaiser's Birthday. Flags flying and German Gottesdienst. Someone cut the rope on the flagpole they've put in "Trafalgar Square" last night, so there is a rare row. All to stay in barracks till the man is found. Added to this the police force has been dismissed. This because a pro-German giving commissions to someone at the head of a line at the canteen, and ordered off by the policeman on duty, objected to the Commander. He took whole as manifestation of anti-German feeling. Hence dismissal. Police taken on again later. Great excitement is caused by having to dodge soldiers with guns in going to the *chalet de nécessité*, where much smoking is done. Lined up outside and given sausage outside barracks. In the C. de N. a soldier out for smokers; as he comes in one end all pipes out, as he goes out all on again. If man doesn't own up by nine tomorrow morning all will be kept in for three days. Men content themselves with saying, "the time will come." By nightfall forgiven.

The temper of the men will be noted; they were in no mood for apologies, and the culprit was not betrayed. Instead, confinement to barracks provoked a revival of collective behaviour that recalled the earliest days. In most barracks loud singing, shouting, and laughter continued all day; forbidden patriotic songs such as "Rule, Britannia!" were defiantly sung, and parties from other barracks en route to the latrines were saluted with cheers. The barrack guards were quite unable to quell the demonstrations and found the day a trying one. This pattern was followed, with ingenious additions, whenever mass punishments were decreed in the future, and the camp authorities became increasingly reluctant to impose them.

The flag episode, added to the previous rows about pro-Germans and the smuggling of letters, meant that the month closed in an atmosphere of greater tension than Ruhleben had witnessed since its opening weeks. And February brought little improvement. Burton continues:

Feb. 1. Freezing. New order that no cards are to be sent out for eight days. Loaf of bread has now to last us three days, and 50 pf. loaf at canteen is increased in price to one mark. Received news today of arrival of son and heir.

Feb. 2. 28 fresh arrivals this morning from Brussels, and 40 in the afternoon from Berlin. New departure in the feeding, each man receiving a piece of meat separate. This is certainly an improvement, but it takes longer to serve. Still, you are sure of having a taste of meat, even though it is small.

Feb. 3. Lots of people today on the sick list, supposed to be a sort of poisoning caused by the meat. Not being used to it. Rounded up in afternoon by fire bell and all bread examined. Those who had more than enough for a meal had it taken from them, and this was distributed among those who were short. We are certainly getting on short rations now. Skilly for tea again. All incoming mail stopped until further notice.

Feb. 5. Several fresh arrivals today, Colonials. The German Admiralty report of intended "blockade" of England posted in the yard. This threat is to take effect on the 18th. Debate "Press vs. Pulpit" in grandstand this evening.

Feb. 6. 150 new arrivals from Hamburg, including M.S. from the hulks, who brought with him my banjo.

Feb. 7. Lots of snow. All the liberated Colonials are now back again.

Feb. 8. Man in Barrack 4 cut his throat this morning. However, he didn't make a good job of it and was able to walk to hospital. 24 fresh arrivals from Dresden.

Feb. 9. 16 fresh arrivals from Brussels. Mail recommenced, both in and outward.

Feb. 10. Our barrack had no bread today until after tea-time. Better late than never.

Feb. 11. White rolls at canteen stopped.

Feb. 12. Report this evening that they have captured 26,000 Russians. This is a very nice supper to go to bed on.

Feb. 17. Flags up again, victory in East Prussia. 50,000 captured Russians. Surely there can be very few Russians free by this time.

With food diminishing and an influx of new arrivals the prisoners were restive and anxious, while the Germans, whose submarine blockade was launched with a *"Gott strafe England!"* campaign, were in an uncompromising mood. However, further new barracks had been started on February 14 to cope with the growing congestion, and on the 20th a newly installed boiler house began supplying hot water for tea—a greatly valued boon. The diary continues:

Feb. 21. All bread stopped at canteen.

Feb. 24. Some 900 small Graham loaves brought into canteen. Four queues instantly lined up, full length of the compound. Only one loaf sold to each customer. I managed to get one and scoffed it. No bread for breakfast.

Feb. 25. One of our Tommies (4th Middlesex Regiment), wounded, was brought in here temporarily and caused quite a commotion. Our keepers got kind of nasty over this and lost their wool. Cookson was reported for special mention, and awarded 48 hours cells for laughing.

Feb. 27. Had today the first instalment of 4 marks which is to be a weekly allowance from Chancellor of the Exchequer, and which is to be paid back later when able.

Feb. 28. Snow again. Started today on new bread system, giving it out one third of a loaf per day per man, and rotten stuff at that. Getting pretty hungry.

This was the hardest period in Ruhleben's history, but in spite of short rations, tighter control, and anxiety about the war the men were still trying to pass the time constructively. Language study was increasing; Abbot writes on February 13: "I have now got into a set programme of study, four hours of Russian, one of German and one and a half of French. This fills up the day very well." And a week later he says of his mess: "We are quite a happy little party, making the best of things." Public activities, too, were kept on, though without much extension in this difficult month. Religious services, as at any anxious time, were well attended, and evening prayer on the open grandstand became a daily event. On February 3 a notable service was held on the theme from Donne's sonnet, "Death, thou shalt die!" The orchestra played Bach, the choir sang the Hallelujah Chorus, and Matthew Prichard, a man of remarkable influence in the camp, gave the address. Serious lectures are also recorded, those of Professor Patchett on "Religion" and H. S. Hatfield on "The Aims and Methods of Science" being particularly mentioned. And the Debating Society continued to approve of Compulsory Education and reject Women's Rights even when the speakers had had but little supper.

Burton seldom reports rumours, but from other diaries we learn that February was marked by a wave of war rumours too extravagant to be passed over. The Germans have lost 148,000 men to the Russians at Thorn, the British have captured Ostende, Ghent, and Zeebrugge (twice), six German battleships have been sunk in a great naval victory, the United States Embassy has packed up to leave Berlin—these are a few of them. There was also a sharp eruption of exchange rumours. Cheering rumours regularly appeared when the men had most need of them, and these outbreaks, which had no factual foundation, probably reflected the general strain and discontent.

The hard winter was ending, however, and March 1915 brought the first real hope of better times. The American Ambassador paid an official visit on March 3, and great efforts were made to acquaint him with the worst features of Ruhleben. Burton says: "American Ambassador here today in person for the first time. Someone wrote on the back of his car, 'We want bread.' He was all around our 'beautiful' village, and was cheered on leaving." Ruhleben was only half an hour's drive from the Embassy and the visit might well have been made earlier. However, Mr. Gerard proved to be a vigorous and outspoken man, who insisted on seeing everything and roundly condemned much that he saw. Two days later the captains were able to announce a list of promised improvements, and on March 6 a party of German "brass hats" came to see for themselves and found the camp, as described earlier, completely flooded out. The improvements were slow in appearing, but official recognition of the need lightened the atmosphere.

The same week saw other important events. After March 1 the men were allowed to write four postcards and two four-page letters each month, the letters giving them their first chance to converse at any length with their families. March 1 was also the day on which a young businessman, Wallace Ellison, suggested a scheme of municipal organization that was later substantially adopted. And on the 8th two reputable dailies, the *Berliner Tageblatt* and *Vossische Zeitung*, were put on sale. Although they failed at first to stop the flow of war rumours, their relatively objective reporting ultimately had its effect. Nor was this all, for it was on March 8 that a band of enthusiasts, who had been rehearsing under fantastic difficulties, produced Ruhleben's first play, Shaw's *Androcles and the Lion*. In spite of makeshift stage, costumes, and scenery the play was a hit and had to run for five nights. New possibilities of entertainment were revealed—and well exploited, as 128 subsequent productions showed. The first of these, a revue, was staged on March 28. The Debating Society had already put on an excellent Mock Trial, and the concerts were growing more ambitious. The territorial societies, dormant since Christmas, began to hold meetings, and the Arts and Science Union was running two lectures a week on such topics as Dietetics, Heredity, Modern Greece, and the Renascence in Italy.

So much activity might suggest choosing the first week in March as the end of the period of settlement and the beginning of a more expansive one. But public events do not tell the whole story; Burton shows why a later date is preferable:

Mar. 6. Presents of underclothing from Queen Mary raffled in the barracks this afternoon. Finished my whack of bread this evening, nothing for breakfast.

Mar. 7. Nothing to eat till 10 A.M. when I had a slice of black bread. It is snowing heavy, and I'm hungry all day and miserable too. Military are reckoned to be taking over the catering, and we are supposed to be in for better times. Hope so!

Mar. 16. Snowing heavily all day. In the afternoon our corner was collared for more "Arbeit" and had to pull cart-loads of potatoes all the afternoon in the snow. Cold, wet, miserable, hungry and *angry*.

Mar. 21. Change in the dinner programme. Having potatoes and gravy and a separate and distinct piece of meat. As a set-back to this it was announced that our loaves have to last us five days in future.

Mar. 22. Commenced on new ration, one fifth of a loaf per day. Guess we will go hungry often.

Not all the men were on such short rations, for the canteens still sold some food and a considerable number of parcels arrived this month. But there were close to two thousand, like Burton, whose only resources were the four marks a week "relief money"; if we recall this when we read of concerts, debates, plays, and lectures on dietetics (of all subjects) we shall better appreciate the spirit of the first winter.

By late March, however, the days of hunger were almost over, thanks to a stream of food parcels from England; and this with two other events brought a dramatic change in Ruhleben life. The first, owed to the British Government and the United States Embassy, was the renting of half the centre of the racecourse as a recreation ground. This space for exercise and sport was of incalculable value to the men, physically and mentally. The second, owed to powers superior to governments, was the coming of spring. Seldom was a spring so longed for as this one; when it came, suddenly and precisely on time on the morning of March 22, the prisoners felt that they had literally been released. "I cannot describe how we rejoiced in the mildness and sun," wrote Denton next day; the winter's gloom was flung off with its overcoats and sweaters, and hope, which is not unrelated to meteorology, took fresh roots in the camp.

One further point must be made. On March 4 Powell had announced that all exchange negotiations were at an end, and rumours of release had almost dried up. There was, of course, still the possibility of an early end to the war, but that was remote. The new hopes of the spring of 1915 were thus significantly different from any that preceded them; they were in great measure hopes of a better life *in Ruhleben itself*. Through the promise of physical improvements, through the revelation that the camp could become self-sustaining, socially, intellectually, and artistically, the readjustment which is the key-note of this period had actually been achieved. The men were at last ready to believe in their city, and so to make it real.

The memoirs of an aging celebrity are often prefaced with a rather early portrait, the author feeling that later ones somehow fail to do him justice. And Ruhleben cherished throughout its history a deeply felt preference for the self-portrait painted during the first winter. It depicted the men as they wished to see themselves—united, patriotic, courageous —and became an important collective symbol. Certain features of the portrait were taken for granted by diarists and hence have been some-what neglected in the preceding narrative; the remainder of this chapter deals with these, and then outlines the administrative and economic backgrounds of the period.

The men's outstanding achievement in the opening days was of course their solidarity, particularly because it was not inevitable. The Germans might have been thought of as interning 1,400 seamen, 200 Jews, 50 jockeys, and so on; instead, they were felt to have interned 4,000 British. The sweeping definition was soon modified, but retained great emotional importance. Without it "Ruhleben" would have been merely a place-name instead of standing for a body of men to which each prisoner was proud to belong.[1]

The camp, then, was first and foremost a *British* camp, and the term as we know early acquired a moral significance. Indeed, as differences within the population became more obvious, "British" came to refer almost exclusively to conduct. It stood for all the social virtues—courage, generosity, honesty, justice, fair play—and this breadth of meaning made it a powerful instrument of control. "Britishers!" became like "Comrades!" among communists, a constant reminder that group norms must be upheld. The following notice (*IRC* 7, p. 16) is worth quoting, though it dates from September 1915:

TO BRITISHERS

As announced in our last number we have organized a collection . . . to endow a "Ruhleben Bed." Let us now seize this opportunity of showing that AS BRITISHERS we sympathize with those at home who are in worse plight than ourselves. The Relief Officer of your barrack will keep the box for a month. As a Britisher you will go to him, you will not expect him to come to you, and make your sacrifice.

Some of the heavy emphasis here was due to the spring's disclosure of a large pro-German party, whose norms of conduct were presumably at the opposite pole, but "British" was already being worked to death before the pro-Germans emerged as a group. If a boxmate objected to lending his soap, "Aw, come on, be British!" might cajole it from him. And all winter the boiler house was covered with posters urging the reader to keep the compound tidy, have his pipe engraved by some "artist," patronize Sunny Smitty the Shoeblack, or buy a copy of Mortimore Howard's new patriotic poem—nearly all bearing the ubiquitous "To Britishers!" at the top. The climax was a sheet protesting some injustice and headed, "IS THIS BRITISCH?"[2] The spelling was quickly underlined with venomous comments by the many unofficial censors, and the notice helped to bring about a reaction in some circles. During the spring floods of 1916 the magazine, under a new editor, made gentle fun of the phrase (*RCM* 2, p. 22):

A water-polo club has now been formed, and a successful season is anticipated. A committee has, of course, been formed, and a suitable pitch secured

---

1. The pride was long-lasting; even in November 1960, forty-two years after the camp was dissolved, forty-five Ruhlebenites gathered in London to recapture the old "we" feeling.

2. The unfortunate who penned this notice may well have been one of the German-reared minority who tried to become British. It was a difficult task, for after the pro-Germans declared themselves in January 1915 the camp became hostile to any sign of a German background.

on the plot lately occupied by the Hockey Club. "TO BRITISHERS!" Why not sign your name?

And after 1916 the cliché was replaced in official announcements by "To the Camp" or "To the Men of the Camp."

The rank and file, however, were less sensitive to banality and remained British to the end, particularly when they were most censorious. The final criticism of any objectionable practice was that it was "not British"—above all when it savoured of special privilege, like the serving of officials out of line at the canteens. Here the altered meaning of the term is clear, for Britain is not entirely devoid of privileged classes. What the Ruhlebenite had in mind was obviously not his homeland, with its long-established social differences; it was the equality, fraternity, and even liberty he had enjoyed in Ruhleben itself during its first weeks. That period had already become a golden age to which the disgruntled looked back nostalgically—just as today's criers of "un-American" and "un-British" look back to a time that has passed forever.

As Figure 3 shows, a heavy flow of rumours characterized most of the first winter, implying a continuance of tension and suggestibility.[3] There is support, however, for the opening and closing dates suggested for this period—a sharp break in both exchange and war rumours early in December, and an unmistakable turning point at the end of March. The former may be attributed to the starting of new barracks and the admission on December 3 of the *Berliner Zeitung am Mittag* or *B.Z.*; the latter, however, is a sign of more fundamental changes. Something obviously happened in the spring of 1915 that reduced the flow of rumours, except in July of each year, to little more than a trickle. There is no doubt what it was; camp life became so satisfying and full of interest that the need for illusory consolations largely vanished. The midsummer outbreaks will be discussed when we come to them, but the winter's rumours deserve notice in connection with the effects of information.

It was of course *war* rumours (shown separately in Figure 3) that were chiefly affected by the availability of information, since news-

3. The rumour chart was constructed as follows: Each month was divided into ten three-day periods, represented by vertical columns, and a dot was entered for every specific rumour recorded in diaries or letters. In the case of letters the date of the letter was used. Obvious variants were excluded, but some duplication was inevitable. On the other hand, scores of rumours must have circulated without being recorded by any informant. General statements ("lots of rumours lately") were given one dot; a few stronger ones ("Rumour fever very intense") two dots. Thus the figures are only approximate, though the general pattern may be taken as reliable.

papers rarely referred to interned civilians. And admission of the *B.Z.* on December 3 does seem to have banished them for a fortnight. Information, however, was only one factor, the other being the strength of the prisoners' need for good news; hence the winter's discontents (plus the notorious sensationalism of the *B.Z.*) soon produced further war rumours and raised them in February to an all-time peak. It is more surprising that they should have continued after March 8, when two responsible dailies went on sale, each carrying the Allied war communiqués as well as the German. However, at least half the prisoners, including nearly all the seafarers, could read no German; these men got their war news by word of mouth, and most of them viewed its German origin with unalterable suspicion. There was also intense excitement during March about the British assault on the Dardanelles and the expected adherence of Italy and Greece to the Allies; many of the rumours bore on these unresolved issues. In short, the prisoners were still so "rumour prone" that the newspapers had little effect. With the spring, however, the expanding life of the camp diverted interest into new channels, the need for good news lessened, and war rumours dropped to a low and constant level for the remaining years. This final stabilization was much aided in the fall of 1915 by daily publication in English of the official war reports, and also by a regular supply of smuggled British newspapers.

Exchange rumours were affected by information in two directions; any report that could possibly be construed favourably set off an immediate explosion, while unfavourable news, if sufficiently authentic, discouraged rumours at least temporarily. The negative statements by von Taube on December 15 and Powell on March 4 are duly followed by "dry periods" on the chart, though in each case other inhibiting factors were also operating. Information about exchange, however, was always exceedingly scarce; hence the incidence of exchange rumours was basically a function of the psychological climate of the camp—a stormy and changeable one in the first winter, but stable thereafter except for the mental crisis each summer.

Besides rumours and a somewhat captious patriotism, the high spirits of the crisis period also carried over into the winter. In the barracks the whole gamut of schoolboy jests was run, from water fights and booby traps to sewn-up pyjamas under the straw pillow. This horseplay, with its disregard of adult conventions, made for a lively sense of solidarity; Leslie writes in April 1915: "It is not everywhere that a respectable businessman on the shady side of thirty-five is tickled as he gets into bed" (p. 54) and the boarding-school atmosphere was heightened by the provocative presence of the German "housemasters":

> In our box in the first winter we often used to sacrifice a 30 pf. mug at night by dropping it on the stone floor, just to bring a howl from the barrack and hear Unteroffizier Pass tear out of his room and bellow "*Ruhe da!*" We would wait quietly until he was back in his den and then drop the broken pieces again from the top bed, with the same result. It simply infuriated him. Of course the noise echoed all down the corridor so that he couldn't tell which box it came from. (L 42)

A more adult tone prevailed in subsequent winters, both because life had become more conventional and because the guards were no longer in the barracks. The civilian captain who replaced them was not a "public enemy" and ragging him had little point.

Life in the first winter was brightened by high spirits, patriotism, and deceptive hopes, but it was a hard life, and concerts and lectures could not hide its crude and graceless character. The prisoners' world was made up of barbed wire and sentries, stables and kitchens, rain and mud, food, sleep, and excretion; it was painted in the harsh contrasts of friend or foe, hunger or satiety, "guts" or contemptible weakness. Existence was on a primitive level, and clothes, conduct, and speech were rough and uncompromising. Garments were as warm and durable as possible; these were the only standards, and no one tried any longer to dress fashionably or eccentrically. Wooden-soled clogs, procured from Germany by the canteen, were universally worn, and the prisoners' movements were heavy, flat-footed, and marked by incessant clumping and scraping. Heads were wrapped in knitted helmets, and full beards and whiskers added a further pioneer touch.

Comradeship was not felt to require politeness, and in the congested barracks contacts were forthright and brusque. A man entering a crowded doorway uttered no "Excuse me!" but simply shouldered his way in; if a messmate left his property on your bunk you threw it on the floor. When conflicts arose, words were quickly followed by action, and there were of course many fights. A teacher, about thirty when interned, stated: "I'd never had a fight from the time I was sixteen until I went into the camp, but I had several physical fights in the first six months. After that there were no more, we had worked out a system of living together" (M 29). The whole atmosphere, in fact, reflected the shifting of middle-class standards towards those of the forecastle.

Rations, as Burton's reports suggest, were well below the forecastle level. Generalization is difficult, since some prisoners (especially those domiciled in Germany) began getting food parcels much earlier than others, but my own box was probably near the average:

Our first parcels arrived from England at Christmas 1914, but contained chiefly such "extras" as chocolate, Oxo tablets, and biscuits; little substantial food reached us until April. None of us was on relief, but we had to husband our funds and canteen purchases were kept to a minimum. For breakfast during most of the winter we had mugs of the official "coffee" with condensed milk and sugar from the canteen; German bread, biscuits, or sometimes canteen rolls; butter or margarine, and jam. Dinner was the kitchen soup, flavoured with Oxo or curry powder from parcels. For supper we had whatever the Germans served except skilly—sausage, porridge, tea, cocoa— and bread with meat paste or sardines from the canteen. A godsend after February 20 was tea from England, brewed at the new boiler house; tea was scarce, so we added a few fresh leaves to the pot each day, emptying them about twice a week. Although parcels became more frequent as spring approached, the canteen shortages, higher prices, and especially the cutting of the bread ration made life even more difficult.

Speech was blunt and crude, as the endless profanity implies, and it was in the first winter, too, that a distinctive Ruhleben vocabulary crystallized. It took shape like all argots in innumerable social contacts, through imitation, selection, and group sanction, and it was again the seafarers who set the standard. They were of course the largest single group, their earthy language was well fitted to the conditions, and assimilation may have been facilitated by admiration of their cheerful bearing.

In any case most of the prisoners quickly found themselves speaking a dialect that was heavily larded with nautical terms. Everyone fetched his "spuds," "skilly," or other "grub" from the "galley" in a "billy-can." Porridge was "burgoo," a pudding was a "duff," your portion was your "whack." Those who ate together formed a "mess," servants were "stewards," and each man's "gear" had to be kept in his own "bunk." The betting-booths became "cubby-holes" and the latrines "bogs." With this marine vocabulary was blended a good deal of German, especially the guards' repeated ejaculations: *Aufstehen! Antreten! Essen holen! Heraus da! Los! Weg! Ausgeschlossen! Nichts zu machen!*[4] And German verbs were often anglicized: "Come on, let's *hole* our *Essen!*" The combination had a unique flavour, tasted anew at every gathering of the Ruhleben Association.

The most vivid picture of this raw, primitive period is found in the doggerel poems that were constantly being sung and written in autograph books. This version of the "Ruhleben Alphabet," the chorus of

4. "Get up! Line up! Fetch your food! Get out! Quick! Beat it! Out of the question! Nothing doing!"

which was given earlier, evidently dates from between Christmas 1914 and the opening of the field in March:

> A is for all of us locked up in here,
> B for the Bastards who won't give us beer,
> C for the Canteen you never get near,
> D for the Dust-heaps—they don't smell, no fear!
> E for Exchange that you hear of each day,
> F for the Football they won't let us play,
> G for "Gott mit uns," at least so they say,
> H for the Hope that we'll get out some day.
> I for the Ikeys, all Englishmen true,
> J for the Jails that the British go to;
> K for the Kaiser and all of his set,
> L for the Licking we hope they will get,
> M for the March, and it is a damned bore,
> N for the News we don't get of the war;
> O for the Odours that come from the bogs,
> P for the Pork in the soup, fit for hogs;
> Q for the Queues in the mud and the cold,
> R for the Rumours a hundred times told.
> S for the Skilly they feed us again,
> T for the Trucks that we look for in vain;
> U stands for Eunuchs we might as well be,
> V the vexation on tasting the tea.
> W the Wash in the morning so cold,
> X for the Xmas well spent, we are told;
> Y is an Englishman kept like a dog?
> Z is the shape you assume on the bog.
> This is the end of the Ruhleben song;
> We'll sing it in England before very long.
>   (H)

There is the camp of the first winter; a volume could not describe it better.

The barrack organization functioned well during the winter. The vice-captains, postmen, cashiers, and police carried out their unpaid duties conscientiously and were generally respected. Their mere existence, however, introduced obvious inequalities of status and power. No matter how informally the man with the button did his work he now had a measure of authority; even the postman, handed a letter after closing time, could accept or refuse it. He was still a fellow-prisoner, but equality did not extend to his official functions.

The captains, too, ran their barracks conscientiously, but in their wider role as camp administrators they were increasingly criticized.

Between January and March 1915 they took over the hot water service, the kitchens, and the canteen; though the prisoners profited by these changes, they also blamed the captains for shortcomings and for delay in further improvements. The direction of the criticism was significant, for it meant that the camp no longer consisted of two opposed bodies, British and German, but of three; and the third, "the captains," was acquiring formidable power. It was now through Powell, Captain of the Camp, that military orders reached the prisoners, and they in turn had to present complaints or requests at the Captains' Office. How this "third force" grew so powerful will be discussed later, but it was already viewed with misgiving. For the captains were not only exercising control undreamt of when they were accepted as interpreters; Powell was also dealing with German, American, and British authorities as the official representative of the prisoners. None of the captains had been elected to any such functions, and the affront to democratic principles caused three years of bitter agitation.

The role of the German military can be summarily dealt with. The maltreatment of prisoners was a favourite propaganda topic during the war, and some accounts of Ruhleben paint a grisly picture. In 1914, however, war was still a relatively civilized activity, and by more recent standards the internees were not badly abused. The worst crimes committed against them—and they were bad enough—were their internment *per se* and the deficiencies of food and accommodation; there was no attempt to break their spirit by deliberate brutality. The higher officials in Berlin were often harsh and arbitrary, but the officers of the camp, with certain noted exceptions, were usually fair and even considerate. The tone was set by the first Commandant, Graf Schwerin, who made no secret of his regret that civilians should be interned at all. He addressed the men in an early speech as "my dear wards," and several times protected them against Berlin, once threatening to resign unless a ban on smoking were rescinded.[5] The white-haired old gentleman was regarded with respect and even affection. The actual administration, however, was largely in the hands of the *Lageroffizier*, Baron von Taube, who was not unsympathetic but had a hasty temper that often betrayed him. He was susceptible to flattery, however, and devoted to his young wife; after she had presented the prizes at the first Sports Day, and had been cheered and given a silver cup, he was never very hard to manage. The remaining officers need no mention, though every Ruhlebenite would be glad to see a tribute to Freiherr von

5. See Powell and Gribble (38), Chapter 4, which contains good sketches of all the German staff.

Mützenbecher, the first censor, and a verbal slap at the callous Lieutenant Rüdiger, who controlled furloughs and releases. After the opening months, however, the German officers had few contacts except with the civilian captains; the ordinary prisoner had little to do with them.

Among the company of soldiers who served as guards there were a few ugly customers; the rest were ordinary fellows, pig-headed but seldom vindictive. Some nasty incidents occurred during the first winter, but these became fewer as the original guards were replaced by low-category and wounded men. A source of much friction was removed when the fatigue work was delegated to paid working parties under their own foremen, and in September 1915 the guards were withdrawn from the barracks and the prisoners saw little more of them. Towards the end of the war, indeed, the roles were reversed, and German soldiers begging for food were sometimes greeted in Prussian fashion with, *"Nein, nix zu machen. Weg gehen! Los!"* ("No, nothing doing. Get out!")

Ruhleben's economy was a mixed and changing one. Most of the prisoners' support was provided in kind, first by Germany from the camp kitchens, and then increasingly by Britain in the form of parcels. But a great deal of money also circulated, most of it ultimately reaching the canteen and thus the German economy. Individual prisoners had two sources of funds. Families who could afford it sent money by mail through neutral countries; this was converted into marks at some profit to the authorities and a maximum of ten marks a week was paid out to the recipient. The other source was the "relief money" provided by the British Government through the American Embassy and administered by the captains; when this commenced in February 1915 more than half the interned applied for the four (later five) marks a week. In addition, a considerable amount of British money was advanced to the captains to finance structural improvements and the wages of a growing number of paid workers.

Until regular relief payments started, half the population was almost destitute while the rest had money, and this gave rise to a flood of pecuniary transactions. For the wholesale sharing of the first few days almost vanished with the appearance of community groups; not that Ruhleben's generosity had dried up—it was always there to be called on —but because new social barriers made men reluctant to accept help save from their own circle of friends. It smacked of "charity." The trade in goods from Berlin was therefore supplemented by the sale of personal belongings—shoes, sweaters, watches, knives, curios—and a great deal of barter also took place, especially after parcels began to come. Much of the latter was handled for a small commission by Mortimore Howard, a bearded lion tamer, in the "Exchange and Mart"—a business which proclaimed itself, "Recognized as a Public Institution, Patronized by the Captains of the Camp." A damper was put on commercial enterprise by the banning of private trading early in 1915, and the introduction of systematic relief greatly reduced the economic pressure. In March 1915 the captains took over the canteen and other services, and from then on most of the prisoners' money passed through this state monopoly.

Three questions were asked of every Ruhlebenite on his return home, and again of returning prisoners in 1945: "What was the camp like?" "How did they treat you?" and "What did you do all the time?" The first two have been answered sufficiently for the moment; more details will be added as required. That the third question should be asked at all shows that common sense psychology is sometimes ahead of the scientific variety, for psychologists have only recently recognized the significance of boredom.[6] Ordinary people, however, have always known how intolerable it can be, and that is why every Ruhlebenite was asked with real curiosity, "What in the world did you *do* for four years?" The reader knows how the question will be answered; Ruhleben life became almost as busy and active as life anywhere else.

That expansive life did not really begin until the spring of 1915, but one unchanging type of activity was established in the first winter and had important effects. This was the daily routine of living, which occupied a surprising number of hours. Merely getting meals was a lengthy business; Jarvis wrote in April 1915: "Meals demand a lot of time here, as one must line up with one's barrack to march to the kitchen, or go without. And lining up always takes a very long time." But there was more to routine than this, and Cohen's graphic description may be quoted:

Rising at half-past six every morning, lining up at the tap to get water for a wash, lining up on parade at seven, crowding round the parcel lists, lining up at the boiler house for hot water for breakfast, lining up for a newspaper, lining up for a parcel, or a library book, or a theatre ticket; then a couple of hours reading, or study, or sport, or lounging; lining up for dinner, crowding round the postman, lining up at the canteens for sugar, or cheese, or sardines, and at the stores for cigarettes, and lining up again at the newspaper shed, and again at the boiler house for hot water for tea; and the evening spent at a lecture, a concert, or play, followed by a monotonous

6. See, for example, D. O. Hebb, "Drives and the C.N.S. (Conceptual Nervous System)," *Psychological Review*, 1955, 62, 243–54. S. E. Asch discusses the theoretical implications of interest in the external world in his *Social Psychology* (New York: Prentice-Hall Inc., 1952), pp. 289–310.

perambulation up and down the parade, until we were roused and dispersed by the fire bell, and lined up again for the second parade, and wandered mechanically back to horsebox or hayloft, and retired at nine; such was our daily programme, seldom varied except by the latest extravagant rumour, or seventy-two hours in the cells or "bird cage" for smoking in a loft. (P. 190)

Cohen's picture, however, though accurate in detail, is seriously misleading in tone. There were men, no doubt, to whom these tedious routines were the outstanding feature of internment, but there were hundreds of others who found them only a vexing interruption of the real current of life—a current no less strong for being confined to a stableyard. To some of these prisoners Ruhleben was so intense an experience that recalling it makes them lose track of the present:

Your questionnaire arrived a fortnight ago, and has given me one of the most exciting shake-ups I have ever had. I don't know from where you got your questions, but they have dug in pretty deep. They seemed to touch some internal spring, and have called up the most amazing quantity of memories. I really seem to have been back there in spirit, so vivid has it been. I have fortunately retained a sort of microscopic view of it—I could walk straight back into the life there without being conscious of a break. (L 79)

Here again is the authentic note of Ruhleben. Whatever experiences were embedded in this man's memory, they were of something more stirring than routine.

6

COMMUNITY STRUCTURE: THE BARRACKS

THE OUTSTANDING DEVELOPMENT of Ruhleben's first winter was the growth of a community structure. Not the formal organization of each barrack under its captain, necessary as that was, but the gradual, unplanned grouping of the prisoners on the basis of their spatial location. They began the winter an undifferentiated crowd, responding en masse to every current of emotion; they ended it members of a multitude of groups in which each individual was physically and mentally anchored. The men were still excitable enough to "drag anchor" on occasion, but the scope of suggestion was limited and life had a generally settled character.

Underlying the emergence of the community pattern was a more basic aspect of settlement: the "adaptation" process through which camp life, at first strange and disturbing, came to seem a normal mode of existence. Adaptation occurs in any organism capable of learning, and consists in a progressive modification of its responses to continuing or recurring stimuli. "Getting used to it" is the usual phrase, but the process is more active than this implies. A cat, for instance, gets used to a new home, not through the mere passage of time, but through coming to respond in habitual ways rather than with the emergency behaviour prompted by strangeness. To elicit such habitual responses our grandparents buttered the animal's paws; this was sound psychology, for it evoked the reflex action of licking them—in itself calming—and then the rewarding behaviour of swallowing the butter. These pleasantly toned habits were incompatible with terror; hence the cat had made a start at settling down.

The Germans did not actually butter the paws of the Ruhleben prisoners, but a similar process took place. Anxious as the men were, they had built-in needs to eat, sleep, and excrete, and repeated performance of these pleasurable acts in the new situation inevitably robbed it of its alarming character. One cannot feel frightened while downing a litre of cabbage soup. Unfamiliar behaviour like marching to the kitchens was at first disturbing, as the accompanying cheers showed, but with repetition it too became habitual and the cheering was not needed. Thought kept pace with behaviour; the idea of being imprisoned, once startling and incredible, became commonplace, even boring. "Everything getting very dull and stale," was Burton's comment after three weeks of adaptation, and such jests as the address on a November tea invitation, "Convict Jones, Cell 22," soon ceased to raise a smile. The fact of internment had been absorbed. This is the significance of the routines described in the last chapter; they show that many camp situations were recurring ones, so that habits had been formed in connection with them—lining up, for example. But a situation that can be dealt with on the basis of habit is no longer alarming; it is felt to be under control.

The most important feature of the adaptation process, however, was its social character. The routines of life were established, not by individuals, but collectively, through the convergence of many on common ways of acting. This method of establishment gave them a social sanction; lining up was not merely a way to get hot water, it was the *right* way. That made it a group norm. And the men were lining up mentally as well as physically; it was "right" to despise Germans, "wrong" to be down-hearted. Conformity of this type was very different from the emotional unanimity of the crowd, for it rested on lasting habits and attitudes. In adapting collectively to their new circumstances the prisoners had thus created the very basis of community—a body of accepted customs. Thanks to this, the ensuing social differentiation did not leave the camp a hodge-podge of unrelated groups, but occurred within a more inclusive unity that was "Ruhleben."

All social development involves both breaking down and building up —differentiation and integration—and it was through these universal processes that simple solidarity became a complex social order. The original mass was broken down into a multitude of smaller, interrelated groups; at the same time, each of these became a social unit in itself and an in-group to its members. The dual process began as soon as the camp opened, accelerated rapidly in the spring and summer of 1915, and was much reduced thereafter. The resulting structures fell into one of the two familiar categories: *community groups*, such as barracks and boxes, and *associations*, like the dramatic, musical, and Lancastrian societies. The community groups arose out of mere physical proximity, so that membership was seldom a matter of choice; they were typically heterogeneous in composition and were formed with no specific aim, reflecting simply the universal human tendency to establish ties with others. The associations, on the other hand, were formed voluntarily on the basis of common aims and interests, and were therefore in some respects homogeneous. The distinction is not absolute—some community groups were deliberately set up by friends who messed together —but it is convenient. For the community groups were products of the first winter and are therefore discussed now, while the associations were not fully developed until the summer of 1915 and will be treated in Part IV of the book.

The historic basis of community is kinship, but Ruhleben was of course not built on the family. How many prisoners had blood relations in the camp is unknown—among the respondents the figure is 4 per cent—but kinship was in any case a negligible factor. Brother and brother, father and son, found themselves in a community where such relationships had no function and tended to become dormant; of six pairs of brothers known to me, only three chose to live together after moving became possible. Indeed, a faint embarrassment about blood relationship was often detectable, as it is in boarding schools; it was an unrecognized category, and those concerned avoided calling attention to it.

Spatial proximity, on the other hand, played a larger role in Ruhleben than in most urban communities, chiefly because of the lack of physical barriers. Those who were thrown together in the same barrack, loft, or horse-box were forced to act towards one another, adjust to one another's behaviour, and do many things co-operatively or in common. As a result they came to think of themselves as "we," as belonging together and sharing certain characteristics. This integration, however, entailed a simultaneous differentiation from those not included in the new unit; they were perceived as outsiders, different from "us" and requiring different treatment. The in-group and out-group categories, used first of British and Germans, were now being applied within the British group.

The community groupings followed the spatial pattern of the camp. Each prisoner was assigned to a barrack and definitely located within it. He was either in a stable and quartered in a box or loft, or else in the Tea House or one of the added huts called "wooden barracks." The latter had no permanent partitions, but their occupants divided them into "corners" with beds and screens. All these divisions gave rise to community groups and aroused some measure of identification; they will be described in their logical order of barracks, lofts, and boxes or corners. They did not emerge in that order; in the 1914 diaries and postcards, "we," "us," and "our" refer either to the camp as a whole ("we had another real good concert on Sunday night") or to the box groups or messes ("we five have stuck together"). But the barracks, though later in developing, were units of great public importance and so provide the best starting point.

Although there was little to distinguish one barrack from another except its number and location, it was not long before every prisoner thought of himself as belonging to a particular barrack, sharing in its character, and being to that extent differentiated from his fellows elsewhere. He had "belonged" to it of course from his first day, but in only a formal sense; personal identification developed more slowly. He lived so much of his life in the building that it soon became familiar and even homelike, but his real identification was with the men who occupied it with him, and this had to grow out of shared activities and experiences.

From the start the barracks were administrative units; each had its military guards and its civilian captain and other officials. The men were lined up by barracks for counting and military orders; damage to barrack property was assessed against all the occupants. And the inhabitants often acted as a group; they marched together to the kitchens and around the racecourse, and the singing and shouting that solidified the camp also made each man more aware of his barrack attachment. Every day, too, the corridors and lofts had to be swept, rubbish removed, and the ground outside tidied, and these tasks involved a good deal of co-operation. All this shared activity made belonging to the barrack more than a formal matter.

Competition with other groups is a notorious spur to identification, and competition soon appeared. Even in the earliest days certain barracks singled themselves out as more noisy and daring than others, and barrack concerts evoked some mild rivalry. Competitive games, however, were the great rousers of local patriotism—though the first contests between barrack teams, in December 1914, did not excite the spectators unduly; owing to the ban on ball games they were confined to chess. On March 28, 1915, however, Baron von Taube kicked off for the inaugural football match on the newly opened playing field, and more robust games came into their own. From then on the field was in constant use and the two major sports, "soccer" and cricket, were organized entirely by barracks. Competition was extremely keen and barrack sentiment, which had been forming all winter, shot up to its greatest heights. While twenty-two men played football there were often twenty-two hundred cheering on the side lines; the success of a man's barrack became his own success, its defeat his own failure. That is what identification means.

The facts are so familiar that they no longer arouse the curiosity they should. What, for instance, *is* this barrack whose fate is being decided between the goal-posts? Not the stable itself, and not the individuals who live in it, for both were already present when there was no such thing as a "barrack." Something has been added to them of which the barrack is only the symbol—a new group relatedness, a new sense of belonging together. What this means to the men is suggested by Mahoney's comment on the first "Cup-tie" match: "One would have thought, from the deafening final cheer which went up from four thousand odd throats, that the British army was crossing the Rhine, instead of its being a paean of praise to the crack football team of an internment camp" (3[?], p. 201). This was on May 17, 1915—the day when the prisoners read a sharp American note about the sinking of the *Lusitania*. But they were now building their own world, and its activities were beginning to obscure what was happening outside.

The most vivid signs of what has occurred are the shouts of the spectators: "Come on, FOUR!", "That's the game, TEN!" Only last November these barrack numbers were empty syllables with no emotional overtones; all the early teams that played in the compound were called after English clubs. From 1915 onwards, however, teams are known exclusively by their barrack numbers; simple digits like "Four" and "Ten" have gathered so much significance that no other names are ever considered. They stand for what the barrack now means to its members: something greater than themselves, but of which each is proudly a part. Thus Ruhleben now contains *more* than its four thousand inhabitants, for through their interactions they have created a series of new social forms, and created them, like gods, out of nothing. Sixteen "barracks" are now in existence—soon there will be more—but the raw materials are quite undiminished.

Even God, however, is said to have repented some of his creative efforts, and men never build a social structure without paying a price for it in individual freedom. The Ruhlebenite was no exception; when he breathed life into his barrack he lost some of his independence. He discovered that he had acquired obligations towards the thing he had made; his barrack had an honour he must defend, a reputation he must maintain. Its teams had to be "supported" in critical games, money was levied for sports equipment, players were expected to turn out when called upon. The first write-up of field hockey, never a major sport, complained wistfully about men who felt that "that elusive thing, their duty to their barrack," compelled them to subordinate hockey to football (*RCM* 1, p. 34). "Elusive" was not always the word, for social pressure was strong; Ewing, busily studying in 1918, wrote in his diary: "N. and L. after me *again* to turn out for cricket. Sure I ought to steer clear of it this year, but they insistent, made me uncomfortable."

The excerpt, however, dates from a period when barrack identification had been weakened by conflicting interests and loyalties. It was different in the spring of 1915; the barrack was then dominant and the typical prisoner strongly identified with it. In meeting its claims he therefore felt no loss of personal freedom; on the contrary, he was doing just what he wanted to do, for the barrack was an extension of himself and its demands were his own. All were included under the general rubric of "loyalty," and loyalty was not exacted from him—he gave it freely and gladly. In return, his life became far richer, for this expansion of the self gave him a fresh sense of belonging, new interests, and new aims.

Barrack loyalty was soon enhanced by the art of the sports writer, for camp publications devoted many pages to sport. A pre-season cricket forecast in one of the magazines (*IRC* 3, p. 39) brought a letter to the editor which perfectly illustrates the change that had occurred:

Sir: Will you *very* kindly inform me:

1. Why you consider Barrack XI's chances at cricket so slight that you have the damned impertinence to pat them on the back for good sportsmanship—the usual consolation prize—before the season has started, and before we have lost a match?

2. Why you favour Barrack III's chances? Do you think the presence of a lot of would-be actors, artists, authors and other sub-men in that barrack will improve the form of its players? Or are you in the team yourself?

3. Whether you think that because Barrack IV have the stamina to win a tug-of-war competition against a rotten camp, it follows that they necessarily have the skill to win the cricket championship?

4. What the dickens is the good of a first rate wicket-keeper to Barrack II if they have no one to bowl straight to him?

Let me tell you, Sir, that if the championship can be won, Barrack XI is the barrack to win it.

Yours,
ELEVENITE

When this letter was written Ruhleben was only eight months old. But the writer—and there were hundreds like him—already had other and more healthy concerns than himself and his internment.

His derision for other barracks is a reminder that identification has a negative side; as we are absorbed into one group we inevitably draw away from others. They are now out-groups, and attitudes towards them are aloof and critical. Cohen-Portheim has an acute observation on the division of Wakefield camp into three compounds:

> The barbed wire divisions created hostility, distrust and dislike, which went on increasing as the years passed by. . . . There were all the absurdities of nationalism; you must prefer your own "country" to the others, you must not profess too much admiration of their institutions or characteristics, you must stand up for your "own people" against the "strangers." (P. 102)

Such attitudes are invariable results of segregation and were not lacking in Ruhleben, even though no barbed wire separated its inhabitants. Praise of another barrack often evoked the well-worn retort: "If you think so damn much of Barrack 3, why don't you go and live there?" On the other hand, the absence of physical barriers permitted inter-barrack friendships, and these usually took precedence over barrack loyalty. A friend might disparage his own barrack, but the tactful visitor would find something to praise, if it were only the convenient nearness of the latrines.

The earliest evidence of out-group attitudes was the loud cry of the first winter: "Stranger in the barrack!" It is a startling cry, for how have the comrades of November become strangers to one another? If we knew when it was first raised we would know when the wholeness of Ruhleben began to break down. It was certainly early, for the cry was originally a warning against sneak thieves, and petty thieving quickly disappeared. During the whole four years, however, any visitor to a strange barrack was likely to hear the old cry echoing after him— ironically now, of course, but with undertones that suggested he was trespassing.

And so he was, for the barrack pattern had actually limited his spatial range. Wire fences were not needed to keep the men apart; the fact of segregation was enough. As Denton put it in September 1915, "E. M. is a very nice chap, but we are in different barracks and don't see much of each other." In the questionnaire sent to ex-Ruhlebenites they were asked:

(a) Which barracks did you visit "fairly frequently"?　(3.5)
(b) Which did you visit "very seldom"?　(8.5)
(c) Which can you never remember entering at all?　(3.8)

Some could not answer and many replies were vague—not surprising after fifteen years. But fifty-six men tried to be specific, and the average number of barracks they listed is shown in brackets. The figures are of course unreliable, but even if that for (a) were doubled it would still be strikingly low, for there were twenty-three barracks, the camp was little larger than a city block, and the men never left it for four years. Most of the untabulated answers suggest the same restricted movement, at least for social visiting:

I rarely visited any. (Q 32)
Only visited other barracks occasionally and with definite objects. (Q 55)
Apart from my own barrack I don't think that I ever, or very seldom, visited any other. (Q 68)
None socially, but most of them in connection with hockey. (Q 69)

The camp was no longer a mere cage full of prisoners; it was a spatial pattern intersected by many barriers, barriers invisible to an outsider but real and effective to the men. Shut up in a small place by the Germans, they had proceeded to make it even smaller. It was part of the process of "getting not to know one another," and the existence of the barracks determined where the broadest lines would be drawn.

The barracks, however, were too large and heterogeneous to become fully integrated groups. They could arouse loyalty and exert control— only the most hardened roisterer would defy shouts of "Pipe down, there!" from disturbed slumberers—but genuine interaction took place chiefly in smaller groups. Barrack opinion, for instance, was seldom clearly formulated except on such clear-cut issues as apologizing for the flagstaff "outrage" on the Kaiser's birthday; Burton reports: "In the evening a petition was taken around with the object of begging for our release. This was not signed by our barrack." It was signed, in fact, only by the captains of the camp and of the Jewish barrack, and a quotation from it will suggest why: "We are all indignant at the action of the coward who by hiding himself has brought disgrace upon us all" (H). This was a matter on which "British" prisoners would all think alike; on more controversial issues consensus was rare except in the relatively homogeneous barracks described later. The captains did consult their barracks on certain moot questions, decisions being reached by show of hands at a meeting in the corridor, but such occasions were infrequent.

And, as the camp grew older, the relative importance of the barracks declined. The prisoners' interest was increasingly absorbed by associations that cut across barrack lines; this tended to blur boundaries, with a consequent weakening of the barracks—just as our local communities have been weakened by mass communications and mobility. In spite of their diminished importance the barracks remained the political and administrative units—again a parallel with Western democracy—but their political role finally vanished with the new constitution of 1918, which provided for direct election of a camp government. Barrack sentiment was thus largely confined to sport, and even here it was limited, for the later sports of golf and tennis seem never to have run barrack competitions. They are of course individual rather than group games, and their popularity from 1916 onwards was one sign of a growing individualism.

Periodic attempts were made to revive and exploit barrack feeling, but with relatively little success. In the campaign to endow a Ruhleben Bed in a British hospital each barrack contributed separately, and competitive sacrifice was certainly not discouraged. The scheme, however, like everything that affected relations with the home government, aroused controversy; only 1,200 marks were collected and the money was never sent to England.[1] An "Eisteddfod" in the fall of 1915 included competitions for barrack choirs and soloists but attracted few entries; accustomed by now to good music, the men were uninterested in local efforts. The Ruhleben Horticultural Society, formed in 1916, awarded prizes for barrack gardens, but these were the work of a few devoted individuals, not of the barrack as a whole. The camp Y.M.C.A. did succeed in reviving the spirit of the early barrack concerts in its 1916 programme, and Denton wrote in April: "Barrack XI gave a concert in the Y.M.C.A. on Saturday which was a howling success. Alick produced the mock play out of 'Midsummer Night's Dream,' which was fine. Quartets, solos, and an excellent comedian, a Scotch engineer with natural humour, completed the bill." Sectional pride was unequal to the strain, however, and only half a dozen barracks took part. After the visit of two American evangelists in 1916 the Y.M.C.A. also organized prayer-meetings on a barrack basis—though not, presumably, on a competitive one. Denton reports again:

Feb. 20, 1916. The Y.M.C.A. Week gave a fine new impetus to all our work here, and we now have in every barrack of the camp (21) a daily prayer-meeting which is well attended.

Mar. 5, 1916. All our religious work has had a great boom since the Y.M.C.A. Week; there are fourteen different barrack prayer-meetings which take place daily.

As will be noted, the meetings dropped off rapidly, few of them surviving the summer.

1. The problem was a down-to-earth one; if the prisoners started sending money to England would England not cut down their relief money?

Although the barracks thus lost much of their public importance, the men never ceased to identify themselves with them emotionally. They supplied, of course, the "address" that everyone needed in a large town, but barrack feeling went deeper than that. Its strength was probably due in part to the emotions involved in competitive sport, and even more to the fact that a prisoner's barrack contained his real camp home, the little box or mess group in which he was most permanently rooted. In any case, the elderly gentlemen who now attend gatherings of the Ruhleben Association all wear lapel cards which show, as a matter of course, their barrack numbers as well as their names.

Differentiation is progressive, divisions give birth to subdivisions, and the barrack was far from being the final community unit. Wherever physical barriers existed within it they had their effect; the men concerned began to lead segments of their lives in common and thus form groups of greater or less significance. Each of the stables contained its boxes downstairs and its two lofts above them, and, since the stairways were out of doors, contacts between floors were not intimate. A box dweller writes: "I can remember a good many of the boxes and their members (though I am often stuck for names) but I hardly remember any of the men in our lofts, though I must have seen them often" (L 59). This was probably typical, and the obverse would hold for "lofters."

The boxes, with their greater comfort and privacy, were usually preferred to lofts and wooden barracks; in the questionnaires, "Chance to get in a box" is the reason most frequently given for voluntary moves. Hence any vacancy in a box allowed some selection; congeniality was the first requisite in a new member, but financial resources and a good parcel record were not overlooked. Mahoney states indignantly that boxes were sold for a hundred marks in the early days (3[?], p. 268) and some undesirables were certainly paid to vacate in favour of a friend. Hence selection tended in time, though with many exceptions, to make the boxes a kind of "upper economic area," and this combined with their spatial separation from the lofts to give to mutual attitudes a slight out-group flavour. The box dwellers felt themselves a shade more civilized than their neighbours overhead, and the lofters in return looked down on them as men of weaker clay with a touch of snobbishness—though this did not prevent their moving down when opportunity offered. Some distinction in character also became apparent; the boxes, with their more intimate, private life, tended to become conventional, and to prize the middle-class virtues of quietness, respectability, and minding one's own business. The lofts, on the other hand, preserved more of the first winter's characteristics; they were more ruggedly "British," more informal, outspoken, and rowdy. The wooden barracks, which housed a third of the population, were enough like lofts to need no separate description.

In these open units the men were separated only by makeshift partitions; this favoured general discussion and gave rise to an active public opinion, typically conservative in tone. A barrack captain, referring to a proposed reform, once remarked to me: "A lot of the boxes are for it, but the lofts are solid against it." Both "solid" and "against" would characterize loft opinion much better than box opinion. Farwell, after commenting on barrack loyalties, ends his 1933 letter thus: "Anyway, if Providence, or the Deity, or somebody, should decree say another Great Flood or earthquake or other calamity, my first comment would probably be this: 'Such a decision will be extremely unpopular in MY loft!' "

"My" loft, however, refers not to the loft as a whole but to one of its two sections, and socially these were the stronger groups. But even they could not hold together against the specialized associations that grew up, and their decline is nicely illustrated in this complaint from a magazine in the summer of 1915:

All honour to Loft B, Barrack 2, for the excellent example they have set us with their tea-meeting. Unfortunately we have too little of the tea-meeting spirit in the camp, we sneak away into boxes and cubby-holes, we gather in cliques and groups lacking that "all good pals together" spirit which one would expect to find in a British *Gefangenenlager* [prison camp]. (*IRC* 3, p. 11)

Editorial tears for the vanishing ways of yesterday are familiar, but this lament is noteworthy, both for its engaging use of "British" to denote the universal comradeship of the first weeks, and for its reluctant testimony to the social change that was occurring.

The quartering of Ruhleben's inhabitants in a dozen different buildings was not only a determinant of their social attachments; it also had marked effects on the picture that each man formed of the camp. Besides perceiving his own barrack as "his" and therefore somewhat superior to others, the prisoner also perceived the remaining barracks as differing significantly from one another. Each acquired its distinctive character, more or less clearly recognized by those outside it.

This extension of the differentiation process beyond the in-group, out-group categories was due to the same need for an organized mental world with an easily grasped pattern. Wherever groups are separated spatially there is a tendency to differentiate them qualitatively as well;

any differences that can aid discrimination are therefore emphasized in perception. As Cohen-Portheim said of the compounds at Wakefield: ". . . the divisions created a conviction of essential differences and in time differences actually came to exist. . . . The difference would have, I imagine, been invisible and incomprehensible to an outsider, but it was a reality to the people concerned" (p. 103). Physical separation at Ruhleben was far less complete, but it caused all important barracks to be distinctively labelled.

The labels were of course stereotypes, products of the human tendency to perceive all members of a distinguishable group as basically alike and to describe them in a few simple terms. All Scotsmen are parsimonious, all Frenchman amorous. As in the case of these familiar stereotypes, labelling in Ruhleben was a collective process; the characteristics of a given barrack were discussed and debated, gossiped and joked about, until an acceptable definition gained currency. The real differences between the barracks could have been discovered only by careful research into their composition and typical behaviour, and the Ruhlebenites were not social scientists. Where no clear-cut differences met the eye, they seized on any available cues, however tenuous, and fashioned the barrack stereotype. Once formed and sanctioned, it was extremely durable, colouring the camp's perception of a barrack's occupants as long as internment lasted.

In the case of four barracks, stereotyping was made easy by official segregation. The first was that of the orthodox Jews, who were separated from other prisoners within a week of internment, ostensibly for dietary reasons. Between two and three hundred stepped forward when called upon, others preferring to remain with the Gentiles. After some days in the nearby Emigrant Station they were tranferred to Barrack 6, the oldest and dirtiest of the stables, where the humiliations of ghetto life soon outweighed the advantage of kosher meals from Berlin.

Had the Jews not been segregated, anti-Semitism would have been almost unknown in Ruhleben. There was nothing in camp experience to give rise to it, and many Jews in other barracks were scarcely recognized as such. Segregation, however, marked Barrack 6 off as a distinct social unit, and it was immediately labelled in terms long traditional in Britain. Israel Cohen, a member of the barrack, writes:

Barrack Six was a sort of by-word in the camp, invariably uttered in a tone of contempt. On the only occasion when I visited the camp Cinema Palace there appeared upon the screen the figure of a grey-bearded old Jew gloating over a heap of coins, and at once somebody called out "Barrack Six!" and a guffaw of laughter swept the room. (P. 206)

The music-hall comedians got many laughs by similar means, and even the Y.M.C.A. at a 1916 concert included a song with a topical verse on Barrack 6. It brought down the house, but was later protested and apologised for. The first camp magazine also found the Jews a ready target for cheap wit: "LOST: Guide to Jerusalem. Finder requested to return same to Homesick, Barrack 6." (*IRC* 1, p. 10.) And a later issue contained a drawing of a highly Semitic face, composed entirely of 6's. No such gibes could have been thought of had Barrack 6 not existed.

Many of the themes were part of British folklore, but Ruhleben provided some additions. The daily kosher meal sent by a Berlin congregation, though at first much better than camp fare, deteriorated with Germany's food supply until orthodox Jews were profaning the Sabbath by cooking. The camp, however, always pictured Barrack 6 as living in luxury while Christians lined up at the soup kitchens. Over half of the barrack's inmates were businessmen—the largest proportion in the camp—and some of them early set up as dealers in everything from cups of tea to jewellry. Private trade was suppressed in March 1915, but "Vant to buy a vatch?" had long since become a catchword. Business connections led naturally to the smuggling of liquor and other contraband; the guards raided the Jews' barrack and one of them coined another popular phrase, "*Immer Baracke Sechs!*" ("Always Barrack Six!"). Armed with this, the Ruhlebenite could blame any new military restrictions on the lawlessness of one group. The Jews were also widely suspected of German sympathies—many spoke with accents and were German residents—but this suspicion is emphatically denied by Cohen.

Special privileges, outlandish customs, shady deals, dubious patriotism, these were elements in the stereotype applied to all members of Barrack 6. Never was a group less suitable for mass definition, for it was the most heterogeneous in the camp with respect to origin, language, and educational level. Along with its Polish tailors and cheap hucksters it contained musicians, actors, scientists, and scholars who contributed greatly to Ruhleben life; they were regarded, however, as exceptions and did not alter the stereotype. Even the fact that Barrack 6 ran creditable football and cricket teams in 1915 did no more than keep prejudice at a relatively harmless level; the Jews remained an out-group as long as they lived in their barrack.

Social isolation is directly reflected in behaviour, for those who are denied full participation in a group are also cut off from its norms and values. The Jews' barrack, it will be recalled, was the only one to sign the rather abject apology for the flagstaff incident, and this "un-British" conduct was hotly denounced. The signers, however, had not only a different cultural heritage; they had also been kept at arm's length by the rest of the camp during the very period when its norms of conduct were taking shape.

The loft of Barrack 6 was condemned by the American Ambassador in March 1915 and cleared three months later, and in November 1916 the rest of the barrack was vacated. A good many German-born Jews had already been released, and the remainder were scattered through the camp. Barrack 6 became the Camp School, and its name ceased to be a byword. In the later magazines there are scarcely any jokes about Jews, partly because of growing restraint, but chiefly because they were no longer perceived as a separate unit that required a differentiating label.

It is possible that Barrack 6 conferred more benefits on the rest of the camp than were recognized by Gentiles, for a licensed target for ridicule is a great convenience in any community. Life in the crowded stables, especially during the first winter, generated constant irritation, and some of this may have been vented in sneers at the Jews rather than in quarrels with boxmates. Even so, this was poor compensation for the humiliation inflicted on one group of prisoners. And the outlet does not seem to have been necessary, for when the Jews' barrack ceased to exist the jokes and gibes simply dried up. Nor was aggression merely diverted to the pro-Germans, for they were segregated in April 1915, while *In Ruhleben Camp*, with its many anti-Semitic witticisms, did not start publication until June.

All this is written from an outsider's standpoint; the inside view of Barrack 6 was of course totally different. Cohen describes it in interesting detail, and emphasizes the hurt astonishment of these men when they found their fellow-prisoners acting as persecutors. Segregation, however, also engendered a group spirit among them, symbolized by the Passover celebrations in their incongruous setting, and expressed in occasional protests against prejudiced material. A magazine item reads: "We throw a bouquet at the Barrack 6 members of the Debating Society for preventing a 'Fagin' scene being included in the programme of the Dickens evening. We like to see the little 'uns sticking up for themselves." (*IRC* 4, p. 23.) The protest reflected the hypersensitivity that a rejected group always displays, and the editor's patronizing tone suggests the gulf that segregation had set between two groups of prisoners. The division was regrettable, both for its denial of Ruhleben's original solidarity, and for its repudiation of shared experiences in the present in favour of stereotypes borrowed from the past.

The second special barrack dates from December 17, 1914, when eighty coloured men were brought in and quartered in the new Barrack 13. Most of them were from British Africa and the West Indies, but there were also East Indians and Arabs; almost all had belonged to ships' crews. Later arrivals swelled the numbers to over a hundred, but fifty were repatriated at the end of 1915—the Germans taking sardonic pleasure in exchanging coloured Britishers for white Germans—and the barrack was emptied a year later.

Barrack 13 was invariably known as the "Niggers' Barrack," but the term was merely a colloquialism, condescending, but implying no prejudice. Denton, for instance, who conducted church services in the barrack, wrote home in 1915, "All my dear niggers are going to another camp." The barrack had its own cricket team in 1915 and there were coloured men on certain other teams; only one prisoner, a South African, refused to play against them. The camp regarded them as amusing and irresponsible children, ignoring such exceptions as the Arabian scholar who sat all day instructing pupils in the Koran. The primitive games that were played outside the barrack, the wild music that emanated from it, the well-known characters who set up laundries, shoeshine stands, and peanut stalls—all this added a pleasingly exotic touch to the Ruhleben scene. There was nothing to arouse hostility.

Few outsiders knew anything of the inner life of Barrack 13. Mahoney spent many hours teaching illiterates the alphabet, and Wallace Ellison was for some time captain of the barrack, but the only book that deals seriously with the group is that of O'Sullivan Molony. He paints some appealing portraits, but his account of a fatal battle between Arabs and Negroes lacks any corroboration. The general camp definition was a superficial one, and is well conveyed by Gribble. He is writing of the summer of 1915:

The hardships had meant less—and the amusements meant more—to them than to most of us. Their teeth and their digestions seemed to be better adapted to the diet than ours were. . . . It may be, too, that those of them who came, as the majority did, from ships, found their barrack as comfortable as the fo'c'sle, and were relieved at having comparatively little work to do. In short, as long as the sun shone—and it shone through that summer almost without a break—these coloured fellow-citizens of ours appeared as happy as the day. And it is a fact that one of them—we called him "Peanuts" because he drove a roaring trade in these comestibles—finding his name on a list of prisoners to be exchanged, actually hid himself in a dark corner of the camp in order to escape repatriation. (22, pp. 313–14)

The most notable separation carried out by the military was that of the pro-Germans, or "P.G.'s" as they were always called. This took place on April 18, 1915, after several earlier incidents. A large number of internees, as mentioned in the Introduction, had spent most of their lives in Germany. "Scores of such men," say Powell and Gribble, "looking like Germans, talking like Germans, and behaving like Germans, were raked into Ruhleben in November 1914" (p. 26), and were naturally looked at askance by the other prisoners. They were still mere individuals, however, objects of curiosity, not of antagonism; even in those days of high patriotism there was astonishingly little friction. Hughes, writing of November 1914, says: "Some of the Germans used to air their minds incontinently without upsetting the humorous tolerance of their fellow-prisoners" (p. 667). Hostility had to await their emergence as a clearly defined group.

Clashes did occur, of course, and these foster children of Germany must often have been stung by the sentiments they heard around them. Not until January 1915, however, did one of them complain to the Baron, the specific charge being that prisoners constantly referred to the German nation as "bloody Germans." What followed has been often described; Burton's account is brief and contemporary:

Fri. Jan. 15. All hands lined up this morning at 10.30 A.M. and each barrack separately harangued by the Baron, about supposed insults to Germans in the Camp. The whole affair arose out of the misinterpretation of the use of the word "bloody" which had been used in relation to Germans, and translated into German language means "blood-thirsty." We were, however, told by the gentleman referred to that he called us "blood-thirsty Englanders" who were the instigators of this war. "Thank God, however, Germany was winning all along the line and would continue to do so." The gentleman was in a great rage, and finished up by ordering all those with German sympathies (*Deutschgesinnt*) to stand out. A very large number were then revealed in their true colours. They were retained for special instructions whilst the "Englanders" were ordered indoors. This was repeated at each barrack. In the afternoon a deputation consisting of Professor Delmer, Mr. Butterworth and Capt. Brown waited upon Baron von Taube and explained away a lot of misunderstanding, and it is inclined to have blown over, though the camp is now very much divided and the "pro" element is certainly in power.

Much amusement was caused by Mr. Delmer's success in persuading the fuming Baron that "bloody" was, in English idiom, a term of endearment; but though this closed the incident it left the camp, as Burton says, very much divided. The seven or eight hundred who stepped out of the ranks ceased to be individuals of somewhat unconventional views; they were at once defined by the remainder as an alien group of formidable size, a foreign body in the community. The effects were immediate. In mixed boxes, easy-going tolerance gave place to hostility; men who had stepped out were asked to mess separately, or treated with cold reserve. "P.G." became a popular term of abuse; if a man had his hair clipped short, or showed too much partiality for German sausage, someone was sure to exclaim, "You damned P.G.!" And in April the "British" prisoners were sewing small silk Union Jacks[2] on their lapels—the in-group was sharpening up its boundaries.

Matters continued thus until April 18 when the Baron, on orders from the War Office, again addressed the barracks, this time in more subdued tone. The definition was now made physical; the *Deutschgesinnten* ("German-minded") were to dwell in separate barracks. Henley describes the scene:

April 18. Pro-German trouble. All Britishers turned out of Barracks 1, 14, 15 and Tea House and P.G.'s turned in. The turn-out was awful and resembled Petticoat Lane on a Sunday morning—bedding, clothing, footgear, jam, bread, butter, all being dumped in the yard until the unfortunates could find quarters. About 600 P.G.'s altogether, 70 from Barrack 7. The P.G.'s who were allocated to Nos. 14 and 15 were allowed to take their own bedsteads, but the Britishers who left there had slept on the wooden floors. An awful mess.

On the whole, the move was a wise one. Once the pro-Germans had emerged as an out-group they could not again have been assimilated; segregation clarified the situation and tended to reduce friction.

The choice made by these men was a hard one, for most of them had ties with both the warring countries. And their lot in the camp was not enviable; they got no parcels from England, and the military, when it came to the point, showed little sympathy with divided loyalties. Gribble says:

The German authorities made them as uncomfortable as possible, hoping thus to persuade them to join the German army in order to escape from their discomfort. A good many of the younger men among them did so, and a good many of the older men were released to do work judged to be of national importance; but it was we *Stock-Engländer*, as they called us, who enjoyed the respect of our custodians. (22, p. 310)

The camp's definition of the P.G.'s was a simple one: they were on the enemy side. That was no topic for jokes, and the magazines scrupulously avoided it. The linguistic difficulties of German-speaking prisoners are touched on in one or two later cartoons, but the only reference to

2. They were sold by the resourceful Mr. Mahoney, who does not state how he secured them.

the split is among some facetious "Publishers' Announcements," a notorious renegade being listed as author of *Under Two Flags*. The men's attitude was strictly correct; P.G.'s were not molested in any way, they were simply ignored. As Powell and Gribble say: "Such incidents, as was inevitable, fixed a great gulf between the two ends of the camp. The English did not visit the pro-Germans; and the pro-Germans were not encouraged to visit the English." (P. 36.)

Isolation, by removing opportunities for conflict, ultimately turned antagonism into indifference, but the affair left its traces on the camp, and particularly on the seamen. The segregated pro-Germans could be ignored, but it was a different matter for anyone in the British barracks who spoke with an accent, had been long in Germany, or otherwise lacked a clean bill of health. A young man brought up in Belgium and not interned until 1916—in itself cause for suspicion—writes: "My first impression was one of aggressiveness towards me. I was perhaps rather un-English, but I did not find it easy to speak to anyone" (L 116). This was not Ruhleben's typical attitude to newcomers.

On the other hand, the camp never developed the hatred of all things German that prevailed elsewhere. The German department of the Camp School was an active one, German plays were staged periodically until June 1917, and Lutheran services in German were held until 1918. Study of German literature and music was never defined as disloyal; in this respect Ruhleben was an enlightened community. As for the pro-Germans themselves, they were gradually released into Germany, and by 1917 the remainder were too few to arouse any attention.

The last separation of a particular group occurred on June 15, 1915, when the "Boys' Barrack" was opened in the western half of Barrack 22. Though the order of internment applied only to persons of seventeen or older, there were many younger boys in the ships' crews; four children under twelve were sent home after two weeks, but others not much older remained. No attempt was made to sort them out, and they spent the first six months wherever they happened to be. In the spring of 1915 the captains recognized their physical needs by supplying them with daily egg-nogs, but lofts crowded with a mixed lot of men were not an ideal environment for them.

On the other hand, the boys were also a menace to the camp. Awed at first by what had happened to them, they recovered all too rapidly; the freedom of the early months went to their heads and they became the street urchins, the *gamins*, of the community. Products often of seaport slums, they were prone to rowdiness, vandalism, and fighting: their language was appalling even by Ruhleben standards, and they feared no one but their own officers, who could not possibly keep track of them. After a fracas they would vanish into the crowd, and few knew their names or in what corners of the camp they lived. In snow-balling weather their marksmanship and aggressiveness were terrifying, and their favourite victims were those Teutonic figures with Homburg hats and fur collars who later inhabited the pro-German barracks. Indeed, after one storm it was reported that some of these gentlemen had been unable to reach the latrines for two days. The boyish gangsters thus amused the camp as well as irritating it, and their presence greatly enlivened the compound. A 1933 letter from one of them, a ship's apprentice, is worth quoting at length:

My first day was miserable and lonely, my only chum Jock D., for we were the only two boys in the ship. We cried together at first, it was with real disappointment, for we had planned to join up in different names as we had previously signed a "Parole" which we had no intention of keeping. [They had thought they were being sent to Holland, not Ruhleben.] After we got over this we wandered about, we had no money, yet our plans were "Could we escape?" We had sufficient brains to soon realize that this was impossible, so we eventually became a pair of loafers.

Very soon we, the sea-faring boys in Barrack 8, got together and we used to roam around together, getting into all the trouble we could and making fun in every way we could think of, although I think we got most of our kick out of the men who were socially better than us, who used to consider us a rough crowd, although we really looked well in our brass-buttoned uniforms. These we had discarded for "going home" in favour of corduroy pants.

I can't say just what the student class thought of us at first for they were well dressed and in their ways the "perfect gentlemen," but I know they had plenty of pluck for on many occasions after being deliberately offensive to them they stood, fought, and often won, although we young sailormen thought ourselves tough, and yet I recall it was these rough-houses as we called them that started many friendships. (L 49)

Some men laughed at this rowdyism, but the sea captains were not amused; to watch a lot of ships' boys running wild offended their very souls. The camp captains agreed with them, the military were consulted, and in due time half of Barrack 22 was partitioned off and some forty lads of eighteen and under moved into it. They quickly drove out the two landsmen who first took charge of them, but treated the ship's captain who followed with respect if not always with obedience.

Segregation had come rather late, and its benefits were not immediately apparent. The boys, it is true, were now under some sort of control and concentrated at the extreme west end of the compound, but segregation also marked them off from the camp and gave them the most formidable esprit de corps of any group in Ruhleben. They kept scornfully away from religious and educational activities, their barrack resembled a dormitory in a poorly disciplined reform school, and strangers approaching it were often greeted with missiles and lurid profanity. During the winter many of them had begun to assimilate to the general population, but once defined as "boys" they played the part and refused to grow up. As the apprentice said later: "Putting us in 22A made us think we were a lot younger than we really were" (L 49).

A change gradually took place, however, and the boys were slowly integrated into the camp. They prided themselves greatly on their football teams, and when the youngest were sent home in December 1915 their successors in the barrack were chosen with a shrewd eye to football ability. Quite a number settled down periodically to study in the Camp School, and some took part in the cultural activities of the Y.M.C.A., though giving its religious efforts a wide berth. Denton writes in March 1916:

> I have just come in from the most successful Y.M.C.A. Social we have had yet, an evening by the "Boys' Barrack," the home of some 40 apprentices and ships' boys. They acted a little play, written by one of their number, and acted it with such charming naiveté and earnestness that an audience of about 500 had one of the funniest evenings of their lives, although the play itself was a melodramatic tragedy of the deepest hue.

The change had various causes, but the most important was the transformation of the camp itself. By the end of 1915 it had become a highly organized society, exerting a great deal of control over its members but also offering them a wide range of satisfying activities. In such a society there was no room for delinquency.

Though the boys were no longer a menace, they did not let their reputation die. They still conducted great snow-ball raids and were ever ready for a scuffle. When the compound was flooded in winter they dug holes and covered them with flimsy camouflage through which the unwary fell into deep pools of water. And on one occasion when rumours were unusually vivid they hoisted over their barrack the Blue Peter, the sign that a ship is about to sail—and were threatened with wholesale court-martial for signalling to hostile aircraft.

The end of the Boys' Barrack was spectacular. On July 14, 1917, fire broke out in a small barn close to it, destroyed the adjoining artists' studio and musicians' shed, and gutted the boys' end of Barrack 22. Its inmates were scattered through the camp and their two years' segregation was ended. Many of them were now over twenty, but the old definition was slow to change, and to most of the prisoners they remained "boys" as long as Ruhleben lasted. This was more than the mere persistence of a stereotype, for the camp's total lack of young children produced a curious distortion in the perception of age. Denton writes at the age of 22: "We get all mixed up here as regards ages; chaps of 40 or so seem like kids, and I call many by Christian and nicknames. And the 16 and 17 year old boys seem such babies, about 12 years old. I can't make out why it is." And later, of the Boys' Barrack: "We still call them boys, though I suppose there are none of them under eighteen now. Our sense of proportion is getting spoiled. I suppose by the end of camp the Boys' Barrack will contain all under thirty!"

The absence of children, like that of women, led to the creation of substitutes, and endowed even "roughnecks" of twenty with some of the appealing qualities of childhood. After the boys were dispersed many were informally adopted by older men, who took them into their messes, taught them mathematics or golf, supplied them with luxuries, and generally looked after them. The relationship was usually above suspicion, being merely an outlet for some of the tender emotions that internment had dammed up. "Have started lessons with young Brown," Irwin wrote in 1918, "he wants to be an engineer and is very keen to learn. The lad makes a sort of substitute for my own 'kid brother' and I am getting fond of him."

Ruhleben's German, Jewish, and Negro quarters, together with a kind of boys' camp, gave the community much of its vivid colouring. And other barracks added their share, as Farwell pointed out in 1933:

What about the queer "local patriotism" so many of us developed for our own barracks—football and cricket teams, barrack mascots like the wonderful wooden rabbit-bird that always accompanied one of the teams to the football field, Prichard "hoodoo-ing" the Barrack Ten team to make it win, and so on? It often amused me in camp. Of course there *were* differences; think of the associations connected with Barrack Ten (public school atmosphere), Barrack Three (Supermen), Barrack Eight (sailors), let alone Barracks Six and Thirteen! The thought of Barrack One (pro-German) still makes me shiver with horror. I was in a good barrack myself, but if I had not been there I would have chosen Barrack Eleven.

These were the accepted definitions; there would be less agreement about most other barracks. Even where no clear-cut label emerged, however, every barrack was felt to be different.

The most obvious clue to a barrack's character was the make-up of its population, but, since this was not accurately known, small but conspicuous minorities had a disproportionate effect. The actual distribution of the main occupational groups is shown in Figure 4; the barracks

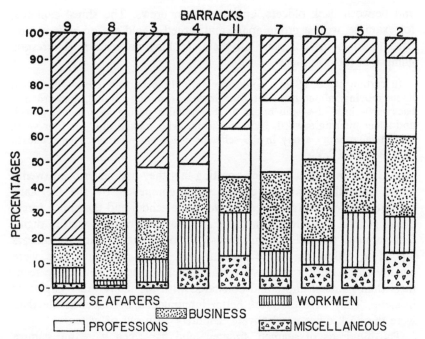

FIGURE 4. Main occupational categories, in percentages, in each of the nine largest barracks.

shown are the nine large stables which were first occupied and contained two-thirds of the population. Seafarers were a highly distinctive element, and Barracks 9, 8, and 4, in which they were heavily represented, were duly called "sailors' barracks." But, as Farwell's letter shows, the typical sailors' barrack was always felt to be Barrack 8, with considerably fewer seafarers than Barrack 9. This was because it contained a large contingent of officers, whose uniforms were a more conspicuous cue than the sweaters and dungarees of seamen. Similarly Barrack 3, though clearly a sailors' barrack, was known instead as the home of the "supermen" or high-brows. Its supermen could have been numbered on the fingers of one hand, but their addiction to modern art and literature became so notorious in 1915 that their barrack was never able to live them down. Such biassed definitions, of course, were never taken seriously in the barrack concerned, but they prevailed everywhere else.

And there were other discrepancies. Landsmen, for instance, tended to lump all sailors' barracks together on the basis of such overt cues as uniforms, jerseys, and provincial dialects; only seafarers were aware of the wide differences existing between "real" seafarers and fishermen, and between deck officers, engineers, and crews. The ships' captains, for example, were a group apart, and turned a cold eye on anyone who tried to force his company on them. Molony gives us a picturesque glimpse of them at night:

> In certain places all one could see were three or four curious little red lights moving, about five feet four inches from the ground, forward and backwards in a line—the briars of sea captains pacing an imaginary deck and never uttering a word. I know of some who walked thus for four years some twelve hours a day in the selfsame place and scarcely ever spoke to their fellows. (P. 26)

And Govett mentions captains boasting that they had never been twenty yards from their barrack except when compelled by the Germans (p. 458). A few captains were active in the school and the police force, but in general they did not mix in camp life, preferring to wait in dignified patience for the coming British victory. Higher ranking officers tended to follow the same pattern, and some chief engineers were equally aloof, but the interests of the junior engineers were more technical than nautical and could be shared with the many other engineers in camp. They were therefore better integrated into Ruhleben life than were the deck officers, who were definitely "fish out of water."

The hundreds of seamen, firemen, and fishermen were the camp's proletariat, and staffed the working gangs, kitchens, and similar services. Those not so employed were universally "on relief," but their lot was not a particularly hard one—some freely admitted that they had never been so well off. Their quarters were as comfortable as the forecastle, their food adequate after the first winter, and they were free to spend all their time as they chose, playing and watching sports, studying navigation and other subjects, reading and card-playing, and attending concerts, plays, and movies at minimal cost. Sailors suffered like landsmen from confinement and separation from home, but, accustomed to shipboard life and long absences, they were perhaps better fitted to endure them.

Without its seafarers Ruhleben would have been a very different camp, softer, less virile, top-heavy with intellectuals. It was their courage that set the first high standards, and their healthy Philistinism that kept the later cultural life in balance. They were tough in language and manner; disputes with seamen quickly led to fights. The two great sections of the camp were fortunately never arrayed against each other, but if they had been the sailors had no doubt of the outcome: "One seaman can handle five landsmen any day!" Their patriotism was unwavering: Gribble says: "There was one section of the community which never doubted; our sailors were always confident, even in the darkest days" (19, p. 62). They cared little whether the Germans reached Paris or Moscow; what difference could it make while England held the sea? Their faith was unshaken even by the first alarming reports of the naval battle off Jutland; they simply refused to believe them. Above all, the seafarers were a stabilizing influence in a restless and mercurial population. Grumblers by profession, they damned the conditions of the camp in the foulest terms, but at the same time bore them more philosophically than the landsmen. Not easily enthused about anything, they were equally hard to depress; their common sense, steadiness, and ironic humour were of incalculable value to Ruhleben. As Henley wrote in 1914: "The sailors are a fine lot and keep the spirit of the whole camp up."

The barracks not dominated by seafarers were, with the exception of Barrack 10, less clearly defined. Barrack 2 contained some famous jockeys and trainers; the Ruhleben racecourse, however, was not much help to them. Barrack 5 was outstanding in sports, and Barrack 7, with its rustic arbours and gardens, was sometimes called the "millionaires' barrack." Barrack 11 was undistinguished save for the "originals" sent to Ruhleben in September 1914; like Barrack 2, it had many horse-racing characters.

Barrack 10, however, was the glory of Ruhleben. It was invariably thought of in terms of the "public school crowd," and actually contained more dons, students, and schoolboys than any other barrack. The stereotype still ignored most of its population, but was justified by the fact that these young men were better known by name and sight than any similar group. For this there were several reasons. Barrack 10's early prestige was gained through cricket, its team—largely composed of these dons and students—winning the league in 1915 and then defeating the camp in a memorable four-day match. But athletic skill was not all; when Barrack 10 was playing, college blazers, white flannels, and beautiful style combined to give the dusty field the air of Lord's at the inter-varsity match. Members of the same élite were familiar in other settings; for instance, J. C. Masterman of Oxford, whose history lectures drew Ruhleben's largest audience, and M. S. Prichard, the eccentric philosopher, with his band of young disciples. Some of the schoolboys made attractive "girls" at the theatre—again a conspicuous activity, with more than a whiff of romance. And on the stage and at the Parcels Office, which was largely staffed by this group, every prisoner could hear them speak in the inimitable accent of the English public school, the hall-mark of social status. No mere facts, however, can convey what

Ruhleben meant by "the Barrack 10 crowd"—who were largely and atypically loft-dwellers. It was something aristocratic and yet warmly appreciated by the lowliest seaman; exclusive, but rarely felt as snobbish. Its members were a clique, but they neither held aloof from camp life nor lost caste by participating. It was something, in short, understandable only in terms of the unique relation between social classes in 1914 England: on the one hand, superiority so effortless that it seemed a fact of nature; on the other, deference sweetened by pride and admiration.

The pre-eminence of Barrack 10 was clearly the joint product of athletic prowess and social superiority, and the same factors probably determined the relative status of all the non-segregated barracks. The importance of sport was natural, for it possessed high prestige and was also the sole means of directly measuring a barrack's success or failure. The other determinant, however, shows that Ruhleben's initial solidarity had not wiped out class consciousness. Barrack 9, for instance, though always formidable on the sports field, was not a "good address"; it was solidly seafaring, and the sailors' barracks (except Barrack 8 with its array of captains) were unmistakably lower class. They were not at the bottom of the ladder, however; that was reserved for some of the wooden barracks, nondescript in population, and so small that they had to combine to raise teams.

The labelling of Ruhleben's barracks was more than a psychological curiosity; it had definite effects on the individual. Everyone who lived in a higher class barrack carried a faint aura of superiority, while it was hard to think of any member of a "tough" barrack as socially or intellectually outstanding. The stereotypes were of course set aside as individuals became known, but they were effective enough to cause more than one prisoner to move to a barrack more in keeping with his public role. And the definitions were permanent; if a barrack was "highbrow" in 1915 it remained so to the end. Indeed, the men's picture of Ruhleben was completely drawn in the first year of internment; their eyes were fresh then, their minds receptive, and the first impressions of the city they had created were never effaced.

7 RUHLEBEN'S FAMILIES: THE BOXES

THE HUMAN BEING has this much in common with the plant, that to survive and grow he must take root. Not in the soil, as is sometimes said of peasants, but in the richer earth of other human lives. Alone he withers, but thrown within reach of others he thrusts out tentative shoots towards them and they towards him. The little fibres take hold, extend, multiply, and intertwine to form at last a living community, in which each is a part of many others. And the Ruhleben prisoner, borne by harsh winds into a desolate place, had hardly got his bearings before he found himself forming new ties with those about him.

These ties differed from general solidarity; they were social relationships, developing through repeated interaction with specific individuals. And they were of vital importance to every prisoner. Solidarity had given him his initial security, identification with his barrack would give him sectional pride and perhaps recognition as an athlete or official, but only in some smaller, more intimate grouping could he know himself valued personally, not for his achievements but for what he was in himself. Some such grouping had to be found if internment was to be bearable, and most men found it ready made in their box or mess.[1] This was a natural unit—often an inescapable one—and during the first winter there were scarcely any alternatives.

The hundreds of men quartered in horse-boxes were forced to live as groups of six—a manageable number, if slightly above the optimum. And a common impulse prompted the greater numbers in lofts and open barracks to sort themselves quickly into similar though somewhat smaller units. No suggestion was needed; they were human beings, and therefore social ones. These voluntary groupings contained from two to five men, their size being limited not only by physical factors but by the intuitive

1. "Box" was a broad term. Referring originally to the horse-boxes, it was extended to the groups inhabiting them, and sometimes to what were more often called "corners" in the lofts and wooden barracks. "Mess" referred specifically to those who pooled their food and ate together; some horse-boxes contained more than one mess. "Box" is used here as the general term for any group who lived together; messing arrangements are specified where necessary.

knowledge that larger groups might split into cliques. Previous acquaintances were chosen when available, but strangers combined just as readily; Henley, whose group of five "stuck together" on the cold stone floor of the grandstand, knew none of the others before his internment. Changes in membership of course took place, especially in the lofts and open barracks, but once a box had settled down it became remarkably stable.

The most apt description of the box group is to call it the Ruhleben family. It had of course no sexual origin, it contained no women or children, and the bonds that held it together had nothing to do with kinship. But its members slept in the same small space, sat around the same table, shared the same food, and did much else together, and it is this common life rather than sexual or blood ties that makes a family. As it developed in the box it gave the prisoner something he could seldom find elsewhere: easy, habitual relationships with a small, familiar group, whose members knew him intimately and accepted him fully. "Acceptance," rather than mutual attraction, was the core of these relationships. Though they began in an atmosphere of comradeship and often developed into permanent friendships, they were basically workaday relationships, built on the prosaic tasks and mercilessly close contacts of the first hard winter. As such, they left no room for illusions and plenty for disputes and criticism—and this, of course, was the source of their lasting strength. For the most durable ties are those that have withstood many strains and tests.

Like the family again, these household groups aroused a deep sense of identification. "We" and "us" were used of them within a week of internment, long before barrack identification appeared, and they were still used regularly in 1918 letters. Even in 1933 many informants were still in touch with some of their boxmates, and a note appended to one questionnaire reads: "The 'Kitty,' as we called our mess of three, is still maintained to date in an informal way" (Q 86). Such strong identification with a group reflects the number of needs that are satisfied in it, and more of the Ruhlebenite's physical and social needs were met through his box group than in any other setting.

"Family" might still seem a questionable term if the men had not constantly used it themselves. Ironically at first, they began to refer to their boxes and corners as "home"; from that to "family" was a natural step, and in time even the quotation marks were often dropped:

Oct. 18, 1915. The bedsteads we have knocked up are much warmer than our old style of sleeping. The work in our "home" has rather spoilt study lately, but I am settling down again. (Abbot)

Nov. 2, 1917. Evans is a very nice fellow and we have been good pals for years now, even if we do have occasional "family" differences. (Abbot)

Feb. 22, 1917. Our family has shrunk since I last wrote, Arthur having left us to join friends in another barrack. We miss him, but he wanted to go and the extra space comes in handy. (Denton)

And Jarvis's diary contains regular financial reckonings, headed simply *Family Accounts.*

Whatever the prisoner's role in Ruhleben's public life, in the box he was simply a member of the family, and his status hinged entirely on how he fitted into this small circle. No amount of public recognition could quite make up for the fact that a man did not get on with his boxmates; Graham wrote after a box quarrel: "We are all quite good friends again; in a place like this it would be hell to be living on bad terms with people." There were of course a few "hermits" in the camp, and others who used the box only as a dormitory, messing with friends elsewhere; the latter, however, were not exceptions—their family was the second group. Letters, diaries, and later reports all leave the impression that a satisfactory relationship with the box or some similar group was almost indispensable to happiness in Ruhleben.

How satisfactory, then, were these relationships? How well integrated did the boxes become? These are broad questions that only a contemporary study could have answered adequately. Letters and diaries give full-length portraits of a few boxes, but the only general information is in the answers to the 1933 questionnaire, which contained a page of questions about box life. Eighty men answered these completely; though not a representative sample, they provided some illuminating material. The groups described are usually those in which the informant lived longest, and range in size from two to six members. Since accommodation and circumstances were roughly similar, the main difference between groups was in their composition, and this is given for the eighty boxes, at least as regards ages and occupations. Owing to the arbitrary allotment of living quarters there are some odd mixtures, and it would be strange if all these ill-assorted groups were happy ones. Men of widely different backgrounds and habits, crammed together for years in a tiny space, can make life almost unbearable for one another. From the retrospective reports, however, it appears that the common need to get along together was usually enough to overcome apparent incompatibility.

Membership, of course, was not entirely haphazard even in the horse-boxes; though moves between barracks were forbidden for over a year, exchanges within them were possible by mutual agreement. And in the lofts and wooden barracks it was relatively easy to break up a jarring group. Nor were the original occupants always strangers, for men from the same town or ship were often brought in and quartered together.[2] On the whole, however, chance played the major role in the first winter.

The demands made by box life were drastic; each man had to adjust himself to a collective life far more intimate than in most families, shared with companions he had seldom chosen, and lived under conditions of squalid discomfort. Reading the questionnaires with this in mind, one can only wonder at the number of groups that held together for years with so little apparent friction.

The boxes described varied widely even in the factual matters reported on, while in atmosphere and personal relations each was of course unique. No attempt will be made, therefore, to distinguish an "average" box or sort the eighty cases into categories. Instead there follows a running description of the range represented by the sample, from the "best" boxes to the "worst," with some twenty boxes used as illustrations. The emphasis is on signs of integration: pooling of parcels or a common mess fund, shared activities, the appearance of group norms, whether the informant's best friends were boxmates, how many "big rows" almost disrupted the box, and how long the group lived together. Some of the illuminating comments added by informants are quoted also.

If the questionnaires can be believed, many boxes got along for years without a single serious row—which should perhaps disqualify them as "families":

Q 55. Four men in their 20's, professional and students. Two long acquainted previously. Together in a loft for 42 months with no serious rows. Pooled all parcels, usually went to theatre and concerts together, tended to think and act as a unit in camp affairs, informant's closest friends were in box. "Our mess was a group held together by purely personal relationships; it was not an *affaire de convenance.*"

Another man says that his closest friends were not members of the box, and that the group did not go out together or act as a unit. It was, nevertheless, clearly a "good" box:

Q 17. Four men, aged 36 to 39. All seafarers, none previously known. Together in a box for 46 months.[3] No serious rows; "certain squabbles over war news and county partisanship." Common mess fund. "We always got on well together, shared all our parcels, and were quite a happy little family. I would like to meet them all again."

_____
2. This was not necessarily an advantage; one informant wrote of his boxmates: "Only knew one before—the first to be quarreled with!"
3. In these condensed summaries "box" refers specifically to a horse-box.

In the younger groups there was often much good-natured ragging:

Q 35. Five men, 19 to 24. Engineer, two business, two students. None acquainted previously. Together for 29 months. "We had had over 2600 meals in that box before I left and were always the best of pals. I left only for a special reason and remained on the best of terms with the others, often going back for meals. We were all high-spirited and some of our rags led to rows, but they never lasted long, with one exception. We always went to the theatre as a party, and none of us had very close friends outside the box, at least for the first two years."

Here, however, is a good box which presents a puzzling contrast if the closing statement is taken literally:

Q 57. Four men, aged 19 to 28. Three students, one professional. Two previously known to informant. Together in a box for 48 months. Common mess fund, tended to act as a unit, went to theatre together. Informant's closest friends were members of box. "No serious rows—minor quarrels with trivial causes due to frayed nerves. But our group was lucky—we could pass many weeks in each other's company without speaking."

Even these four examples suggest the many factors involved in good integration. Similarity in age and background was certainly helpful, similarity in camp interests probably so. Temperament and disposition were of course more important, but lay beyond the scope of questionnaires. There are some comments upon them, however. Leslie writes of a boxmate in 1916: ". . . nothing could surpass the beauty of his mind, and he has never given unnecessary pain. Imagine what it means, Mother, to be able to say this of one with whom you have been living for a year and a half in a horse-box shared by three others." (P. 170.) And one informant says: "I had the misfortune to be in the box of one Dr. J. I will say no more, his name speaks for itself."

Ages were fairly similar in the above groups; where the age range exceeded ten years, integration seems to have been more difficult. There are exceptions, however:

Q 37. Six men, aged 20 to 40. Two previously known. Two musicians, two students, one business, one chemist. Together in a box 30 months before informant's release. Common mess fund and system of duty, tended to act as a unit and keep up standards, usually went out together. Informant's best friends were among the group. No big rows.

The following two messes varied both in age and in camp interests:

Q 24. Three professional men, aged 25, 28, 40. Together for 48 months. "I happened to fall in (in the military sense) outside the jail at E. with two men with whom I remained all the time without any quarrels. We were at first in Y loft; later, after a "General Post," we got into a box with three strangers. We later swapped one undesirable party for someone more congenial, and carried on quite well amongst ourselves and with the three strangers until the end. I don't know whether this constitutes a record, and whether we deserve the Dunmow Flitch. Our party of three did not by any means act as a unit in camp affairs—we were all doing different things—but I think we loyally supported each other if any occasion arose. We all had friends in other barracks, and except for meals were not often to be found together. I still keep up my friendship with one of the party, but the third has drifted out of my life."

Of the second there are three independent reports, which agree almost completely:

Q 111. Six men, including members of two boxes. Aged 20 to 40 (five over 30). Three professional, two business, one student. All had met at a German city. 48 months together. Camp interests spread over whist, gardening, languages, sports, administrative work, and literature. Common mess fund and system of duty; two report that they were very active as a unit in camp affairs, all three that their best friends were members of the mess. "Box life was kept on a high standard; language was fairly bad but not obscene; domestic arrangements were strictly upheld and no slacking was allowed." Two report no serious rows, the third writes: "One member refused to do his share of the work and was asked to leave."

The success of these groups suggests that variety of interests, within obvious limits, might reduce friction rather than otherwise.

A general similarity in social background characterizes all the groups so far described; wide differences in this respect could make integration difficult. Such differences are not perfectly indicated by the men's occupations, but that is the only index available. The next three groups are more heterogeneous in background, but all pooled their parcels—a sure sign of good integration—and all stuck together for the full four years:

Q 63. Six men, aged 18 to 22. Art student, engineer, correspondent, student correspondent, two waiters. None known before. In a box. No rows.

Q 105. Five men, all in their thirties. Traveller, correspondent, photographer, secretary, butler. All previously acquainted. In a loft. A few big rows.

Q 112. Four men, aged 21, 26, 31, 41. Clerk, correspondent, two factory workers. None known previously. In a box. Two big rows on account of drunkenness of one member.

The following letter from a student describes a still more mixed group:

Nov. 25, 1917. We have a pleasant little mess in Barrack D. Tommie is the son of a wealthy ship-owner in Liverpool; with him live Alex Palmer, a Cambridge student, and Jim Hopkins, a stoker from Hull and a great footballer. Besides me, Jack Simpson now occupies a prominent position in the mess. He worked as a pit-boy in the mines from 13 to 15, and then went to sea as an extra hand. Funny mixture, our mess, isn't it? But we are all like one little family.

When men of widely different backgrounds shared a horse-box the group might include two or three messes, or each individual might prepare his own food. Recalling the dimensions of the boxes and how long the prisoners had to live together, the latter arrangement may seem to denote intense mutual dislike. That is not necessarily so, however. The habitual reserve of the Englishman, while discouraging intimacy, is entirely compatible with politeness, good feeling, and regard for others. And it involves, further, a high degree of self-control—invaluable in avoiding such quarrels as often convulsed more intimate boxes. The four following groups were markedly heterogeneous and each contained more than one mess, but they were stable groups and not seriously discordant:

Q 76. Six men, aged 23 to 45. "Private gentleman," printer, two clerks, fitter, engineer. One known previously. Together in a box for 38 months before informant's release. Little common life, informant's best friends not members of box. Occasional rows. "I expect ours ought to be put down as one mess because, although each man almost invariably brought his own food, we were social enough to take our meals together regularly; in fact, taken all round, we were quite a harmonious lot and got on together."

Q 78. Six men, aged 25 to 48. Pilot, textile designer, author, ship's carpenter, musician, student. None known previously. Shared a box for 48 months. Three separate messes. Little common life. Best friends not in box. No big rows.

Q 61. Six men, aged 21 to 42. Scientist, factory manager, circus clown, two ship's engineers, one unspecified. None known previously. Together in a box for 28 months. All messed separately, no common arrangements or activities. Informant's friends all outside box. No big rows.

Q 73. Six men, all in their thirties. Sailor, brewery worker, vaudeville artist, stockbroker, golf professional, race-horse attendant. None known previously. Together in a box for 21 months. Three separate messes. Little common life, but "some attempt to keep up standards by moral suasion and force." Best friends not in box. Two big rows.

The above boxes were certainly not strong social units, but some common pattern of living must have been worked out in each. Otherwise their incongruous members could hardly have shared their modicum of space so long without disaster.

Though living in such mixed groups might sometimes be trying, it could also be stimulating and broadening. There follow letters from two men, each of whom spent the full four years with boxmates whose backgrounds were widely different from his own. The first, an art student whose boxmates are listed under *Q 63* above, writes:

> The experience in Ruhleben has given me lots of food for thought these last years. When war broke out I was an extremely shy, backward youth, and though I had a certain amount of confidence I was no good in the social life. Being thrown forcibly into contact with every possible type in camp did me a lot of good. I forgot myself more or less. Best thing of all I got from Ruhleben was the liberal education from my fellows. I found myself, I believe. (L 63)

The second man, interned at 22, had been brought up in a strict sectarian circle with scarcely any contacts outside it. In Ruhleben he found himself sharing a box with an old variety artist, a jockey, a clerk, and a cabinet-maker, whose ages ranged from 18 to 53 and whose outlook was worlds removed from his own. The jockey had been living happily with a mistress and was supporting an illegitimate son by another mother; the informant says:

> By all the standards I had been brought up by he was a villain of the first water: the fact that he was as cheerful as a sparrow, scarcely ever grumbling and generous to a fault, set me thinking vaguely that perhaps a kind heart, without adherence to any code of morals, was worth more than strict morality divorced from a kind heart and cheerful spirit.

The variety artist was an equally foreign type, who "had run away to sea when he was fourteen . . . dressed more shabbily than most tramps, grew a beard, and was a hopelessly dirty eater." The others were scarcely more congenial, but the informant lived with them in the box for four years and recalls only two major quarrels, caused by "trivialities arising from strained nerves." Of his relations with the group he writes:

> I had always been curious to find out things and to learn, and although I found it extremely difficult at first to establish anything approaching satisfactory contacts with any of my box-mates, I did eventually succeed in doing so, although our relations were never really cordial. The effort which this demanded of me, and the resulting self-discovery, has been of inestimable service to me since. (L 32)

Problems of this kind were not always tackled so successfully, and the decisive factor was clearly the attitude taken towards them. When marked discrepancies of age or background were accepted from the start as precluding any satisfactory relations they naturally did so; but when they were regarded simply as obstacles to be surmounted they could become an actual source of strength to the group. That so many ill-assorted boxes did achieve a *modus vivendi* may perhaps be put down once more to the solidarity generated in the early days. To take in cold blood some of the groups listed here and force them to live together for years in a ten-foot space would seem like an invitation to murder. The Ruhlebenites, however, were not thrown together in cold blood, but in warm comradeship, and that made all the difference. The spirit of the first winter was a spirit of making the best of things, socially as well as physically.

A good observer remarked on a closely related point about arrangement:

There was another phenomenon which seemed to me to be established—that those boxes which arranged themselves according to social status, education, friendship, etc., came to grief and smashed up through quarrels, whereas those which remained as they happened to be—with the possible expulsion of one undesirable party or so—continued to get on tolerably well. (L 24)

This observation was often confirmed, and its meaning is obvious. When a prisoner managed to get into a "hand-picked" box he was apt to feel that no further exertion was required, that things would now go well automatically. This was a grave error; so many irritations were inherent in what Cohen-Portheim calls "that monstrous, enforced, incessant community" (p. 85) that only sustained and unselfish efforts could keep friction below the danger level. In the unselected box such efforts were imperative. It might even be suggested that the intense vitality of Ruhleben's public life in 1915 was in part the product of a "home" life that daily and hourly demanded of each man the best he had to give. Leslie, well known for his public activities, wrote in 1916:

You would think that relationships had a tendency to become stereotyped when you had lived well over a year in the same box with four others, but such is far from being the case. I may have written about H.T. before. He is as unselfish a person as one may well conceive. He is the only member of the box who never offends your taste and never hurts your feelings, but whose whole life is an encouragement to act. (Pp. 158–9)

Relations did of course become stereotyped in time, but by then integration was usually so well established that the group functioned almost automatically.

Leslie's letter reflects an admiring friendship, while the previous quotation listed friendship as a dubious basis for building a box. There is no conflict, however; it was one thing to secure your friends as boxmates and quite another to make your boxmates friends. Fifty informants say that their best friends were members of their boxes, but more than half of them knew none of their boxmates before internment. Box life was fatal to many "imported" friendships, but those native to it were remarkably hardy. Friendship has various meanings, however, and it may be noted here that the romantic attachments familiar in camp were poor foundations for box relations. They were too emotional and transitory; when the inevitable break came, continued life together became torture. The following comment is apt: "I always thought that living with people in a box was very like marriage. Whether you feel comfortable with people is more a question of compatibility of temper than of strong affection. The two don't always go together" (L 31).

We have seen some very happy boxes, and others in which relations, though more distant, were still amicable. Occasionally, however, no better accommodation could be reached than a sort of armed neutrality, hiding silent but powerful hatreds. One businessman of 35 shared a box with five men, none of whom he had known before: two other businessmen, a carpenter, a clerk, and an itinerant teacher, whose ages ranged from 32 to 41. Not an impossible combination, it would seem, but this is what he writes:

> It is obvious that six persons, indiscriminately cooped together and unable to avoid each other, must in general become hateful to one another. Personally I was confined with people with whom I had *no* interests in common and who, leaving me out of account, had no common interests among themselves. A particularly unfortunate box, but by no means an exception. I think the U.S.A. would define this as "mental cruelty." Anyhow, people in Reno are regularly divorced on much less definite grounds. I hated the people in Box 40 more than I ever hated anybody. Mind, I am not blaming them, but I never want to see any of them again. (L 85)

Set the last two sentences beside the earlier quotation—"We were quite a happy little family; I would like to meet them all again"—and the top and bottom notes in the gamut of box relations have been sounded. And at each end of the scale the writers fall naturally into the language of marriage and the family. This prisoner spent forty-one months in his box; there was no common mess-fund or system of duty, no shared activities, but "constant bickering and incompatibility." No wonder he later calls his internment a nightmare. He does not blame his boxmates; lest he be blamed himself, it may be added that his German business was ruined by the war, he was distracted by family worries while in camp, and he was unemployed when he answered the questionnaire. Ruhleben, he says, meant "a kind of holiday for some, but ruin for others"; it is not surprising if the latter did not always settle down to build groups out of unpromising material.

The darker aspects of camp life should not be minimized, and this man's box may have been, as he says, "by no means an exception." But among the hundred boxes of which some report was given it *is* an exception—the outstanding one, for there is no other statement like it. One man says his boxmates were "uncongenial" and that he spent his time elsewhere, and a few others imply something similar. But that is all. Those with unpleasant memories may have ignored the questionnaire; there is no way of telling. And the prisoners' generalizations are of little value, for each man's judgment was coloured by his own experiences.

There is one parallel to this ugly picture, but we have to go to Wakefield to find it. Cohen-Portheim's account deserves to be quoted, if only as a suggestion of what long internment could be like:

The hatred engendered inside the camp between its inmates was terribly concrete. Every man, almost, is full of little foibles and more or less unpleasant mannerisms which his fellow creatures smile at or mildly object to in normal, everyday life. When human beings live together, as in married or family life, these easily lead to friction. It is not the men of bad character or morals you begin to hate, but the men who draw their soup through their teeth, clean their ears with their fingers at dinner, hiccough unavoidably when they get up from their meal (a moment awaited with trembling fury by the others), the men with ever-dirty hands, the man who will invariably make the same remark (every day, year after year) as he sits down—the man who lisps, the man who brags, the man who has no matter what small defect or habit you happen to object to. You go on objecting quietly, for one does not quarrel about such silly trifles, and the thing gets on your nerves, becomes unbearable by the simple process of endless repetition, until you hate the cause of your torture with a deadly hatred. (Pp. 88–9)

No doubt L 85 would endorse this as an accurate picture of Ruhleben. As it happens, however, the passage was copied out and sent me by another ex-prisoner, not as an interesting parallel, but as a puzzling curiosity. These are his comments:

It exhibits, to a Ruhlebenite, such a completely incomprehensible state of affairs that it should be studied in detail. Were it not for the fact that Portheim is, in many other cases, apparently quite objective in his description, I should put it down as the product of a disordered imagination. (L 79)

No final judgment is possible, but in my own opinion, for what it is worth, Portheim's account is not a fair picture of Ruhleben. Perhaps not of Wakefield either, for he was an artist, sensitive, and with no congenial companionship.

On the other hand, L 79 is also generalizing; the pent-up irritations that Portheim describes would be far from incomprehensible to many Ruhlebenites. Graham writes to his wife as follows:

> *May 4, 1917.* You can see that I have little news. Just the same old place, the same old talk, and worst of all—the same people always. How sick we are of one another! It is a great relief to divide life between these two boxes as I do, and certainly makes the people in one's own box seem less objectionable.

> *June 15, 1917.* And how sick we are of the sight of one another! To know you have got to meet and see certain people and cannot get away from them is trying, I can tell you.

Graham, however, remained on good terms with his boxmates and makes no complaints of them in fourteen subsequent letters. Ewing's diary contains the following on April 15, 1918:

> Tried to write, but Bert came in and lay down on his bed. His is a presence that makes itself felt to a terrible extent with me, he doesn't know how to efface himself temporarily and give the other chap a rest; I feel sometimes as if living with him were going to *smother* me.

These two men, however, were still close friends in 1933, when each of them sent in a questionnaire. Other such statements could be given; for the most part they seem to express passing moods, recognized as such and often fought against. Again a matter of morale, and the morale of Ruhleben seems to have been definitely higher than that of Wakefield. It will be noted, too, that all these extracts date from the later years, when the camp's collective spirit was weakening.

My judgment may be biassed by my own pleasant experiences, but it is at least based on reports of more boxes than any one prisoner can have known. How many of them should be called "good" cannot be estimated, but the following questionnaire replies are relevant; the percentages are based on the 80 complete reports:

Questionnaire Item	*Per Cent*
9. Usually went to theatre, etc., with boxmates	67.5
10. Closest friends in camp were boxmates	62.5
11. Group tended to think and act as a unit	47.5
12. Group efforts to check swearing, loose talk, or otherwise keep up standards	30.0
13. Informant remembers *no* "big rows" which actually or nearly broke up the group	66.3

Only fourteen men replied negatively to all five items, so that over 80 per cent reported at least one positive index of integration. Three of the fourteen add comments depicting quite friendly groups, and most of the remainder are reporting on boxes in which they only slept or ate, their social contacts lying almost entirely outside them.

A favourable view is also supported by the stability of the boxes, as shown by the men's changes of address. A prisoner could of course move into another mess without shifting his quarters, but he could also change his address while keeping the mess intact, as Q 24 did, so that mobility is a fair index of box stability. In view of the incompatible groups first compelled to live together, it might be expected that when permission was given half the camp would want to move; indeed, it was probably for fear of this that transfers were so long forbidden. The fear was groundless, however, most of the men having settled down well enough in the first months to be content to remain. In one hundred instances the men reported their various addresses, how long they remained at each, and their reasons for moving. The average number of moves is 1.34 per man, but many were forced moves, due to the opening of new barracks, segregation of various groups, and similar causes. If these are subtracted the average number of moves falls to .56 per man, just over half a move each. Fifty-four of the hundred prisoners had only one address throughout their stay, and one after another writes "Never moved," "Stayed there all the time," or "Only box I lived in."

Although some early moves may have been forgotten, the figures suggest that the Ruhlebenite "stayed put" rather remarkably. Admittedly, it was the easiest thing to do; mutually satisfactory exchanges, at least until 1916, were difficult to arrange. Over eleven hundred men, however, left the camp during 1914 and 1915,[4] thus providing many vacancies, and in later years the difficulties were chiefly psychological. Leaving a box where one had lived so long meant a new uprooting; it was a drastic step, reflecting on all concerned and causing comment among the neighbours. One of the men wrote as follows:

The only change in the box was when Bill Walker left it about 1916 to live with Potts in Barrack Y. He had been spending all his time there, so is wasn't exactly a surprise. We were having supper when he said there was something he wanted to say to us, and rambled on about changing interests and so on until Curry, whom you may remember, broke in and said, "You

---

4. The number seems large, but is based on official records. Powell and Gribble supply much of the explanation in Chapter 3 of their book. Two categories of prisoner might petition for release into Germany: those who had sons serving or willing to serve in the German army, and those suffering from chronic illness. "Leave of absence" (often indefinitely extended) might be given those willing to volunteer for the army, and those whose presence was required in a business or industry. The last provision, in particular, accounted for many departures from Ruhleben.

mean you want to leave the box?" Bill said he supposed that was it, and Curry was pretty huffy and said, "Then all we can say is we're sorry." And that was all we did say. We were a bit hurt, as we'd all been together since the beginning. When he left we talked about seeing each other often and so on, but of course we didn't. (L 126)

Abbot expresses similar compunction about breaking old ties:

Apr. 20, 1917. As I think I have already mentioned, there has been a slight split in our "family." Between you and me, Mr. Bernard often has moods like our old friend P.B., and while in one of these moods he expressed a wish to be left to himself, so I now grub with Slater in his new quarters and sleep in our old corner. Please don't mention anything to Mr. Bernard's people about our split. It upset me rather at first as we had lived so long together. I told him straight what I thought and we are now quite good friends again.

Although the boxes showed such resistance to disruption, they were by no means free from violent quarrels. "Box rows" ranged from half playful arguments to furious fist-fights; usually they were quickly forgotten, but sometimes they changed the whole complexion of the group. The mere congestion was a constant source of friction; Cohen writes:

There was hardly a box without an occasional row, which was inevitable when six men were confined with their beds and baggage in an area ten feet square, and when some of them would be simultaneously engaged in such incongruous occupations as late breakfast, shaving, violin practice and language-study. (P. 112)

Irwin appended to his 1933 questionnaire:

"Rows" with other members of the box were mainly due to relatively trifling causes, such as personal uncleanliness, selfishness in grabbing luxuries from the common pool, etc. The main source of irritation was undoubtedly due to cramped quarters and lack of privacy.

And Denton wrote in a 1915 letter: "The boxes are terribly cramped in winter; if four people want to play cards, Heaven help the other two." In later years many rows were due to mere weariness of one another's company, as we saw earlier, or to the general gloom caused by such events as the onset of another winter:

July 28, 1917. There have been some rows in this box lately—in my absence fortunately. We really are a great trial to one another and it is time that we had a change. It is all very well to be treated like schoolboys, but we ought to have some holidays. (Graham)

Oct. 16, 1917. It has turned very cold tonight; we were all so depressed at tea that we didn't speak a word until Harry knocked Fatty's tea over. Fatty threw the cup at him and wet me, and I responded with a loaf that got the teapot, and in a moment we were all at it hammer and tongs. Then we had a good laugh and cleared up the mess, and now feel much better. (Denton)

Serious quarrels sometimes led to a long breach of relations between two members; the difficulties and constraints may be imagined. The camp was fond of the story of two learned professors who, after a quarrel about the use of a clothes hook, occupied the same box for eighteen months without speaking to one another. And an informant, in listing his boxmates, attached to one name the following note: "Left mess after a series of violent quarrels, and though in the same box for three more years was not on speaking terms with self and B" (Q 86). This must constitute an endurance record.

The camp magazines naturally found box rows better copy than the humdrum of peaceful life. A "Ruhleben Intelligence Paper" contains the question: "Two bodies of fixed but diametrically opposed views occupy a finite space (B.O.X.) for an indefinite length of time (W.A.R.). Estimate the amount of heat produced at the end of two years and six months." (*RCM* 6, p. 51.) In the *Mikado* Parody "NHO-Gho" says to a new arrival:

I am afraid, young man, you are not accustomed to Ruhleben society yet; but I warn you, it is no use being exclusive here. In Concentration Camps, remember, extremes meet. For instance, I know a donkeyman who shares his tinned salmon with a minor poet. Yes, we're all very good friends here; except those men who happen to occupy the same box. They are never on speaking terms. (*RCM* 5, p. 17)

And "Phoebe," always censorious, notes a familiar contrast between public and "home" conduct:

"Here a man seems to have two characters, a box character and a camp character, and they are never a bit like one another. Why are people so different in their boxes?"
"Why do people treat their wives differently when other people are present?"
"The fact is," said Phoebe, "the people here are British in every way, and they are proud of it."
"Hear, hear," I murmured weakly.
"Except one."
I started. "What is that?"
"Their behaviour in the secrecy of their boxes. There are feuds in nearly every box. Tyrannies, coalitions, autocracies, plutocracies, cabals, boycotts, quarrels, riots—just get out the dictionary for a moment!"
But I had fainted. (*IRC* 8, p. 4)

As against this pessimism there are the many reports from ordinary, inconspicuous prisoners who lived with their little groups for two, three, or four years with only the occasional quarrel. Time may have mellowed their memories, but the long series of contemporary letters leave the same impression. Somehow, with many setbacks, most of these small units were able to find a level at which they could function smoothly, and thus provide their members with the most solid sense of belonging that Ruhleben could provide.

Simple belongingness was by no means all that an integrated box provided; each member also enjoyed a personal status that larger groups could not supply. He held a distinctive position, played a distinctive role, and these gave him unique value in the eyes of other members. He might be relied on as a cook or carpenter, looked up to for his experience, cherished for his sense of humour, or teased about his letters from girls; however defined, he had a place that was his alone, and without him the group would not be the same. These interrelated roles were the very essence of box life; they were often compressed into nicknames whose use, even years after release, immediately re-created the box atmosphere.

No status hierarchy existed, however, for all roles were regarded as equal. Solidarity demanded this equality, and it was jealously adhered to. "Jones" might be a notable figure in England or in camp affairs, in which case outsiders frequently referred to the box as "Jones's." Within it, however, he enjoyed no preferred status, but had to take his turn with the rest at sweeping and washing up. One informant in 1933 was still resentful of a boxmate who assumed that the importance of his camp role should excuse him from household chores. Nor did box life itself produce a hierarchical organization with leaders and followers; the group aims that could give rise to it were lacking. Certain individuals undoubtedly played major roles in solving internal problems and setting the prevailing standards, but this informal leadership was seldom recognized as such and carried no authority with it. The Ruhleben families were strictly equalitarian.

They were also marked, however, by the most pervasive social control found anywhere in the camp. Its essence was, as always, the subordination of individual to group needs, and it was manifested in the norms that governed every aspect of box life. In a good box the necessary rules were jointly worked out and respected as a matter of course; in a poor box they were frequently disputed about and contravened. Many of the rows that disrupted boxes are reported as due to "selfishness in grabbing luxuries," "laziness of one member about fetching hot water," "lateness for meals," or "failure to line up for spuds"—all reflecting the existence of a common mess. But it made little difference if members of a horse-box messed separately; at such close quarters there were scores of other questions on which agreement had to be reached and enforced. Among men of similar backgrounds many standards needed no discussion; they were tacitly understood and followed almost unconsciously. But in mixed boxes generally accepted norms were more difficult to reach, and in the first winter drastic action was sometimes taken. A schoolmaster stated in 1933:

It took time to reach a satisfactory basis for life, for new conventions had to be made for the new conditions. There were all sorts of matters that had to be dealt with which would not arise outside. For instance, there were those people who objected to others washing and dressing while they were eating their meals. And then there was a man in our box whose bed smelt; the rest of us talked it over and we took his bed and all his clothing and threw it outside into the sun. We told him what we had done, and said nothing would be allowed back into the box until we had passed it; he took it very well, and brought his things back one by one. (M 29)

A man's private life was no longer private in such grotesquely cramped quarters; untidiness, uncleanliness, drunkenness, and "intolerable snoring" are all mentioned as causes of quarrels. Standards of course varied greatly from group to group, but without some degree of co-operation and acceptance of majority rule no box could long survive.

The fact that only 30 per cent of the informants reported "group efforts to keep up standards" (see table above) need not be taken seriously; the low percentage was due almost entirely to the unfortunate phrasing of the question. Misled by the reference to swearing and loose talk many occupants of fully integrated boxes replied, "No need in our case," "Not necessary," or in one instance, "No, we were *grown-up!*" The answers actually mean, of course, not that a social code was lacking, but that it was so completely accepted as to make overt enforcement unnecessary. The methods of control reported include such sanctions as "Put money in box" and "Extra turn for hot water," but these obviously refer to minor offences like swearing; for standards in general, "moral suasion," "bawling out," and "a telling off" were the commonest methods. And in the best boxes even they were seldom needed; each member was so identified with the group that consideration for others became second nature.

Most boxes were united enough to arouse in-group loyalty in their members, and this was heightened by the playful feuds of the first winter with their raids and water-throwing. In the lofts and wooden barracks there were more serious quarrels about space, one group being accused of edging their bunks into another's territory; in such cases even a discordant box would stand together. And it was striking how rapidly the prisoners came to feel that they should not criticize members of the family to outsiders; they did so, of course, but not without the apologetic clause, "I hate to say this about a boxmate, but. . . ."

Pride in the box was an important cohesive factor, and its most concrete source lay in the periodic "improvements" that were made, particularly after numbers were reduced. In later years many horse-boxes were almost unrecognizable; curtains and stained woodwork hid the walls, beds were curtained off, cosy corners and alcoves built. In lofts and wooden barracks improvements were more modest, since fire regulations prohibited structural alterations, but even a new bookshelf, tea set, or tablecloth was a matter of group pride. Improvement of the box was also an index of integration; where no unity existed a joint plan could not be worked out, though individuals might "fix up" their own bunks. Three-quarters of the informants report that the group spent money on such improvements; a few more say "only individually," and several state that they could not afford it—wood, in fact, was so expensive that in 1917 the camp school had to cancel its carpentry classes.

The Ruhlebenites were talkative people, and more communication probably took place in boxes than anywhere else. Long hours were spent sitting over meals, and in the first winter boxmates commonly passed the whole evening together; at such times a steady hum of talk rose in each barrack. Govett points out the many arguments that took place:

> We would have grown even duller had it not been for the ceaseless arguments indulged in in the boxes. We argued about the most impossible subjects and often about exceedingly fine points. But at least we "set our minds against the minds of others." Small talk, on the other hand, was almost non-existent; one wondered what one had ever found to say to casual acquaintances in the past, or would find in the future. (P. 458)

Small talk was indeed pointless among men who knew one another so intimately; this may explain the long silences reported in one box.

True communication, however, is more than chit-chat or hairsplitting; it involves the actual sharing of experiences, beliefs, and feelings. A vast amount of such communication took place in the boxes, though only glimpses are recorded. Leslie's published letters are full of references to conversation with boxmates and other friends; in June 1915 he writes of a close companion: "We discuss, we talk and we work, we think and we feel, but we hardly ever oppose one another" (p. 66). And Denton says of his boxmates in two 1915 letters: "We spend much time talking of the flowers and things at home, each chap describing his own favourite scenes"; "We sit on the grandstand in the evening and read 'Venice' aloud, and simply float right away over the wire netting until we are in gondolas on the Grand Canal."

Such sharing was more important to the box than anything else that occurred in it. If the men became a close-knit group at all, it was through this mental intermingling; in it they discovered one another, through it they converged on those common attitudes that made collective life possible. Wherever we have heard of a good box we know that communication was full and spontaneous. And communication created its typical products; new symbols appeared that stood for the group and helped to hold it together. The nicknames were such symbols, compressing into a word the perceptions and feelings attached to one member. And there were catchwords such as "Make way for His Lordship!" and "Don't chew the fat!", habitual phrases like "Let's clean up the sty, pigs!", private terms for objects and situations, and a growing store of common memories evoked by the words, "Remember when . . .?"

Although these group products were often trite or vulgar they were highly valued, for they belonged to all members jointly, thus sealing their comradeship. A nickname was a sign of affection; however opprobrious it might sound, the bearer knew what it meant—that he was unreservedly accepted. Many of the stock phrases were facetious, referring back to incidents when tension had been resolved by laughter; their use re-established the same relaxed atmosphere. And each repetition of these symbols of previous solidarity reminded the group of the many things that bound it together. It is not hard to understand the Ruhlebenite's reluctance to move from an established box. And, as distinctive patterns of speech and action took form, the box like the barrack acquired its own character, recognizable at least to near neighbours. There were noisy boxes, quiet boxes, friendly, tough, and "classy" boxes. In returning his questionnaire in 1933 Burton wrote: "I well remember you and your box, the Post Box, famous (or notorious) for noisy rags and keeping respectable citizens awake at nights."

Above all, communication in a good box was the medium of personal growth and change; no one could take part in it for years and remain the individual he had been. The most obvious example of change was the levelling and converging that produced the box norms, but the process went deeper than that, for in communication the Ruhlebenite discovered not only others but himself. When he found himself disturbed

by a boxmate's views he was learning something about his own preju-
dices; when he stated his opinion on an issue he was discovering, perhaps
for the first time, what it really was; when he argued for it and noted the
reaction of others he was learning how much it was worth. And in the
process he himself was changed; his outlook broadened, his system of
values altered. He was growing. This opportunity for mental growth was
the great advantage of being thrown with unfamiliar types in Ruhleben.
Not everyone could avail himself of it, but we have seen the letters of
two prisoners who clearly did so, with results that each described in
terms of self-discovery. How many boxes provided a climate for such
growth cannot be guessed at, but it must have occurred wherever men
were still flexible and the group even partially integrated. As long as
individuals were thus changing, box relations could never become
stereotyped.

Ultimately, however, box life was weakened by the same forces that
affected the barracks. The prolific growth of associations after the first
winter drew men into new relationships that not all their boxmates
could share. Sometimes this led to a move that brought fresh blood into
one or more boxes. In any case, the resources of these small groups
were not inexhaustible; sooner or later each member was so completely
known that all his responses were predictable. When this happened,
relations did tend to become stereotyped, and communication perfunctory, almost mechanical. The box continued to fill many essential needs,
but its members, like grown-up children, took the "family" for granted
and found their vital contacts elsewhere.

We now leave the community structure and pass to more complex
developments. Already, after five months of internment, the camp is
vastly changed; the visitor will still see thousands of men in a small
enclosure, but the Ruhlebenite sees a settled community, divided into
many neighbourhoods, each crowded with family dwellings. A camp
address now has social significance, for every citizen is defined to some
extent in terms of where he lives. His barrack has its distinctive reputation, his box is unlike any other, and within that he has a place that is
peculiarly his own. Differentiation has thus produced four thousand
unique individuals, each rooted in his particular social niche. And the
prisoner now plays a variety of roles that add new interest to his life;
he is one person to his boxmates, a slightly different one to his barrack,
and again to the camp at large. He has "found himself" in his new world;
he knows, and others know too, who he is and where he belongs.

Spatially, too, he is well oriented, for every salient feature of the compound now bears its familiar name. The canteen alley is "Bond Street," the gateway to the grandstands the "Marble Arch," the area inside the main entrance "Trafalgar Square." Fittingly enough, the latrines have German labels; the western one is "Spandau," the eastern "Charlottenburg." The names, like so many other products of the first winter, were collectively created—hit upon by some individual, picked up and repeated by others, and finally fixed as customs.

Men do not bestow nicknames on objects to which they are indifferent, and these labels are enough to show that the winter has done its work, and the prisoners have made themselves at home in Ruhleben. "Yes, man is a pliable animal," wrote Dostoievsky, who knew his prisons, "an animal who gets used to anything";[5] even while the men yearned to get away from their racecourse it was secretly taking hold of their minds and affections. Molony writes of the eve of his escape: "Feelings almost sentimentally absurd surged within me as I took what I believed to be my last bearings of those sheds, barrack-lofts and corners" (p. 126). And many others shared his feelings when they left Ruhleben for the last time.

We know now what these feelings signified. The buildings were nothing in themselves, but each barrack and box had been touched with the glow that only the deepest social experiences can give. The men had grown together, become involved with one another, in a life that was often rich in friendship and discovery; in leaving their prison, with all its trials and heartaches, they were leaving part of themselves behind.

5. *The House of the Dead* (Everyman's Library, 1929), p. 9.

PART IV | Expansion

8

PHYSICAL IMPROVEMENTS: PHYSICAL AND MENTAL HEALTH

THE THREE PRECEDING CHAPTERS might be summed up in one sentence: "During the winter of 1914–15 Ruhleben was *settled* by the British." For a settled territory is one where the land has been parcelled out among its inhabitants so that each is specifically located, and where the settlers enjoy enough security for life to take on a routine character. Both statements were true of Ruhleben by the spring of 1915.

The prisoners, of course, were not in reality a whit more secure in March than they had been in November, but they had a *sense* of security previously unknown to them. The establishing of settled routines and relationships had made life so orderly and predictable that the early atmosphere of crisis—the feeling that "anything might happen"—was dissipated. No one can really believe in an emergency if it does not interfere with his habitual way of living. The men still knew that a world war was being fought, that its outcome was dubious, and that they themselves were helpless in enemy hands. But intellectual knowledge had little force against the concrete reality of a daily life that had become customary and repetitive.[1]

The camp might conceivably have remained on the settlement level; the men might have eaten, slept, and talked in their boxes, gone out to fetch food or look at the weather, and returned to eat and sleep again. A dull existence, but early Arctic explorers spent their winters in much this fashion. Ruhleben life, however, was different from the start and conspicuously so from the spring of 1915 onwards. A wide range of activities—unnecessary to survival but invested with great importance —united the men in what are called associations, and a new, independent layer of organization was superimposed on the community structure. It was this added dimension that made the camp a full-blown society.

---

1. Civilians far from the combat areas in the Second World War were constantly accused of "complacency" by returning servicemen, who complained: "They don't seem to know there's a war on." They knew, of course, but they were still living much as usual, so that their knowledge was largely intellectual,

The community growth was natural and inevitable, bound to happen if the men remained together, and requiring no specific leadership. It occurred uniformly among seamen, intellectuals, and businessmen, and the resulting groups showed a general similarity. The new activities, however, were not inevitable but voluntary; they were therefore more representative of the varied interests of this heterogeneous population. And their initiation and development, though markedly spontaneous, involved a good deal of leadership, both by particular elements among the prisoners and by specific individuals. These activities and the social institutions that took form around them will be our chief concern as we pass now to the period of expansion, April to November, 1915.

As the social structure grows more complex it can only be described piecemeal, certain aspects being ignored while attention is focussed on others. The community life of barracks and boxes of course continued, but that must now be taken for granted while fresh developments are dealt with. Underlying them all was a substantial improvement in living conditions, and the rest of this chapter will be devoted to it, and to the related topics of physical and mental illness. Chapter 9 will then summarize the history of the period and the emotional fluctuations that marked it, and Chapter 10 will describe the explosion of new activity that gave it its essential character. Then in Chapters 11 and 12, we shall come to grips with the central topic of this section: the elaborate organization that all the activities underwent, and the consequent creation on the racecourse of a "substitute world" of extraordinary reality and interest. Chapters on leadership, government, and the changed atmosphere of the camp will complete the story of Ruhleben's great period of growth.

Ruhleben could hardly have reached its full social development without some amelioration of physical conditions; the daily struggle against the hardships described in Chapter 1 would have absorbed too much energy, at least during the winters. Every improvement secured was therefore important to the expansion of life that followed, and some of the prisoners' most significant attitudes were also related to the rise in their standard of living.

Arrangements made by "top brass" in wartime are not easily altered, and Ruhleben was no exception. Some of the credit for the changes ultimately made must go to the American Ambassador, acting for the British Government; some to the Camp Commandant, who often interceded with his superiors. The chief credit, however, belongs to the prisoners themselves and the captains who spoke for them. Firmly and persistently they pressed their demands for better food, accommodation, and facilities; when refused by the Berlin authorities they offered to make essential changes themselves at British expense; if this were forbidden, the Ambassador sometimes intervened successfully. The Germans found many pretexts for delay and evasion, but in the end importunity was effective. It was the Commandant himself who said to an American visitor in 1916: "You mustn't suppose that the camp was always like this. When the men were first brought here, the place wasn't fit to keep pigs in. All that you have admired in the camp they have themselves created" (38, p. v).

The official intermediary between prisoners, Germans, and ambassador was the Captain of the Camp, and Joseph Powell was commendably vigorous in his protests and requests. His book (38) makes clear the many difficulties encountered and the amount of pleading, cajoling, and even threatening required to overcome them. The other captains, too, were kept busy, since almost every improvement involved new responsibilities for the interned which had to be planned and organized. The short-lived Camp Committee was a valuable spur, and after its dissolution some members continued their pressure as individuals. Details of how all the improvements were secured are no longer of interest; the following pages summarize the most important changes, and indicate what living conditions were like in the later years of the camp.

The intolerable crowding had not been relieved by the erection of Barracks 12 and 13 in December 1914, since they were needed for new arrivals, but ten smaller huts were added in the spring of 1915, six behind the grandstands and four in a strip of land annexed to the west end of the compound. This made 23 barracks in all, including the Tea House. New prisoners poured in heavily during February 1915, but steady losses were also occurring, small groups of invalids, old men, and boys being repatriated and large numbers of "Germans" quietly released. No more barracks were built, but as releases continued the population fell from 4,168 in May 1915 to 3,771 in July 1916, and 3,256 in July 1917. This permitted the horse-boxes to be reduced to five and later four inmates, and the lofts to be similarly thinned out, with a great increase in comfort. In the spring of 1918, with population down to something over 2,300, the middles of the lofts were entirely cleared of beds and some horse-boxes had only three men in them.

Meanwhile the prisoners had shown much ingenuity in making their quarters more habitable. In the horse-boxes, bedsteads were set three tiers high and curtains and other furnishings installed. In the lofts and wooden barracks double-decker bunks were built and the spaces they enclosed made as comfortable as possible. Mattresses could be bought through the canteen as early as June 1915; those who could not afford them learned from the seamen to make netted rope beds. By August so many of these were being fashioned that there was a string famine. Extra blankets, sent from England or ordered through the canteen, made the winter nights more tolerable.

Candles in safety holders were permitted in the boxes in October 1915, and in November small accumulators, re-charged in the camp, came into general use. This greatly relieved the light shortage; the bulbs were tiny, but men could at least read by them. The lighting wires which ran just outside the loft windows were a permanent temptation to interned electricians; those caught tapping them were severely punished, but some methods were never detected.

New latrines were constructed in June 1915, and showers and laundry tubs installed on their old site in August. The barrack taps were moved and so fitted that the corridors were no longer wet, while the new barracks had their own wash-houses. Only cold water was available in taps and showers, but hot water for shaving could be got from the new boiler house.

Interned engineers set to work on the grounds in April 1915, putting in drainage where possible and building elevated cinder roads between barracks, kitchens, and latrines. Though these did not banish the mud, they at least prevented it from coming over the tops of men's clogs. The labour was provided by work-gangs of sailors, paid out of camp funds.

The large restaurant or "grandstand hall" was heated and opened during the day, providing a smoking-room in bad weather, and in March the sports field on the race-track was rented from the Ruhleben Company. This was available for about six hours a day, when sentries were posted around it; it was closed in fog and bad weather. The loft of Barrack 6 was cleared and handed over to the Camp School in June 1915, and in 1917 the whole barrack was remodelled into classrooms and laboratories. On December 24, 1915, the International Y.M.C.A. opened a large hut in the centre of the camp; this was used for religious services, reading, writing, and studying, and also housed classrooms and a reference library. Thus even in winter the men could spend much of the day away from their barracks.

The long delays in some of these improvements were due less to the military than to the racecourse owners, who were averse to structural changes. Rent had to be paid for any property not included in the original lease to the War Office, and cash deposits and fire insurance premiums were demanded. With the backing of the British Government, however, the financial problems were surmounted and Ruhleben was adapted as far as possible to its new functions.

None of this would have helped much if the food supply had not improved, and during the first winter it was steadily deteriorating. The bread allowance was progressively cut, in line with the rations of German civilians, but they could supplement their diet with other edibles, while bread was on many days the only solid food the Ruhlebenite received. Foodstuffs were disappearing from the canteens, their prices were exorbitant, and Herr Griese's kitchens were still serving their watery soups. Resentment of this semi-starvation was high, but the military were touchy on the subject and protests brought only temporary improvements. Finally, however, the authorities were persuaded to make a radical change, and on March 7, 1915, Griese's contract was terminated and a staff of four inspectors and thirty paid workers, all prisoners, undertook to prepare the food. The change made a difference from the start as Henley notes:

Mar. 7. Military took over kitchens. We find cooks and labourers and work out our own salvation with material provided.

Mar. 10. Marked improvement in food this week. Sausage, etc., now being given out each tea-time almost. Can now tell the difference between tea and coffee, which was formerly impossible.

The problem was not solved, however, for the amount allotted for food remained constant while German prices were rising and many foodstuffs becoming unprocurable. The official rations were perhaps enough to sustain life—though Dr. Alonzo Taylor's 1916 report threw doubt even on this[2]—but they were so skimpy and unpalatable that they would certainly sustain nothing else. The bread supplied was often uneatable; several men made museum collections of the straw, stones, potato peelings, and other objects found in the sour, soggy loaves.

The prisoners accordingly turned their hopes to parcels from home. British parcels had been arriving since Christmas 1914, but were regarded purely as luxuries; not until the spring of 1915 did the men begin to think of them as sustenance. They did so reluctantly, knowing it was the duty of the Germans to feed them; but when the bread ration was cut in March to 200 grammes a day, about four good slices, every letter home asked for foodstuffs. The writers dared not be explicit for fear of the censor's scissors, and there were many cryptic references. Irwin wrote in January 1915: "Finest opportunity for cultivating our

2. British Foreign Office, *White Papers*, "Miscellaneous," No. 18 (1916) Cd. 8259.

table manners here, twig?" And again in February: "You'll be glad to hear that Little Mary is progressing, but is rather void at times." In March Denton sent more drastic messages through bible passages which the censor obviously failed to look up (the texts are here shown in brackets):

Mar. 15. The services are going well. Our text yesterday was Lam. 4, 9, *very* appropriate ["They that be slain with the sword are better than they that be slain with hunger"]. I try to send you the "text" each week, but cannot always get it right; sometimes I choose it myself! It is nice to think that we have communion of thought even across the sea.

Mar. 23. Mr Williams preached on Sunday, Luke 15, 16 ["He would fain have filled his belly with the husks that the swine ate, and no man gave unto him"]. . . . Condensed milk is not necessary as we can still buy it. If you have some condensed *bread*, now—but perhaps it has not yet been invented. Some fellows have had bread from England, stale, but still edible. Only as a luxury, *of course*, bread being provided here.

These S.O.S. calls, of course, greatly exaggerated the situation. Men were often hungry, but there was no starvation in the camp. There was, however, an ever growing *fear* of starvation—and it took at least six weeks to get a reply from England.

The response was whole-hearted; the 8,000 parcels of January 1915 rose to 27,000 in June. Later figures were still higher, and many prisoners were almost swamped with food. Charitable organizations raised parcel funds, and prisoners whose families could not supply them sometimes got more than their wealthier fellows. There was a great deal of overlapping, and the resulting waste, though never publicly referred to, made some men angry and ashamed. Graham wrote to his wife in 1916:

Jan. 29. At the moment I have at least the equivalent of six of your regular parcels in stock. I can assure you that a lot of good camp food is wasted because people are able to live on parcels and get too lazy or too dainty to go up to the kitchens.

June 30. I wish you would become less interested in giving me an enormous stomach and in feeding others at my expense. The parcels, which really are and ought to be a delight and a great treat, become a d——— nuisance. It is no use telling me to store the stuff up. There is no space, and it simply means waste.

Graham depended upon his wife; those on the lists of patriotic societies had, as he says in August, extra supplies: "One day I shall tell you of the wicked waste I have seen here. Two of my mess-mates are Lancashire and one Shields, and there are committees sending them foodstuffs from both places." Indeed the popularity of the Lancastrian Association was largely due to the generosity of its Manchester committee, and sardonic jests circulated as to the *bona fides* of some of its three hundred members.

While some men wondered where to store their food, others were poorly supplied. Their messmates usually took care of them, but the situation was unsatisfactory and came in time to the ears of the British Government. In December 1916 a new system provided every man with three Red Cross parcels per fortnight, and private donors were restricted to four "personal" parcels a year. Graham writes again:

Nov. 3, 1916. We have seen something about the new arrangements for parcels, and can quite understand it is necessary for the large number of societies, committees, etc. But surely private people will be able to send parcels. No doubt the charity schemes have been much abused.

Dec. 29, 1916. I was devoutly thanking heaven yesterday that there would be an interval with no parcels when to my surprise I got my first standard parcel. Let me say that as parcels sent by a public body they are good.

Most comments are far less resigned than this, but even the loudest critics recognized that some change was inevitable.

Hard times still occurred, of course; the standard parcel contents were not always well chosen, and in 1917 and 1918 they often arrived irregularly. Ewing writes:

Feb. 10, 1917. Things are very scarce at the moment, short rations in everything and completely out of milk and margarine. Not enough of these necessities in the government parcels, but they're very generous in other ways. A large package of *salt* in almost every parcel; we have *12 lbs.* on hand already and still it comes!

Mar. 31, 1917. Since last writing parcels have absolutely stopped, and we've been on our last legs. Been absolutely out of milk and sugar and butter for over a week.

Such shortages, however, were never more than temporary, and were often met by borrowing from neighbours. And the minutes of the Marine Engineers' Association a few weeks later suggest that supplies in general were more than adequate:

May 17, 1917. Committee meeting called to discuss advisability of reducing the number of parcels which are sent by our association. In view of the fact that in response to our notice that parcels were to be had, and to personal investigation by barrack delegates, only four engineers applied, the committee think it our duty to write to the secretary stating the facts and requesting him to reduce the number of parcels.

This is a far cry from the letters of early 1915.

The hot-water house, built in February 1915 and greatly enlarged later, had at last allowed men to make tea and coffee at 10 pfennigs (one penny) a pot, and also to heat canned goods. Each tin was attached to a string with a numbered tag and immersed in a great kettle of boiling water; after fifteen minutes the owner claimed it and paid the penny fee. Corned beef straight from the can is not inspiring fare, but all efforts to secure facilities for private cooking were fruitless until June 1916, when a shed with two large ranges was opened for business. Here the prisoners' own dishes were boiled, baked, fried, or burned at nominal cost by a staff of carefree sailors. The "pot-pie" quickly became a stand-by: corned beef, covered with sliced boiled potatoes from the kitchens, and browned in a gravy of Oxo cubes. Flour began to come in parcels, and pies, pastry, and cakes were baked in the cookhouse. Porridge was a universal breakfast dish; it was prepared in bulk from Quaker Oats and sold at the cost of fuel.

The problem of bread had not been solved by British parcels, since it almost always arrived completely mouldy. But late in 1915 arrangements were made for regular despatch of loaves from Denmark and Switzerland to every prisoner; these came in ten days or less and were usually in edible condition. Around midsummer, when mould was at its worst, hard biscuits made a tolerable substitute. Butter, too, was a commodity that could not be shipped safely; after the canteen ceased to stock it the most common spread was tinned beef dripping, which had a higher melting point.

Save for a chronic shortage of fruit and green vegetables the prisoners now lived reasonably well. Their diet was simple, monotonous, and probably lacking in vitamins, but otherwise it was adequate as long as parcels arrived on schedule. On birthdays and other special occasions regular banquets took place; Irwin contributes the illuminated menu of a dinner given a Russian scholar before his release:

Hare Soup
Beef Pasties
Tongue
Rice and Tomato
Fruit
Coffee

Two additional food sources were among the few advantages enjoyed by well-to-do Ruhlebenites. The first was the Casino, originally a restaurant for the racecourse employees, but converted into mess-rooms for the German officers and enlisted men. One section of this was reserved for those prisoners who could obtain a pass and were willing to pay three marks for a dinner. A single glass of beer was also allowed them. Passes were issued at first only on medical orders and for a limited period, but the privilege was gradually extended; voluntary camp workers dined at the Casino—at the expense of the Camp Fund, according to Cohen—and in later years (when the meals were scarcely worth eating) almost anyone could secure a pass.

The other source was smuggling. Most of the guards, if suitably bribed, would bring in contraband, and as time went on they even competed for the trade. After their removal from the barracks contact was often made in the Casino. Liquor was of course the chief item involved, but at Christmas and on special occasions food delicacies were also ordered, until they became unprocurable in Berlin. Two Christmas dinners described in Kendall's diary provide an illuminating contrast:

Dec. 25, 1915. C.A. got in two geese which we made a great spread with. I made a comic menu, and we had great festivity, all eleven dining in our box. Hot mulled wine (i.e. cheap spiced wine) was served out. About half a cupful was enough to put many under the table.

Dec. 25, 1916. Very quiet Christmas dinner. We went up to the kitchen and got a big slice of bacon, sauerkraut and peeled potatoes. Geese being over 100 marks each and whisky 30 marks per bottle, also Hochschule beer at 80 pf. being vile, deprived us of any beanfeast.

The camp canteen was an important source of food in 1915, for when the captains took over the concession in March they went into business on an unprecedented scale. Buying through German agents on commission, they combed the country for foodstuffs, and their success may be gauged by the sales of food in the last eight days of August 1915:

2,102 lbs. butter	3,286 lbs. sugar
815 lbs. margarine	418 lbs. ham
805 lbs. cheese	119 lbs. bacon
2,300 tins condensed milk	162 lbs. sausage
25,138 eggs[3]	120 lbs. salt

(*IRC* 9, p. 33)

Such abundance, however, could not last. On November 14 Ewing writes that there has been no butter or margarine available for a week, and Cohen's book states: "During the seven months from November 1915 to June 1916, no butter, margarine, or condensed milk was on sale at

3. This figure seems almost incredible, since no letter of the period mentions eggs and there was still no cookhouse. However, Powell speaks of selling up to 10,000 eggs a *day* at reduced prices in the fall of 1915, when a shortage was anticipated (38, p. 92).

the canteen. Eggs were sold only once (at 25 pfennigs, about 3d.) and nobody could buy more than one" (p. 182). As wartime shortages increased in Germany, all such foods were rationed and unprocurable; at times the canteen sold mostly sour pickles and *ersatz* jam. The shrinkage is graphically reflected in the men's purchases of comestibles over three years:

1915 (last 7 months) M 521,819[4]
1916 (12 months) M 194,858
1917 (12 months) M 79,114

The resulting deficiency was filled of course by the parcels, and also by bulk shipment of certain foods from England. The official rations remained unaltered and, as may be expected, the number of prisoners drawing bread, soup, and skilly fell steadily. In the end the Germans were persuaded to put most of their food allowance into potatoes and other vegetables, and these helped to balance the diet.

Food was by no means all that the canteen handled; most of the prisoners' other needs could also be supplied in one of its score of departments. In 1915 these included dry goods, outfitters, tailors, shoemakers, barbers, a watch repairer, and a book and music shop; the boiler house and camp carpenters were also part of the system. Later additions included glaziers, a photographer, and a "special order" department for goods not carried in stock, besides the cookhouse, the accumulator charging depot, and various other services. Cigarettes and tobacco had to be secured from parcels until 1917, when a tobacco shop opened with tax-free supplies direct from England; in spite of the nominal prices charged, its turnover that year was 95,000 marks.

Most of these establishments were housed in a row of little shops on "Bond Street," the initial outlay being financed by the Camp Fund, to which the American Embassy made advances when necessary. The canteen enterprises as a whole were self-supporting, but foods were regularly sold below outside prices and often at a deliberate loss, the deficit being made up by profits on other goods and services. The overall aim of the canteen officials was to break even, and it was well achieved; they ended the four years with a net profit of 0.6 per cent on

4. Turnover for all canteen departments in these seven months averaged 26,000 marks (about $6,500) per week. The prisoners then numbered almost 4,200, of whom an average of 2,600 were drawing relief of five marks a week (*IRC* 7, p. 45). Assuming that this was their only income (somewhat questionable, since no means test was applied), they were not much worse off than the 1,600 men supported by their families, whose canteen expenditures, by these figures, would average eight marks a week each.

a turnover of almost 700,000 marks. Whatever hard things the camp had to say about its captains, their direction of this large retail undertaking could scarcely have been improved on.

Except on one occasion in 1915, when the camp's purchases of eggs were alleged to be inflating Berlin prices, the Germans turned a benign gaze on all this commercial activity. And well they might. For, besides permitting substantial economies in the official rations, it brought a flow of sterling into the country to be profitably exchanged for marks; and in addition the authorities collected a nice little commission of 7½ per cent on every purchase made by the camp!

Britain thus largely fed and supplied the civilians interned at Ruhleben, and all the camp improvements except the new barracks, washhouses, and latrines were paid for with British money. It was well spent, for had conditions remained unchanged many men would surely have been broken in health and spirit. At the same time, it is possible that the sufferings of the first six months were the making of the camp morally, whatever they were physically. Molony has a suggestive paragraph on the subject:

How curious it is to remark that strange feature of prison life by which a prisoner's dependence on discomfort is essential if he wishes to preserve his sanity and health. The more there is of material need in pursuit of which his mind may be diverted . . . the greater is the consequent response. (Pp. 103–4)

The morale of Ruhleben was certainly higher in the first winter than it ever became again, and some who bore with a joke the privations of those months complained bitterly later if parcels were a few days delayed.

One of the best criteria of living conditions is the amount of sickness, and Ruhleben was on the whole a relatively healthy community. This was not attributable to good medical attention, for the German doctors relied on aspirin as a cure-all and the official *Lazaret*, just outside the camp, was a place that no one wished to visit twice. A pure water supply, however, and the men's own care about sanitation, prevented any outbreaks of typhoid, typhus, or cholera, while the open-air life and good food after the first winter were generally beneficial.

There were, however, a number of prisoners in chronic ill health, and no town of four thousand could escape its quota of acute illnesses. The inadequacy of the medical arrangements was obvious from the first, and the prisoners made immediate efforts to supplement them. The Samaritan Club visited and cared for invalids in their barracks, and a relay of interpreters at the doctor's office enabled sick men at least to describe their symptoms. The interpreting was gradually taken over by Stanley Lambert, German agent of a British coal firm, who devoted himself from 1915 until the end of the camp to his ailing fellow-prisoners. Urgent representations in the spring of that year resulted in his being put in charge of one of the new huts, which was set aside as a convalescent barrack and equipped with forty beds and other necessities from British funds. Special diets, good nursing by Lambert and his assistants, and freedom from roll calls and kitchen parades made the barrack a haven for those with minor illnesses or recuperating after a session in hospital. Conditions at the *Lazaret* were also greatly improved that fall, though again only by the expenditure of camp funds for orderlies, cleaners, and equipment.

In the same year Dr. Weiler's sanatorium in Charlottenburg was taken over to accommodate chronic and more serious cases. Here a hundred patients could be treated in two classes, the fees for Class II being defrayed by the British Government. Attention and food were reasonably satisfactory, and the men also received their parcels. Major surgical cases, however, had to go to the Prisoner of War Hospital in Berlin; here conditions were thoroughly bad throughout the war, food and supplies being deficient and bed nursing almost non-existent. Persistent efforts were made to send voluntary orderlies, medical supplies, and foodstuffs from Ruhleben, but all met with flat refusals.

An official list of deaths up to July 1915, covering the worst period of internment, contains 17 names; total deaths in the first three years numbered 50 out of an average population of 3,500 (CC). Since all who could qualify as invalids were sent to Holland in 1918 the final total was probably under 60. Most of the population were, of course, in the robust years of life, 80 per cent of them in 1915 being between 16 and 45 years old.

Gribble wrote a good article on the camp's medical history (21) and his account of the general health of the prisoners is borne out by letters and diaries. The first winter was marked chiefly by colds, coughs, and rheumatism; Ewing writes: "My health is now quite good, we have all got through the winter surprisingly well. I had a bad cough for some weeks and an attack of the 'flu' in January." An epidemic of diarrhoea in February 1915 was not serious enough to be mentioned in some letters. Poorly balanced diet was probably responsible for the boils that afflicted Denton and others in the spring and summer of 1915: "At present I am not taking much exercise, being confined to bed with boils all up my right leg. The doctor slices and treats them but new ones keep appearing." On May 2 Henley reports "many down with measles," and the mild epidemic lasted through the month.

In 1916 the camp was probably better fed than either before or after, and the year was healthy except for the winter colds:

Jan. 26, 1916. The "flu" has been going round the camp—I am just recovering from my little attack. (Abbot)

Nov. 3, 1916. I have had a bad cold this week, as bad a cold as I have had at Ruhleben, and am now getting better of it. The whole camp has or has had colds, so it is nothing extraordinary. (Graham)

In July 1917 there was a serious outbreak of dysentery with some three hundred cases; the worst were isolated in one of the wooden barracks and, thanks to volunteer nursing, no deaths occurred.

A year later, in July 1918, the "Spanish 'Flu" ravaged the camp, fortunately in its early, mild form. In a population that had fallen to 2,336 there were 1,565 cases reported, but only two men died from complications. Those who had recovered nursed their comrades, hampered by the fact that the German War Office chose this moment to divide the camp by a locked gate in retaliation for some English "outrage." Denton, then in the Tea House, gives a brief diary record of the epidemic:

July 1. Barrack 23 opened as hospital. Grippe.
July 4. Forty "Spaniards" in Barrack 4 alone.
July 5. Over 50 per cent of Bar. 12 ill, Spanish grippe.
July 6. Barrack 23 full.
July 7. Spanish Sunday. Appell[5] thinly attended. Three men went off field. Made corn starch for boys and took it up camp. Helped carry Epworth back to 7, very bad. Into Box 10, Fatty still in Bar. 23, others all in bed.
July 8. Plague still raging. Took toast up camp at 8 a.m. Found middle gate shut, not to be opened for less than ten people. Got through, however. Barracks 2, 14, 15, etc. very thin at Appell. Fifty per cent of Barrack 7 down.
July 9. Nine hundred cases. Sent jelly to boys.
July 10. Some 750 away from Appell.
July 11. Tea House mustered only 31. "Flu" slacking off.
July 12. Gate now opened every ten minutes.

There are no more entries, the epidemic subsiding as abruptly as it began.

Something should be added about teeth and eyes. Ewing wrote in April 1915: "I have had a great deal of trouble with my teeth, as has almost everyone. The continued soup and soft stuffs are bad." After unhappy experiences with a visiting German dentist a fully equipped

5. The German term for "roll call," invariably used in camp.

surgery was opened in the camp, staffed by two interned dentists; it could hardly keep pace with the demand, however. Ewing wrote a year later: "I have had a lot of dentistry again; my mouth seems to be falling to pieces." There were also many complaints of eye strain from reading by poor light, and of infections from the dust that blew about all summer. A German oculist was brought in periodically, but some men probably suffered lasting disability.

On the after-effects of four years' internment no judgment can be made. Most men who answered the questionnaire attributed some physical impairment to Ruhleben, but such statements are of course impossible to evaluate. Nervous complaints were most frequently mentioned, followed by gastric disturbances, general debility, and rheumatism; but the lists included everything from appendicitis to baldness. On the other hand, some respondents said flatly that they suffered no damage and a few reported themselves physically improved.

Only the camp itself can be pronounced upon here, and the men's letters leave an emphatic impression of general good health. There was of course a tendency to reassure those at home, but the actual statements ring true. The following are in chronological order:

Jan. 7, 1915. Am in splendid health and spirits despite cold and rain and *much* mud. (Irwin)

May 1, 1915. I am feeling ever so much better than a month ago, less routine work and more exercise. So you needn't worry; I am living in an extra cheap sanitarium, open air treatment and all. (Denton)

June 30, 1915. The camp is in very good health, and everyone is tremendously sunburnt. (Graham)

Sept. 24, 1915. The camp seems in very good health, helped largely by the sports. (Graham)

Jan. 29, 1916. I have a slight cold on me, but I have told you how quickly I seem to be able to throw off such little troubles here. (Graham)

June 1, 1916. All very well here, glorious weather the last ten days and we boys very happy in consequence. (Irwin)

Jan. 29, 1917. We have much to be thankful for in the camp, but the chief thing, I think, is the good state of health. (Ewing)

July 20, 1917. The weather continues favourable for tennis and I have had a number of good games, which seem to help to keep me in good condition. Last summer I often felt like a wet rag, but I haven't experienced the feeling this year. (Abbot)

Nov. 30, 1917. How am I entering upon the fourth winter? Cheerfully enough, thank heaven with a few minor troubles that do not amount to much. I have two or three chilblains, a troublesome toe-joint, a few bad teeth and some possibility of rheumatism. (Graham)

Jan. 10, 1918. All very well here; it is very cold, but skating provides warmth. (Irwin)

There were men who did suffer acutely during their stay, and the long-range effects of Ruhleben are of course impossible to estimate. Under the conditions, however, the record is a good one. Indeed, several men survived four years in the camp only to be killed by influenza almost as soon as they reached home.

Mental health was a different matter, and one of special importance in Ruhleben, for once the physical conditions were somewhat ameliorated the strain on the prisoners was chiefly psychological. This was recognized in the campaign waged by the English press and public for exchange of all civilians at whatever cost. Lord Beresford, speaking of Ruhleben in the House of Lords on October 24, 1916, referred to letters "from which it was clear that a few months more would not elapse before loss of memory, loss of mind, and even madness [*sic*] would be enormously increased in that camp." And a month later Sir Timothy Eden, a recently exchanged Ruhlebenite, wrote as follows to *The Times*:

I will not dwell upon their physical sufferings. They have been many, but no worse than, and in many cases not so bad as, those of countless other sufferers in this war, but I cannot lay too much stress upon the serious mental condition of the civilian prisoners. And this condition is only natural. Suddenly snatched from their peaceful occupations these men have been herded into a racecourse, where they have now lived in crowded stables for two years. For not one single instant during the whole of that time has any prisoner had the slightest privacy.

It is impossible to be alone. There are no past glories to dream about. No consolation in the remembrance of duty done. The men have nothing to think of save their ruined prospects and the hopelessness of their position. Therefore, I say again that the mental state of these prisoners is most serious. And it is imperative if they are to retain their reason that they be set free at once.

These are, of course, *ex-parte* statements and not free from exaggeration. But they should be recalled when we consider the functions of the social world constructed in 1915.

How much mental illness actually occurred is stated only in a proposed memorandum to the British Government, drawn up in Ruhleben by an official committee at the end of 1917. According to this there had been fifty cases of "insanity" and fifty of "total nervous collapse" up to December 1, 1917. The figures are suspiciously round ones, the diagnoses inevitably vague, and there is no indication of what cases were included. Presumably they were those who required medical treatment, in or outside the camp. Considering the unselected population exposed to the rigours of Ruhleben, a larger total might have been expected, and Bishop Bury, after his visit in November 1916, described it as "a very wonderful thing that so few relatively have broken down" (6, p. 35).

A special section of Weiler's sanatorium was set aside for nervous cases; in March 1916 there were reported to be seventy men there, and in November Bishop Bury saw and talked to about that number. Treatment—chiefly rest and frequent light meals—was probably as good as obtainable at the time. Cases diagnosed as psychotic, however, were sent to a public institution at Neu Ruppin, which camp rumours pictured as a typical madhouse, complete with strait jackets and padded cells. Powell stated that he gained "a very good impression" of Neu Ruppin in June 1918, but he only talked to the staff and was not allowed to see any Ruhleben patients (CC).

More concrete information about breakdowns is contained in the letters and diaries, which refer to forty-seven cases, including three suicides and three attempted suicides. Names are not always given and only two medical diagnoses are reported, but approximate ages are known in thirty cases and symptoms are often indicated. From this sample it is possible to learn something of the temporal incidence of mental illness, and also to divide most of the cases into an older and a younger group. That is done on the assumption that the older cases, Type I (nearly all of men 50 or over), were more or less inevitable under the circumstances, while the younger ones, Type II (30 and under), should have been preventable.[6] The assumption is an arbitrary one, but it is based on the fact that age was often decisive for a prisoner's ability to adapt to Ruhleben. The classification will therefore be useful in estimating the prophylactic value of the camp's social life.

The distribution of all reported cases is as follows: 1914–15, 4; 1916, 23; 1917, 16; 1918, 4. Physical hardship was evidently not a factor, since only two cases are mentioned during the first winter. The drop in 1917, when the strain was actually increasing, probably means that many susceptible men had already collapsed and been removed from the camp, while in 1918 all the obviously unfit had been repatriated or interned in Holland. On June 6, 1916, Kendall commented in his

6. Whether by chance or otherwise, the ages between 30 and 48 are represented by only one case, aged 41. Kendall reports him "completely mad," but he recovered, and referred to his illness in his questionnaire as "nervous breakdown or stroke." He is included in Type I.

diary: "The 'French Ambassador' was sent home, he is quite mad. I don't know what they must think of us in England if they judge by the specimens who get sent home. Last month four or five were insane."[7]

The older men, who have been placed in Type I, include two-thirds of the men whose ages are known, and illness tends to appear earlier than among the younger men. Some were clearly predisposed to mental breakdown and would have given way under any severe strain; some were chronically "peculiar"—neurotic, perhaps, or simply eccentric. Of the rest I am assuming that they lacked the resilience necessary to cope with the conditions Sir Timothy Eden described, and with an important additional one: utter uncertainty as to the future, and an endless succession of sanguine hopes and bitter disappointments. General comradeship and high morale seem to have carried most of them through the first winter, but they could not face the strain of succeeding years, usually because of inability to immerse themselves in the camp's social activities. Their illnesses, though of various sorts, may thus be regarded as inevitable, given the personalities and conditions.

The earliest case described occurred in 1914, and portrays one type of man who should never have been interned:

Another of my early boxmates, a distinguished looking, nervous bachelor of some 50 years, found the sudden transition from a peaceful secluded life to that among a heterogeneous, rather noisy crowd too much for his mental stability. He had apparently been somewhat self-centred, to judge by his conversation, and all his thoughts upon internment were concerned with his own safety. And, as he was extremely fearful, he was subjected to a good deal of rough and ready leg-pulling. It was not meant cruelly, but he was so very gullible that he was tempting prey. After a few weeks his mind seemed to succumb to his fears and he developed *Verfolgungswahn* [persecution mania] and had to be removed to a sanatorium where he died shortly afterwards. This gave us rather a shock as we had not realised how terribly his unreasonable fears had preyed on his mind. (L 32)

A sampling of other Type I cases follows: the names given them are of course fictitious:

Sept. 26, 1915. "The man who was going to speak at yesterday's Wednesday service was taken to the asylum today" (Denton). This was an educated man in his fifties, who went into a sudden depression, with delusions. His fate is unknown.

Feb. 21, 1916. A well-known camp character who ran his own business was reported by Kendall as "off his rocker" in the convalescent barrack. "They have given him a piece of board which he opens and shuts like a

---

7. A regular train ran to Holland on the sixth of each month.

trap door and tames lions." The man, about 50, was always mildly peculiar, but he recovered from this attack.

June 6, 1916. A harmless elderly eccentric called the "Lord Chief Justice" caused much amusement by conducting the promenade orchestra from the audience and by sitting out on his stool in pouring rain. "He is an old Etonian and walks about alone, never speaking to anyone; his mind has been obviously unhinged" (Kendall). He was repatriated.

July 27, 1916. "Renison, out of this box, has been taken to the sanatorium with some kind of mental breakdown. He got very thin, though he ate well, was inclined to mope, then he suddenly got worse, talking a lot of rubbish, and finally we had a very bad night with him" (Graham). The man was 48.

Aug. 5, 1916. "Poor old Ball, one of the first to attend our services, is going quite out of his mind. He is 54 and pretty feeble. These are the men who should be exchanged, and not so much fuss about us young chaps" (Denton). Ball's talk was irrational and he created some disturbance at services. He was sent to a German mental hospital.

Aug. 19, 1916. "The old watchman of the Y.M.C.A. building was sent to Weiler's today 'off his rocker.' He has for some time been sitting outside on the steps of his loft at night time wailing and crying" (Kendall).

Similar cases continued to appear through 1917, especially among men over 45, who had been promised exchange at the start of the year but had to wait for it until 1918. Jarvis wrote in his diary for August 8, 1917:

Man in Barrack 3 tried to commit suicide by cutting both wrists and stabbing himself. Terrible, and weak perhaps, but if the 45ers don't go soon I fear others will follow his example. The exchange talk, rumours, facts, hopes, longings and disappointments are torture to the poor devils, who are doing nothing but think and talk about their chances.

The last clause is significant; no one, young or old, whose mind was entirely preoccupied with his own fate could hope to come through the years at Ruhleben undamaged.

The cases of younger men, Type II, were much fewer but at the same time more disturbing, for they all involved men still in their twenties, some of them quite active in camp life. The first recorded is in mid-July 1916, and three more followed that fall; four appear in 1917, and only two in 1918. The record is deceptive, however, for other references suggest that cases of "nerves" among young men were actually increasing in 1917 and 1918. Denton wrote home in December 1917:

The suffering in this camp is mental and spiritual, not physical, and it is becoming more and more severe. Strong, healthy young fellows are losing grip one after another, becoming morose and silent, shunned by their friends and hating them in return, refusing to write letters home, and some of them even to read them.

While this reflected a current concern of the Y.M.C.A. workers, the picture is confirmed, though less dramatically, by other letters. Not many of these cases reached the point of complete breakdown, hence the paucity of diary records. But the symptoms became familiar in the later camp: progressive loss of interest in any occupation, withdrawal from contacts with others, depression, and a more or less complete retreat into the self. In their milder forms the symptoms often yielded to determined efforts by the man's friends; when these failed, a week or so in the convalescent barrack usually brought him around. Concern was justified, however, for similar symptoms marked the onset of the more serious cases, which ultimately became completely inaccessible and irrational. These were sent out of the camp and seldom heard of again, though ugly rumours circulated and several deaths were reported. A man's boxmates would therefore put up with a great deal rather than have him "taken away," but two suicides by young men during 1918 suggest that such forbearance was not always wise. Of the men sent out, at least two in Type II recovered, though only after long treatment in England; a third shot himself there while under treatment. How such social isolation became possible in the once warmly united camp will be discussed later.

Among unclassified cases were at least two where the breakdown was signalized by violent aggression—"running amok"—rather than withdrawal; the men were probably young, but all that is certain is that they were sailors. Another man was repatriated to England in 1916 after a period in the sanatorium, but jumped overboard and drowned as the ship neared Tilbury. His age also is unknown.

Most of these hundred or more unfortunates must be counted out as we follow the camp's developing life; with certain Type II exceptions they took little part in it. How much they suffered before they opened their arteries or withdrew into impenetrable shells may be imagined; this is one of the few dark pages in Ruhleben's history. The breakdowns had their effect on the rest of the camp, though it was less than might be expected. A popular notion, expressed by three informants in their letters, was that *all* the prisoners were going mad together and would not realize it until they got out. This was not seriously believed, of course; no healthy individual really doubts his own sanity. One 1933 correspondent, however, who had come close to a nervous breakdown in camp, mentioned among the debilitating factors of the last year of internment "the permanent fear of some day going off one's head like so many others" (L 58). And Abbot, telling his parents that he was seeking work outside the camp, wrote in May 1918:

Seeing that you have not been shut up for four years, you may not like the idea, but I am relying on your confidence in my ability to decide what is best for myself. After all, there is a limit to human endurance and my chief aim is to return to you sound in body and *mind*, which I don't think will be possible if I have to stick this life of inactivity much longer. I don't want to alarm you, but it may help you to appreciate my point of view.

Abbot, however, was never in any danger of mental collapse; like others, he was in urgent need of a change of scene and occupation, and was defending a decision that was open to obvious criticism.

One source of strain that bore with particular severity on young and well-educated men was directly connected with the physical improvement of the camp. The Ruhlebenite of military age was spending the war in a far safer and more comfortable place than the trenches, and he could not contemplate the fact without a disturbing sense of guilt. During the first winter he could at least feel that he was suffering for his country, but as Ruhleben life grew easier and the war more destructive many letters show signs of mental conflict:

March 19, 1915. The worst of this life is the knowledge that we are doing nobody any good. (Jarvis)

July 31, 1915. It is dreadful to be shut up here while such great things are going on outside. (Merton)

Sept. 26, 1915. We feel as if we would have to hang our heads whenever the war is mentioned for the rest of our lives. I sometimes feel like stopping all parcels just to get a little real hardship like the boys at the front, but even that would do no good. (Denton)

Jan. 26, 1916. It is terrible to be doomed to play a watching and waiting part and not be able to help. (Abbot)

Jan. 29, 1917. Nice of N. to write about me so, but one takes all these comforting messages with a grain of salt. We can't deceive ourselves into thinking we are serving our country; on the contrary, we are only a burden on you all, a public nuisance rather than anything else. (Ewing)

And Irwin stated in 1933, as the "greatest single hardship" he endured at Ruhleben, "the thought that I couldn't help my country in the war." These quotations suggest the emotional problems of the sensitive Ruhlebenite as he contrasted his increasingly pleasant life with that of his countrymen in uniform. As time went on and relatives of his own age enlisted and were killed, the sense of inferiority grew heavier and probably played its part in some of the Type II breakdowns.

For the less sensitive majority, however, the problem was simpler. They met it by a collective insistence that Ruhleben life was *not* easy but bitterly hard, and that the only valid picture of it was that of the first winter. A correspondent wrote in 1933:

No doubt you will have noticed the great importance many attached to the hardships of the early days before parcels, etc. It seemed a way of keeping up their self-respect for when they would go back and meet the men in the army. Remember the trouble caused by Gerard's reports about our sitting in deck chairs and so on—perfectly true of course, but not what we liked to hear. (L 75)

And Ewing refers to Bishop Bury's published account of the camp after his visit:

Mar. 25, 1917. I hear he painted the camp in glowing colours; we haven't had a copy here, but saw some of the English criticisms. Many have been down on him here for it, for their "sufferings" are the men's most prized possessions and they'll give them up to nobody. There will be some dreadful yarns told when we get home by some of our would-be martyrs.

Blood-curdling tales were indeed told by some exchanged Ruhlebenites, and both Ambassador Gerard and Bishop Bury were damned in the camp for merely reporting conditions as they saw them. But the same men who reclined in the sun while the orchestra played Strauss waltzes had previously shivered in the lofts and waded through the mire, and they clung to this earlier picture with a tenacity that was pathetic as well as ludicrous. For they *had* to magnify their sufferings or else endure the sharper pains of feeling themselves useless shirkers.

When permission was given to send home the Christmas 1915 number of *In Ruhleben Camp*, a controversy arose. Although the issue contained some suitably depressing photographs, many prisoners maintained that its cheerful tone would "give a false impression"—or, as the blunter seamen put it, cut down the parcels. Opposition was strengthened by the publication of Ambassador Gerard's first, uncritical report on the camp, but the magazine was finally sent off, though not until mid-February. By the next Christmas, however, the men were less touchy, and four thousand copies of a much brighter issue were mailed to Britain and elsewhere.

Individually most prisoners would have admitted that they were very well off after the first winter, and several letters utter warnings against the lurid reports of repatriated men. Collectively, however, such realism was taboo. No public reference to the camp dared depict its inhabitants except as forgotten heroes, keeping a stiff upper lip in spite of unending hardships. This self-definition coloured every collective symbol that emerged, and was explicit in the "Ruhleben Song" quoted in Chapter 4. Nowhere in this national anthem is there a hint of football, cricket, concerts, plays, or study; these, the outstanding features of life after the first winter, could not be included in the camp's self-portrait. Partly, no doubt, because they did not date from the sacred period of solidarity, but partly too because of their troubling implications that interned life was often enjoyable. Thus on January 14, 1919, when King George V opened the Ruhleben Exhibition in London—a remarkable display of painting, handicrafts, and other constructive work—it was of course the Ruhleben Song that was sung. And it is ceremoniously sung again at every annual gathering of the Ruhleben Association.

9

LIVING CONDITIONS at Ruhleben need concern us no more; like the continuing community life, they now supply part of the background for a more complex series of changes. This chapter gives a running account of the "period of expansion"—April to November, 1915—and describes some important emotional changes. It makes no attempt, however, to deal with the new activities of the period, the real key to its character; so many games, lectures, classes, and entertainments were now taking place that it would be impossible even to list them. The whole development will be summarized in Chapter 10.

We left the men at the end of March 1915, enjoying the new sense of freedom that came with the spring. Spring, however, also brought some reminders that to the Germans, at least, Ruhleben was still an internment camp. On March 28 Walter Butterworth, recently elected a barrack captain, was put in the cells and dismissed from office for "impertinence" to the Baron, and two days later Israel Cohen and a dozen others were imprisoned in Berlin for smuggling out letters. Then the smouldering pro-German trouble flared up. The Baron, complaining that those who had stepped forward in January were not adequately represented, replaced Barrack 15's captain with a stout pro-German. Powell and Beaumont, Captain and Vice-Captain of the Camp, promptly and courageously resigned. They were reinstated in less than a week, but soon another prisoner was accused by a pro-German of offensive remarks about the Kaiser and sent to Berlin for trial. Rumours spread that he would probably be shot, and feeling ran so high that the Baron felt compelled to issue the following notice:

In reference to the case of alleged lèse-majesté in Barrack One, the accused, if found guilty by the Court Martial, will only receive a short term of imprisonment—possibly ten, fourteen or twenty-one days in a military prison, according to the decision of the court.

A message has been received by telephone from the *Kommandantur* that should any case of trouble arise, or interference with the men concerned in the above affair, this camp will be dissolved and turned into a military camp for French and Russian prisoners of war, and the English civil prisoners will be transferred to Döberitz and treated as military prisoners. (H)

While the statement removed some anxiety, its threats against any retaliation on the informer caused profane mutterings.

On April 14 there were two escapes from the *Lazaret*—the first recorded; on the 16th another man was put in cells for joking about an officer, and next day Wallace Ellison, captain of the Negroes' barrack, was sent to prison for "remarks offensive to the authorities." This, however, ended the trouble for some time. The lèse-majesté case resulted in acquittal, giving the prisoners confidence in the courts; the escaped men were recaptured, which pleased the Germans; and on April 18 the pro-Germans were segregated and the greatest source of friction removed.

Apart from their pro-German aspects, these incidents reflect a significant shift in the relative positions of prisoners and captors. The captains were beginning to assert themselves and even to forget how internees should address their superiors, while the German officers were belatedly trying to show that they, and not the British, controlled the camp. In spite of many such efforts, a diarchy was the best they could attain; Powell was already exercising effective control by resigning. As for the pro-German problem, its worst feature was the confusion it introduced into British-German relations; segregation cleared this up and opened the way to better understanding.

April was a critical month in the war. The second battle of Ypres reached its bitter climax in the west, the ill-starred landing at Gallipoli took its toll in the east. In the six diaries that cover this month, however, there are only two references to the war. What is jotted down in a diary is of course only what comes to mind at the moment, and there are letters that show deep concern about the battles. But the fact is still striking, for some of these diaries contained much war news earlier. Spring may have had something to do with it; as Ewing wrote on the 23rd, "It is astonishing how quickly one's troubles evaporate when one can lie on the ground and bask in the sun." But the diarists' concentration on camp affairs was also a sign that Ruhleben was beginning to function as a substitute world. The men could not worry indefinitely about events they were powerless to affect; they were being forced to make the barbed wire their horizon. This reorientation had much to do with their new assertiveness against the Germans; if they had to accept Ruhleben as their world they must secure satisfactory status in it.

With May we find some renewal of interest in the war, together with further efforts to keep the authorities in their place. On May 3 the flag was hoisted for a German victory in the Carpathians and an officer posted up the official list of booty—160,000 prisoners, 25,000 horses, and so on. It was not a tactful act, and deserved its reception. A large crowd gathered around the boiler house, cheering derisively as someone translated the notice, and then breaking into the ditty that was Ruhleben's stock expression of incredulity:

> There was a cow
> Climbed up a tree—
> OH, YOU BLOODY LIAR!

The singers were moved along by the police before trouble resulted. The torpedoing of the *Lusitania* on May 8 aroused intense feeling, and conjectures about its effect on America are recorded in several diaries. There was no public disturbance; but on May 20, when Italy's entry into the war was imminent, the police were warned to prevent demonstrations if the papers should contain good news (Chapman).

Such incidents, however, did not reflect deep antagonism; even in April Denton wrote: "The soldiers are getting to know us better now, and we all get along very well together." England and Germany were at war—that was never forgotten—but within the camp a pattern of coexistence had to be worked out, and these demonstrations were mainly a demand for fair play. If the Germans could cheer for victories, so could the British; if the Germans chose to boast, the British had the right to laugh at them. And when, a month later, an officer posted up a fantastic British account of ill treatment at Ruhleben, the prisoners conceded that a point had been scored against them. The war inside the camp was beginning to resemble a football game.

Good sportsmanship, in fact, was now the cardinal virtue in Ruhleben, as sport was the dominant interest. A short football season had ended on May 17, preparations for cricket were under way, and Whitmonday, May 24, was celebrated with a great programme of athletic events. The kitchens produced a gala dinner of meat, potatoes, gravy, and peas, and Italy's declaration of war on Austria turned the feast into a festival. When the German officers, in spite of the news, turned out in a body for the races, the men agreed that they too were good sports.

April brought social security to the poorer prisoners through official British approval of the relief payments made by the Embassy, and the weekly amount was raised to five marks. It was ostensibly a loan to be repaid after the war, but those who signed the receipts soon did so automatically and no attempt to collect was ever made.

That economic differences still existed, however, was shown by the opening in April of the "Summer House Club" in a small building behind the grandstands. Use of it had been privately granted to some well-to-do businessmen, and there was an entrance fee of ten marks and annual dues of twenty. The club's amenities were modest; a few small rooms for reading and card playing, a fenced garden for deck chairs, and a white-coated steward who served tea, Oxo, and synthetic lemonade. But the quota of a hundred members was quickly reached.

So incongruous an innovation as the "Snobs' Club" aroused much biting comment: "WANTED, by member of Summer House, respectable young man to fan him during the summer months and fetch his relief money" (*IRC* 2, p. 21). And its expensive privacy was directly challenged by the man who posted the following notice:

BURIED TREASURE—WHERE IS IT?

200 paces east of the market place the more exclusive prisoners have erected a pleasure house. Here they find the hours pass smoothly and easily as an idle dream, the sight of their less fortunate companions screened from them by a wooden palisade.

Not five yards from their jealous wall our emissary stopped, drew a five-mark note from his pocket, and *buried* it. Will the finder kindly write his name and barrack at the foot of this notice. Another competition next week. (S)

It was only five months since the internment, and this blatant violation of solidarity was something of a shock. But so much was changing, and so quickly, that all public criticism of the Summer House was humorous or satirical; anything more serious would have seemed *gauche*.

And there was a real demand for such clubs; the Summer House was followed by the Corner House, Phoenix Club, 25 Club, and various others, housed mostly in sheds constructed against barrack walls. Exclusiveness was never the chief motive; to escape from the din and smells of the barracks into fresh, uncrowded surroundings where one could smoke with impunity—this was something like a periodic vacation. Only Ewing among the informants belonged to the Summer House; he wrote in July:

I am writing this in the "Club" of which I have become a member. 100 of us have a small enclosure where one can get a little quiet. The place is really a comfort, one can work in comparative peace, and we have some nice nasturtiums and books.

Exchange rumours were remarkably scarce in April and May; on April 7 there is a solitary item, "release by May 15," but from then until May 25 diaries and letters contain nothing. Then a speech by Bonar Law in favour of exchanging all for all started a flurry, and on the 26th

Henley felt "very optimistic." Alleged confirmation from the usual "sources" kept these rumours alive until June 4; we hear of no more until July. Thus, except for Bonar Law's plea, which would have started rumours at any season, these months of new activity and growth were practically undisturbed. The camp, it seems clear, produced its rumours when they were psychologically needed.

Most of April was cold and wet, but from the last week onwards spring came into its own. May was warm and sunny, the trees were all in leaf by the middle of the month, swallows were building under the barrack eaves, and a chorus of frogs in the little pond kept up an interminable chanting. Many of the barracks had made gardens, and the effect of a few flowers were almost magical.

Spring, however, also had its drawbacks. April's letters are the first to complain of the dust in the compound, and on May 14 a veritable sandstorm broke several windows. It scarcely rained for two months after April 18, and every breeze whirled the dry soil into hair, eyes, teeth, and nostrils. From the middle of May mosquitoes plagued the prisoners, and were replaced in July by millions of flies. To some men spring brought inner discomfort too, by intensifying homesickness. Ewing writes in April: "Carol's card which came yesterday nearly made me weep. Think of daffodils and lunch on the moor! Well, some day." On the whole, however, the spring letters are buoyant, especially when describing camp activities. Ewing had written a fortnight earlier: "The time goes very quickly. Am studying a bit, writing a play and preparing a lecture. Everyone is much more cheerful with the coming of spring. Our next attack of depression will come about August, I fancy." His prediction was surprisingly accurate.

An amusing event of May 11 was the great census. Daily counts were made in each barrack, but the grand total had never agreed with the alphabetical list of prisoners. So the Germans decided to find out once and for all who was in the camp. It was two o'clock on a hot afternoon when the men were marched onto the field and arranged, with tremendous difficulty, in alphabetical columns according to surname. Then the fun began. Count after count was made by the perspiring soldiers, each with a different result. Almost four hours passed before they gave up, the last official figure being 4,168, still at variance with the list of internees. The Lancastrian *Minutes* suggest that the Earl of Perth had been listed under E, under P, and again under his family name of Drummond. In any case, the attempt proved that the prisoners were literally innumerable—at least by German privates—and it was never repeated.

June was a fine month, its first two weeks unusually hot and dry. Summer outfits of light shirts, trousers, underwear, socks, and shoes had been distributed at the nominal price of one mark, and as the heat increased the men left off hats and socks and rolled up their shirt-sleeves. In general they went no further; the sunburned appearance so often mentioned was confined to those areas which could properly be exposed on an English tennis court in 1914—face, neck, and forearms. The cult of sun-bathing was still regarded in Britain as immodest and smacking of "continental morality." In Germany, however, it was well established, and many of the prisoners had been brought up there. On May 26 a group started basking on the racecourse in trunks, and were viewed with immediate disfavour by Chapman: "Watched the cricketers at the nets, then read and dozed and watched the naked fools in the *Luftbad*." The performance was not markedly indecent, and Ruhleben was a male community. But it did contain one woman, Baroness von Taube, and her windows overlooked the field. The lady did not notice the moral lapse— or kept it to herself—until June 2, when she complained to her elderly husband with explosive effect. The whole camp was drastically punished by the closing of the field, which was only reopened on condition that costume be thoroughly *anständig*. Further complaints and punishments followed, however, and the camp police had ultimately to censor the prisoners' dress.

Sun-bathing had everything to recommend it in Ruhleben, and many conventions had already been flouted. Its flavour of impropriety, however, plus the fact that the pioneers were pro-Germans, turned opinion against it. Graham wrote: "Sun-bathing had to be prohibited, and I quite agreed that it was too much of a good thing." The magazines always made fun of the practice: "STOP! Don't throw away that old pocket-handkerchief! We can make complete sun-bathing costumes from it. Apply Wyldmann & Co." (*IRC* 3, p. 43.) And in another issue there is a sketch of a young man whose only offence is wearing abbreviated shorts and leaving the front of his shirt open. But the caption reads: "Miss Maud Allan and the Venus di Medici were respectable young women compared to some of the men in this camp!" Mrs. Grundy had arrived in Ruhleben; a month later she was able to ban a debate on legitimizing "war-babies."

June's atmosphere is well conveyed in this letter from Graham:

June 15, 1915. I feel settled here indefinitely and am quite resigned and comfortable. Cricket is being played on matting wickets on the ground inside the race-course, where football was played up to Whitsuntide. I am sure I am putting on weight, and you would be sorry to see me disgustingly fat as a result of the lazy life here. The fine weather has made everybody sunburnt, and we must look a very healthy lot of people. So I suppose we are. Most of the barracks have made small gardens and have bought flowers to beautify the place, so now one sees crowds of people lolling in deck chairs in the gardens.

This might come from a health resort, and the hundred captured trawlermen brought in the previous day must have found Ruhleben a pleasant haven. The month also brought welcome improvements in the opening of an enlarged hot-water house and of the new latrines—though the apertures in the latter, according to the Lancastrian *Minutes*, revealed lamentable ignorance of British anatomy.

Then June gave place to July and a subtle change came over the camp, unsettling everyone's emotions. Even the weather seemed involved, for after one hot week the long-delayed rains poured down and continued until August. The first sign of unrest was a violent outbreak of rumours, shattering the serenity of the previous weeks and marked by symptoms that became proverbial—a fall in attendance at classes and a sudden rise in the number of tins heated at the boiler house. Rumours are first mentioned on July 2 as "very vivid"; next day *La Belgique* reports that the Dutch Government has arranged immediate exchange; on July 4 they are "very acute," and by the 5th they receive the usual confirmation: "Exchange imminent—Baron's opinion, soldiers say so in P.G. barracks, *La Belgique*, English papers, letters from England, kitchen people not buying any new stuff" (Farwell). On July 10 Henley notes, "Terrible week for rumours of all kinds," and on the 16th, after a short break, the *Reichsanzeiger* announces that negotiations have been resumed. No one, of course, saw any of these newspapers, but their contents were on every tongue and excitement was intense. Then on July 17 Farwell and others report that the Ruhleben lease expires in September and the prisoners are going, not to England, but to Döberitz or Holzlinden. This was a dash of cold water, and no more was heard of exchange for the rest of the summer.

The only negotiations actually in progress were for release of certain chronic invalids, so this outbreak must be mainly attributed to a change in the camp's mental climate. And in its physical climate first—for the precipitating factor, this year and later, seems to have been the men's awareness that the evenings were beginning to shorten, that winter was on the way. Behind the spring's cheerfulness had lain always the cherished hope that the war would end before another winter, but that hope, though no one yet admitted it, was dwindling. On July 1 it was rumoured that *The Times* had summed up the war situation unfavourably, and every day the German papers reported great victories in the east and attacks bloodily repulsed in the west. On July 9 Denton wrote:

> We are all rather depressed here; the family is not very flourishing, is it? Poor old Nick has had his appendix removed, and while Frank and John are working hard, they are not making much, it seems, and expenses are terribly high. Michael really seems to be in the strongest position, and sends a great deal of help to his family and friends. I see that he is at present sending tremendous subscriptions to his friends who are in business with Frank.

The code—Nick for Russia, Frank for France, Michael for Germany, etc.—was a transparent one, but although the letter reports troop movements to the western front (always observable from the camp) nothing was deleted. Letters were "sterilized" by being held ten days before despatch, and actual censorship was often perfunctory.

All are depressed, says Denton—but about the war; no writer has yet put into words the fear of a second winter. That is still only a shadow in the background, kept out of consciousness by the flood of exchange rumours. In mid-July, however, the rumours dry up, the shadow becomes a reality, and every letter refers to it:

> *July 14, 1915.* It has been much cooler lately and we are turning our thoughts to winter. . . . I had a touch of the 'flu or something last week. It is astonishing how black your thoughts get in surroundings like ours when you get run down. (Abbot)

> *July 15, 1915.* After many weeks of dry weather we have now got rain, and the aspect of the camp reminds us of winter, which is not pleasant. (Graham)

> *July 23, 1915.* There seems no prospect of getting out before next summer, if then. It is not nice to think of. We are all a bit low at present; I hope it won't last, but prospects are not rosy. If one could *only* get out and help! Nothing else seems important now. (Ewing)

Such extracts can be misleading, for the same letters contain many cheerful pages about camp activities. On the other hand, what *is* said of emotional tension is usually understatement, most men tending to minimize their worries when writing home. Depression, however, was clearly abroad, and lasted in some cases well into August, perhaps reaching its climax around August 4, when the first anniversary of the war saw the Germans capture Warsaw. Ewing, who seldom conceals his feelings, writes in that week:

> *Aug. 8, 1915.* I am quite well, but find it hard to keep cheerful. Every one of us is feeling the same just now, the reaction after the high hopes of spring, and the more and more certain prospect of another endless winter. Forgive

my writing so sadly; I have put this letter off several days already. I don't expect my depression will last long.

As the days went on, however, and the possibility of another winter became a certainty, it turned out, as always, that the certainty was the easiest to bear. It is when an issue is still unresolved that emotions are most troubling; certainty, of whatever sort, calms us by permitting some definite action. Even early in August, when Ewing was most depressed, those actually preparing for the winter were far more serene:

July 31, 1915. Now, as to clothes. We are all thinking of next winter, more especially as July has been rather a cool, wet month, and the days are noticeably shortening. (Graham)

Aug. 3, 1915. I think October is rather early for this business to end, in fact most of us are making ourselves as comfortable as possible for the winter. (Abbot)

And the letters of later August are quite resigned in tone:

Aug. 15, 1915. Since I last wrote we have had Bank Holiday. Permission was granted for all kinds of shows to be erected, and the recreation field looked like a miniature "Temperance Festival." We were able to take our minds off current events for a day, and I am sure it did us a lot of good. We are doing our best to make our quarters as comfortable as possible before the cold weather sets in, and have been doing quite a lot of carpentry. (Abbot)

Aug. 17, 1915. It is not pleasant to look forward to another winter, but we may be sure that it will be less disagreeable than the last. (Graham)

Aug. 27, 1915. We now have a whole street of shops nicknamed Bond Street. New sheds are going up and there is a rumour of a photographer. . . . We look forward to a prolongation of our stay, not with pleasure, but with resignation and the hope that we are suffering in a good cause. (Graham)

There is nothing to show at what date Ewing accepted the inevitable, but when September and October came, with their busy round of activities, he wrote as cheerfully as the rest.

This was the basic emotional rhythm of Ruhleben, a seasonal cycle, established in 1915 and little altered thereafter. Through each winter the men buried their hopes, busied themselves with camp affairs, and waited for spring. When it came, with its regular Allied offensive, their spirits rose to sanguine heights. But the spring offensives of 1915, 1916, and 1917 accomplished little, and the hopes of victory slowly drooped and died. And in 1918 it was the Germans who attacked. Then came the summer solstice, and with it the unbearable thought of a further winter in the stables. It was in July that the days became noticeably shorter, and each July the same sequence of readjustments began. First an imaginal reaction, a period of delusions; the men said in effect, "We won't believe it," and hid the spectre of another winter behind a cloud of exchange rumours. Figure 3 shows how uniformly this happened. Then, as the rumours evaporated, came an emotional reaction of depression and protest; "We can't face it." Finally there was the practical reaction, "Let's do something about it," and preparation for the winter relieved the tension. Hopes were put forward again, and the cycle recommenced.

The pattern was identical in 1915, 1916, and 1917; in 1918 an actual conference about prisoners set off the rumour explosion a month early. There were wide individual differences; some men struggled for months against accepting another winter, while others started preparing for it as soon as the midsummer madness had run its course. The latter were railed at as pessimists, but in Ruhleben it was the pessimists who were the most contented citizens.

We now return to July 1915 for an important turning point in the camp's social history—the great badge controversy. A number of "territorial" societies had been formed early: Scottish, Irish, Welsh, Lancashire, Yorkshire, Australian, Canadian, and various others. Most of them were primarily "Old Boys' Associations" and had been dormant during the winter, but with spring they began signing up new members in case of a sudden Allied victory. In March a more inclusive society was organized: the Ruhleben British Association or R.B.A., whose purpose was "to keep green in the memory of all our stay here, for all time and all the world over." It proposed to unite all the local societies and its activities were to be well nigh boundless: annual dinners in every corner of the globe, a permanent club in London, employment agencies, "substantial cash discounts" to fellow-prisoners, and so on. In other words, the universal comradeship of the early days was to be perpetuated —an aim with the strongest emotional appeal.

The smaller societies, unwilling to be absorbed, ridiculed the R.B.A.'s grandiose programme, and at a further meeting on March 29 this was more modestly formulated. A Ruhleben directory would be published, dinners held where convenient, and all members issued with a moderately priced badge, "possession of which would be proof of their having been detained as civil prisoners in Germany at the time of this war" (H). The wording was significant in view of the prisoners' guilt feelings, their secret dread of the question, "What did *you* do in the Great War?" The badge was to be their alibi.

"A lot of tall talking," was Burton's comment on this meeting, and no more was heard of the R.B.A. until July. But the idea of a badge was attractive, and eight of the local societies began taking orders for badges of gold, silver, bronze, and "metal," one side to bear a common design, the other that of the society concerned. The Lancastrians were not among them—characteristically, they had decided to "go it alone"—and there was no mention of the R.B.A. On July 18, however, its promoters called another mass meeting in a final attempt to capture the movement. It was a bad moment; the great rumour season had just ended, the men were restive, and a resurgence of old emotions turned them into a disorderly crowd.

Fervid oratory opened the meeting, and amid deafening cheers all the clichés of solidarity were paraded: the utter invincibility of Britain, the cruel injustice of internment, the dauntless courage of the prisoners. When the badge question was raised, however, boos and cat-calls mingled with the cheering. Prices secured from England for the four metals ranged from 2.50 to 28 marks; was this not an invidious distinction, emphasizing differences rather than solidarity? Loud voices were raised against it, and Mr. Cohen aroused frenzied applause with his superb peroration: "*One* Empire, *one* flag, *one* badge, *one* metal, *one* price!" Another worthy, whose guardian angel must have been off duty, argued for the original proposal, pointing out that badges would be worn on watch-chains, and that lesser metals would not look well if the chain happened to be a gold one. His objection was natural, and so was his toying with his own watch-chain as he made it, and the result must have astonished him. From every corner arose jeers and laughter so raucous and prolonged that the meeting had shortly to be adjourned. Not for months was he allowed to forget his innocent remark; the magazine caricatured him with an enormous chain, labelled "GOLD," across his waistcoat, he was incessantly asked the time, and in his barrack someone posted up the hours at which the offending jewellry would be on public view.

Ruhleben, however, was becoming a public, and more sober discussions followed the meeting. A common misgiving is reflected in this pencil notice, decorated with facetious badges:

TO BADGERS!
Men! Why run the risk of stopping your comrades' relief money?
Is it justice to yourselves, your comrades or your country, to spend half a week's money on such baubles?
Any commonsense person will say if you have money for badges you need no relief.
Be men and not mugs! (S)

At the adjourned meeting these criticisms were answered in alarming fashion. The R.B.A., it appeared, had already drawn up a letter to the British Government, asking whether, in view of the money coming into the camp, they would object to funds being sent to England. A grossly impolitic inquiry, it seemed to many, but such a letter was actually sent —it was never clear by whom—and drew a frigid reply from the Foreign Office. And there was worse to come. During the meeting another issue was raised. Perhaps—who knew?—the Government themselves planned to award medals to the Ruhleben heroes, thus making badges unnecessary; a tactful inquiry would therefore be made on this point also.

This was too much. There were still clear heads in the camp, and on July 29 this notice was posted:

RUHLEBEN BADGES
You must hear the short, common-sense speeches on the above subject to be delivered in the Town Hall at 2 p.m. today.
No personal attacks, no ragging. The matter affects your own position with the outside world. (H)

This meeting was brief and businesslike; Mr. Prichard was in the chair and only four speeches were made. The first speaker opened by saying that, if the letter asking about a Ruhleben medal expressed the opinion of the majority, it was time the camp was run as a lunatic asylum. The other speeches were equally direct, and the following resolution passed with one dissentient:

That this meeting calls upon the camp to act consistently with the maintenance of good relations with the American Embassy at Berlin and with the authorities and people in England. It regards as undignified and inopportune the application to external authorities for badges, and trusts that all associations in the camp will agree with this point of view. (*IRC* 5, p. 17)

The camp had come to its senses and the movement was dead. The meeting, however, was only the *coup de grâce*; the mortal blow had been struck earlier by the man, whoever he was, who first referred to the badges as "medals." The label was more deadly than any argument, and it had been so shrewdly used that the meeting of July 29 found the ground completely prepared. *In Ruhleben Camp* took an unequivocal stand; the issue that went to press on July 25 carried a strong editorial, a full-page portrait of the gentleman with the watch-chain trying to pawn it, a series of sarcastic designs for medals, and several further items.

The controversy also produced the greatest flood of anonymous notices in Ruhleben's history, new ones appearing daily on the boiler house and latrines. Most of them were the work of the intelligentsia, arguing cogently against the badge movement, ridiculing its promoters, and displaying witty but insulting designs for the various societies. But the seamen were equally aroused, and two of their productions should be quoted, if only because so little such material has survived. Both are in pencil on small sheets of paper; punctuation is unaltered:

BADGES AND MEDALS

Gussy saw some fine bright medals
Advertised for sale one day,
And he said. I'd like a medal
Just to wear on life's rough way.

Billy heard young Gussy's saying
And he said, there is a way
of getting medals without fighting,
All you've got to do is—pay.

Then a crowd said, yes we'll have them
And we'll wear them on our clothes
But a JACK TAR—cried out boldly
Why, they'll stink beneath your nose.

Don't you know that ITS FOR DUTY
And for fighting for the King
And for love of Home and Country
That ENGLISH die for such a thing.

(S)

MEDAL MANIA

Have you heard the latest news?
If you have, then don't refuse
Going to the meeting "HUGE"
This Sunday morning meet.
Speeches will be made to masses
Which will suit gold medal classes
And to men with brains unsound
Voices will proclaim all round
That medals BOUGHT by prison bands
Are tricks not worthy of the land
Of Valour—known as ENGLAND

Men there are whose fads are great
Some want gold, and others plate
Some want silver, some want bronze
Some enamel, No, that's wrong
Such common stuff as that, won't suit
The Swells that "Golf" with patent boot
But men there'll be who'll plainly tell
Those "medal cranks" to go to hell.

(S)

Class feeling was seldom so openly expressed as in the second outburst, but its appearance is not surprising; gold badges were to cost 28 marks, and the promoters of the R.B.A. were mostly business executives.

The societies fought hard for their badges, but their plaintive tone suggests a lost cause:

> What have the associations done? They have sought to meet the desire of the great majority of men in the Camp for a simple yet pleasing souvenir of their stay here. . . . A souvenir is only a symbol of something . . . a souvenir is not a medal. . . . Between a souvenir and a medal there is a world of difference. (*IRC* 5, p. 30)

And, in a manifesto from seven associations: "We hope our members will not allow themselves to be stampeded by a word" (H). The stampede had taken place, however, and it was a word of five letters that caused it. Chapman's diary is revealing. On July 10 it reads: "Attended meeting of Canadian Club, called to decide on badges." His view is not stated, but the club's decision was favourable. On September 2, however, he writes: "Canadian meeting at 9.30 but couldn't go. Gave them my name as not wanting a medal. Am not in the habit of *buying* medals." The unconscious shift from "badge" to "medal" is nice evidence of social control.

The reaction was fatal, not only to badges, but to the societies; with one exception they passed into oblivion.[1] The exception was the Lancastrian Association, which had been canny enough to hold aloof from the movement. Its unsullied reputation (and generous flow of parcels) gave it three more years of active life in the camp, and on repatriation its executive calmly issued—a badge. It was the only Ruhleben medal ever struck.

The episode marked Ruhleben's graduation from unreflecting solidarity to conscious responsibility. The self-importance and emotionality of the crowd had been again displayed, but this time only to be resisted. The prisoners were growing up; in future, though still susceptible to fads and crazes, they acted like adults in all serious matters.

And even their hankering for badges had a meaning we should not overlook. Three thousand names were once on the rolls of the R.B.A.; to that host of men their internment had not been a nightmare they wanted to forget, but an experience of comradeship so stirring that they

---

1. The present Ruhleben Association is in a sense the legatee of the Ruhleben British Association, but it was founded independently after the war, never issued a badge, and confines its activities to an annual dinner in London on each anniversary of the internment.

wanted to remember it always. If they showed some lack of perspective in their enthusiasm, it was partly because Ruhleben meant so much to them.

The same week that saw the collapse of the medal movement provided further outlet for crowd excitement in the "Ruhleben Bye-Election" arranged by the Debating Society. A proclamation issued over the seal of "Mayor" Butterworth had brought Conservative, Liberal, and Suffragette candidates into the field; committee rooms were opened, and the camp was plastered with posters and banners. The open-air meetings, however, were so rowdy that the captains timidly forbade any more, and the campaign fell rather flat. In the voting the Suffragette candidate obtained a not unexpected majority. His opponents had held out free beer, electric tramways, vast sums in compensation for internment, and similar inducements, but Mr. Castang confined himself to one topic which is sufficiently indicated by his last speech, here given in full:

"Wouldn't you like to have girls, boys?" (Cries of "Yes!"). "Wouldn't you like to have fun, boys?" (Cries of "Yes!"). "Well, then, boys I'm going to give you girls and give you fun—hundreds of girls and buckets of fun! That's my ticket, boys—girls and plenty of 'em. Just you stick to me and you'll be all right. Three cheers for the girls, boys, and bless their little hearts." (Wild cheering.) (RBE, p. 29)

Although this was not precisely Mrs. Pankhurst's programme, it went over well in the camp of 1915.

The rest of the period may be treated summarily. August saw one remarkable event—a strike by the actors and musicians against the captains. Its causes will be dealt with later; like the medal controversy it was a sign of the conflicting social forces now at work in the camp.

The Baron was still using the field as a means of control, closing it on August 21 because of the escape of two youngsters from the Boys' Barrack. They spoke no German, got only to Charlottenburg, and were let off with three days in cells. One of them left a note pinned to his bed, "bequeathing" his relief money to a friend! The field was again closed on August 22 because of a recrudescence of sun-bathing, and when a drunk was arrested a few days later the Baron threatened to close it for good. These tactics were particularly irritating because the field was rented with British money; fortunately the Baron was gradually weaned from their use.

On August 21 a small cinema was opened at one end of the grandstand hall; Powell, who had been in the business, put the project through and arranged a weekly change of German films. This was the sole Ruhleben recreation that was completely passive, and it appealed only to a limited number who could find nothing else to do.

The last two weeks of August were very rainy, but September was a beautiful month with day after day of fine, cool weather. And it brought one change of great importance. On the 15th Graf Schwerin suggested to Powell that the German guards be removed from the barracks and internal control be taken over by the captains and police. Barrack meetings were held, the plan approved, and the captains informally confirmed in office; and next day Ruhleben received a large measure of self-government. It was not entirely a concession to the prisoners; the Graf admitted to Powell that his 250 soldiers were more trouble than the 4,000 British. Some tough customers were always having rows with prisoners, and others were regularly bribed to smuggle in liquor and other contraband.

The chief benefit of Home Rule was the increased sense of responsibility it gave the prisoners. There was little more freedom, for the captains took their duties seriously, police whistles were imperious, and the German guardroom was still in the compound. Orders, however, were less arbitrary, and it is easier to obey one's own officials than aliens. And living in purely British barracks and marching to the kitchens without a military escort gave the men a feeling that Ruhleben was more truly "theirs," and encouraged them to exploit all its possibilities.

September closed on a cheerful camp. No one now hoped to escape a second winter, but the Allies were advancing in Artois and the exchange of invalids had been speeded up. So the sound of whistling mingled with hammer blows as amateur carpenters made their quarters more comfortable. On September 24 cricket ended with Barrack 10's victory over the rest of the camp by the huge score of 673 to 509—a spectacular match, in which G. L. Crosland made 331 runs before a crowd that included most of the camp. Next day football began—the official end of summer for Englishmen—and on the 26th Denton wrote:

I am keeping well, and we are all taking a more hopeful view of things after the terrible August depression. We have to look a year ahead, however, to see any light. Many invalids are being exchanged now; seventy this month. I am afraid I shall not come under that heading. Well, cheer up, it must end some day. We are all delighted to hear about Jack and Frank taking such a good turn, though it does not make things easier here. We would gladly starve, however, if it could go on.

The events of October all had to do with the activities we turn to next; sport, study, and music were in full swing, and after the 20th, when new lighting was installed in the hall, the theatre reopened with unprecedented success. A few extracts from letters will give a final glimpse of the prisoners at this time.

Oct. 3, 1915. The second time I've seen autumn in Germany, and still no sign of the war ending. My month's holiday has certainly been of varied interest, and I shall have reason to remember it. But the peace which must come will come eventually, so cheer up. (Jarvis)

Oct. 6, 1915. Eleven months today and all smiling. I hope you are too— what else is there to do? This morning twenty unfits left by the morning train. There are a good many whose claims are better than mine. . . . Am now going out for a constitutional, then evening papers, then supper at 6, then probably a game of cards, then bed at 8.45, up again at 6.30, and so we go on. (Graham)

Oct. 18, 1915. We have just started the second football season in Ruhleben, and hope that it will be the last. There is much more interest taken in hockey this year. I hope through plenty of exercise to keep fit this winter. Our lodgings we have made very much more comfortable too. (Abbot)

Oct. 19, 1915. All are resigned to this winter now, and hope the spring will end it. We have to have some date to look forward to. I am keeping very fit, and will stick the winter all right. The shower-baths in the morning are nice, though cold, a great improvement over last year. No lights in boxes, however, so the day is very short. Dark today at 3.30, and raining. The meals are not bad now, had really delicious porridge for supper tonight, and the Sunday meat is excellent, if microscopic! (Ewing)

Oct. 20, 1915. A great quantity of carpentering has been going on in the barrack during the last few weeks. Everyone fitting up and making themselves comfortable for the winter. Even the heating of the barracks has begun. We get along well, with an occasional breeze over such questions as having the window open or not. (Graham)

Oct. 31, 1915. "Mr. Preedy and the Countess" had a six days' run last week, and an extra free matinee of it was given yesterday for a number of poor fishermen who had just arrived from Sennelager. They find Ruhleben rather like heaven! We have had a great frost this week, everything ice. Six inches of snow the day before yesterday, still on the ground. But the heating is on, so it isn't so bad. (Denton)

And so November came and winter settled down over the racecourse. On Saturday, November 6, the Ruhleben Express Delivery, an inter-barrack postal service established in July, cancelled all stamps with a special postmark: "One Year of Captivity, 1914–1915." And the same day, after warm farewells and countless repetitions of "See you soon," 140 invalids left for England. Their train started from Berlin, and as it passed the camp again it was white with fluttering handkerchiefs. Those left behind cheered and waved and watched it out of sight; then they turned back to the barracks to begin their second year in Ruhleben.

10

THE COMPARATIVE CHEERFULNESS with which the prisoners faced a second winter betokened a significant change in their mental orientation. Internment had split their universe into two unconnected parts; the great world outside and the little world in which they lived. At first the outside world had been the "real" one, from which they felt temporarily cut off, but in time the balance shifted and camp life became more real than anything else. The shift was predictable, for sooner or later direct experience was bound to get the upper hand over the pale reflections conveyed through letters and newspapers. But it was made relatively easy after the spring of 1915 by a tremendous enrichment of Ruhleben life.

Behind the events described in the last chapter there was occurring an outburst of spontaneous activity that turned the prisoners' interests more and more towards camp affairs. They began exploring the possibilities of Ruhleben, discovered numberless things to do, and set themselves eagerly to organize and perfect the doing of them. And in the process they created a network of social activities so extensive and absorbing that the camp became a world in itself—sometimes *the* world. The causes of this sudden expansion will be best considered when we have surveyed some of its dimensions, and sport will provide a good starting point.

The playing of organized games is so traditional in Britain as to seem almost instinctive, and the Ruhlebenites had not been twenty-four hours in their compound before an improvised football game was in progress. German objections and the snow and mud of the winter put a stop to open-air games, however, and the break lasted until March 1915, when the playing field was rented from the Ruhleben Company. A roar of delight greeted Powell's announcement of the contract on March 20, and a veritable eruption of sport followed.

March lies in the British football season, so football had the right of way—football of course meaning soccer. Two fields were laid out, first and second teams organized in fourteen barracks, and an exhibition match opened the season on March 28; two weeks later Henley tells us that no fewer than eight league games a day were scheduled. There were scores of first-rate players, including several professionals, and the matches attracted huge crowds. Barrack 1, captained by Steve Bloomer, a veteran international player, won the league, and Barrack 4 the cup competition that followed. In June cricket began with equipment from Germany and England, and play was remarkably good. First and second league matches continued until the end of September when Barrack 10, the champions, defeated the rest of the camp in an exciting match. Then, with October, football recommenced amid undiminished interest.

These were the major sports, but enthusiasts for other games clamoured to share the new opportunities. Rugby football began on April 5 and five teams played regularly until the hot weather. Field hockey started on April 25 and was played for three more seasons, and from April 30 onwards the field was opened from 8 to 9 A.M. for the many golf professionals, the "course" consisting of five makeshift holes with criss-crossing fairways.

Tennis players had to wait until near the end of the summer, when the Ruhleben Company allowed seven courts to be laid out on the straight section of the race-track; fees were high, but all costs were covered in the first season and a hundred players entered the September tournament. Again the camp possessed many experts and their matches were eagerly watched. Rounders was played in a corner of the field, lacrosse and *la pelote* were seen on occasion, and from 1916 onwards Sunday baseball games, organized by Canadians, became popular. Bowling and horse-shoe pitching were unknown, but a form of skittles, played in the compound with sawn-off chair legs, was a pastime of the older seafarers.

Periodic programmes of field sports were arranged, and in April there was an invitation hundred yards race which aroused so much interest that one bookie was unable to pay up. Entries for the Field Day on May 24 necessitated four days of preliminary heats; sweepstakes were numerous, an Olympic runner showed beautiful form, and Barrack 7 amassed the highest total of points. Over a hundred men did "physical jerks" every morning, boxing was popular and well organized, and fencing appeared a little later.

Many hundreds of prisoners were now pleasantly occupied, whether as players or spectators, and the whole atmosphere of the camp was enlivened. Gribble points out that the sports "supplied an immediate in place of a remote interest" (22, p. 166) and in 1915, at least, the thoughts and feelings of more men were probably shifted towards camp affairs by the games than by any other innovation.

The prodigious amount of sport was of course partly due to the fact that every day in Ruhleben was a holiday. But it also reflected the keenness that Abbot refers to in November: "There is a lot of keenness in the sports, in fact it is the only thing—bar parcels and letters—that keeps us healthy and in fair spirits." This eagerness for activity brought out scores of men who had not played games or run races since their schooldays.

Team games are highly organized activities, but they can be played without formal organization, and the first football games in the compound were as casually arranged as corner-lot baseball. The programme of 1915, however, obviously required organizing, and sport was soon surrounded by a multitude of clubs, committees, and subcommittees which drew in numbers of additional men. The Ruhleben Football Association, Cricket Association, Rugby Football Club, Lawn Tennis Association, Hockey Club, Boxing Club, and Golf Club were all formally organized, and their many officials were kept busy arranging schedules, appointing referees, dealing with protests, and keeping the grounds in shape. But this was only the beginning, for each barrack was also organized for football and cricket, sometimes in a single society like the Barrack 9 Sports Club, more often for each sport separately. So in every corner of the camp secretaries were calling meetings and writing minutes, treasurers collecting dues and keeping books, and selection committees watching the form of their players and revising the teams before each match.

These formal arrangements, unlike the games themselves, were not the expression of long pent-up energies. The activities of large numbers of men had to be co-ordinated, and the prisoners simply adopted the means familiar to them, that of setting up organizations for the purpose. It was an obvious step, but it was also a critical one, profoundly affecting the activities themselves and changing the whole character of the camp.

The sudden urge to be active which produced such a wealth of sport was equally evident in the intellectual field; indeed, more men participated in educational pursuits than in any other organized activity. We have seen how early some diarists were studying languages, and private work of this sort, though sharply restricted by lack of space, had continued all winter. Leslie writes on March 15:

At the end of the week I am giving a little lecture on Keller to a circle of friends, though for a serious study of the man the books of reference are lacking. . . . In the afternoons I usually work with a college friend of mine, who is studying the same subject as I am. (P. 48)

The pioneer organization in this field was the Arts and Science Union or A.S.U., formed in December 1914 as a body of university graduates. It later opened its membership to all in sympathy with its aims: the arrangement of public lectures and the facilitation of private study and creative work. With space for study unprocurable, the A.S.U. fell back on lectures in the grandstand hall, the first being the address on *Parsifal* that appeared so incongruously amid the hunger and tension of January. There were others in February, two or three a week in March and April, and in May things really began to move. The A.S.U. took over the third grandstand and twenty open-air lecture courses were soon under way. The list was as follows (*IRC* 1, p. 28):

Calculus	Agricultural Chemistry	German Literature
Elementary Physics	Radioactivity	(in German)
Electricity and	Mechanics	Italian Literature
Magnetism	Elementary Biology	(in Italian)
Inorganic Chemistry	Heredity	Shakespeare
Organic Chemistry	Psychology	Euripides
Electrochemistry	Music	Alfred de Vigny
Sugar Chemistry	English Literature	

Most courses met twice weekly, they were well attended, and three "popular" lectures each week drew great crowds.

There was clearly no dearth of lecturers; A. T. Davies speaks of "two hundred interned professors and teachers" (p. 30), Gribble says "enough to staff Trinity College, Dublin" (22, p. 67), and Filmore's "Samuel Pepys" observes: "But indeed there is in this Campe such a collection of Anticke Fellowes who prate on all manner of Subjectes, such as were never before assembled together in one place, nor ever will be again" (*PP*). And the professionals were later reinforced by a large number of men whose first experience of teaching was gained in the camp.

The programme was of university calibre, as Denton notes with pride in a June letter:

The university is in full swing, with excellent lectures on all sorts of subjects by men of great attainments and ability. Bainton, of the Royal Academy, gives an interesting course on music, and I also attend Shakespeare, English Literature, and various popular courses. I have hardly ever a free moment.

And the curriculum was steadily expanded. In June courses were added on the human body, hydrostatics, and conic sections; in July Mr. Pogson began his astonishingly popular class in Mandarin Chinese, and in August Henry Brose, a physics student, started a course on the dynamics of a particle.

The number of science lectures will be noted; they were largely inspired by H. S. Hatfield, an electrochemist of much originality and wide interests. And the Ruhleben physicists deserve special mention. Brose was in his early twenties when interned, as was James Chadwick, who gave the lectures on radioactivity; Charles Ellis was a schoolboy of 19. All three continued their work in makeshift quarters in the camp, and after the war the latter two went on to Rutherford's laboratory at Cambridge. Brose became Professor of Physics at Nottingham, Ellis at London, and Chadwick of course discovered the neutron in 1932 and became Nobel laureate in 1935.

In August, too, J. C. Masterman, now Master of Worcester College, Oxford, began his lectures on "The Development of England as a Great Power"; of these the magazine says in October: "Mr. Masterman's lectures have, without doubt, been the most popular in the camp, and the size of his audience has been no less extraordinary than the variety of its composition." The sudden thirst for learning was not confined to any one group, and Masterman's audiences of around three hundred included almost every element in the population.

The range of intellectual fare was soon widened. In June, after a heated debate, the A.S.U. took over the Monday nights in the grandstand hall, and began a series of literary, musical, and scientific evenings that were among the most rewarding public events in the camp. The usual form was a paper followed by illustrations, and the standard was generally high. The first evening was devoted to English folk-songs and morris dances, the second to modern English poetry. Then there was a French evening with music and a one-act play—"the prettiest thing we have seen yet," according to the magazine—and a recital of English madrigals, the first finished choral work produced. The series continued until a month before the Armistice, with illustrated lectures on the Maoris, evolution, food products, vaccination, and venereal disease; chamber music evenings, two-piano evenings, evenings of modern music, Russian music, Brahms, and Hugo Wolf; and evenings on the Greek drama, Shaw, Synge, Wilde, Chekhov, Ibsen, and many others. A great deal of work of artistic value but limited popular appeal was produced, and groups of men were kept constantly busy preparing future programmes.

Even yet the intellectual thirst was not slaked. Men with particular interests were finding one another out and seeking more specialized and technical discussion than public gatherings could provide. The June 1915 announcement of the A.S.U. stated: "A weekly meeting of biologists, chemists and physicists on Wednesdays at 6 p.m. has been arranged for the purpose of hearing papers on subjects of mutual interest, to be followed by a discussion" (*IRC* 2, p. 2).

Other such groups may have been formed earlier—indeed, the Scots Literary Circle claimed, naturally, to have preceded everyone else. Sticking to the record, however, we read of a Spanish circle early in July, and also that the Marine Engineers' Association (M.E.A.) then held its first lecture, on diesel engines. The audience numbered a hundred —but one of them, Mr. Pepys, should apparently not have been counted: "By mischance I was directed to the wrong chamber, and was compelled, for one Houre of the Clocke, to lysten to a Lecture upon Diesel hys Engynne, to me most tedyous" (*PP*). Italian and French circles soon appeared, the Science Circle was formally organized, and by the end of September at least ten were meeting regularly. As the M.E.A. minutes put it: "Our lecture evening, which we commenced in a very modest way, has grown into a proper craze." Whoever started the movement, it clearly filled a need, for besides those mentioned the following are recorded:

Technical Circle	Shakespeare Circle	Scandinavian Circle
Deutsche Zirkel	Business Circle	Irish Literary and
Banking Circle	Celtic Circle	Historical Circle
Nautical Circle	Old Ships' Circle	Woollen and Worsted
English Circle	Social Problems Circle	(or Textile) Circle
History Circle	Anglo-Russian Circle	

Most circles met weekly for a paper and discussion, and the language circles also went in for readings, debates, and conversation. *Il Circolo Italiano*, under Mr. Prichard's stimulation, set a record by meeting three times a week; it later published its own journal, as did the M.E.A., while the Technical Circle duplicated digests of its lectures. The circles varied in size, and attendance fluctuated, but some hundreds of men at least were provided with new and interesting activity. Three minute-books yield the following figures:

Circle	Period	Members	Meetings	Average Attendance
Marine Engineers Assn.	1915–18	130	23	66
Technical Circle	1915–18	109	92	29
English Circle	1916	50	35	19

Many circles arose independently, but on September 11 all agreed to affiliate with the Arts and Science Union. Space for the winter was secured in the cinema, the circles bearing the cost of sound-proofing the partition between it and the hall.

The specialized nature of these groups suggests the new divisions appearing in the once solid camp; individuals were gravitating more and more towards those of like interests with themselves. In a list of circles published in the fall of 1915, two announce that they are "limited to persons who can contribute in their turn a paper of interest to the circle" (*IRC* 9, p. 2). Selection was already effective in sports and other fields, but this is the first reference to a camp activity from which some of the comrades of 1914 were formally excluded.

The intellectual outburst of 1915 would have led to chaos had it not been organized. The A.S.U. had the usual quota of officers, a large general committee, and various subcommittees, and during this growth period its officials were among the busiest people in the camp. Each circle also had officers and a committee, though with one exception: "The circle which meets to consider the question of social problems has, we feel, already taken a great step in the direction of reform by declining to have a committee" (*IRC* 9, p. 6). Apart from such rare comments, however, the epidemic of organization that attended the prisoners' expanding activities was taken completely for granted.

The impulse to learn was not all absorbed by the Arts and Science Union; another institution, the Ruhleben Camp School, ultimately surpassed it in scope and numbers. The school was originally an offshoot of the A.S.U., but a divergence in aims was soon apparent and mutual references in print are somewhat acid. The A.S.U. was the stamping ground of the "Supermen"—young intellectuals with a passionate belief in education, but little experience of teaching and no patience with fools. There was, however, an enormous demand in the camp, not only for lectures on Dante in Italian, but for straightforward instruction. A "Ruhleben School of Languages" flourished in the spring of 1915, as did a business school organized by Mr. Wimpfheimer; both were later absorbed by the Camp School. But the school was no mere tutoring establishment; its curriculum ultimately ranged from elementary level to first year university work and beyond; its improvised laboratories were startingly effective, and it resembled, as Farmer says, "a mediaeval university more than anything else, for one could learn anything there" (p. 397).

On its organization in January 1915 the school circularized the prisoners to find out what they would like to study. Eleven hundred forms were returned, covering a wide range of subjects and usually asking for three classes—the maximum allowed; for lack of space only a few classes in boxes could then be started. In the spring, however, the school moved to the third grandstand with its broad tiers of seats, and here its growth struck the rapid tempo we have seen elsewhere. By the end of June, 50 classes were meeting, comprising some 500 men, and teachers were urgently needed, especially in languages. A magazine report shows that French classes were most numerous, with English, Italian, Dutch, and Spanish also being taught. German is not mentioned, but Professor Patchett, a bearded and energetic philosopher, was discussing *Faust* in that language before a large audience. (The topic was apparently inexhaustible, for the professor had only reached Part II by the spring of 1917, and the war ended before he could finish it.) Two classes for ships' engineers had about thirty students each, the same number were studying mathematics, there was some elementary physics, and shorthand and bookkeeping had just started.

The school's further progress was meteoric. By mid-August classes numbered 75, with 700 pupils; at the end of the month numbers passed the hundred and the thousand mark respectively; on September 12 more than 1,500 were registered. And numbers were well maintained; estimates of enrolment in 1916 range from 1,000 to 1,400, and a 1917 prospectus lists 246 teachers in 17 departments.

In the fall of 1915 winter accommodation was provided by the handing over of the loft of Barrack 6. It was hastily partitioned into classrooms and gradually equipped with home-made furnishings, students meanwhile bringing their own chairs. A small grant had been secured for running expenses, but the school was forced to appeal to the camp for funds to adapt its new quarters. The magazine remarks:

The Camp School is at present the most popular and, we venture to say, the most useful institution in the camp; will the appeal for funds damage its popularity? We trust not! The School is of far more use than even the Football Clubs, and we hope to see it as readily and generously supported. (*IRC* 8, p. 6)

The appeal brought in 1,500 marks, the A.S.U. transferred its lecture programme to the school, and the latter entered on the winter as the camp's sole teaching organization. The A.S.U. restricted itself henceforth to its cultural Monday evenings, the activities of the circles, and the allotment of betting booths or "cubby-holes" for private study.

This huge programme of adult education required much organization, and the school was well organized. Each department was represented on the governing committee until 1917, when control of general policy was given to a committee of five and the department representatives became the Board of Studies. In addition there were various subcommittees and permanent officials. The chairman of the school committee, until his release in 1918, was A. C. Ford, later of the University of London; his enthusiasm and organizing ability were primarily responsible for the school's success. An enormous amount of administrative work was involved: enlisting teachers, enrolling pupils, securing space, arranging time-tables, keeping records of attendance, progress, and expenses —all in addition to the actual teaching. Scores of men were kept busy and officials were often badly overworked. Practically all this labour was voluntary; a few teachers who lacked funds were paid five marks a week for a time, but almost the whole school budget went for plant and equipment. Occasional donations were made, and from 1916 onwards students were asked to contribute. Ewing writes: "The expense now makes fees of 25 pf. a week necessary; surely there is no school in the world where such instruction can be got so cheaply."

Books were of course needed; the language text-books of Otto, Hugo, and Berlitz were ordered in hundreds through the canteens, and a large amount of reference material was shipped from England under the British Prisoners of War Book Scheme. Ruhleben seems to have been its chief beneficiary, to judge by this 1917 report:

RUHLEBEN—To this, the best known of all the camps, continuously since July, 1915, a steady stream of educational books, numbering many thousands, have been sent for the reference and class libraries established there and also to individual prisoners. An account of the highly organized educational work which has been made possible by these and other gifts would fill a volume. (10, p. 29)

By April 1916 over six thousand such books were in the Reference Library and various departmental libraries.

Though the values of study in internment are obvious, the school's enrolment of 1,500 pupils in a few months can hardly be put down entirely to rational decisions. One out of every three prisoners has this summer been transformed into a schoolboy, and sailors, engineers, jockeys, and businessmen are carrying text-books in their pockets, studying vocabularies in the queues, and struggling with homework in their boxes. It is an extraordinary metamorphosis, and its suddenness suggests that education, like autograph collecting and "medalomania," has become a craze, a matter of suggestion rather than sober choice. This view gains support from a certain instability among the students; the magazine editor notes a "deplorable tendency to coquette with a number of subjects and really to study none" (IRC 9, p. 6), and Govett's "Phoebe" says: "We suffer here from a peculiar migrating variety of the genus pupil. . . . They float about from lecture to lecture, from

language to language, and end up as silly as they started" (*IRC* 6, p. 3).
A September letter from Ewing is particularly revealing: "My Italian
is getting on well and I can babble a little now. I don't know why I'm
learning it, but everyone is studying something." In spite of increasing
social divisions, the prisoners were still impelled to do what everyone
else was doing.

The school's great achievement, therefore, was not the enormous
registration of 1915, but rather the fact that it was able to hold on to
most of these recruits and transform a passing fad into a lasting and
serious pursuit. We shall learn later how this was accomplished.

If the lectures and classes of 1915 gave Ruhleben the air of a university town, there was also enough extra-curricular activity to make
one wonder when people did any studying. The swollen athletic schedule
has been noted, with its league games morning and afternoon every
day of the week. But that was not all; the "students" were also running
a theatre four nights a week, with a good orchestra in the pit and a
brand new production every Wednesday.

The group of amateurs who had been so successful with *Androcles
and the Lion* at once planned further work, having first as a matter of
course organized themselves as the Ruhleben Dramatic Society, or
R.D.S. They, too, had a full set of officers, a general committee, and
a testing committee—indeed, they had several within a few months,
for the dissensions of this lively period were particularly sharp among
intellectuals. The second production was to have been another Shaw
play, *Arms and the Man*; but the German authorities, who kept a wary
eye on the stage, shied at the title and declared that no militaristic plays
would be tolerated. The plea that Shaw was not preaching militarism
but satirizing it did not seem to help; the ban was emphatically confirmed. Undiscouraged, the actors substituted a home-made revue,
calling it in revenge *Legs and the Woman*. Ruhleben's chorus girls,
however, had not yet been discovered, and the sailors pronounced the
title grossly misleading.

On April 18 the R.D.S. produced Galsworthy's *Strife*, and in May
Captain Brassbound's Conversion was very well done. Short plays by
Stanley Houghton followed, and in June a more ambitious offering, the
forest scenes from *As You Like It*, showed that the theatre had real
artistic possibilities. The play was staged against curtains in several
shades of green, to incidental music by Bryceson Treharne, one of
several interned composers. The magazine says: "To many lovers of
Shakespeare it has given an entirely new and delightful conception
of one of the most delightful of the plays" (*IRC* 2, p. 28).

The R.D.S., however, no longer had the field to itself. On April 10 an Irish folk play had been presented with great success, and ten days later the Ruhleben Irish Players were organized and preparing their next production. The music-hall artists staged a variety show in April which appealed vastly to the rank and file, and in May a revue directed by two professionals took the camp by storm and had to run for two weeks. The Ruhleben Song was introduced, to be whistled for months to come, and the first "girl" chorus appeared, captivating the audiences with its costumes, dancing, and falsetto singing. The lyrics, set to current rag-time, had a direct appeal:

> Down in Ruhleben, there I want to be,
> Four thousand boys would be enough for me!
> For we're the girls, girls, girls,
>   And we would charm you
> With our curls, curls, curls—
>   We wouldn't harm you
> But we'd kiss you now and then,
> You could tell us when,
> We'd fool around and fool around
> And then we'd kiss again!

There was of course a great reservoir of responsiveness in the male audiences, but this does not account for all the pride that the Ruhleben "girls" aroused. The camp had many good-looking boys, a professional ballet master, and unlimited time for rehearsal; under such circumstances female impersonations can be startlingly successful. Denton wrote: "I wish you could see our 'girls' and their costumes and acting. They are really marvellous. The new arrivals refused to believe they were not real."

Then at the end of May, only six weeks after the pro-German trouble, a musical comedy in German, *Der Fidele Bauer*, was skilfully produced, well attended, and heartily applauded. And by September the Ruhleben Society for German Drama and Literature had joined the array of dramatic societies, which now also included the Société Dramatique Française de Ruhleben. The magazine commented: "We cannot vouch for the authority, but we are informed that forty new theatres are being put up in the camp in order to cope with the supply of Dramatic Societies" (*IRC* 2, p. 15). By April 1915 the theatre was already "full" —that is, enough productions were offered to keep it running continuously—and it remained so, apart from incidental interruptions, until 1918.

The high level of performance maintained over three years required a well-developed technical organization, with its stage managers and make-up men, prompters and property men, scene painters and shifters, costumers, wig makers, call-boys, carpenters, electricians, ushers, and ticket-sellers. Adding to these the actors and producers (32 of the latter attended a 1918 meeting) we have a good-sized body of men now busily and purposefully occupied. Nor must the audiences be forgotten; dozens of letters attest the theatre's contribution to Ruhleben life. Graham writes in December 1915: "Most of us, including myself, are well and lively, and I expect we shall have a jolly Christmas. We are to have a grand pantomime, and indeed I find an occasional visit to the theatre the best relaxation."

Music, as we know, was one of the men's first recreations; unlike sports and education it needed no more space than the grandstand hall could provide, and by April the concerts had developed considerably in scope, if not in finesse. Letters still speak of the orchestra and choir as "Adler's," but the existence of other conductors was no secret and there was an undercurrent of criticism. Ruhleben in fact was more richly provided here than in almost any other field; a whole flock of British musicians and students had been caught at Bayreuth and elsewhere, at least a dozen of them well known then or later as conductors, composers, or performers.

On Good Friday, 1915, orchestra and chorus presented the Haydn *Passion*, following it on Easter Day with a Stanford *Te Deum* and Mendelssohn's *Lobgesang*. The closing concert of the "season" took place on May 23, and Adler, after handing the magazine an ambitious programme for the fall, disbanded his force until September. It was a tactical error, for in June the orchestra was re-assembled under a Scottish conductor, J. Peebles Conn, and a series of open air "Promenade Concerts" began. Each Tuesday evening that summer the musicians sat on the first grandstand, with the prisoners around them or on the promenade below, and Mr. Conn conducted overtures, waltzes, and other light music. The magazine's editor was delighted: "Real good popular music it was, and played in first-rate style, too, and didn't it go down with the people!" (*IRC* 3, p. 7). In October the winter season started again, with concerts every Sunday night—orchestral programmes every third week, chamber music and recitals between them.

A change had taken place, however; the musicians had organized and Adler's monopoly was broken. The magazine describes gleefully "the curious spectacle of a band of musicians trying to be businesslike while they founded a society of their own," and adds: "It is rather regrettable, by the way, that they forgot to give their new society a name—still, you can't remember everything" (*IRC* 2, p. 41). Owing to this oversight the society, which had some forty members, was sometimes called the Ruhleben Musical Society and sometimes the Ruhleben Society of Professional Musicians. It now took charge of the concerts and gave all qualified conductors their chance with the orchestra. Later it also secured facilities for practice by building a shed and renting a piano; this partially met a need that had been acutely felt, for instrumental technique is highly perishable. From now on music was a constant feature of camp life, the musicians keeping in form and gaining experience, the prisoners enjoying a series of first-rate concerts until a few weeks before the armistice.

Art was less strongly represented at Ruhleben than music, but a few professional painters and a number of students and amateurs were interned. They, like others, had been finding one another out, talking their own brand of shop, and longing for the feel of brush or pencil in their fingers. Only heroes could have worked under the winter conditions, but spring released the artistic impulse as it did so much else, and men began sketching in uncrowded corners. In June the fever that was raging struck here also, and Ernest Hotopf wrote to his colleagues asking them to submit work for an exhibition. To some the suggestion seemed fantastic, but musicians and actors were doing remarkable things and it almost appeared that nothing was impossible in Ruhleben. So the artists got busy, the exhibition was held from July 12 to 14, and the catalogue listed over two hundred items, many of them humorous sketches that sold well. And the show was a popular success; Chapman's diary reads: "Went to Art Exhibit but didn't go in because of the crowd."

This venture established an esprit de corps and encouraged the group to tackle their chief problem, that of space to work in. In the fall of 1915 they built themselves a studio at the west end of the compound, and it became the centre of the camp's artistic life. It had at most some twenty-five members, not all active, but the amount of work turned out was astonishing. There were at least ten more public exhibitions, every theatrical production was advertised by striking posters, and the magazines contain page after page of sprightly and well-executed drawings. Few small towns since the Middle Ages can have had so productive a group of artists.

Besides the above activities, which either began or grew enormously in 1915, the debates and religious services continued to occupy a number of men without noticeable expansion. One might expect the formal discussion of shopworn topics to lose its attraction as new pursuits appeared, but the Debating Society had actually a longer life than any other camp institution except the church. Beginning in December 1914, meetings continued until October 21, 1918, and regularly drew good crowds. This was partly because the debates were free, well run, and varied with literary and musical evenings, and partly because they appealed to a section, mainly of seafarers, whose needs were somewhat overlooked by other organizations.

About organized religion only one thing need be said: that the wave of enthusiasm which swept men in hundreds to games, lectures, plays, and concerts passed religion by. Its mass appeal had been earlier, when the prisoners were hard pressed and anxious; in this period of buoyant activity Protestant congregations at least were dwindling, and magazine advertisements plead for better attendance. Development was taking place, but it involved only a restricted circle and consisted chiefly in multiplying the services and elaborating the rituals. These trends will concern us later.

Camp jobs increased rapidly during this period and contributed their share to the "full employment" that Ruhleben had come close to attaining. The municipal organization adopted in May 1915 brought fresh faces into the bureaucracy, the heavy flow of parcels doubled the parcel staff, and when Home Rule was granted in September the police force was reorganized and enlarged. By that date there were close to two hundred "civil servants" keeping the community running.

Their status and duties were proclaimed by badges; postmen, parcels post staff, and many junior officials wore large buttons in their lapels, each policeman had a numbered button plus the blue and white striped arm-band of the London "Bobby," and the captains were resplendent in white arm-bands embroidered in red with their title and barrack number. So much British regalia must have threatened to outshine the Kaiser's uniforms, for on June 17 the Germans guards convulsed the camp by themselves appearing in red, white, and black arm-bands, stamped with the numbers of the barracks they controlled.

Badged officials worked without pay, but 1915 also saw a great increase in paid jobs as new fatigue parties were formed, the kitchens and canteens taken over, and hot water and other services established. The wages came out of the camp fund, which was underwritten by the British Government, administered by the captains, and kept in balance by the profits of theatre, canteens, and other enterprises. Pay was nominal—around ten marks a week at most—but some prisoners were glad of it, and the jobs also provided occupation for those who had no urge to study French or discuss social reform.

Ruhleben was now an extraordinarily busy town—how busy is suggested by two other developments of this summer. The Ruhleben Express Delivery or R.X.D. was established in July by an imaginative entrepreneur; stamps of several denominations were printed in Germany, postboxes in each barrack were cleared six times daily, and the same number of deliveries were made to the recipients' addresses. The first magazine announcement says: "WHY WASTE TIME in rushing around the camp looking for your friends? Drop a note in the R.X.D. letter-boxes; it'll only cost you ½d." In its opening month the R.X.D. handled 5,151 pieces of mail—secretaries of organizations found it invaluable—and business improved so much later that parcel post, registered letters, and even special delivery were added.

Then in August we find a full-page advertisement of the Ruhleben Supplies Delivery, offering to buy and deliver canteen orders for busy prisoners on a 5 per cent commission. "No more waiting in line for an hour! No more long queues in the cold & rain! No more breaking engagements!" (*IRC* 4, p. 44). Six messengers were employed (twelve on Saturdays) and by the end of the month the R.S.D. was also paying its way and had established a record of 260 orders on one Saturday. Had an internal telephone service been possible it too would have prospered in this humming internment camp.

The explosion of activity that marked Ruhleben's first spring and summer was a turning point in its history, for it settled the camp's final character—that of a busy, productive, and highly organized society. Apart from personal friendships, Ruhleben is best remembered for its thrilling football and cricket games, its notable lectures, concerts, and plays—for these, and for the men who achieved fame in them. None of these activities, however, was decreed by the Germans, none was necessary to survival; one may well ask, therefore, what drove the prisoners into them.

Various answers have been given, for the phenomenon was not confined to Ruhleben. Cohen-Portheim describes rather cynically the sports, lectures, and plays at Wakefield, and Vischer writes: "In the civilian camps in the early days great eagerness for activity reigned; clubs and schools were founded, organizations created" (p. 22). The ordinary person asks no explanation; he takes it for granted that idle prisoners will seek occupation, and only wonders what they found to do. Psychologists should be interested, however, and in Ruhleben the outburst was so sudden and intense that the prisoners themselves were curious about it. We saw Ewing's puzzlement as to why he was studying Italian, and in August 1915 an anonymous poem put the same question to the organizers:

WHY

Thank you, thank you,	Which was,
Captains all,	Compared to what shall be,
Supermen, and Button-men,	Or e'en now is,
Deans of Universities,	Thank you.
Thank you I must	But why?
When I think on that	Why do you do it? . . .

(*IRC* 6, p. 34)

The motives of leaders will be touched on later; what about the mass participation sketched in this chapter? Suggestion may explain the rapid spread, but that is all, for no suggestion is accepted that does not meet some need. What need? Vischer plumps for a Freudian answer: at the beginning of internment the *libido sexualis* is still lively and impels a passionate search for substitute activities. This is too general to be helpful, however, since it would account equally well for any form of human activity. The same is true of Cohen-Portheim's observation that "people unable to continue their real work in life . . . would go mad without some sort of occupation" (p. 94); it at least suggests why civilians are particularly affected, but "some sort of occupation" misses the point. For it is clear that just doing something was not enough for the prisoners; it had to be something "interesting," and that raises further questions.

What a given person will find interesting clearly depends upon his previous experience; the musician is more likely to be interested in Bartok than the accountant. More specific statements are hazardous, for the precise meaning of "interest" has always eluded psychologists. But the activities that the Ruhlebenites found so interesting in 1915 had at least two things in common; they all provided *changing* stimulation, and they all involved *purpose*.

No one will doubt that the prisoners needed a change after the first winter; the varied excitement of the opening days had soon given way to routine, and even box relationships tended to become habitual, though slowly and with many exceptions. In any case, nothing could prevent the days being tedious while everyone was waiting—waiting for something he could not hasten by one minute. Certain events, however, stood out sharply against the general monotony—the pioneer concerts, lectures, and plays; and when these were extended in the spring, and sports added to them, waiting was often forgotten and boredom almost banished. For these were activities of a different type; so changing and unpredictable in themselves that they could never become matters of habit, and offering as well almost unlimited scope for further development. Whatever "interest" may be, it is such constant change of stimulation that sustains it.

Even a movie, however, provides unceasing change, whereas the camp cinema, after its first few shows, was usually sparsely attended. The prisoners needed something more; they needed to be active, and their activity had to be *purposeful*. The social disruption of internment had been largely made good, but not the temporal disruption; the men's future was still unstructured and they lacked any concrete goals. The universal goal of release was of no energizing value except to the few who planned to escape; for the rest it was only something to wait for. What was urgently needed were goals on which the men's powers could be immediately directed—attainable goals, like winning a game, learning a language, putting on a play. And these were what the spring provided.

The purposeful activity that followed did more than make camp life interesting, for purpose is the great organizing agent of the personality, establishing priorities among its motives, giving direction and focus to behaviour, and so unifying and stabilizing the self. An aimless life is a disorganized life, and ultimately a demoralized one, for without some goal one way of acting is no better or worse than another. These were of course the chief dangers of a long, meaningless internment, and the series of mental breakdowns showed their reality. Only an infusion of purpose could avert them, as Sir Gilbert Murray asserted in commending the British Prisoners of War Book Scheme:

> The reports which I have heard . . . have almost always the same burden: the men who fill their days with some purposeful occupation come through safely; the men who cannot do so, in one way or another, break or fail. The occupation must, as stated above, be purposeful; it must not merely while away the time, like playing cards or walking up and down.

We have yet to see how the paltry goals available in a prison camp acquired enough value to arouse any whole-hearted purpose, but when they did so the men possessed a sovereign remedy against the worst ills of internment. How welcome it was after the winter's stagnation was shown by the huge popular demand, and enthusiasm was heightened by a sense of limitless possibilities as the rich resources of the camp came to light. Here were four thousand people, equipped with most of the knowledge and skills of civilization, and faced for the first time in their lives with a cultural vacuum. No wonder they rushed in to fill it.

A more personal need, too, often underlay the search for new activity —the desire for fresh and more stimulating contacts. Box life could itself be stimulating, but it had to be conducted on a level appropriate to all, and in mixed boxes this meant subordinating some individual interests. The neglect was not felt during the crisis period, but after that the past gradually reasserted itself and individuals began to seek for others who shared their previous interests. The man whose thoughts had for weeks been monopolized by stable life and rumours of release began, as things settled down, to recall that he was not only a prisoner of war but also a professor of music. Here and there he found others with similar backgrounds and spent increasing time with them, talking less of the dreary racecourse and more of Covent Garden or Arnold Schönberg. It was a refreshing change; he began to feel that he still counted for something as an individual. A rich growth of these informal contacts preceded organization in almost every field, and "shop talk" often led on to group undertakings.

Thus the need for activity also reflected the deeper need to re-discover one's self, to emerge as a person from the anonymity of the crowd, the jealous equivalence of the horse-box. Reminiscent conversation was not enough, since former achievements had lost much of their meaning; for full self-recovery the individual had to act in and on the present, and that is what great numbers were now doing. It is through such purposeful action, however, that the self is formed and developed; hence participation in camp activities had unforeseen consequences. Instead of merely recovering their old selves in the new surroundings, the active prisoners created somewhat new selves, Ruhleben selves, often differing substantially from those they had left behind. And for many this was a revealing and exciting experience.

If Ruhleben, as was suggested earlier, ceased to be a prison, it was because of the organized activity that this chapter has described. One cannot be consciously a prisoner while playing centre forward on a football team or translating Goethe in class. In so far as the men immersed themselves in the new roles offered them—and on the whole they did so eagerly—they ceased to feel themselves prisoners. Not all of them and not always, of course, but many of them and for much of the time. How this change of roles was actually brought about is our concern in following chapters; meanwhile the reader will not be startled by the assertion that Ruhleben was, during much of this period, a surprisingly happy camp.

11 | THE ORGANIZED CAMP

TO BE REASONABLY HAPPY a good part of the time was no small achievement in Ruhleben; few human beings, however situated, can do any
better. And the factors most obviously responsible were the new activities of 1915. Activity as such, however, possesses no magical powers;
had the Germans *forced* the prisoners to play games and attend classes,
these would have seemed only outrageous impositions. What actually
made internment bearable and even enjoyable was therefore a change in
the men's outlook; things that could be done in the camp had suddenly
become important and well worth doing.

To understand this change we must turn to social conditions; once
physiological needs are met, it is they that determine attitudes and
behaviour. Personality of course plays its part; some men cannot respond to even the most favourable conditions. But in Ruhleben, where
severe strain threatened even the strongest personality, the emphasis on
social factors was strikingly vindicated. That so many men found their
internment a stimulating experience and so few, relatively, were broken
by it must be put down squarely to the social climate of the camp. To
its general friendliness first, no doubt, but still more to the invigorating
changes that occurred in 1915. That, at least, is the argument of this
book.

A wealth of new organization had sprung up around the expanded
camp activities, and we are now going to look at it functionally, for its
effects on the prisoners. These were complex and far-reaching, but their
net result was that the men could lead a *purposeful* life in internment
and thus preserve their mental integrity. This was no simple matter, and
requires a brief discussion of what was involved psychologically, of the
changed character of camp activities, and of the vital role played by
organization. Then we shall turn to Ruhleben's chief institutions—sport,
education, and the rest—for a concrete picture of how camp life became
purposeful and satisfying.

To form a purpose is to have a goal, and the problem was to find goals within the camp that would be acceptable to men whose only wish was to get out of it. Once accepted, such goals would set up tensions in the individual that could be released only on achievement, and this would keep him alert, active, and mentally sound.

What sort of goals were needed? Long-range ones wherever possible, since prolonged, directed effort makes for stable mental organization. And the goals had to be attainable ones; the common goal of freedom set up plenty of tension, but the tension was destructive, since nothing could be done to reduce it save by those planning escape. Too easily attainable goals, however, would not serve either; some uncertainty was required to arouse tension and effort. The goals offered by the new activities—football leagues, dramatic productions, courses of study—clearly met these criteria; they were long enough in range to create sustained purpose, and their attainment was fraught with stimulating uncertainty; the game might be lost, the play flop, the student fail to master French verbs. Finally, to be seriously pursued, the goals had to seem important and worth the effort; they had to be "values." This was the crucial problem, for what real value could attach to the petty diversions of a prison camp? The solution was of course a social one: through group participation and elaborate organization, what had been mere ways of killing time were imbued with high importance and value.

The acceptance of long-range goals required that the prisoners do something they had never done before the spring of 1915: look forward to an extended future in the camp. This implied more than the weakening of belief in quick release; it also implied the existence of a stable social order. Only a fully organized society could provide a predictable future, and so encourage long-range goals; and only such a society could supply the incentives and controls that inconstant human beings need to keep them steadfastly at work.[1] Thus the complex social structure in which all the new activities were embedded had psychological as well as practical functions.

Relinquishment of the hope of early release was a drastic readjustment; some men were never able to make it, and most of the Type I breakdowns (see Chapter 8) were probably found among them. But the relative absence of exchange rumours after early March shows how profoundly the general attitude had altered. Fresh outbreaks came only with the intolerable prospect of each further winter; otherwise exchange rumours practically disappeared. Each passing month, of course, had

1. S. E. Asch emphasizes the dependence of purpose on social organization in a remarkable chapter, "The Transformation of Man in Society," of his *Social Psychology* (New York: Prentice-Hall, 1952).

been a silent argument against the likelihood of complete exchange, and March 3 brought an official statement that negotiations had been broken off. Its effect, however, would have been short-lived if it had not been followed by the outburst of activity described in the previous chapter. Interest was directed into new channels, the longing for release became less urgent, and the balance was finally tipped by a startling development: the explicit condemnation of rumours by the prisoners themselves.

Even in January *The Oracle* had headed a column of "DON'TS" with: "DON'T spread rumours—DON'T listen to them!" And, as more and more men became purposefully occupied, they sensed the inherent contradiction between their healthy activity and the seductive hopes of repatriation. Moved by sound instincts, they resolved it by putting a ban on rumours. Mahoney describes this as the work of "the more level-headed members of the community," who administered punishment to offenders ([3?], p. 43), and active prisoners were certainly the first to feel the danger of rumours. But there is no other report of sanctions, and the development was almost entirely spontaneous. The men simply found themselves indignant at rumour-spreading; it had become a reprehensible act, almost an immoral one.

This was different from the protective scepticism adopted by many during the winter, for to communicate a rumour now aroused definite feelings of guilt. What had emerged was another group norm, a collective response to a new group need. The social world that the Ruhlebenites were now building rested on the shaky premise that the camp would last for some time; exchange rumours denied this premise and so had to be outlawed. Though they embodied the dearest wish of every individual, they were a threat to the group, and the group placed a taboo on them. It was of course broken, but even the transgressors bore witness to it by their new formula: "Now, *this isn't a rumour*," they began, "but one of my boxmates heard the Baron say to Mohr . . ." and so on in the familiar strain.

Rumours might be effectively controlled, but uncertainty remained, for the Ruhlebenites were serving an indeterminate sentence. If there was no news of exchange today, there might be tomorrow, or the war itself might suddenly end. This was the greatest obstacle to the development of the camp, for it tended to rivet the men's attention on time and how to deal with it, thus reducing their activities to the status of *pastimes*, devoid of intrinsic value. That is precisely the picture that Cohen-Portheim gives of Wakefield Camp:

One need do nothing, but doing nothing is possible only to very wise or half-witted men. . . . So everyone almost did something and occupied himself in some manner. Time here really had to be *killed*, for it was the arch-enemy, and everyone tried to achieve this as best he could. (P. 91)

To Portheim, as may be supposed, all the busy activities of his fellow-prisoners were futile and meaningless. Vischer's conclusions are no different; the feverish activity in civilian camps is only a way of passing the time and sublimating sexual drives; it quickly flags and reveals its emptiness. At least one writer, Geoffrey Pyke, described Ruhleben in similar terms—though he was, significantly, one of the few who escaped to England. And a deadening sense of the futility of camp occupations was often felt by others; a busy prisoner would look up from his work, catch a glimpse of the world outside, and ask himself: "Why am I doing all this? What good is it?" Almost invariably, however, he turned to his work again, partly because of his obligations to others, but also because camp pursuits had somehow been lifted above futility and invested with real importance.

They had no such importance initially; apart from the utilitarian tasks of officials and traders, none of the early activities had been more than ways of passing time. An exception must be made for active participants; the Christmas *Messiah*, for example, was an important event to the players and singers. To the camp at large, however, it was a mere curiosity of internment; except for two perfunctory references, the letters and diaries ignore it completely, as do the *Camp News* and *The Oracle*, which appeared early in January. Most of the men's attention was still focussed on food, physical conditions, and the prospects of release.

In the summer of 1915, however, a momentous change took place; camp activities ceased to be simply pastimes and became, for many and for a long time, absorbing and valued pursuits. The change is well illustrated in Leslie's letters to his mother. In April 1915, after describing his informal studies and some early French teaching, he added: "You see, there is no lack of interest, but much of it is a mere attempt to fill in the time with a minimum of loss to oneself and others" (p. 53). Here, however, is what he wrote in April 1916:

I have not yet told you of my paper to the Historical Circle on Jeanne d'Arc. . . . The writing of it has been a revelation to me. Of course I am not interested in the politics of the period for the sake of historical knowledge; what is really helpful is to have been brought face to face with this beautiful, sincere, pure, clear and simple figure. (P. 144)

And again, three months later:

Several of my friends who speak French well and love it, have now under-taken to give fortnightly lectures to my class. . . . My chief aim is to make others feel that their study of French is leading them towards something which nothing but France can give, and that they can already make French thought a living help. (P. 163)

Both Leslie's scholarly eagerness and his long-term aim for his class are worlds removed from any "mere attempt to fill in the time"; study and teaching are now values in themselves and means to further values. The same metamorphosis occurred in every field of activity; instead of wondering how to pass the time, hundreds of men wondered this summer how to find time for all they wanted to do. And winter brought no slackening; Denton wrote in December, acknowledging a parcel of books: "Your books were very well chosen, though Scott requires a great deal of time, which is the one thing we have *not* got here!"

The transmutation of pastimes into values was obviously the saving of Ruhleben; the busy, keen prisoners of 1915 and 1916 were as solidly protected against mental deterioration as if they had never been interned. The change was not effortless; to avoid thinking about release often required great determination. And it was made possible only by the deeply social character of all the new activities. Goals already sanctioned in British culture were set up afresh and jointly pursued by *groups* of prisoners, working together; and the common enterprises were given importance and stability by formal organization. It is no accident that Leslie's first statement refers to teaching that was still scarcely organized, his others to a circle and a Camp School class, respectively.

All long-term purposes are caught from groups, which generate values and goals that have, like other norms, immediate validity for every member. British values, whether concerned with "keeping the chin up" or producing Bernard Shaw, could thus have no force in Ruhleben until they had been re-discovered—in fact, re-created—in the crowd or in some smaller group. Even the earliest purposeful activities bore this social hallmark; men with kindred interests got together and hatched out in common the plans for a service, debate, or play. Leadership was of course involved—someone always made the first suggestion—but the plan had to be "ours" rather than "his" to arouse sustained purpose.

The early activities were social in a second sense too, for their primary aim was to brighten the hard winter for others. Until music, plays, and lectures became institutionalized this was their chief driving force; indeed, only men whose motives were altruistic could have faced the disheartening obstacles encountered. Both these social incentives are mentioned in the letter of a scientist who was one of the first lecturers: "I personally lectured because of my love of the work and because I like studying in company—and also on account of a desire to help" (L 37).

Such pursuits as painting or carving ship models could of course absorb a prisoner without group support, but only if he had already acquired the goals and skill; even so, he nearly always gravitated into some congenial circle. And few of the men who began studying "on their own" would have persisted for long without the massive backing of the Camp School. Thus the problem of infusing serious purpose into as many prisoners as possible appears in a new light; it was a problem of getting them into groups, the purposeful groups called associations. And that meant organization, and on a heroic scale.

To many people the word "organization" has dreary connotations—of tedious committee meetings, perhaps, or of the forbidding organizational charts so dear to big business. This is a pity, for every scientist knows that organization is actually the key to the understanding of the universe, from its basic constituents to the nature of life itself. Electrons, atoms, cells, are only building blocks; all the endless variety of nature depends on how they are organized together. For organization results in the emergence of new properties; oxygen and hydrogen "behave" differently when combined as water, and water accordingly has properties that neither oxygen nor hydrogen possess. And similarly, the motives, perceptions, and behaviour of human beings alter when they are organized into groups, and the groups themselves behave in ways not wholly reducible to individual terms.[2]

The transforming effects of organization are nowhere better seen than in the team game. A score of boys randomly kicking a football about are not organized; what they are doing is pleasurable, but it is clearly a pastime, of no felt importance and arousing little purpose or effort. They act as they feel inclined and quit when they are tired. Organize a game, however, and the whole picture changes. Two "teams" take form, each made up of individuals playing differentiated but co-ordinated roles. Purpose appears, the winning of the game, and its pursuit is regulated by the rules and conventions of football. The boy's attitudes change dramatically; personal inclinations give way to team play, and each one strives towards the common goal. And, depending on the degree of integration, each team behaves like a single unit rather than a collection of separate individuals.

2. These facts explain, of course, why the laws of physics are of little help in predicting the behaviour of living organisms, and why the sociologist or political scientist need not be a psychologist. Every level has its own distinctive phenomenon.

What accounts for the increased drive shown by the players, their sudden keenness and seriousness about the game? Each is now part of a valid, if temporary, social organization, and is therefore functioning under the most stimulating conditions known to us: he has acquired identification with a group, a distinctive role within it, norms to observe, and a goal to achieve. The goal is a group goal, which immediately makes it a value to him, and the tension that urges him towards it is sustained by the fact of organization itself. For the game is a temporal as well as a social organization, binding into one inclusive pattern everything that happens from the first whistle to the last. Until it ends, the pattern is incomplete; it cries out for what the Gestalt psychologist calls "closure." This sets up strong psychological pressures towards completion, the stronger because two incompatible forms of closure are possible, each desired by one side. Hence the players put forth all their skill, the bystanders cheer them on.[3]

This familiar illustration epitomizes what happened to the Ruhleben prisoners in the spring of 1915. Organized social goals aroused high motivation, and everything the men were doing gained fresh significance in relation to them. A fumble by a cricketer was "important," for it might lead to an extra run, the run was important for its bearing on the game. But was winning the game really important? It was quickly made so by simply extending the temporal organization, so that the game was only one of a series culminating in the "championship." Much more than sport was affected, of course; every committee meeting, school class, and circle session was now part of some larger social and temporal organization. And no one, fortunately, questioned the ultimate goals of these institutions—whether winning the *championship* was important, for instance. The mind has its limits, and once an organization is sufficiently extended in space and time the value of its aims appears self-evident. That millions of people are more exercised about the World's Series than about averting nuclear destruction may seem like blindness, but it shows the effects of elaborate organization.

And in Ruhleben, with its special problems, these effects were wholly beneficial. The men's sole defence against four years of deadly futility was to discover real importance in their camp occupations, though even a glance at the warring world made them seem trivial if not reprehensible. Study and artistic work could be partly justified by their intrinsic

3. The game as a temporal organization is discussed in my paper, "Time, Values, and Social Organization" (*Canadian Journal of Psychology*, 1951, *5*, 97–109).

value, but sport—"playing games while humanity was crucified"—was deeply vulnerable. Ewing, a cricketer, but with a brother in the trenches, wrote home in July 1915: "One doesn't have much heart for games, but they are good exercise, and it is our duty to keep fit, I suppose." The prisoners were no social scientists, but they did spontaneously, as so often before, just what the situation demanded. Turning their gaze from the external world, they heaped on their petty activities the visible importance that complex organization confers. Sport, appropriately, received the most elaborate treatment, but all the major activities were built into large and impressive institutions. The goals sanctioned by these commanding organizations acquired unquestioned validity, and the prisoners could pursue them with zest and a clear conscience.

Organization, of course, does not need to be built; it grows of itself wherever a small group, as in the Ruhleben boxes, interacts over a period of time. All that the prisoners did was to short-cut this natural growth by creating *formal* organizations, in which roles were specifically allotted, clearly defined, and hierarchically arranged. Formal organization becomes inevitable when groups are large, and when complex tasks cannot wait for an appropriate structure to form. The little group who produced *Androcles* were informally organized or they could not have put on their play, but as soon as a series of productions was planned, with a consequent increase in membership, they became the Ruhleben Dramatic Society, with its elected officers and written constitution. And the lengthened time perspective and wholesale participation of 1915 had the same result in every major field.

Formal organization, then, created nothing new; the activities were functioning before organization overtook them.[4] Nor did natural growth cease; though their outward forms were fixed, the societies continued to grow and change internally, and changes in their formal structure sometimes followed. Within each group, for instance, there grew up an informal organization, somewhat independent of the formal one, but often exerting a decisive influence.[5] And in the larger bodies a progressive centralizing tendency became apparent. In education, the almost complete autonomy of the original teachers was first replaced by departmental control; then, in 1917, policy decisions were transferred from

4. Sport seemed an exception, since football was formally organized in advance of the actual opening of the field. But the exception was only apparent; many football games had been played in November 1914.

5. The functions performed by informal organizations within formal ones are well discussed by Chester I. Barnard in *The Functions of the Executive* (Cambridge, Mass.: Harvard University Press, 1948).

the department heads to a small executive committee who did little teaching. Many universities have recently passed through a similar evolution. It owes little to conscious planning; organizations, once established, seem to follow an inner logic of their own, and adjust to every new problem by further concentration of power at the centre.

This apparent autonomy is due, of course, to the fact that an organization's behaviour is the end product of a multitude of interactions, and rarely conforms to the original intentions of any one individual. It results, however, in a widespread tendency to regard the large institution as in fact a super-personal being, pursuing self-chosen ends that even its leaders cannot alter. This is of course an illusion; economically useful—what would we do without the fiction of the corporate personality?—but dangerous when exploited politically. It is almost inescapable, however, once the size of an organization obscures its individual components; we are compelled to speak of "the Government," "the Company," and the verbal habit soon becomes a mental one. Officials seldom try to dispel the "institutional fiction," as F. H. Allport called it;[6] it is too useful to them. By facilitating identification among the rank and file it promotes compliance with institutional demands; sacrifices are more readily made for a personified country or church than for those who happen to be its current leaders. And when such drastic action as the expulsion of a member is necessary this can be done anonymously, by the institution, without anyone seeming to be personally responsible.

Although only the Camp School among Ruhleben institutions was so large and well integrated as to evoke any actual personification, formal organization raised all but the smallest associations somewhat above their members. The practical results will be seen later, but the implications of formality itself deserve a brief comment here. Many customary formalities, the requirement of an "introduction" to strangers, for instance, had appeared as soon as the period of crisis was over; they reflected the effort made by every society to preserve social distances and thus reduce friction and disruptive emotion. The new organization of 1915, however, introduced formality into numberless transactions among officials and between officials and members; this placed a large segment of camp life on a new level, most aptly described as one of "play-acting." For the function of formality is to depersonalize social contacts, to make clear that those concerned are not moved by personal considerations but are playing prescribed roles. The formal phrasing of official pronouncements is therefore no mere fashion of speech; like the

6. *In Institutional Behavior* (Chapel Hill, N.C.: University of North Carolina Press, 1933).

masks worn in classical drama, it proclaims that a play is being acted, and that the roles portrayed must on no account be confused with the individuals who are playing them.

The distinction thus drawn between the human being and certain of his acts was perhaps man's most daring social invention, and an essential one if society was to develop beyond the kinship group. For without the immunity and "replaceability" it gives to the functionary no complex and lasting institution could conceivably operate. At a deeper level, however, the assumption of impersonality also reveals the surpassing value placed on the principles enshrined in social institutions. For what it boldly attempts to do is to raise these man-made structures above their makers, to assert their freedom from human emotion and error, and thus to give their aims and practices a more than human sanction. The formality of the courtroom, for instance, is a way of assuring the prisoner that he is being judged, not by a fallible fellow creature, but by a superhuman agency, the Law.

We may doubt today the divine origin of either law or morality, but one thing we cannot doubt: that certain principles discovered by men in their long efforts to live together—justice, truth, brotherhood, for example—seemed to them so precious that they tried to set them above time and change forever. And when Ruhleben's simple activities were clothed with formality the goals they embodied were similarly exalted; they became what the prisoners most needed in their internment, genuine and lasting values.

12

THE WORLD OF SPORT

BY THE SUMMER OF 1915 the camp was teeming with activity as never before. Its prolific inhabitants, not content with producing a host of community and family groups, had now engendered a more lively progeny, a hundred or so formally organized bodies. These were purposeful units which energetically pursued their aims, co-operating, competing, and quarrelling with one another, and releasing a profusion of interaction that raised life to new intensity. Activities were extended, improved, subdivided, and elaborated to the point where Ruhleben became a world in itself, something too vast to be explored by any individual, and hence offering him apparently limitless horizons. It was an ordered world, but an immensely complicated one, for each larger division was itself of world-like proportions; and it was brimming with present interest and plans for the future—if Ruhleben should have a future.[1]

In this highly organized world the prisoner's life reflected the ageless paradox of society: he was both bound and free. He was controlled as he never had been in the winter, but he was also faced with so wide a choice of activity, such long vistas of opportunity, that he felt a new and invigorating sense of freedom. This is the general picture we shall see in sport, education, and other fields.

The programme of sport outlined in Chapter 10 was novel only in its magnitude; indeed, the prisoners took pains to make every detail as much "like home" as possible. The very familiarity of such organized programmes, however, tends to blind us to their significance, and a close look at this miniature model may be rewarding. The most obvious effect of formal organization was to introduce order into what would have

1. My statement is in interesting contrast to Sir Timothy Eden's sentence in his letter to *The Times*: "The men have nothing to think of save their ruined prospects and the hopelessness of their position" (quoted in Chapter 8). Which statement was "true" depended on whether or not the individual concerned could immerse himself in camp activities. That is why the organization of 1915 was so decisive for the mental health of the prisoners.

been a chaotic situation. Four thousand men could not conceivably use a small field except through the detailed arrangement of hours, areas, and matches in advance; indeed, the need to co-ordinate the activities of large groups is usually the first stimulus to organizing them formally. External order, however, is reflected in the minds of those exposed to it, and the organization of sport in March 1915 was one of the early factors in the mental stabilization of the prisoners. Each of them now knew what barrack teams would play today, tomorrow, and for weeks ahead; he was living in a better organized world, and was therefore less governed by impulse and suggestion.

The achievement of order implies something more important, the establishment of control. Control is of course inherent in social organization; the mere fact of interdependence—that all roles are mutually related—sets limits to self-determination. With formal organization this diffuse control is concentrated and channelled; roles are no longer regarded as equal, but fall into a hierarchical pattern that gives a few persons control over many. Thus the organizing of sport meant a redistribution of power, the prisoner paying for his new aims and interests with the loss of some of his personal freedom. What he lost was absorbed by new organizations: all extensions of himself, as it were, but extensions over which he had little control. The Sports Control Committee, itself a subcommittee of the Captains, took over the playing field in his name and allotted space on it without consulting him further. The football, cricket, and other associations then decided what barracks should play and when. And the barrack clubs, by their selection of teams, determined who were to enjoy the privilege of actually kicking or hitting balls.

Few human activities are as natural and impulsive as the playing of games, but in Ruhleben the impulse to play was now hedged about with many duties and restrictions. The man who felt like a game of football could no longer go out and start one; he had to await his barrack's turn, pass an evening of suspense while the Selection Committee deliberated, and then see if his name was on the list. If it was not, he had to do without his football; if it was, he was expected to play, though bad weather might have quenched his enthusiasm. It would be unthinkable for him to join in the game if he had been left off the team, and equally unthinkable for him, if he played, to stop when he had had enough. His wishes, indeed, seemed not to matter.

They mattered as much as ever, but they had been profoundly altered in that expansion of the self that is called identification. A rash of new "we's" in letters of this period—"we have a hard game tomorrow," "we finished up third in the league"—shows how closely the individual was identified with his barrack team. Its goals, and the norms governing their achievement, were now his own; thus it was a matter of course for him to finish a hard game in spite of a sore ankle, put team play ahead of his desire to score himself, and accept being dropped from the team without protest. Control of this sort is at the opposite pole from regimentation; it is self control in its most effective form. No wonder organized games are thought to produce good citizens!

Self control through identification is the ideal of every society, but it is nowhere fully realized. In small, informal groups the inevitable lapses can be dealt with by persuasion, criticism, or, in extreme cases, ostracism. In large organizations, however, informal control is less dependable, and is partly replaced by another social invention, that of "authority." The nature of authority is beautifully illustrated by a small pencil notice, headed "Barrack 20," and dated November 4, 1915:

> The Selection Committee has decided to suspend [John Doe] indefinitely from taking part in practice games and matches on account of a most unsportsmanlike display in the match against the Boys yesterday. Further that during the time of his suspension he shall not be allowed to use the club property for Rugby or other games. (H)

This is control of a sort new to Ruhleben; had the offence occurred in November 1914 it could only have been dealt with by argument or force. Twelve months later, however, it is handled quietly and far more effectively by posting a notice on a barrack door. The formal wording is significant; this was not how the internees addressed one another. But it reveals that social development has reached its final level, and now requires some elaborate play-acting. John Doe's suspension must appear as the work of superior powers, untainted with human frailty; the committee therefore make their announcement completely impersonal.

It is a piece of barefaced make-believe on their part—everybody knows Doe—but a necessary one, for the authority they are wielding is itself a fiction and would evaporate if they failed to play their stylized roles. The natural, human reaction would be to tell Doe: "Your conduct yesterday was disgraceful, and we're damned if we'll let you play any more!" But this would muffle the voice of authority, and an angry altercation might follow. As it is, the culprit can make no reply.

Who is in fact preventing him from playing? Not the secretary who posted the notice; he is probably a weedy individual whom Doe could knock out with one hand. What Doe is up against is an abstract entity impervious to blows, the carefully capitalized Selection Committee. Behind it stands another abstraction, the Ruhleben Football Association, and behind that the whole four thousand prisoners. For sport is now a social institution, its aims and code are collectively sanctioned, and the men will see that they are upheld, by force if need be. No force will be needed, however, for Doe will make no attempt to play. Football means less to him than continued acceptance by his fellows, and that is conditional on his submission to recognized authority, however profanely he may criticize its application.

Formal control of this kind is so familiar that we take it for granted, but to see it actually coming into existence is a startling experience. Only a year ago Ruhleben was a place of absolute equality, and hence of wide individual freedom. And, so far as the Germans are concerned, the men are still free and still equal. But they themselves, by means of which they are scarcely aware, have fastened new restrictions on their conduct, restrictions enforced, not by the Germans, but by fellow-prisoners playing formal roles. It is an astonishing development, but it means that there is now a full society on the racecourse.

Closely related to control was the remarkable stability of Ruhleben's new institutions. All the important activities of 1915 were still running in 1918, and running along almost identical lines. Human impulses are proverbially fickle, but the control implicit in organization holds them in check and harnesses them to established norms. With individual variability thus ironed out, the behaviour of the organization itself becomes highly—one might say "inhumanly"—consistent. Its operations are jointly performed by many individuals in interlocking roles; hence they cannot be altered piecemeal or reorganized over night. Change must occur if the organization is to survive, but never sudden change, for that would disturb the balanced relations between its parts and set up acute inner tensions. Hence the lengthy time perspective of institutions, their constant concern with past precedents and future policies. Since abrupt change may destroy them they are compelled to take the long view, and the larger and more complex they are, the further they must plan ahead.

When Ruhleben sports were institutionalized, therefore, they became highly predictable; if the Sports Control Committee announced in June that football would begin on October 3, it began that day, though the weather might still be sultry. Long seasons were played out to the last tedious match, football and cricket succeeded each other regularly for four years and might have done so for several more. But if the prisoners, as they faced each further winter, could always say confidently, "Well, at least there'll be the football," this was due to no dependability of human nature, but to the time-binding character of social institutions. The stable environment thus created was of immense value to the prisoners, for it permitted them to form long-term purposes themselves. In May 1915 one pessimistic barrack club seriously tried to book the field for October 1, and a 1916 letter tells of the writer's decision to play hockey rather than rugger "next season." All organized activities were similarly affected; Abbot, toying with the idea of studying for university credit in the school, wrote on November 2, 1917: "At any rate I shall not start until Easter, when another matric exam will be held." Easter was still six months away.

The stability of institutions explains their reputation for conservatism and may, at periods of rapid change, prevent their meeting new needs that have arisen. Ruhleben's institutions were inevitably conservative, but most of their leaders made some attempt to adjust them to the changing needs of the camp. In the final two years, however, there were clear indications that the stability so valuable in 1915 also had its drawbacks.

The size and complexity of a large organization, its manifest power over individuals, the machine-like regularity of its operations—these make it an impressive object and shed importance on all its components. They are no longer perceived in isolation but as essential parts of the structure, and so gain new significance. When, for example, Barrack 5 met Barrack 11 in cricket on July 23, 1915, the spectators did not see merely twenty-two men playing with a ball; they saw two teams, each representing a barrack, and both being parts of a widely extended whole comprising all the teams in the league, the array of officials and committees, and the whole tradition and *ethos* of cricket. And just as this sentence acquires meaning from its context of paragraph and chapter, so the match of July 23 drew significance from the wider perspective in which it was seen. The game might be dull, but it was not trivial, for it was an integral part of something whose importance was obvious. So many teams appearing at the appointed hours, so many men seriously acting their parts as players or officials—all this clearly proclaimed that cricket was a matter of real consequence.

The time perspective was equally potent, and this match was of course part of an extensive temporal organization; one with no adequate name, but generally called "the cricket." What was meant was the ever shifting pattern of wins, losses, and team standing—a pattern charged with stimulating uncertainty, since its final shape could not be known until the season ended. Much of the game's importance derived from this future reference, and much of it also from the past. For the match was not seen as a newcomer would see it, but in a context of beliefs and expectations based on the teams' previous records. And when predictions were confounded by Barrack 11's unexpected victory the compound hummed with talk, Barrack 5's supporters were heckled, and settled opinions were revised. Heightened uncertainty had its stimulating effect; as the magazine put it:

The interest in the cricket has once again risen to a high pitch on account of Barrack Five's defeat at the hands of Eleven. Barrack 5 and 10 have now lost one game each and it seems hardly possible for either team to lose again before the season is out—but cricket is a funny game and it is hard to say just what will happen. (*IRC* 5, p. 43)

Against the background of all that was occurring that summer, few events could be less important than this game in an internment camp. In its own context, however, it *was* important and therefore of great psychological value. For the prisoners now had something definite on which to focus their interests and emotions, something more wholesome than the insoluble problems of war and release. And it was organization that gave it to them.

Once sport had achieved institutional status its importance was rapidly increased by circular mechanisms resembling those that reinforce all organic growth. One of these was publicity. The mimeographed journals of January 1915 totally ignored the beginnings of what are here called camp activities. Except for a single item ridiculing Adler's musical exploits—in itself significant—they contained only news of military orders, canteen supplies, and promised improvements, together with facetious paragraphs about rumours, the Negroes, the mud, and the flooded compound. On the other hand, the first issue of *In Ruhleben Camp*, which appeared on June 6, 1915, devoted more than three-quarters of its pages to sport, music, education, debates, and plays. And this proportion was more than maintained in later issues.

The contrast emphasizes the radical change that spring had brought, for in both cases the editors simply reflected the camp's chief interests. The public re-echoing of current interests, however, in turn spreads and intensifies them, and every prisoner who read the paragraph just quoted was inevitably struck by the attention given to cricket and moved to keener interest in it. Many pages of similar material appeared—reports of matches, critical comments, seasonal reviews and predictions—and the full schedule of games and standing of teams were posted on official boards and in many barracks. Through this constant reiteration of its importance sport was invested with higher prestige than any other activity, and hundreds of men were led to talk, think, and even dream about it. The publicity was admittedly trifling by present standards—but then nobody was making money out of Ruhleben sport.

There were other forms of circular reinforcement. No one, for instance, would think of training for a mere pastime, but organized competition soon led to regular training and practice, and play reached a
very high standard. This drew large crowds to the matches, and this in
turn heightened their importance and made competition keener.

As a result of all these converging factors games were taken with
immense seriousness in Ruhleben. Indeed, apart from golf, the craze
for which later reached absurd proportions, sport is the one public
activity never ridiculed in camp magazines. A traditionally British attitude, of course, but of obvious value to the prisoners. For their mental
safety depended, as has been suggested, on the creation of a substitute
world. It had to be a "real" world, however, one that *could* be taken
seriously, and that is what organization was accomplishing.

The prestige of an activity is directly reflected on those who take part
in it; hence the men who are exerting themselves on the field or in committee now have the further incentive of public recognition. Players,
committee men, referees, time-keepers, scorers, even the boy who runs
out with barley-water for the cricketers—all are conscious of playing
roles in an important institution and hence of possessing some importance themselves. And the individual is beginning to relish such distinction. Outstanding players, of course, receive it in full measure: as
Douglas Sladen says: "There is no surer passport to being influential
and respected in the Ruhleben Camp than proficiency in sports"
(p. 252). The first issue of the magazine praises sixteen men by name
for athletic prowess, and lists twenty-eight footballers as worthy to
represent the camp against a hypothetical outside team (*IRC* 1, p. 11).
Differences in status have existed since the community took form, but
almost solely between groups; now organized sport is providing ladders
by which individuals may climb to fame. This is something new in
Ruhleben, something that changed the whole texture of its population,
and every organized activity is contributing to it.

As soon as a collective activity attains institutional status it becomes
the focus of new needs and satisfactions. As a social value it is revered
and cherished, particularly by an inner circle of devotees. The manner
of performing the activity becomes important; it must be dignified and
formal, not casual. In time what appears fitting becomes ritualized, and
so inseparable from the activity as to seem a necessary part of it. The
many formalities connected with British sport were of course familiar to
the Ruhlebenites, and even in internment they felt impelled to introduce
them.

The footballers might have played in any available shirts and shorts, but instead they were clad in regulation uniforms, supplied from England in distinctive barrack colours. Cricketers made great efforts to turn out in flannels, umpires wore the traditional long white coat, official British score-books were used, and the progress of the game was shown in large figures on a "telegraph." Then there was the formal kick-off by the Baron at the commencement of each football season, the noisy procession of certain barracks to the field, headed by their mascots, and the ceremonious cheers for each team when the match ended. Cohen reports similar formality in the Empire Day sports:

All the arrangements for the competitions were modelled on those observed at athletic festivals at home. The distances were carefully measured; the competitors wore distinctive colours and a prominent number on back and breast; the starting was done by pistol shot; and the winners and times were announced through a megaphone by Mr. Tom Sullivan, the champion sculler. (P. 237)

The wearing of distinctive uniforms is a proverbial aid to identification, and all this embroidery undoubtedly made the games a more enjoyable spectacle. But it had a further function too. When children play at being soldiers or cowboys, something in the way of properties—if only a wooden gun or a string lasso—seems necessary if the roles are to be fully realized and the desired illusion created. And the chief function of Ruhleben's football uniforms and other frills was a similar one: to make camp sports so "real" to the prisoners that they could play their new roles with conviction.

When decorative adjuncts begin to multiply about an organized activity, their source is typically the functionary; his tasks are chiefly administrative and he tends therefore to identify with the institution as such. It is he who tends, cultivates, and promotes it; it becomes his hobby, his "child," and he delights in enriching its functions and embellishing its activities. There is voluminous evidence of these secondary motives in the case of Ruhleben sports, much of it in printed or mimeographed form—the official's chief means of expression.

There is, for example, the *Handbook* of the Ruhleben Football Association, a neat brochure of 48 pages, printed at some cost in Berlin in September 1915. It contains a review of the first season, interviews with team captains, biographies of leading players, and of course a complete list of the Association's officers and committees. Hardly necessary in a prison camp, but the kind of thing officials like to see, gratifying to those whose names appear, and a boost to the prestige of sport. Then there was the "Concert and Presentation of Medals" that wound up the first season: a gala evening arranged by the Association, at which the

values of football were loudly extolled and the importance of its functionaries was incidentally established. Twenty-two silver cups and 122
silver medals—bought in Berlin, engraved by Mr. Mahoney, and paid
for from camp funds—were presented to flattered players amid thundering applause; skill was being recognized, the status of sports enhanced.

Nor was that all that a cynic might detect in the ceremony. For every
time a footballer bowed to accept his award from some dignitary on
the platform, was he not symbolizing the power relationship now existing
between the administrator, as patron and benefactor, and the player
as his humble dependent? The suggestion would have been scoffed at
by the prisoners, at least in 1915, and perhaps it does go too far. For
Ruhleben's games and players were not controlled by financial tycoons
in the background; the top football officials were mainly ex-professionals
and generally admired in the camp. None the less, as organization grows
more elaborate there is always a tendency to exalt the administrator
at the expense of the performer, and, in glorifying the institution as such,
to obscure the purposes for which it exists.

As for the amount of silverware distributed (at which the editor of
the magazine raised his eyebrows), that may be attributed both to the
professional background of the officials and to the special enthusiasm of
the first season. That such splendid football could be produced in internment came as a revelation to the camp, and no tributes to game or players
seemed excessive. And perhaps the organizers were wiser than they
knew, for in 1915 all the new institutions were still fragile enough to
need some bolstering. Both handbook and medals did this for sport, and
neither seems to have been repeated in later seasons.

The Ruhleben collection at Harvard includes a quantity of mimeographed programmes for special football, rugby, and cricket matches;
every prominent player was well known by sight, but formal listings
added something to the lustre of the occasion. There are also programmes and rules for field days and tennis tournaments, regulations and
forms for booking tennis courts. The Golf Club contributes membership
cards, lists of "local rules," booklets of printed score cards, and R.X.D.
postcards stating the member's handicap. The Barrack 9 Sports Club
has its applications for membership, bylaws and regulations, election
ballots, and receipts for fees all mimeographed; the Tennis Association
has luxuriously printed membership cards in keeping with its 20-mark
fee, and the Barrack 5 Sports Club outshines everyone else with its
specially printed stationery for official correspondence. Rules for booking the sports grounds, passes to let officials on them out of hours, and

all sorts of other items reflect a wealth of elaboration, some of it useful, some chiefly symbolic.

The world was at war, and Ruhleben was a concentration camp. To find cricket officials in one stable communicating with those in an adjacent one by writing letters to them is itself startling, though a flood of such paper work was necessitated by organization. To find them, however, writing these letters on specially printed club paper seems evidence of some form of insanity. And much of this behaviour has of course its psychiatric parallels. It was not a sign of mental breakdown, however; on the contrary, it was the one sure protection against it. For these very extravagances tell us what we have long waited to hear: that the men who were snatched out of one social world have succeeded, under difficult conditions, in building another.

Ritual and ceremony, though technically superfluous, are of deep psychological importance; by dramatizing man's petty activities they rescue them from insignificance and endow them with dignity and value. And the dressing up, the formality, the whole apparatus of make-believe that surrounded the playing of games in Ruhleben, were decisive factors in making those games what they were: a key point in the camp's system of defences. For when men lavish time and thought on embellishing an activity we know it is not a mere pastime to them; it is one of the values that give meaning and purpose to their lives. Social values of this sort are not given but created, and created by the kind of *mise en scène* we have been watching. The few values man starts with concern only his physical survival. To transcend them he has to become both dramatist and actor, for life beyond the animal level is a play or it is nothing.

The organized sports of Ruhleben were often called the "salvation" of the prisoners, mentally as well as physically. It was not running about on a field, however, that kept them unscathed. It was rather the fact that they were playing their roles in a social world that had become as real and absorbing as that outside. It was a substitute world, admittedly, but not a pathological one, for it was a *shared* world, similarly perceived by all. And that is our only criterion of reality or sanity.

13

THE BASIC PATTERN sketched for sport held good for all Ruhleben's social institutions. First came the felt need for some purposeful activity, and spontaneous group efforts to meet it; then rapidly growing numbers and more ambitious plans. These necessitated organization with its far-reaching effects: the activities were ordered and given continuity, standards of achievement rose, formality and elaboration appeared. Camp life was enriched and stabilized, and much of it was conducted on an impersonal level. For the prisoners, the change meant new and absorbing interests; pervasive control, lightened by identification and personal recognition; a great seriousness about most camp pursuits, and a consequent escape from the emptiness of internment.

Within the general pattern, however, wide differences existed, and these are apparent when we turn from sport to the only other institutions of comparable size, those concerned with education. Education began with a signal advantage over almost any other activity: whatever the men gained from it was relatively permanent. It could also count, at least at the higher levels, on the intrinsic pleasure of intellectual exploration—though games were no doubt equally pleasurable to those proficient at them. On the other hand, education provided little or nothing that could rank as entertainment, and so lacked the wide popular appeal of sport and the theatre. Unsupported by audiences, it depended entirely on the interest of actual participants, and to sustain this in Ruhleben was not easy, particularly since learning is in essence an individual rather than a social task. Once the stampede of the first summer was over, education had to be "sold" to the camp, and again organization turned out to be a good salesman.

The earliest educational body, the Arts and Science Union, was at first dominated by prisoners with little interest in organization, the so-called "supermen." Like all intellectuals, they found their own studies absorbing enough without external props, and they tended to assume the same independent motivation in others. While they controlled the

A.S.U., organization was kept to a minimum; believing in the creative potential of the individual, they were also convinced that academic formalism would quickly stifle it. Such control as they exerted over the A.S.U.'s lecture programme was completely informal, and always subordinated to their main objective: the fullest possible opportunity for individuals to express what was in them.

Much can be said for this attitude, but it was scarcely a practicable one in the summer of 1915. Men flocked to the lectures, but largely because of suggestion and the need for change, and lack of organization tended to keep participation on that level. The programme resembled the caucus race in *Alice in Wonderland*, with lecturers starting and ending courses when they saw fit, and listeners attending or not as they felt inclined. Chapman's diary recorded in August: "Went to a lecture on mathematics, but found it to be one of a series on Shakespeare by Ford. He was on Richard III and was good. Stayed on for a lecture on the Development of England by Masterman." Uncertainty of a further winter was admittedly discouraging to long-range planning, but the mass of prisoners could form no serious purposes in so casual an atmosphere.

The A.S.U. was a large and heterogeneous body, and artists and scientists, supermen and academics, rarely saw eye to eye on policy. These internal feuds were clearly apparent at general meetings, when reports were rejected and committees thrown out with alarming regularity. One issue that divided the factions was class teaching, and the Camp School, though a branch of the A.S.U., lacked consistent support. The school, however, was headed by a small, businesslike committee; they had a mandate from the 1,100 prisoners who had applied for classes in January, and they were determined to fulfil it. There was much friction during the summer, but clear aims and sound organization won out, and in September the school absorbed the whole lecture programme and emerged as the only teaching body in the camp.

The circles and the Monday night programmes remained under the A.S.U., and much of Ruhleben's intellectual and artistic life was channelled through them. The circles, however, really ran themselves. Each was a distinctive unit, with its own officials, its own group life, projects, and problems; relatively unnoticed by outsiders, it helped to make internment meaningful to its members. The Monday evenings were handled by a small committee, which sought out men who could give programmes and arranged the schedule. All forthcoming events were announced in advance, to circle members or to the camp at large, and the A.S.U. thus helped to organize the prisoners' future.

The Camp School had been operating alongside its parent body since the spring, but its atmosphere was significantly different; aims were more limited, but they were specific, and their attainment was planned out in detail. Every prospective pupil was interviewed, graded for his previous knowledge, and assigned to a small class as soon as a teacher could be found. Over a thousand were thus enrolled in the ten weeks following July 1, 1915; this meant securing teachers, space, and hours for ten new classes a week.

As numbers grew, organization developed; departments were set up under qualified heads and given a good deal of autonomy. And all changes in policy or organization were discussed and voted on at frequent meetings of the full teaching staff. By the time classes moved to Barrack 6 for the winter, organization was already paying off; education had lost its hit-or-miss character, teachers were regarding their work as a professional task, and students were selecting their courses intelligently and putting real work into them. The structure thus set up was amazingly durable: on November 8, 1918—the day before the Kaiser abdicated—Farwell noted in his diary, "Took my German class, work as usual."

The time dimension was the critical one for all camp institutions; serious purpose could only exist when the future was firmly structured. And what leagues and championships did for the sportsmen was accomplished for students in August 1915, when the school announced a scheme of fixed terms and vacations. Until then temporal definition had been vague; classes began as soon as teacher and pupils were brought together, and ended no one knew when—presumably on release. From the fall onwards, however, work fell into a rhythmic pattern of three twelve-week terms a year, accented by enrolment days and examinations, and men all over the camp began to set their mental clocks by the school's opening and closing dates.

Such arrangements seem so obvious that it is hard to realize the courage and foresight they demanded. The school's chairman, A. C. Ford, had been one of the first to recognize the central fact about internment: that its dangers could be averted only by ignoring rumours and preparing for a long stay. He first struck this note at his May lectures, and the incredulous reaction of his audience shows what a rare note it was:

> When I started my first course of lectures on Shakespeare I announced that I proposed to lecture twice a week and that the course would take about 120 lectures. This was greeted with a howl of derision. But of course I finished these, gave a similar course on Milton, and was well started on a third on Bernard Shaw before the end came. (M)

Mr. Ford required the same courageous pessimism from his hundreds of teachers, demanding that they start work each fall on the explicit assumption that they had at least another year to put in. And of course a school with fifteen hundred students could not operate in any other fashion.

The school's insistence on the long view permeated the camp largely through its publicity; a printed prospectus was issued before each term, and the magazines published frequent announcements. Its leaders were also realistic enough to recognize that even prisoners, whose deadliest enemy was *ennui*, must be enticed into serious work; along with the general catalogues, the Ruhleben Collection contains more detailed syllabi issued by departments, and complete outlines of various lecture courses. Mr. Ford commented:

> We found that it was necessary to be specific. It was not enough to announce a course of lectures, we had to tempt the men to come by making them sound attractive. We found by experience that if we advertised, say, a course on French Literature we got very few applications; but if we drew up a syllabus on de Musset, showing just what each lecture would cover, then they came. (M)

A future predictable in so much detail was of course a great aid to purpose.

Salesmanship would have been of no avail if the goods had been tawdry, and every effort was made to build a sound teaching programme. The lecture courses taken over from the A.S.U. were largely of university standard; these were added to and extended as needed, and supported by a multitude of classes at lower levels. The curriculum soon became too extensive to be outlined here, but a summary from the prospectus for the summer term of 1917 will suggest its ultimate scope.

> Seventeen departments and 247 teachers are listed. French is the largest of the language departments, each of which covers a range from beginners' classes upwards. French is taught in five grades by 43 teachers, with a daily *conférence générale* or a lecture on *le pays de France*, which all students are urged to attend. The German staff of 17 suggests the lack of prejudice against that language; it carries students to the matriculation level and on to *Faust* and the lyric poets. English includes everything from elementary grammar to matriculation authors and Old English philology; advanced Italian students are reading the *Inferno* and modern comedies; Russian, with 13 teachers, has a class reading Tolstoy; and eight other languages are taught, including Irish and Welsh.
>
> Science is most remarkable for its laboratory courses in heat, light, sound, electricity and magnetism, statics and dynamics, chemistry, and botany, the last using Ruhleben *flora*. Certain apparatus was secured in Germany (Einstein is said to have donated some), but many pieces were ingeniously built

from scrap by an interned instrument maker. Mathematics goes as high as the optional papers for the London matric; History and Philosophy are relatively small, and are combined in one department; Music includes harmony, counterpoint, and a great deal else; and a full programme of commercial subjects is offered.

The Nautical Department teaches everything required for navigation and seamanship certificates, and adds naval architecture for good measure; the Engineering Department has a wide range of courses in mechanical, electrical, marine, and construction engineering. Finally there is the Handicrafts Department, with metal, leather, book-binding and woodworking sections; by 1917 it had 22 teachers and was of growing value to men who had lost interest in other activities.

All told, there is enough to keep any prisoner profitably occupied; Jarvis, later a successful engineer, enrolled in January 1918—his fourth year in camp—for classes in volumetric analysis, machine drawing, building construction, and technical German.

The work of the teaching staff can hardly be overpraised. There was a strong academic nucleus including many brilliant scholars, and these men, with scores of schoolteachers, students, and amateurs, gave their time freely over long periods. Ford's record has been noted, and Patchett's tireless examination of *Faust*; M. F. Liddell taught languages even longer. Brose gave more than two hundred scientific lectures, and Masterman, who began his first history course in June 1915, lectured unbrokenly until August 3, 1918. On that day he failed to meet his class and was found to have escaped. Like most such ventures he was recaptured two days later.

These, however, were only a handful of the hundreds of men who stuck patiently to their teaching against distracting pressures—the sudden upsurge of rumours, the utter lassitude that sometimes drugged the camp, and the private anxieties from which few were immune. To explain so much unselfish devotion we must look beyond scholarly interest to social motives: the simple wish to help, the stimulation and support of colleagues, and the compelling obligations incurred by all who form part of a complex organization. These will be touched on shortly.

Work in so excellent a school had a real bearing on post-war life, and this was a powerful incentive to students. In October 1915 Graham wrote to his wife, "I am speaking four languages now in this camp, and only wish I had had this little experience twenty years ago." From the start the school made use of this potential value, confirming the student's sense of progress by examinations and records of study. And in time more tangible criteria were arranged for. The Royal Society of Arts and the London Chamber of Commerce permitted their examinations to be written in camp, work in the Nautical Department was credited towards masters' and mates' certificates, and from 1916 onwards Ruhleben was a local centre for matriculation at the University of London. Abbot, who studied almost continuously from 1915 to 1918, writes home: "I have still another result of my studies here. I sat for the Royal Society of Arts exam in French (intermediate) and have just seen from the results that I got a first class pass." Such outside testimony to the soundness of the school was immensely helpful; like all Ruhleben's institutions, it had been hastily constructed from local materials, and its foundations were anything but deep.

Though the aims of study were thus more realistic than those of sport, sustained purpose was undoubtedly harder to instil. The goals were more remote, and they were individual rather than social goals. The student was neither part of a team nor identified with a barrack, his efforts brought no cheers from the sidelines, and the emotional drive of group competition was lacking. With all these difficulties the school had somehow to cope.

The long road was divided into manageable portions by the time-tested method of grading classes from elementary to advanced, with examinations at each level. And the three school terms also helped; many a prisoner gained proficiency in a language after beginning by "trying it for a term."

Nothing, of course, could alter the fact that learning was ultimately an individual process, but it received strong social support in the school setting. All instruction was in very small groups, and their atmosphere was far less formal than in most schools of the period. Much depended on the teacher, but faced with adults and fellow-prisoners he was seldom tempted to rely on authority. His usual role was that of guide and helper in a common undertaking, and this made for warm personal relationships, as many letters suggest:

Mar. 9, 1917. Five of the elder students of Russian gave a little informal dinner to Mr. Morozoff, our oldest teacher and now head of the Russian Department at the School. Each of us made a short speech and we gave him a book with an inscription and our signatures. (Abbot)

Apr. 6, 1917. The School holidays have come, but I have a real good Italian teacher and we are going to keep on a reading class all through the holidays. (Graham)

July 28, 1917. I have finished a term of teaching Spanish, and one of my pupils brought me a couple of eggs as a parting present—one of them was bad and the other helped to make a rice pudding. (Graham)

In congenial groups of this kind the purpose of the individual, whether student or teacher, received constant social support.

There were still times, however, when goals grew dim, aspiration weakened, and studying or teaching became a burden. At such times the control generated in a large institution showed its strength, and kept men working almost in spite of themselves. There is no record of suspensions or expulsions—perhaps Ruhlebenites never cheated in exams —but positive controls were ever present in that network of mutual expectations and obligations that organization creates. The immediate obligations were towards the individuals with whom a man worked and whose expectations he felt compelled to meet, but in time obligations were also felt towards the school as a whole. No one from the humblest student to the department head was exempt from them, and the higher a man's status the more was expected of him—and the more, because of his fuller identification, he was prepared to give. The working of these obligations is clearly reflected in the following letters and diary entry:

June 2, 1917. My Italian teacher expects a lot, and I have to do my best as he takes a lot of trouble. (Graham)

May 4, 1917. Yesterday I had a shock, the Camp School people have asked me to take a Spanish class, and I felt unable to refuse, in view of the benefits I have had from the School at such small cost. . . . I hate the idea but shall do my best, and hope thereby to learn myself. (Graham)

Jan. 10, 1917. Called in to Y.M.C.A. room by Duncan-Jones and informed that I have just been unanimously elected chief of the [. . .] department of School, though not a teacher. Started work at once, seeing teachers and trying to arrange times. (Farwell)

Farwell gives us here a revealing glimpse of how institutions approach their functionaries: in one hand the plum of personal recognition, in the other an immediate increase in work and responsibility. And the approach was sound; for the next twenty-two months he toiled indefatigably for his department.

The school's remarkable success in keeping its members at work also reflected the more centralized form of control available to institutions that have attained independent existence. For the school, more than any other organization, came to be thought of as an entity apart from the men who composed it. Graham refers above to the benefits received from "the School," and his capital "S" is significant. A few early letters speak of "the school," but after 1915 it is capitalized as regularly as the names of persons.

No one planned such a reification, but nothing could have prevented it. This assemblage of two hundred teachers and officials acted unmistakably as a unit; it was also the largest such body in the camp. It had its own name, and even a building—the dingy loft of Barrack 6—to give it physical embodiment. It received and spent money—its own money, not Ford's or anyone else's. Each student received on enrolment a membership card headed *Ruhleben Camp School* and divided into squares; when he paid his weekly 25 pf. fee one square was imprinted by a functionary with the school's official stamp. All this made the institution a social and mental reality; the student felt responsibilities, not only towards particular teachers, but (as Graham's letter shows) towards "the School."

The development was a direct product of organization and a great aid to its smooth functioning. Teachers and officials might quarrel—even Ford was once the object of a vote of censure—but their loyalty was to the school and was therefore unimpaired. And the submissiveness of students towards a great institution made them far easier to handle. When discipline was required—at formal examinations, for instance—such a reserve of unchallengeable power was indispensable, and its complete impersonality lessed resentment when it was exercised. Abbot, planning to take a first-year university course, wrote in March 1918:

I have been politely informed that if I wish to take any of the higher exams *in the camp* it will be necessary to take the Matric again. . . . It is rather annoying to find that one has not passed the Matric after all, though I am assured that the exam I did pass was stiffer than the regulation Matric.

Whatever the problem was, no individual had to accept responsibility for Abbot's disappointment or bear the brunt of his annoyance. The "School" was responsible, and the "School" did not make mistakes.

Impersonal control was most often used as a routine convenience—to secure compliance with the many regulations which a huge registration made necessary. Here are two paragraphs from the *General Notices* in a 1917 prospectus:

The Summer Term begins on May 7th. The enrolment of all students, old and new, in all Departments takes place in the Loft of Barrack 6 on May 1st and May 2nd, 9 to 11 A.M. and 2 to 4 P.M.
BEFORE enrolment every student must obtain personally at the Office a Card of Membership which admits to all Classes and Lectures. When getting this card the student is expected to subscribe to the School Funds.

This, with its tone of formal authority and its deluge of capital letters, is a typical institutional statement. Seen against the perfect equality of 1914, it is also an outrageous one. On what meat have Ford and his colleagues been feeding that they dare address their erstwhile comrades with such lofty formality, let alone the bare-faced imperative, "every student *must*"? The prisoner, however, read these sentences without the least irritation, went to the appointed place at the prescribed time, and lined up to pay his fee. For the formal phrasing told him at once that this was no fellow-prisoner speaking; it was the voice of the "School."

Possessing so much intrinsic prestige, and standing for such durable values, the school had no need to bolster its importance with the decorative rituals that we saw in sport. Although its teaching was often of university standard there were no graduation ceremonies, and academic costume was seen only in magazine cartoons. More regrettable in retrospect is the fact that the school never awarded any honorary degrees; the spectacle of Captain Powell and Mr. Prichard being solemnly capped would indeed have enlivened the camp! The fact is that the school's elaborate organization was wholly devoted to the job of education—a situation that many of our colleges may envy.

The school thus weaned an unstable camp from the notion that learning fell like rain on all within sound of a lecturer's voice, and redefined it as an end to be steadfastly pursued. It did not succeed with all—some dropped off when they saw the long road ahead of them—and its shaky foundations were revealed by the sudden drop in attendance at every rumour season. But the school grew in size and scope for two years after its founding, and even in September 1918, when Germany was clearly collapsing, the enrolment days saw students lined up to register for another term.

Whatever the long-term results of organization—and they are not all beneficent—Ruhleben's educational institutions had made interned life real and purposeful for a great many men. They were laughed at, of course; the sudden earnestness of young and old seemed ridiculous to those untouched by it, and the magazines are studded with skits on "The Ruhleben Language Factory" and its half-baked products. But the informants tell a different story; when asked in 1933 what one thing did most to make Ruhleben bearable or enjoyable, they mention study more often than any other activity, including sports. And among those aspects of internment felt to have been of most value since release, study comes second only to the social lessons of tolerance, forbearance, and understanding of others.

A later chapter will suggest what the educational opportunities meant to certain individuals; here a tribute from a magazine writer may be quoted—a backhanded one, to be sure, but good evidence that the substitute world was functioning:

Oh yes, we all know that you're having the time of your life here. Stick you down anywhere where you can gas about the Arts and Science Union and addle your brains by learning half a dozen languages at once and you'd be quite happy. You don't care whether you ever get back to England or not, do you? (*IRC* 9, p. 13)

The Ruhleben theatre was also an institution of great public importance, but the nature of dramatic activities made its pattern different from that of either sports or education. Though half a dozen groups were engaged in production, competition between them was less direct than in sports and their relative standing was a matter of opinion. Nor did any of them attain much stature as organizations; insiders might judge a play as the work of a certain society, but to most of the audience it was merely a good or bad show, well or poorly acted.

As a money-making (or losing) institution the theatre was subject to more control than were non-profit organizations. The producer of a play enjoyed the usual freedom, but not until his plans had been passed by his own society, the Entertainments Committee (a subcommittee of the captains), and the German censors. The society was concerned mainly with the merits of play and producer, the Entertainments Committee with cost as against probable box-office takings, and the censors with military and political considerations. Even the first hurdle might prove difficult, as this published letter of June 1915 shows:

DEAR HATFIELD,
I am instructed by the committee of the Ruhleben Dramatic Society to give you the following reply to your application for permission to produce *The Master Builder*: "The committee of the R.D.S. have considered Mr. Hatfield's English translation of *The Master Builder* and regret that they are unable to pass it, as they do not think it fit for Ruhleben. The play as translated possesses no dramatic merit, it is absolutely deficient in action, and the dialogue, in the opinion of the committee, does not attain the necessary level to compensate for these deficiencies."
Yours,
W. J. CROSSLAND BRIGGS, Sec'y.
(*IRC* 2, p. 10)

This withering rejection (to which the editor appends, "Poor Hatfield—and poor Ibsen too!") was partly the result of a feud within the R.D.S., and the play was produced under the A.S.U. in November. But the letter vividly reflects the consequences of organization: authority in full control, formality and deadly seriousness surrounding the putting on of a play, officials depersonalized—and all within three months of the first stage performance. Crossland Briggs is no longer Hatfield's fellow-prisoner or even a human being; he himself is acting a part, and has donned the appropriate costume.

The stringent attitude of the society was due in part to more plays being offered than the theatre could hold; in a sellers' market it might have been less high-handed. Thus the power of organizations, in this and other fields, was a direct product of the men's urgent need for purposeful activity; by the time that need had been largely met the institutions had gained such momentum that their disappearance was unthinkable. This involved a significant change in the motivation of camp activities. As for the theatre, its stability is sufficiently shown by its 128 productions, the last actually opening after the 1918 armistic.

As soon as enough productions were offered to require precise scheduling, the theatre, like other institutions, helped to settle the prisoners by giving them a predictable future. The April 1915 issue of *La Vie française de Ruhleben* lists plays up to mid-July, a letter of September 1916 speaks of looking forward to *The Mikado* at Christmas, and Denton writes in May of that year: "We started rehearsing the Pirates of Penzance today, it is to come off in the *autumn*! Terrible prospect, isn't it? But we have to be prepared for the worst." July's wild rumour epidemic intervened, but rehearsals continued all through it—they had to, to meet the schedule. On August 5, 1916, Denton speaks of attending a rehearsal and a Y.M.C.A. meeting, giving a lesson, playing in a second-league cricket match, and having "no time" for an Assault at Arms and a Promenade Concert, all on that day. So much pre-arranged activity inevitably made the men less easy to stampede, and it is no coincidence that Denton ends his letter thus: "We are still hearing rumours of release, etc. but don't let them unsettle us."

Publicity and technical improvements contributed much to the theatre's importance. *Androcles* had been announced on a sheet of brown paper and played in home-made costumes on a makeshift stage, with cotton hangings for scenery and candles for footlights. In a few months, however, such primitive conditions were recalled only with amusement. Striking posters from the studio proclaimed each week's entertainment, and the magazines were filled with advance advertising, dramatic criticism, heated discussions of censorship and admission prices, and feature articles on the theatre and its equipment.

How elaborate the productions became is suggested by Bishop Bury, who saw a 1916 production:

I can only describe the whole evening as one of the most wonderful I have ever had. Two visitors had come in from Berlin. . . . The place was filled to its utmost capacity. The stage was beautifully draped and very long; the members of the large orchestra were all in their places, the conductor ready to begin. . . . The overture then began, Offenbach's "La belle Hélène," which was magnificently played. Then the curtain rose—a drawing-room scene, with shaded lights and beautiful furniture all made by the men. It might have been a bit of Mayfair and not the lower part of Ruhleben grandstand. My neighbour on the right, a graduate of Oxford—though a German, visiting the camp for the evening—exclaimed, "Wonderful!" (6, p. 46)[1]

Costumes were made in the camp by a corps of amateur dressmakers, or else hired in Berlin or shipped from Britain. Conventional scenery and properties were built, a sliding curtain hung, and a complete lighting system installed by camp electricians, with footlights, spotlights, colour screens, and dimmers. This traditional apparatus, though deplored by the purists, made the theatre seem "the real thing" to the mass of prisoners, who were soon racing to the box-office after Monday morning roll call to book their seats from a numbered plan. And for the privileged few invited to the dress rehearsal there was the rare pleasure of passing judgment on the play before lesser mortals had seen it.

Like other institutions, the theatre made tireless use of the mimeograph, and in the Ruhleben Collection are stacks of programmes, with their ceremonious listing of everyone remotely connected with a production, bundles of tickets priced from 75 pfennigs for a "stall" downwards, passes to dress rehearsals signed by the producer, lists of entr'acte numbers for the orchestra, permits for all involved in a play to get their suppers early at the kitchens, and pass-out checks for patrons who wanted to stroll between the acts. Technical conveniences, these, but far from unimportant; even more than the performances they led the men to take the theatre seriously as a solid institution in their midst. A given play might be disappointing, but the theatre was more than any play; it was an integral part of Ruhleben's world.

Dozens of references show how well the theatre succeeded in amusing

1. This performance was on Saturday, November 25, 1916. By a startling coincidence, *The Times* of that same date published a released artist's plea for the exchange of the Ruhleben prisoners which read in part: "People who have not been there cannot realize the misery in that Camp. . . . The feeling there is —Hell could not be worse." Nothing could better illustrate the deep contradictions surrounding the prisoners' situation, and the difficulties experienced by such visitors as Bishop Bury in reporting on it truly as well as acceptably.

and entertaining the camp, and this was its most obvious function. But more serious dramatic aims were also achieved on many occasions. After the performance of *Captain Brassbound's Conversion* in 1915 the magazine speaks of "men to whom 'Captain Brassbound' was not merely an evening's 'entertainment' but something that has arrested their attention and compelled their thought" (*IRC* 1, p. 10). Three years later, when many of the best actors had been exchanged, Irwin writes: "Saw last night Masefield's 'Tragedy of Nan.' English drama is looking up when plays like that are written." And Ewing's diary says of the same production: "A terrible play; even so poorly done it shook me up very badly. Felt depressed all evening."

These tributes came from the audiences; for those who took part, dramatic work was both more arduous and more rewarding. Standards during the three years were genuinely high; Farmer says: "The theatre became almost professional and the quality of the performances was really remarkable" (p. 397). This meant an enormous amount of voluntary work, and not all was inspired by a sense of public duty. For the theatre became in Ruhleben what it always tends to become: a world in itself, with its own code, traditions, and jargon, its friendships and bitter feuds, its gossip and scandal, and its own intimate, exclusive, and utterly fascinating life. In the Ruhleben Collection, for instance, are illuminated invitations to the gay supper parties on the stage that followed each closing performance—love-feasts given by the producer, graced by the presence of the cast in costume, and marked by relaxed good humour, witty speeches, and a wonderful sense of accomplishment.

These were private affairs, but the theatrical world also offered great rewards in public recognition; the star of a dramatic hit became a celebrity overnight. And what could be pleasanter, after weeks of furious toil and frustration, than to read something like this:

"La Petite Chocolatière" was a great triumph for its producer, Mr. Bell, whose work I cannot sufficiently praise. The casting and the scenery (designed by the producer) left nothing to be desired, and the acting was such that I can only say I have never seen better in Ruhleben. (*IRC* 10, p. 9)

Nor should such tributes be discounted on the supposition that prison-camp criticism was bound to be favourable; praise was the sweeter because the critics were so often scathing and satirical. Here are two other samples:

Its poor humour has not even the false brilliance of the average London society-play; the works are painfully visible, the characters boring at the height of their appalling funniness. The playlet [*Fancy Free*] was badly produced and badly acted. (*RCM* 3, p. 33)

The gentleman who was heard to applaud at the performance of "General John Regan" is requested to hand in his name (in confidence) to the secretary of the Irish Society. (*RCM* 6, p. 4)

Criticism in the camp was real criticism because the theatre itself was real, not make-believe. A paradox, but only part of the great paradox of Ruhleben. For all the prisoners were engaged in the very task to which the actor must devote himself: that of making the play real, and reality for the time an illusion. And so when the lights went down in the Ruhleben theatre, the curtain rose, and the audience leaned forward to follow an absorbing plot, they were immersing themselves in what was in fact a world within a world, a play within a play.

To the camp musicians, organization was only a necessary evil. The secretary of the musical society wrote in 1933: "No, I have no minutes, and I very much doubt whether any were ever written. After all, we were musicians, not politicians!" Music to these men was already a value and required no dressing up to give it importance. Organization was needed to arrange concerts, rent pianos, build the studio, and allot practice times, but it was kept to a minimum and the society achieved no symbolic status. Most business was handled by the executive, general meetings were perfunctory—save once, when an extravagantly lethargic committee was voted out of office—and formal control was notably absent.

Music conveys few political ideas, so German censorship was never a problem, and the concerts cost so little that the Entertainments Committee was seldom troublesome. The society's control of conductors and recitalists amounted to little more than giving each his turn; most of them were professionals and happy enough to perform, if only for the sake of practice. Some reluctance developed in later years, but persuasion from a colleague was usually effective, together with the universal motive of giving some pleasure to the men. This sense of obligation was nowhere stronger than in the musicians, and the camp's unquestioning assumption of a continuous series of concerts was in general cheerfully met, in spite of the hard work involved. This was largely because most of the professional musicians saw enough of one another outside their public appearances to form a distinct group. There was no Music Circle, but there was the Corner House, a club that included many musicians and artists and had a piano in its shed. Here shop talk whiled away the hours, the seeds of future concerts were planted, and many evenings were brightened by informal music. Ensemble playing was perhaps the most complete of all possible escapes from Ruhleben, and those who shared in it, actively or as listeners, were seldom insensitive to the plea that they also help out with the concert programme.

It was in the amateurs who made up most of the orchestra that a real conflict between duty and inclination arose, and its result was the camp's only trade union, the Ruhleben Orchestral Society. The players gladly gave their time at first, but by the fall of 1915 they had to protect themselves. Not only were concerts planned for all year round, with almost daily rehearsals and much private practice, but theatrical producers expected an overture and interludes at each of the five weekly performances—work of no intrinsic interest, which interfered hopelessly with other activities. So the players organized—the only body of "employees" who ever did so, though schoolteachers and even footballers might have been driven to it if the war had lasted longer!

The "union" quickly arranged for a small theatre orchestra with alternating personnel, and secured for the players a permanent voice as to the nature and amount of their work. Issues were settled amicably, but the tone of subsequent rehearsal calls is studiously placatory, and a sheet headed: "Ruhleben Orchestral Society: Decisions of the Concert Committee re Promenade Concerts" (H) shows that by 1918 the players had effective control. Other mimeographed items—lists of future fixtures, weekly call sheets for orchestra members, tickets for obtaining meals and hot water out of hours—suggest the considerable amount of planning needed in even this small sector of Ruhleben life.

Musical events soon lost all resemblance to that unforgettable first concert in Barrack 6; tickets were sold in advance, annotated programmes prepared, and the audiences behaved with Queen's Hall decorum. With many established professionals available, the level of performance was generally high, and Farmer says: "Some of the most delightful concerts I have ever heard were given in Ruhleben, and many were introduced to good music for the first time" (p. 400). The orchestra of about fifty was never complete in the wind section (gaps were filled by a powerful harmonium), but under first-rate conductors it performed remarkably well. And chamber, choral, and solo works were often beautifully done. The magazine summaries written by Benjamin Dale, the English composer, review a wealth of good music from folk-song and lieder to concertos and the lighter symphonies, and from Byrd, Bach, and Mozart to Debussy, Holst, and Vaughan Williams. And the seriousness of the criticism, both of the works and of their performance, is enough to show that a musical world, with its own set of values, had taken shape in the camp.

Painters can usually scoff at organization, for their work is not only meaningful in itself but also less dependent on co-operation than almost any other activity. Like the musicians, however, the Ruhleben artists were compelled to organize for two purposes, the building and maintenance of their studio and the arrangement of art exhibitions. This brought them together as a group and had significant results.

When an exhibition was planned, circular letters were sent out by the secretary-treasurer, and the entries submitted were judged by an *ad hoc* hanging committee. The shows were always well attended, and the "private view" which preceded them was a social event of the utmost importance. As one artist says, "The censors, Rüdiger, Mützenbecher, Powell, and the very cream of Ruhleben society were conducted round with pomp" (L 105). Most of the studio's other business was financial, for, while professional musicians played for nothing in camp, the artists, though mostly amateurs and "part-time" painters, were earning money. Numbers of pictures were sold at the shows and many portraits commissioned; prices were low, but sufficed to pay for materials and leave something over. The chief expense was the cost of constructing the studio—two studios, in fact, since the first was destroyed in the 1917 fire. Both were frequently rented for evening parties to help raise funds.

Economic incentives, however, were of small importance to the artists in comparison with their delight in painting and modelling and their lively sense of public responsibility. The latter was given full scope by the ceaseless demand for posters, and for drawings and cover designs for the magazines. All magazine work was contributed freely, while the painter's reward for a theatre poster, often a stunning piece of work, was one free ticket and ultimate possession of his masterpiece—if he could get it ahead of rain or a souvenir hunter. Even then he often gave it to the producer.

More than half the content of the later magazines consists of clever and well-executed drawings, and much of the stimulus to this outpouring of time and effort must have been social. In the studio the artists worked side by side, and this prolonged common life, with its daily discussions and criticism over afternoon tea, was probably the decisive factor in making them so public-spirited. Every mere prisoner who went to plead for a poster will recall his experience: the studied ignoring of him by the half-dozen men at work, the foreboding silence or grunts of "too busy" that followed his timid request, and then, when he had been sufficiently tried, the half-grudging offer by someone to "have a go at it"—and the final reward of something more beautiful than he had dared hope for. It is worth noting that one of the magazine editors, while praising the artists for their yeoman service, complains of poor support from the many writers in camp (*RCM* 1, p. 23). And, apart from the witty contributions of a few men like Filmore of the *Punch* staff, the writing is markedly inferior to the art work. The reason must surely have been that Ruhleben's writers were never organized, never got together after the production of *Prisoners' Pie* in 1915, and so never felt themselves a group with a group's obligations to the community.

Hundreds of Ruhleben sketches in the homes of ex-prisoners show the camp's appreciation of its artists. Much work was of purely topical interest, but some excellent portraits and landscapes can be seen in the pages of the camp magazines, the *International Studio*, and elsewhere. Ruhleben also had its "contemporaries"—of 1914 vintage, of course—and ten of Stanley Grimm's charming impressions were reproduced in *In Ruhleben* (43).

Working with professionals in the studio was of obvious benefit to the part-time painters, who greatly improved their style and technique during the four years. And a group of beginners who studied under Healy Hislop in the school achieved remarkable results and had their own exhibit in 1918.

Turning to religion, we meet a striking contrast. Though the first services had been initiated by the men themselves and thronged with eager worshippers, the early crowds fell away without creating any vigorous, growing organizations. The need for emotional reassurance in 1914 was not replaced by any surge of purposeful activity in 1915; it simply ebbed away. Nor was the gap filled by any general sense of obligation; many business and professional men were frankly indifferent to religion, the sailors (apart from a few elderly men) had grown up without meaningful church contacts, and those who keep most religious bodies going—the women—were of course totally lacking. Thus, while many bourgeois conventions were being re-established, churchgoing was not among them; indeed, all important sporting events were scheduled for Sundays during service hours.

More was involved than this, however. Though all creeds had worshipped together on the cold grandstand in 1914, the end of the crisis brought an automatic splitting into five independent groups: Anglican, Nonconformist, Roman Catholic, Jewish, and German Lutheran. What such fragmentation would have done to sport or education need only be imagined. Except for some overlapping among the Protestants, each body went its own way, cultivating its members but having almost no impact on the camp at large. The Y.M.C.A. branch established in 1916 made various attempts to draw in the indifferent, and there was a tremendous emotional response to Bishop Bury's visit that year, but the effect of such efforts was short-lived.

Thus in 1915, when great numbers of men were finding purpose and enjoyment on the sports field or in study, and many others learning to act, play in an orchestra, debate, or do handicrafts, only small groups of the devout were developing fresh insights into the meaning of their faith. This was not due to shallow exuberance, for an immense amount of serious discussion was taking place. M. S. Prichard, the philosopher of art, Cecil Duncan-Jones, a disciple of Rudolf Steiner, Reginald Ramm, an occultist interested in theosophy—all had their followers, as thoughtful prisoners tried to understand what had happened to their world and themselves. Denton, an ardent Anglican, wrote in May 1915 for church publications, saying: "We are flooded with Futurism and New Thought, and I want some backing for the old." The old, however, had lost much of its relevance.

The inner life of the various groups needs little description, and few materials are preserved. German Lutherans held only occasional services with an outside *Prediger*; Jewish observances are well depicted in Cohen's book. The Roman Catholics had their resident priest who celebrated Sunday mass, and a permanent chapel under the first grandstand where daily services were held. Their musical director was the well-known organist, Quentin Maclean; one of his choristers writes: "The liturgy was as carefully carried out as in any great cathedral, every week we had a new two-part Mass to learn" (L 116). And a hundred Nonconformists sang hymns and listened to speakers on Wednesday and Sunday evenings—usually the same hundred.

The Anglicans, as the "established church," were the largest denomination. Here a zealous group gave themselves devotedly to performing and embellishing the rituals, and one of them writes of attending *seven* services at Easter 1916. The Sunday services, conducted by the Berlin chaplain or an interned missionary, were fully choral and drew regular congregations of 150 to 200 men. And the small inner group who met at the daily devotions developed a sense of fellowship and spiritual growth that their letters show to have been deeply valued. Similar needs were met in the other bodies, and all religious activities seemed important to those long accustomed to them. But in comparison with what was going on in the camp they seem, in retrospect, static and ingrown.

Religion should have had more to offer to this town of isolated men; after assuaging their fear and loneliness in the first weeks, why could it not also express their later cheerfulness, courage, and deep-lying comradeship? The answer must be sought in the other-worldliness and rigidity of ecclesiastical institutions. They had their eternal aims for the human soul, but what was their purpose for the social body that was Ruhleben? Absurdly divided as they were, they could obviously have none. The aims most commonly stated were individual consolation and moral support, but the men had now settled cheerfully into camp life, and few felt that their morals needed attention; indeed, they regarded themselves as a pretty decent bunch of Britishers. In practice, the purpose of these institutions turned out to be the repetition of the same rituals, in much the same way, week after week—a sharp contrast to the diversity and movement found in sport, the theatre, and other fields.

And there was a more significant contrast. Much of the drive and enthusiasm that characterized the secular institutions rose from the fact that they were genuine products of Ruhleben. Each had started from scratch in the camp, freely adapting old patterns and creating new ones; each had grown directly out of real and present need, and each had the unique appeal of having been formed and shaped by the men themselves. Religious practices were in a different category; too sacred to be dissolved and re-created in the new situation, they remained the least indigenous of all camp activities, and therefore the least capable of arousing men to eager, purposeful effort. Their forms were set, the authority of their functionaries unquestioned, and their members, when they prayed for a spiritual rebirth in the camp, conceived of it only as a return to the pieties of the past.

Two years later a small religious movement arose that abandoned tradition and tried to base itself squarely on the obvious needs of the prisoners. But in 1915 the only person who envisaged anything like a Ruhleben religion was Matthew Prichard; his conception—the expression of social unity through integration of the arts—was scoffed at by the churchgoers as outlandish paganism.

"Ruhleben was an amazing affair," a journalist wrote in 1933, "seven [sic] thousand men of all classes . . . achieved a social organization and became a sort of miniature state."[2] Their major institutional achievements have been sketched, but scores of other societies existed. "In course of time," Cohen says, "the Camp was literally honey-combed with these societies—intellectual, artistic, social, professional, and athletic—and their prominent members became our celebrities of greater

2. The clipping was sent to the author without source or date. It celebrated the appearance in the same week of three ex-Ruhleben musicians on B.B.C. programmes, and was probably from *The Listener.*

or less magnitude" (p. 111). Only such pastimes as card-playing, chess, table tennis, and gambling seem to have escaped formal organization, and the first three (if not the last!) were often sponsored by the Y.M.C.A. and other organizations.

But what is "amazing" about this? Social organization was not invented in Ruhleben; the prisoners merely reproduced, with appropriate modifications, a system long familiar to them. What so impressed this journalist and others was that the whole process was the work of the men themselves. Every human being is born into a pre-existing social structure, and can seldom re-shape even a fragment of it; these men, however, had the unique experience of building a society *de novo*. Without women or families, and cut off from most of the world, they yet created for themselves the only habitat in which man can live contentedly—a working social order.

There was nothing extraordinary about the forms or practices of the new society, and much of its striking vitality must have been due to its indigenous character. War had confined the Ruhlebenites physically, but it had also set them free; free from the daily necessity of conforming to old traditions, of doing what was expected of them; free therefore to do for a time what they themselves *wanted* to do. And what every human being wants to do is to act, build, create; not at the command of others, but of his own free will. It was an artist who wrote the following, but it would apply to many others:

Completely freed from all my responsibilities, I did all the things I had never previously found time for. The days were too short. I enjoyed every day of my internment simply because I was let alone to do the things I wanted to, irrespective of praise or blame. (L 105)

And the waiter's reference to "the freedom to do almost as one wished, mixing with people, doing and seeing everything different" will be recalled (Chapter 3). It was this experience, increasingly rare today, that breathed life into the prison-camp world, making it so attractive that its stop-gap nature was seldom remembered.

The Ruhleben prisoners were no revolutionaries; it was mere chance that presented them with a *tabula rasa*. But they set to work on it with all the fervour of child architects on a clean, tide-washed beach. And their pride in the city they built was like that of the Chinese in their new communist state; it was no Utopia, certainly, but it was their own, as no society ever had been or would be again.

14

RUHLEBEN COULD NOW SUPPLY most of the prisoners' psychological needs. New dimensions of belonging and status, new and changing experience, and purposeful accomplishment were now available to all who sought them. Bishop Bury wrote after his visit: "One thing which struck me very much was that no one need be unoccupied, that everybody could find something pleasant or interesting or profitable to do, if he chooses" (6, p. 42).

Not all shared alike in these benefits, however, for the extended organization of 1915 was a further differentiating agent, sorting and sifting the population along new lines. Choice of a particular field of activity labelled certain men as primarily athletes, teachers, or musicians; their relative proficiency classified them further as good or mediocre performers; and ability and personality combined to determine who would be leaders and who followers. The broadest differentiation, however, which took precedence over all others, was between those who participated actively and those who did not.

The active elements have so far been emphasized, for they gave the period its character and seemed at the time to include almost everyone. But a small minority remained aloof from almost all camp activities, and a much larger section was relatively passive, merely swelling the audiences at games, theatre, or cinema when "something good" was offered. Of the 116 men who filled out the questionnaire, 5 per cent say they were "definitely uninterested" in camp activities, and 17 per cent that they were primarily "interested spectators," and the figures would certainly be higher if the sample were a representative one. To such relatively inactive prisoners organization could offer few new roles or purposes.

Two readjustments were necessary before a man could play his full part in Ruhleben's new life: he had to come to terms with the privations and inconveniences of stable existence so that they were not a permanent distraction; and he had to detach himself sufficiently from the outside world to accept Ruhleben and identify himself with it. The latter, in particular, involved a mental reorganization that was much more difficult for some than for others.

Six per cent of the respondents say that their characteristic mood in camp was "fairly constant depression and worry"; to such men, harassed by ill health or private anxieties, full acceptance of Ruhleben was obviously impossible. And, apart from them, it seems apparent that both the required adjustments would be most easily made by the younger and unmarried prisoners. Older men, more settled and less flexible, often found the conditions of camp life a perpetual trial; Graham, aged 44, wrote in July 1916: "It is no joke for elderly men with their set habits to have to live together in such close quarters and rub up against each other without the chance of getting out of the way." Older men, too, were more likely to be economically established and to worry about business losses and later re-employment. And if they were married these problems were intensified; to men whose wives and children depended on their earnings, internment could seem only a disaster. Most British employers, it turned out, behaved generously to both the interned and their dependents; even so, however, Ruhleben could be only a partial world to husbands and fathers cut off from their families. Graham put it feelingly to his wife in September 1916: "You say you miss me more than ever. Well, without you I feel that only a part of me is here, and how I long to see you, morning, noon and night."

Younger men, in contrast, adapted quickly to the physical hardships and sought new interests; they usually had less at stake in the war than older men and fewer worries about the future. And single men lacked the responsibilities and emotional ties that tormented the married; one of them, after describing himself as "quite contented" with camp life, added: "I was a bachelor, age 40, with no dependents, and an orphan too. Two brothers and two sisters were sympathetically interested, no doubt. But apart from that my return or failure to return could affect no one. Hence 'worries' were entirely absent." (Q 3)

These impressions are borne out by the questionnaire replies summarized in Table I; it is based on the hundred forms containing fewest omissions in this section. Internment, it is clear, was a much more shattering experience to older and married men than to the young and single (Item 1); younger men were more likely to focus their attention on camp affairs (Item 2) and to play an active part in them (Item 3); and it was particularly the young and single who viewed camp activities as of real importance and value in themselves (Item 4). All but three of the married respondents fell in the "older" group, so it was

TABLE I

ATTITUDES OF 100 EX-PRISONERS BY AGE AND MARITAL STATUS WHEN INTERNED
T = Total; Y = Young (27 & under); O = Old (28 & over); S = Single;
M = Married

Questionnaire Item (slightly condensed in some cases)	Percentage checking each answer				
		Y	O	S	M
	T	(*N* 50)	(*N* 50)	(*N* 65)	(*N* 35)
1. *In my first few days at Ruhleben, I thought my internment was:*					
(a) More amusing than serious, rather a lark	16	28	4	19	6
(b) An exciting adventure, to be long remembered	31	38	23	40	16
(c) A very serious blow, but bearable	47	32	62	35	69
(d) A catastrophe—the end of everything	6	2	11	5	9
2. *The major portion of my thought and interest in camp was given to:*					
(a) Camp life and its problems	30	45	16	30	27
(b) The war and outside events	27	19	34	32	17
(c) My release, and plans for the future	43	36	50	38	57
3. *As regards the multitude of camp activities, I:*					
(a) Threw myself energetically into them	22	27	17	20	23
(b) Took an average part	55	56	54	58	50
(c) Was an interested spectator	17	13	22	18	20
(d) Was definitely uninterested in them	5	4	7	4	7
4. *I regarded those activities in which I participated as being:*					
(a) Of real importance and value in themselves	66	75	56	70	56
(b) Interesting, but without any real importance or value	28	21	35	27	31
(c) Mere ways of killing time	7	4	9	3	13
5. *Looking back on Ruhleben now, it all seems to me:*					
(a) A valuable experience which I am glad I had	48	54	36	56	24
(b) An interesting interlude, but rather unreal	27	30	27	30	30
(c) A bitter experience which has left its mark	22	11	33	11	40
(d) A bad dream, which I want to forget	4	4	4	3	6

not possible to separate the two factors completely. But it is clear, in spite of many exceptions, that being married and past one's first youth tended to militate against full acceptance of Ruhleben.

This was to be expected; the notable point about the figures is the way they confirm, for this biassed sample, the transmutation of pastimes described in the previous chapters. After fifteen years of freedom, professional and businessmen might be expected to view their Ruhleben activities with a trace of cynicism that would colour their answers to Item 4. But two-thirds of them (and three-quarters of the younger group) asserted that these activities possessed real value for them at the time. The importance of this is obvious, for if a man spent his Ruhleben years in pursuits that were meaningful and important to him, internment could not harm him mentally and should rather be a period of growth and development. And that is what Item 5 of the table shows. The distribution of answers between classes follows the familiar pattern; what is striking is their relationship with the answers to Item 4: no fewer than 37 (80 per cent) of the 47 men who checked 5a had also checked 4a. In other words, the odds are four to one that a prisoner who later looked back on his internment as a valuable experience was also one for whom camp activities possessed reality and importance. In contrast, only one of the six men who regarded activities as "mere ways of killing time" (4c) thought Ruhleben a valuable experience, and he was a youngster for whom intense personal friendships seem to have been the dominant interest. And, of the four men who looked back on Ruhleben as "a bad dream" (5d), one had been invalided home after a nervous breakdown, a second spent most of his internment in hospital, a third suffered a personal crisis that caused him to shun public activity, and only one, who held a routine camp job, seems to have been normally active.

Letters also confirm the direct connection between purposeful activity in camp and later attitudes towards the internment. All three of the prisoners whose tributes to Ruhleben closed Chapter 1 of course endorsed the a answers in Items 4 and 5. And the refusal of a businessman who "couldn't be bothered" with the questionnaire implied the same connection:

> One point of information I will give you if it interests you. Although at the time I regarded my internment in Ruhleben as a very distinct nuisance, I took my activities in the camp quite seriously at the time, and I now regard it as one of the most interesting experiences of my life, and one which I would not willingly exchange for any other period that either preceded or succeeded it. (L 128)

On the negative side, of several men who asked to be excused because they wanted to forget their internment, none seems to have been at all active. One wrote: "I took little part in the general life of the camp . . . the internment had very little physical or psychological effect on me"; another, who pleaded that answering the questionnaire would "re-open old wounds which time has kindly alleviated," was a professional pianist who steadfastly refused to play in camp. In Ruhleben, too, the differences in attitude between active and inactive men were often noted; Leslie wrote in October 1915:

Those who are working, who are teaching, or in some way constantly occupied with doing what share they are called upon to carry out in the work of the whole, are usually easy to get on with, and easy to please, while those who are lazy or selfish are, of course, the everlasting grumblers. (P. 107)

It seems well established that only as camp activities acquired real value could internment become a rewarding experience instead of a dire catastrophe.

Besides age and marital status, education was an important factor in sorting out active participants. With the single exception of sport, all the new activities bore the imprint of the intelligentsia; the first lecture was on a Wagner opera, the orchestra began with Purcell, the theatre with Bernard Shaw. The camp, however, was no congress of highbrows; seamen, fishermen, workmen, and others with only primary education made up almost two-thirds of the population. Had these men set out to organize Ruhleben it would have been a very different place; instead, the lead was taken from the start by the better educated minority. Farmer comments: "The less educated classes were of course in a numerical superiority and could, had they wished, have made life very trying for the rest of the community. What actually took place was just the opposite." (P. 402.) The ambiguity of the last sentence was of course unintentional, but there were times when the intelligentsia *did* make life rather trying for other classes:

DEAR MR. EDITOR,
We read with regret that long-haired devils wish to pump Ibsen, further Shakespeare, etc. into this Lager. We wish these people were anywhere but here; where Box Office receipts would be a more immediate and definite reply from the public than is the case here, where the poor prisoner sighing for "Charlie's Aunt" would rather bear Elizabethan plays or Ibsen than boredom. Can nothing be done to muzzle these people? (*IRC* 6, p. 46)

A series of such protests soon modified the dramatic fare, but such pursuits continued to be dominated by those who had started them and were most active in them, the better educated men.

They were of course unusually numerous for a town of four thousand, but the reasons for their activity were psychological rather than numerical. Liberal education, with its constant demand for adjustment to new facts and relationships, had rendered them flexible enough to enjoy dropping conventions and fraternizing with sailors, to accept Ruhleben with its frustrations and hardships, and to perceive the many possibilities it offered. And the educated men *needed* intellectual and aesthetic stimulation as well as food and shelter; they were thus impelled to transform the compound into a cultural centre, while many of their fellows would have been reasonably content with parcels, physical improvements, and simple pastimes. The other prisoners were not necessarily any less intelligent; they had merely been denied the same opportunities for mental growth.

Games of course were enjoyed by all, and camp jobs were an outlet for many with limited education. But the aspiration to act, play in an orchestra, study physics, or paint pictures was foreign to most working class homes of the period, and hundreds of prisoners came from them. The remarkable thing was the number who developed such aspirations during internment; for many it was their first taste of a richer existence, and often also their last. Few sailors and workingmen filled out questionnaires, but the descriptions of boxmates include a dyer's apprentice who took singing lessons, a locksmith who acted in plays, and a brewery worker who divided his time between sports and lectures. And the waiter whose appreciation of Ruhleben's "freedom" has twice been quoted, used his freedom thus: he studied bookkeeping, French, and the Hotel Industry, went in successfully for football, running, and boxing, was founder and secretary of the Ruhleben Boxing Club, and "took an active part in lots of the concerts and revues" (Q 113). After the war he went back to waiting; to the question, "What seemed to you the greatest hardship you had to endure in camp?" he answered simply, "There were none to me."

While many such men seized on Ruhleben's cultural opportunities, others—and particularly the older men—said in effect, "These things are not for the likes of us." Besides the poverty of their education, one peculiarly British handicap must be remembered, that of speech. Lecturers, most teachers, and actors in other than character roles spoke in the rarefied accent of the aristocracy, and those lacking it were apt to feel out of place among them. They could act in music-hall sketches, play instruments, study what they pleased, and teach commercial and nautical subjects as well as handicrafts, but in other areas a subtle barrier existed; even Canadians were usually restricted to American roles on the stage. The perennial popularity of the Debating Society was largely due to its freedom from this class distinction; every dialect of the British Isles was equally at home in what one enthusiast calls "the only democratic institution in the camp" (*RCM* 3, p. 8).

Closely related to education was the factor of occupational experience. Interned athletes, scholars, musicians, and artists were in a highly congenial climate, engineers could at least pursue the theoretical aspects of their work, and there was a steady demand for the skills of shoe-makers, tailors, carpenters, watchmakers, and other tradesmen. But for two of the largest groups, the businessmen and the seafarers, little appropriate employment existed. Small entrepreneurs had a field day until private trading was abolished, but general business experience was an asset only in administrative jobs, and these could absorb relatively few. Younger men studied and played games like everyone else, but the older established businessman, with certain notable exceptions, merely put in the time at Ruhleben. The seafarers were even more handicapped; of all the camp institutions only the Nautical Department of the school catered specifically for them. Sports interested nearly all of them, ship's engineers had their professional association, and some deck officers were active in administrative posts; but a thorough adapta-tion to Ruhleben could hardly be looked for from men who described all occupations but their own as "shore jobs." Again, however, this applies chiefly to the men with years of voyaging behind them; young sailors, firemen, and stewards merged easily into the general population and often developed new interests and skills.

None of these factors operated inevitably; Graham, though a business-man of 44, married and with children, was adaptable enough to study and teach languages throughout his camp career, and such exceptions were numerous. On the other hand, even young and well-educated men might be inactive under special circumstances:

Being naturally of an optimistic temperament, I could not bring myself to initiate things while in Ruhleben. I always expected to be out within a few months. Although a scientist (lecturing on chemistry at that time) I was not keen on pursuing my subjects and could not settle down. (L 67)

The only thing I thought worth while in Ruhleben was to get out of it; this I was lucky enough to accomplish and to serve as an officer in His Majesty's forces before the end of hostilities. My ambition was achieved, and the events of the camp were of no interest compared with this. (Q 10)

So much for general responsiveness to Ruhleben; what about specific interests? As the massive participation of 1915 settled into the steady rhythm of later years, it became clear that every activity was a further differentiating medium, winnowing out its devotees and adherents from the camp's population. Each began to draw its regular quota, swollen on special occasions and sometimes altering as the years passed, but still highly predictable. The Rev. H. M. Williams, who came to conduct Anglican services, never found a congregation that could not be accommodated, nor did he ever preach to an empty hall. And they were much the same people each Sunday; the appeal of Anglican rites, like that of field hockey, piano recitals, or history lectures, had become selective, affecting some but not others. Choice was imperative, for no one could take part in all the camp activities; but complete specialization was late in appearing, and 1915 was remarkable for the variety of interests which men managed to sustain. Abbot combined regular hockey and rugby games with twelve hours of classes and nine of teaching each week, and also sang in Adler's chorus; Denton, besides conducting the music at all Protestant services, managed to practise a little, study Italian and Greek, write for the magazine, and play cricket for his barrack.

In time, however, most prisoners restricted themselves to one or two fields, and this ultimately affected their social contacts. Leslie wrote in 1916 of a pre-war friend: "I do not see him constantly or even daily, for our spheres of action are different and one meets few except those with whom one's activity forms a natural link" (p. 165). This is a far cry from either solidarity or community groupings; the expanding life of Ruhleben, like the expanding universe of Jeans, was drawing its constituents apart from one another.

Most of the choices made were the obvious ones; men followed their previous interests and did what they were good at. But not always; a surprising number of prisoners adopted roles in camp that had little relation to their previous lives. The convalescent barrack was set up and devotedly supervised by Stanley Lambert, a coal exporter, the lending library by a chartered accountant, J. H. Platford; *Androcles* was produced by an engineer, *The Master Builder* by a research chemist; all the early theatrical costumes were designed and made by a distinguished biologist. Administrative work provided many examples; the chairman of the Entertainments Committee was an Otis Elevator executive, the Chief of Police was a golf professional, and the kitchen inspectors, who supervised the catering, included at various times a real estate agent, a church organist, a director of the Remington Typewriter Company, a dentist, a master mariner, and an eminent Berlin singing teacher. And, for contrast, "one of Lambert's assistants, who did valiant work in the lazarette and was a really fine fellow, had kept a brothel in Paris" (L 111).

Though shifting of roles was most frequent where professional training was unnecessary, many men who had never taught in their lives became excellent teachers and lecturers, ships' boys made themselves formidable golfers, and rank amateurs developed into capable actors, singers, and orchestral players. Men can learn almost anything if they really want to, and the camp of 1915 not only provided a host of opportunities, but also aroused a real eagerness to seize them.

The variety of roles played by individuals during the four years may be illustrated by a few cases from questionnaires:

Mining engineer, age 34 when interned, visiting relatives in Germany. Studied bookkeeping, electricity, analytical geometry, book-binding; played cricket, football, rugby, lacrosse, track sports; introduced and played baseball. Treasurer of barrack sports club; police constable; assistant in lending library. (Q 117)

Waiter, age 20, working in Cologne. Acted as steward to various boxes; studied French, Spanish, Russian; police constable; main interest gardening; barrack gardener and member of the Ruhleben Horticultural Society. (Q 91)

Army cadet, age 18, studying German. Active in organizing sports; played football; vice-captain of barrack; member of A.S.U.; studied languages, handicrafts and science; helped build and maintain chemistry laboratory. "After the war I became a chemist; study of science and association with scientific men had disinclined me for army life." (Q 57)

Schoolboy, age 17, studying German. Parcel post worker, vice-captain of barrack, kitchen inspector, manager of cinema, member of Entertainments Committee; helped start Irish Players, member of Ruhleben Dramatic Society, successful actor. After the war became actor and director of a school of drama. "No intention of stage before the war; adopted it afterwards in desire to 'earn' artistically." (Q 52)

To explore fresh fields in this way often proved so stimulating that men found more enjoyment in their temporary roles in Ruhleben than they had in their previous occupations. And, as the last two cases suggest, this sometimes had lasting effects on their lives.

Many of the occupational shifts were in a sense forced ones. For the sailor, businessman, or jockey, internment was a kind of technological unemployment; he might work at a camp job for years just as "something to do," and on release go back, essentially unaltered, to his old occupation. But such men, though numerous, were far less important than those others who found their sudden unemployment an exciting release, and who came to regard their camp jobs, not as stop-gaps, but as absorbing occupations in which they could develop new abilities and new conceptions of themselves. These men were in the forefront of the 1915 expansion, creating its infectious atmosphere, and inspiring others by their willingness to "try anything." And, with so wide a range of choice, no occupational choice could be strictly a forced one; if it seemed so, it was because hide-bound schooling and a compulsive social system had turned the individual into a robot.

Further divisions appeared as soon as those in a given field began to interact; men of similar views formed parties, and individuals who stood out for their drive or ability became leaders. Not surprisingly, it was chiefly in the intellectual fields that competing factions appeared. The supermen's struggle against the academics in the Arts and Science Union has been touched on, and they were soon battling in the Ruhleben Dramatic Society, this time against giving the camp "what it wanted" rather than further Shaw, Ibsen, and Shakespeare. Here their opponents voted them down and broadened the society's programme to include thrillers and farces.

No one was certain how these young intellectuals acquired the "superman" label—it must have had something to do with Nietsche—but its meaning to Ruhleben was simply "high-brow." They were a very small group; H. S. Hatfield, a chemist with an absorbing interest in literature, was the outstanding member, and he was supported by R. H. Pender and Norman Kapp, with the novelist Duncan-Jones and the musicologist Leigh Henry more loosely attached. That so few men could cause so much controversy is a tribute to their convictions and courage. Most of them were of a type taken for granted at universities today—uninterested in games, excited by contemporary art and literature, rebellious against bourgeois standards. In Ruhleben, however, they stood out sharply, for their *avant garde* views were publicly expressed in lectures, reflected on the stage, and ridiculed in the magazines and elsewhere. Leigh Henry, a disciple of Gordon Craig, was a particularly easy target; he dressed eccentrically, wore a beard even in summer, and daringly lectured on composers from Schönberg to the Italian Futurists. Marinetti's dictum, "art has nothing to do with beauty," would be controversial in a small town today; at Ruhleben in 1914 it was an atomic bomb. The magazine announced (*IRC* 4, p. 22):

BANK HOLIDAY ATTRACTIONS
Arts and Science Society on the Third Grandstand at 7 A.M. Mr. STARBOARD HARRY will deliver the A.S.S. popular weekly Lecture
MUSIC AND THE CALCULUS
This lecture will be illustrated by selections from the Masters' Works on the slide rule, patent integrator and pantograph.
Bring your own smelling salts.

Similar lampoons were so numerous that the next issue stated: "TO CONTRIBUTORS. Kindly note that we do NOT require any poems, jokes, pictures, articles, or anything which has the Supermen as subject. The Camp is fed up with them and so are we!" (*IRC* 5, p. 32)

The supermen believed that the ordinary man need only be exposed to the best to respond to it, and that Ruhleben was a priceless opportunity to act on this belief. The conviction did them credit, and the group was largely responsible for the high standards set at the beginning. The diet, however, was too strong for the stomachs of most of the men, and their complaints were often voiced:

We're not an intellectual race and what's more we're the mugs of the British Empire or we shouldn't be here. Of course we *pretend* to enjoy the brainjuice of the supermen, nobody's got the courage to say they don't for fear of being styled "hignorant and huneducated" by his neighbours, but give us an entertainment needing no mental strain to suck it in and we applaud it uproariously. There's the plain truth. (*IRC* 3, p. 21)

The ridicule poured on the supermen was not entirely unjustified; like most young iconoclasts they were a little cocksure, a little contemptuous of other opinions. The criticism was unfortunate, however, for it made them a rather self-conscious clique and ultimately drove them almost out of public life. But the A.S.U. Monday Nights gave them an outlet for at least two years, and were a great contribution.

Another important group formed around the Bergsonian philosopher Matthew S. Prichard. Prichard was perhaps the most remarkable character in a camp well supplied with them. Although over fifty when interned, this art critic and linguist made light of discomforts as "aberrations of mere matter" and devoted himself to enlarging and stimulating the minds of a coterie of young men who attached themselves to him. He was a gaunt, beak-nosed figure, usually attired in a black corduroy suit with a light blue sash and scarf, but his personal charm and the originality of his thought made him almost irresistible to those he chose to cultivate. Leslie refers to him as follows in August 1915:

If you have noticed a more deeply optimistic tone in my letters . . . it is in the main due to one man, of whom I have not spoken before, but to whom I owe more than I can tell. . . . His name is P - - - d, and W.U.S. and I are linked to him by ties of deepest friendship and respect. He is more than twice our age. It was he who was the centre of that little group into which I was introduced on my second day in camp, and which read Bergson's "Le Rire" under the most extraordinary conditions. I cannot say more about him now, but here is a beautiful mind. (Pp. 93–4)

Prichard's greatest singularity was his practice of releasing the *élan vital* in himself and others by intense mental concentration, often accompanied by peculiar wafting movements of the hand; by this means he cured his friends' illnesses and even ensured the victory of Barrack

10's teams by gestures from the side lines.[1] But he was also a highly cultivated scholar; he had reached a view of the social functions of art that had much in common with Durkheim, and he was an expert on Dante and head of the school's Italian department. It was no wonder that his young followers listened to him with something like reverence.

The camp identified Prichard with the supermen and treated him with the same ribaldry. But there were wide differences between them. Prichard's mystic views repelled the tough-minded intellectuals, and his flat rejection of all art since the Renascence and all music since Mozart offended their modernist tastes. The supermen, too, were radicals who became convinced internationalists during the war, whereas Prichard, a member of the British squirearchy, despised Germans as totally devoid of culture and drew all his disciples from the Public School élite. Unlike most scholars, he was a skilled politician, whose followers often controlled the A.S.U.; he was frequently asked to mediate between warring factions, and was even elected captain of Barrack 10 in a vain effort to drive Powell from office. Ruhleben had no more influential figure.

This brings us to specific leadership. What kinds of men started Ruhleben's activities and kept them running successfully? A partial answer has already been given, for all were inevitably active participants, who had accepted Ruhleben as a reality with which they could for the time identify themselves. They differed widely in roles and personality, however, and the initial distinction was between the "pioneers," who first opened up various fields, and the later leaders, who organized and cultivated them.

Pioneering in Ruhleben required men of special qualities, for the obstacles to any serious activity in the first winter were formidable. There were no facilities for rehearsal or performance, the prisoners were engaged in an unending struggle against cold, wet, darkness and hunger, and their mood was by turns glum, turbulent, and facetious. Those who launched classical music, a formal debate, a lecture on *Parsifal*, and a Shaw play into such a camp needed their share of boldness. Their contribution, however, should not be exaggerated; development might have been delayed by their absence but it could not have been prevented. Had Adler not arranged his concert or Norman Kapp produced *Androcles*, someone else would shortly have done something

1. Prichard's eccentricities became more marked as he grew older; when I last saw him in 1933 he was even controlling the English weather! His peculiarities were minor matters, however, and when he died in 1936 anonymous tributes to his character and influence filled more than half a column of *The Times*.

similar. The pressing need for meaningful activity was bound to bring a response.

Those who responded first may be described in terms of two extreme types: the "pusher," whose personal needs were paramount, and the "creative leader," whose outstanding trait was sensitivity to the needs of others. Most pioneers of course had their share of both characteristics; it was the balance that made the difference.

The pusher was marked by self-assurance and aggressive, dominating tendencies—traits often associated with business success. Ruhleben's businessmen, however, showed relatively little initiative; Kendall wrote: "It was remarkable how the big successes of the commercial world did practically nothing in leadership in the camp" (L 111). This ignores such atypical businessmen as Walter Butterworth, who pioneered in several fields, and also excludes the captains who set up the community organization. Culturally speaking, however, Kendall is substantially correct; the only enterprises that can certainly be credited to business were the promotion of the Ruhleben British Association and its counterparts, and the editing of In Ruhleben Camp by a briskly articulate advertiser. The pushers in general were apparently moved by a strong individual drive, not only for success, but for personal recognition. The flat levelling of the winter had acted on them like a goad, impelling them to emerge from the crowd by some form of conspicuous achievement. Certain of these individualists were prominent in the early stages of sport, music, the theatre, and education, and they surmounted many obstacles. They were seldom top-notch men, however, and their itch to shine personally unfitted them for team work. Hence many were pushed aside as organized groups took control.

The "creative" pioneers were of a different type; well educated, often brilliant, they were marked above all by flexibility, imagination, and wide-ranging interests. Not one was a specialist who could be readily pigeon-holed; they stood on the border line between fields, or had developed avocations that overshadowed their professional interests. Such were Duncan-Jones, the novelist, poet, dramatist, and mystic; Prichard, a mystic too, but also a linguist and art critic; Stafford Hatfield, a research scientist with a powerful literary and humanist bent; Walter Butterworth, a successful businessman whose deepest interests were in art, literature, and human welfare.

It was men of this sort who found internment stimulating; they were by no means all young, but they were genuinely youthful in their positive adaptation to Ruhleben and their absorbing interest in others.

To them the mass of idle, restless men was a challenge, not to assert themselves, but to discover, invent, or improvise something in the way of healthy and pleasurable occupation. Such men were the catalysts in Ruhleben's intellectual transformation, in education, science, literature, the theatre; they accomplished far more than the pushers because they incited others to activity rather than driving them. Most of them remained active, but some could not stomach the later institutional developments and retired into small circles of intimates.

The full organization of activities created new conditions and demanded a new type of leader. With physical facilities improved and participation heavy, experience and team play were more sought after than initiative or imagination. Organization also brought individuals together in a context where their respective capacities could be compared, and this led to intense competition, sometimes concealed, sometimes open and bitter. The broad result was the replacement of many pioneers by specialists—not necessarily by professionals, who were lacking in some fields, but by men of ability who were also acceptable to their associates. On the whole it was the less capable who were gradually weeded out, and this had much to do with the steady rise in standards. Unfortunately, however, not only the mediocre were crowded out, but also certain pioneers whose views did not fit traditional moulds. For when men met in committees differences about policy and programme tended to be resolved in the easiest way, by adopting practices long familiar in similar organizations elsewhere. To a few creative leaders this seemed a betrayal of their visions for Ruhleben, and they dropped out of further participation.

Why was specialized leadership so relatively late in appearing? Partly because the real expert is usually a diffident person, who prefers not to push himself forward but to wait for the recognition that is bound to come. It is not the most notable figures on a ship's passenger list who orate in the smoking room or monopolize the lounge piano. Partly also because specialized training is apt to make a man somewhat dependent on his familiar setting. The scientist who had discoursed to hand-picked students in his laboratory, the soloist accustomed to the perfect arrangements of the recital hall—such men were sometimes unable to imagine themselves attempting anything under the conditions of the first winter, and a few retained this attitude permanently. Thus, while distinguished British musicians listened with secret horror to some of Adler's concerts, it was not until the fall of 1915 that they produced anything better. Whatever the shortcomings of certain pioneers, they at least demonstrated what could be done in Ruhleben. A talented prisoner wrote on some of these points:

> As to "leadership," under our conditions the pusher probably came first. The fact that a certain pianist could consistently refuse to play because he considered it worthless in such a camp is illuminative. The many who were pushing eagerly forward were not a company I wished to join. It was clear that when those who were merely showy had had their innings, any other would find an audience able to distinguish between sincere power and its clever simulation. (L 135)

This final sorting of Ruhleben's population was a gradual process, not completed until early in 1916. One by one new faces appeared in public, new names on committee lists, while various early celebrities slipped back into obscurity. Like the other siftings described, it was a direct result of the spring's activity and its embodiment in organizations. Only as men were spurred into action could their abilities be displayed, and only when they were brought together could their respective positions be determined. Organization thus performed in Ruhleben the function it fulfils everywhere; it was the "casting" medium for the social drama, the means through which the individual was allotted his role as planner or performer, star or supporter.

The mechanics of the process should be noted: with the significant exception of religion, every activity was controlled by majority vote. As it was organized it came under a committee, whose members were nominated and elected at open meetings—a glaring contrast to the over-all government of the captains. The process was open to all the familiar abuses of democracy; cliques and pressure groups contended for power, meetings were packed, rebels were flattened by official steamrollers. But the method was adopted without question; it was the only fair and "British" one.

Democratic procedure, however, failed to make the replacement of so many pioneers painless; ousted committee members prophesied black ruin under their successors, frustrated individuals brooded over their wrongs and sometimes refused to participate further. When an organization of musicians finally removed the concerts from Adler's sole control, he sent the following letter to the magazine (IRC 5, p. 47):

SIR:
In No. 1 of your magazine you announced my intention of opening a new winter season on Sept. 5th by the rendering of "Hiawatha." It is with great regret that I have to inform you that owing to the very unfortunate attitude adopted with regard to my work for the Camp by my fellow professional musicians, it will be quite impossible for me to proceed with my concert

work and do justice to myself and the Camp. On the other hand, immediately fairer treatment and a proper co-operation is accorded me, I shall throw myself heart and soul into the work of providing entertainment for the Camp in the coming winter as I did throughout the last. . . .

Yours,

F. CH. ADLER

The aggrieved conductor, however, later reconsidered his stand and took his turn with the rest.

The activities that flowered in the spring of 1915 were so obviously desirable that to inquire into the motives of those who started or directed them would have seemed ridiculous. By midsummer, however, the sheer multiplicity of organizations was raising the question "Why?", as in the poem quoted earlier, and the competitive struggle between groups and individuals was causing motives to be openly stated, impugned and defended. To judge by public utterances, the discussion was pointless; everyone was working simply and solely for "the Camp" (invariably with the capital "C"). The R.D.S. existed to provide for the dramatic interests of "the whole Camp,"[2] the Protestant services were run "by men in the Camp FOR the Camp" (*IRC* 2, p. 36), and captains, canteen workers, musicians, and medallists were all inspired by this single motive. Adler's letter is a perfect example of public statements on the subject.

The actual motives of pioneers and administrators were of course like human motives anywhere—mixed, often unconscious, and as various as the personalities concerned. Pride, emulation, and the enjoyment of prestige and power were inevitably interwoven with more socialized drives; one prisoner remarked: "In my opinion, vanity and rivalry inspired a good deal of what was done in the camp, as well as the effort to follow previous lines of conduct" (L 135). Even so, three points already made should not be forgotten. First, that "the good of the Camp" was no meaningless phrase, but reflected a sense of responsibility for others that had existed since internment. Ford's statement of his own motives is a striking example:

What I did in the camp I did quite deliberately and after careful thought. I realized, and I used to say the same thing at the teachers' meetings, that there we were, unable to fight, unable to make munitions, or do anything to win the war. But one thing we could do; these four thousand chaps would later be part of the material of our country, and any way in which they could improve themselves during those years would be just so much gain. (M 29)

---

2. Advertisement of the Ruhleben Dramatic Society, mimeographed, issued as Stop Press section of *In Ruhleben Camp*, No. 1 (June, 1915).

Altruistic aims were not always so dominant, but no one devoid of them was permanently acceptable as a leader. Even their constant flaunting against critics reveals the high value placed on them, and those who professed them were under such close observation that the impostor was soon detected.

Secondly, the active men were doing what they had freely chosen to do, and therefore enjoying their work; this was an important source of motivation, at least until late in the internment. And finally, individual leadership, where it existed, soon gave way to co-operative groups in which the "leader" was only the first among equals; here the sharing of tasks and the stimulus of like-minded colleagues made work more of a pleasure than a burden. Captains of teams, chairmen of committees, heads of departments—all those charged with co-ordinating the activity of others—were, in Ruhleben, compelled to become experts in what is called "group work." Not only were they dealing with subordinates still jealous of their heritage of equality, but they lacked the autocrat's economic weapon—not one of their "employees" was paid. Hence the only recourse was to treat them as co-workers, sharers of responsibility, problems, and rewards. This knit the group together in loyalty to one another and to their joint aims; once that occurred little further motivation was needed. Professor Brose's statement, already quoted in part, touches on most of these points:

I personally lectured because of my love for the work and because I like studying in company, and also on account of a desire to help. Hatfield largely inspired me to do so. I felt that the time spent in study could only be profitable from every point of view—progress, health and general understanding. (L 37)

Work so inspired was in the fullest sense voluntary, and the will to do it was greatly strengthened by its social character. To be one of a congenial group pursuing a worth-while goal was a precious thing in this camp of isolated men—how precious many of them discovered for the first time. And the desire for it underlay much of the sorting and sifting described in this chapter; individuals joined an Italian class or a dramatic society as much because they had friends in it as through interest in the work, and when a qualified man dropped out of some activity it was nearly always because of a crisis in personal relations. As a result, the permanent groups were "groups" in the true meaning of the word: informal bands of co-workers, held together and kept on the job by common interests and warm mutual regard.

The power of such factors was particularly apparent in the "civil service," where the work had little intrinsic appeal; the parcel post staff, the kitchen inspectors, and the police force were veritable clubs, each with its treasured bit of exclusive space, its own lore and folkways, and its private yardsticks for the selection of new members. Even among paid workers, congenial company was as important as the money; no one lasted long in cookhouse or work-gang unless he fitted in with his mates.

TABLE II

THE 26 PRISONERS MOST PROMINENTLY MENTIONED IN CAMP MAGAZINES, 1915–17

The list includes all prisoners who received 10 or more significant references in editorial material. Each name is followed (in brackets) by the man's previous occupation, where known, and then by the camp activities on which most of his references are based. Bracketed figure at end is number of references found.

1. Henry, Leigh (dramatic production, music critic). Pioneer intellectual, lecturer, producer, "superman." (25)
2. Adler, F. Charles (student conductor). Pioneer conductor, actor. (22)
3. Conn, J. Peebles (conductor, violinist). Conductor, violinist. (22)
4. Powell, Joseph (business). Captain of the Camp. (22)
5. Bainton, E. L. (principal, Conservatory of Music). Conductor, pianist, composer. (20)
6. Butterworth, Walter (business, local government). Pioneer in community organization, welfare, debating. (20)
7. Ford, A. C. (schoolmaster). Lecturer; chairman, Ruhleben Camp School. (20)
8. Hatfield, H. S. (research chemist). Pioneer in A.S.U., theatre, literature; "superman." (18)
9. Pentland, F. B. (professional footballer, coach). Football. (17)
10. Duncan-Jones, Cecil (novelist, poet). Pioneer in drama, literature, philosophy. (16)
11. Prichard, M. S. (art critic, philosopher). Intellectual pioneer, education, philosophy, religion. (16)
12. Bloomer, Steve (professional footballer, coach). Football, cricket. (15)
13. Weber, Charles (singer). Singer, conductor. (15)
14. Kapp, Norman B. (engineering student ?). Pioneer in drama, literature; "superman." (14)
15. Masterman, J. C. (history tutor, Oxford). Lecturer, education, cricket, tennis. (14)
16. Pender, R. H. (student). Pioneer in A.S.U.; "superman." (14)
17. Bodin, A. H. (philosophy tutor, Glasgow). Religion, education, football, medals movement. (13)
18. Welland, Archibald (student of drama). Actor, producer, costumier. (13)
19. Cohen, Israel (writer, Zionist official). Debating, bye-election. (12)
20. Thorpe, John H. (business). Barrack captain; chairman, Entertainments Committee; actor. (12)
21. Crossland Briggs, W. J. (?). A.S.U., drama, medals movement. (11)
22. Lindsay, William (piano student). Pianist. (11)
23. Pauer, Waldemar (piano student). Pianist, conductor. (11)
24. Cameron, John (football manager). Secretary, Ruhleben Football Association. (10)
25. MacMillan, Ernest C. (organist, studying music). Conductor, pianist, actor. (10)
26. Merritt, George (actor). Actor. (10)

This brief discussion of leadership may be ended with a glance at Table II, which lists the twenty-six Ruhlebenites most often referred to in the camp magazines, with something of their backgrounds and camp roles. A total of 162 men, roughly 4 per cent of the population, were considered by editors and contributors to deserve some kind of specific comment, informative, laudatory, or satirical, and the table shows all who received ten or more such references.[3] The list obviously reflects prominence rather than leadership, and favours men who happened to make good copy—the controversial supermen, for example. But all the outstanding leaders are there, though a few influential men do not score quite enough to be included, and are replaced by conspicuous performers in one or another field.[4]

In spite of its shortcomings, Table II is worth noting, for it shows the kinds of men on whom public attention was focussed, and so tells us a good deal about the city of Ruhleben. And an extraordinary city it was, with three-quarters of its most prominent citizens engaged, not in government or business, but in education, the theatre, music and literature. There can have been few parallels since Athens in its prime. Versatility is much in evidence, almost half the men listed being active in more than one field—though this, of course, increased their chances of being referred to in print. And it was also a remarkably youthful city; data on age are incomplete, but at most three of these men were over fifty in 1915, and at least ten were still in their twenties.

The part played by educated men is clear, for professionally trained prisoners, who made up 18 per cent of the population, supply a good 75 per cent of its leading public figures. Business, on the other hand, contributes only three names, and not a single seafarer is included. These proportions are little altered if men with five or more references are added, extending the list to 73 names. One seafarer appears—the head of the school's Nautical Department—and nine more businessmen, as against at least 25 further professional men and students. Of the whole 162 names found, 70 per cent were referred to in connection with

3. All 16 issues of *In Ruhleben Camp* and *The Ruhleben Camp Magazine* (692 pages in all) were searched. Prominence was measured by the number of meaningful references in editorial material—articles, verse, reviews, jokes—and in the form of portraits or caricatures. "Reference" was narrowly defined; it required that something be said or implied about the individual beyond the mere printing of his name. Hence lists of teams, casts, and committee members were ignored, as were repetitions of a name in a single reference.

4. The list is also a poor predictor of later eminence, especially in science. Sir James Chadwick, Sir Charles Ellis, and Professors Brose and Vincent (all in *Who's Who*, 1940) do not appear; they were still students when interned and their camp roles were largely confined to the school.

cultural activities, 15 per cent in connection with camp administration, and only 9 per cent in connection with sport—perhaps because writers and artists were not deeply interested in it.

It is rather startling that only one out of every twenty-five Ruhlebenites should ever have been written about or caricatured in the magazines, but one important reason lies in the remarkable stability of camp leadership. It had seemed probable that any list based on the magazines would be seriously unbalanced, since the ten issues that appeared in 1915 fell to five in 1916 and to one in 1917. No problem arose, however, for the list of 162 men was virtually complete before the end of 1915 was reached. The 1916 and 1917 issues added substantially to existing scores, but produced only nine new names, none of them important.

This finding has two implications for the camp's social history. It shows first how thoroughly Ruhleben's resources were exploited in 1915; no field that might have brought new faces into prominence remained for later development. The society was thus complete before it was a year old, its patterns of activity were defined, its social groupings established, and its leaders discovered. And all the men's most lasting impressions were formed in that exciting year; the landmarks were named, the barracks labelled, and the few nicknames that came into general use—mainly for actors and "actresses"—adopted. F. C. Reynolds, who played the title role in *Androcles*, was still addressed as "Andy" in 1918, Mr. Hart was always called "Preedy" after another 1915 production, and the same unforgettable season christened "Skin-the-goat" Wilson, "Gertie" Underwood and (probably) "Polly" Welland. The men's favourite catchwords, too, originated in the first year: "Stick it, Jerry!" came from a music-hall sketch; "Hold it, Edwin!" from Steve Bloomer's favourite ejaculation on the football field; "God bless Mr. Kemp!" celebrated an interned missionary who doled out tobacco and tracts to seamen, and "Jam's in!", referring originally to receipt of stock by the canteen, came to stand for any piece of good luck. All these, along with the morale-boosting slogans of the first winter, are recorded in 1915, and no new ones seem to have appeared later. It may be wondered whether a society that flowered so precociously would keep its bloom for long.

The paucity of new names after 1915 signifies, too, that leadership had become thoroughly institutionalized. The competitive free-for-all of the first summer was never repeated; it left a hundred or so individuals in control of most camp activities, and they continued to control them. When release or resignation created a vacancy, it was typically filled from within the organization by someone long connected with it. This was the natural method, and ensured continuity in institutional policy. But the lack of new blood was discouraging to innovations and tended ultimately towards something like stagnation.

No account of Ruhleben can escape the bias that results from 4 per cent of its inhabitants being more conspicuous than the remaining 96 per cent. All that can be done is to keep in mind the hundreds of men who took part in games and debates, lectured, taught, sang, played, and acted without ever receiving special mention. It was they who kept the whole elaborate machine going, and without them leadership would have been meaningless. Nor should the larger number be forgotten who watched the games, attended the lectures, and formed the audiences at plays and concerts. Not much can be said about them, it is true, but they were essential to the balance of the system. The present history inevitably stresses the active minority, but this at least can be said for it: that not one of the twelve men whose letters and diaries are quoted, and only three of the 116 who returned questionnaires, can be found in Table II.

Prominence in Ruhleben meant just what it means elsewhere: that a man was recognized wherever he went, treated with respect by many, toadied to by a few. Such attention is pleasing and it undoubtedly inspired a good deal of public activity. For Ruhleben was no longer a mere community, and prominence in it required that the individual be re-defined on the basis of his public performance. The new definitions were inevitably superficial ones, for few but their boxmates knew that a brilliant actor was stingy with his parcels, or that a tedious orator was also a kindly soul, always doing more than his share of the work. But they were of great importance to the many who were now seeking the honey of public recognition.

Social status, however, was not identical with prominence; though affected by public activities, it was not based on them alone. It would be pleasant to report that class distinctions vanished in Ruhleben, but it would not be strictly true. The class system is an extremely resistant phenomenon, embedded in the deepest attitudes of those reared under it; after the first days of complete solidarity, it played a definite though minor role in the camp. Those who belonged to Britain's élite were distinguishable only by accent and manner, but they were distinguishable, and no one was unaware of the status they enjoyed at home.

In so far as a status system existed in the camp, it was a simple one. Of the three major occupational groups, professionals, businessmen, and seafarers, the last were generally felt to occupy the lowest position. Ships' officers were exceptions, but the status of seamen, firemen, and fishermen was accurately symbolized by their monopoly of the camp's manual work. With them were grouped factory workers, stable-hands, and the like, while the white collar classes, including most business employees, ranked considerably higher. Then came, on the one hand, the substantial businessmen—directors, entrepreneurs, and managers— and on the other the strictly professional class; its status was generally higher, but there was much overlapping. Over all stood the public school élite, closely identified with the academic professionals, but aligned against business by the aristocracy's old disdain for "trade" and its practitioners. This social cleavage accounted in part for the hostility of the élite towards the camp captains, who were mainly in business, and also for the tendency of upper-class prisoners to fraternize with seafarers while avoiding businessmen. Sailors represented no threat to the traditional ruling class in 1914.

But, though Ruhleben was not a classless society, it was far from being a class-ridden one, for the lines were broken as sharply by intern-ment as by the bombing of Britain in 1940. A professional man could not ignore the differences between himself and a kitchen worker, but he regarded them typically as differences in education that should not affect human relationships. In many mixed boxes social differences were completely subordinated to group solidarity, and the same was true of teams, school classes, and other such groups. Indeed, the arti-ficial and misleading nature of class distinctions was one of the chief lessons taught by internment; here are some of the 1933 answers to the question: "What aspect of your Ruhleben experience has been of the greatest value to you since release?"

Meeting and living with all sorts and conditions of men. (teacher)
Intimate contact with all classes of men. (artist)
Rubbing shoulders with men of all classes. (student)
Mixing up with so many types of men. (chemist)
Association with men of all classes. (businessman)
The fact that one saw human character without social veneer. (banker)
Experience gained through contact with so many different types. (dyer)
That some of the lower element had the whitest hearts. (manufacturer)
The unique opportunity of meeting on level terms all classes and types of Englishmen. (engineer)

Two men used extra space to elaborate:

To have been in close contact with so many men of varying origin, educa-tion, experience and outlook, and to have learnt to understand and appreciate their outlook on life and apprehend how they arrived at it. (businessman)

I am glad that I mixed with people and found that it is a great mistake to be influenced by the knowledge that a man has either done hard labour or has obtained a good social position. (engineer)

A letter from Ewing in April 1917 may also be quoted:

> But oh, Mother, I wonder if the people in England are learning, as we are, how artificial and harmful all barriers and divisions are, and whether the equality of service and sacrifice at the front will find its natural consequence in equality of opportunity and responsibility after the war. . . . To be governed by a comparatively small, respectable, wealthy class is not enough.

These statements, however, while repudiating class distinctions, also recognize that classes existed in Ruhleben. There were thus two somewhat independent status systems operating, one based on camp achievements, the other on class membership. Though the first was the more conspicuous, the second provided an unchanging background for it. There was little conflict between them, since the educated classes also supplied most of the active leaders. And the aims of these leaders were so obviously unselfish that class antagonism was kept at a low level. Remarks about "snobs" were common in the sailors' barracks, but these were chiefly evoked by individuals whose expenditures on food, furnishings, and clothing were needlessly and tactlessly conspicuous.

The "complete disappearance" of class distinctions in Britain during the critical days of the Second World War aroused much admiring comment; less was said about their subsequent reappearance. And the impressive social democracy of Ruhleben was also a temporary thing, vanishing, except from memory, on the men's return to conventional society. The waiter who could recall no hardships in internment was asked in 1933 with how many fellow-prisoners he still kept in touch; his answer read: "Meet quite a number in my business, but socially they are above me" (Q 113).

15

GOVERNMENT AND POLITICS

WITHIN A YEAR of the internment Ruhleben was a totalitarian state; every aspect of its corporate life was governed, directly or indirectly, by the Captains' Committee. Ultimate authority still rested with the Germans, but it amounted in practice to little more than veto power, and this was seldom exercised. How a small group of prisoners, unremarkable as individuals, came to control both their four thousand fellows and also, to a considerable degree, the German authorities is an intriguing study in the dynamics of power.

The captains, initially, were the ten men who stepped out of the ranks as interpreters on November 8, 1914. Others were added as further barracks were opened, and in September 1915 the committee numbered seventeen, including J. P. Jones, the Camp Treasurer. The only qualification originally needed was fluency in German—plus, it might be added, enough self-assurance to come forward at the Baron's request. Cohen speaks caustically of the interpreters as "presumptuous enough to recommend themselves" (p. 38) but this is unfair; some volunteered only reluctantly, because no one else did so. On the other hand, Powell's assertion, "the elections thus improvised were quite informally conducted" (p. 12), is a masterly understatement; the "electors" were given no chance to express their preferences. For obvious reasons most of the volunteers were businessmen resident in Germany; not only did they know the language, but dealing with Germans had been their *métier*. It should be stated that not the slightest objection was taken to these appointments at the time; the interpreters' functions appeared purely formal and internment was expected to be a matter of days.

Ruhleben lasted for four years, however, and chance had put these men in a potentially strategic position. Control of human beings, when not exerted by force, rests on communication, and effective control on reciprocal communication. In the camp, however, communication between Germans and British was obstructed by two barriers: the language difficulty, which affected more than half the men, and military etiquette, which made the officers relatively unapproachable by prisoners. It was at these barriers that the interpreters had been placed; though their functions were not important, their location was extremely so. Like the British at Gibraltar, they sat astride of a vital channel of communication, where a minimum of power can have maximum effect.

Their position was strengthened by several circumstances, the first of which was a mere linguistic error: use of the word "captain." The official title was *Obmann*, meaning "spokesman" or "representative," and the Baron is said to have used it at some barracks. The word, however, was unknown to most prisoners, and was widely mistaken for the familiar military term *Hauptmann*, or captain. The *Obmänner* made no effort to correct the error; they promptly equipped themselves with buttons and arm-bands labelled "Captain," and the designation was adopted without hesitation. Perhaps it made no difference; "spokesman" might in time have gathered the same connotations of authority that "minister" (originally "servant") has in parliamentary democracy. But "captain" at least suggested a higher status than *Obmann* would have implied.

The essential factor in the rise of the captains was the existence of a power vacuum in the camp. To remain intact, authority must be effectively exercised; after the first few days, however, German authority was slighted even in matters of immediate military concern. An absurd number of rules had been laid down, and enforcement was inevitably sporadic and inconsistent. The prisoners were unused to discipline and contemptuous of the Prussian variety, while the soldiers, dull-witted and without a word of English, could conceive of no other method of managing them. When barked commands were ignored, or only sluggishly obeyed, they began by knocking men around and throwing them into the cells. Physical violence, however, brought protests to the Commandant and not infrequently a reprimand; hence most of the soldiers ultimately reconciled themselves to a kind of semi-authority, accepting dilatory line-ups, sloppy marching, and endless talking after "lights out" as the price of a tolerably peaceful atmosphere in their barracks. Their removal in September 1915 was a belated acknowledgment that British civilians were best left to run themselves.

The chief power vacuum, however, was due to the fact that the Germans never attempted to control more than a small segment of the prisoners' lives. Interned civilians were exempt from the manual labour required of captured soldiers, and the Germans could hardly prescribe route marches, physical exercise, and similar occupations for every hour of the day. As a result, the men's spontaneous activity in organizing their community and its later institutions was almost untouched by military control, and this had momentous consequences. For it was through organization that the forces diffused through four thousand vigorous men were focussed and gathered into relatively few hands, a situation that made direct military rule impossible. A disorderly crowd can be dominated by a handful of armed men, but a united and well-organized community, as would-be despots have often learned, can be safely handled only through its own leaders. It is to the German officers' credit that, far from trying to interfere with Ruhleben's internal organization, they watched its autonomous growth with frank admiration; only later did they discover what a weapon had been forged against them. The captains moved in at the summit of each organization, where power was most concentrated, and their consequent control of all camp activities enabled them many times to bring the Germans to heel.

Government by the captains operated at two distinct levels. First was the individual captain's control of his barrack, which rested, at least after September 1915, on authority delegated by the Germans. In general, this was tactfully exercised and good-humouredly accepted. Secondly, there was the control of the camp's growing institutions—financial, economic, recreational, cultural—by the captains as a body. This rested on no clear authority but was an outgrowth of circumstances; its fortuitous origin was resented, and it was often challenged. In addition to control, the captains acquired important representative functions; they were recognized by the Commandant as representing all the interned, and in time the same recognition was given them, at least *de facto*, by the United States Embassy and the British Government. Internal control plus external recognition made their position almost impregnable, and they were never dislodged from it.

The barrack captain gained authority over his three hundred prisoners swiftly and inevitably. Even in the first week he was no mere translator, for the Baron, rather than address a dozen barracks in succession, sent his routine communications through the captains. And when one of them stood in the corridor and requested silence for a military announcement, he was already exercising control; when he explained it or suggested compliance he was exerting a little more. He was now the accepted link between the German staff and the barrack—the soldiers were merely a nuisance—and men inured to receiving orders through him found it natural, before long, to accept orders from him. Communication, moreover, was a two-way process. Innumerable inquiries and requests were directed to the captain; some he duly transmitted upwards, but with others he was soon able to deal himself. It was he, too, who appointed the postmen, cashiers, and other officials, and to him that they looked for instructions. The captain's box quickly became the busiest spot in the barrack and required a notice stating his office hours.

In short, the barrack captain was compelled by circumstances to act *as if* he had authority; this evoked old habits of compliance and so made his authority real. For authority resides, not in its supposed possessor, but in the willingness of others to accept it.[1] When removal of the barrack guards left the captain in sole charge, the change did little more than confirm the status quo; the soldiers were already as superfluous as they were irritating. It did heighten the captain's status symbolically, however, for he and his vice-captain now set a distance between themselves and other prisoners by moving into the soldiers' rooms.

Barrack administration was soon a matter of routine, and barrack captaincy as such carried no great prestige. It was important politically, however, since it was the only means of entry to the central government where real power resided. Powell resigned his captaincy of Barrack 10 when Home Rule was granted, and the Camp Treasurer never represented a barrack, but they were the sole exceptions. The system was traditional—even prime ministers must represent some constituency—but it was somewhat illogical, for the two spheres had little in common. The 1918 constitution recognized this and provided for the direct election of a five-man camp executive, but until its adoption in the last month of internment Ruhleben was governed by the barrack captains. But not by all equally; as their number increased there appeared what Powell and Gribble call "an informal and unofficial Inner Cabinet" (p. 42) which decided policy and drafted agenda in advance of the full meetings. When action by "the captains" is referred to, it is this inner cabinet that should mainly be thought of. The grounds given for thus dividing the committee—unwieldiness and the presence of pro-German captains—are reasonable, but it is noteworthy that only staunch supporters of Powell were ever included in the inner group.

How did the captains acquire their power over the camp? On page 14 of *The History of Ruhleben* Powell and Gribble state: "the captains were resolved to let slip no opportunity which might present itself of getting the administration of the camp into their own hands," and the assertion is subsequently twice repeated. It is, however, chiefly a product of hindsight. The authors say later that most of the captains' early

---

1. That authority comes "from above" is, as Chester I. Barnard points out, only a necessary fiction; its actual source is in its voluntary acceptance by the individual concerned. For an able analysis of the problem see his *The Functions of the Executive* (Cambridge, Mass.: Harvard University Press, 1948).

actions were "tentative and provisional—based upon the assumption that the war might come to an end at any moment" (pp. 221-2), and this is nearer the truth. No definite aim to take over the camp could be formulated until its probable permanence was recognized, and the recognition came slowly, even to captains. What actually happened is clear: the captains' early efforts to cope with immediate problems started them on paths of action which were bound to lead them to power, whatever their intentions.

They first met as a group on November 9, 1914, elected Trinks as chairman and Powell as vice-chairman, and discussed the camp's most urgent problems: sickness, destitution, lack of essential supplies, the dangerous condition of the latrines. The attempt to deal with these emergencies carried them in two directions: into collecting money to have the latrines cleaned—the beginning of autonomous administration; and into getting permission to telephone the American Embassy—the first step towards outside recognition. And similar moves followed. Each captain appointed barrack officials and raised a small fund to buy brooms and pay cleaners, while Trinks's phone call resulted in his being allowed to visit the Embassy a week later.

An even more significant step was the organizing of a police force on November 13. The motive was simple; it was clear that if the guards remained in sole charge of the prisoners riots would occur. The Commandant must have been impressed by the argument, for a body of thirty men was enrolled under an inspector and two sergeants. They had mainly routine duties, but they were a *force*, and a force that took its orders from the captains, not the Germans. This was no small concession under military rule, and all the captains' early accomplishments— organizing the barracks, cleaning up the camp, getting funds from a reluctant embassy—reflect determination and outspokenness. The blunt forcefulness of some of these businessmen, and particularly of Powell, was much criticized later, but it justified itself in their early dealings with the Germans. Powell's book says truly, if defensively, "If they had been unduly modest and retiring, they might long have remained a mere group of unrelated spokesmen-interpreters" (p. 13).

Though the captains' control was for some time limited to communal organization at the barrack and camp levels, the prisoners were already opening up new fields of activity. Within a few weeks teachers were advertising for pupils, services, debates, and concerts were being held, and all sorts of pastimes had sprung up. There was no logical reason why the captains should control these new activities, but their position was already so strong that no other outcome was possible. As each activity was organized it came under a hierarchical series of committees, and by the spring of 1915 the captains were firmly entrenched at the top of each hierarchy.

They got there by virtue of two potent weapons, derived from American and German recognition respectively. The first was financial. Most activities required supplies from outside; besides the traders, who were ordering in everything from milk to mattresses, scores of individuals were clamouring to buy text-books, dictionaries, slide-rules, chess sets, footballs, and musical instruments. Beginning by ordering urgently needed goods on behalf of individuals or groups, the captains quickly became large-scale buyers, and found themselves saddled, of course, with financial responsibility. This was intolerable without control; after a brief nightmare as mere go-betweens, they persuaded the Germans to ban private trading and went into business themselves as a commercial monopoly.

There was no necessity for them actually to operate the cultural and recreational institutions; these were already well organized, and their financial needs ensured control. Heavy orders of sporting and theatrical equipment could only be financed through the Camp Fund which the captains administered, and this gave them a deciding voice in policy. And similarly, when in the fall of 1915 Powell persuaded the embassy to advance M 3,000 for education—chiefly for remodelling Barrack 6 into classrooms—it was a certainty that the school was no longer controlled solely by academics. Institutions that accept public money usually find it wrapped in a list of regulations, and the school was in fact already under a subcommittee of the captains.

Financial power is familiar everywhere, but the second form of control was peculiar to Ruhleben: the captains' control of *space*. This was already effective before pecuniary questions arose, and would have ensured their power over camp activities even if these had cost nothing to run. For space was the scarcest commodity in the compound, far scarcer than money, and this made it the object of intense competition. There were quarrels in the lofts about two inches of floor space, boxmates fought over the use of a shelf or clothes hook, and the billeting of a new arrival in an unfilled box was bitterly resisted. Deprived of the mobility that enables animals to solve such problems by migration, the prisoners were reduced to the level of plants, struggling for *Lebensraum* in an overgrown garden.

In their living quarters the men reached, by mutual concessions, an accommodation not possible to plants, but the commencement of public activities raised the problem in a new form. With the opening of the grandstand hall in December 1914 someone had to decide whether debaters or musicians should have it on a given evening, when the A.S.U. might hold a meeting, and when the church choir could rehearse. The Germans merely made the space available and left its allocation to the captains, who thereby secured a firm hold on all organized activities. Since no public function could be held without applying to them for space, none could be held without their consent. Some such system was patently necessary in the interests of order, but again order was synonymous with control. Thus the presence of a camp policeman at religious services, entertainments, and public meetings was more than a safeguard against disturbance; it was also a stamp of approval by the captains.

As pressure for space increased their power grew with it. The little storage sheds in various corners of the compound were coveted by many organizations, the artists and musicians wanted sites on which to erect their studios, and a growing number of private clubs sought permission to build sheds against the back walls of barracks. Some daring individuals constructed little huts out of packing cases and maintained squatters' rights to them, but German approval was essential to any substantial project. The officers sometimes complicated things by dealing direct with favoured prisoners, but in general they yielded space, if at all, only to representations from the captains, whose sanction thus became necessary. And when Powell negotiated the lease of the sports field—the only important new space ever acquired—it was placed as a matter of course under a committee controlled by the captains. Ruhleben's economics were in fact economics of space as much as of money, and in both fields the captains had almost a monopoly.

It was, however, a surprisingly long time before the powers they exercised in so many directions were clothed in any appropriate organization. The Arts and Science Union, Debating Society, and Camp School were all organized before February 1915, and by April they had been joined by a horde of athletic, dramatic, and other associations. The captains, in contrast, were still trying to deal as a group with the multifarious activities of a growing town. A couple of *ad hoc* committees had been set up and certain captains had been assigned special functions, but Powell was loath to delegate power and areas of authority were far from clear. The situation must have been trying to the captains, and it was certainly confusing to the prisoners. A captain could not cross Trafalgar Square without being buttonholed by suppliants, and one might give Adler the hall without knowing that another had reserved it for a seafarers' meeting. For businessmen, they were extraordinarily remiss about organizing their own work.

One of them was finally moved to action; in the first week of March Wallace Ellison, then serving as captain of the Negroes' barrack, handed Powell a memorandum urging a municipal form of organization. His preamble read:

We have in this camp of 4,000 a town in embryo. Especially is this the case now that the internal administration is largely in our hands, and the suggestions which I am bringing forward are in essence an appeal to the captains to perfect the organization of the camp by copying those features of English municipal government which would be of advantage to the camp at large. (H)

The plan was simple: the setting up of a number of departmental committees "for greater efficiency and prevention of criticism," control being retained through the chairmen, who would be captains, and through appointment of the remaining members. It is curious that an "appeal" should be needed for so obvious a step, and that a captain should use the term to his colleagues. But it is very suggestive of the relations between the inner cabinet, of which Ellison was not a member, and the rest of the body.

The appeal was ultimately acted upon, and by the end of May camp affairs were in the hands of eight committees: Finance, Kitchens, Canteens, Watch and Works (Police), Sanitation, Sports Control, Education, and Entertainment. (A plan of the organization is shown in Figure 5.) All eight chairmen and five of the vice-chairmen were captains, as was one of the committee members, and the remaining thirty-six were captains' appointees (*IRC* 8, pp. 37–8). In the case of sport, education, and entertainments an effort was made to select fairly representative men, but there was no pretence of their being elected. The distribution of offices among the captains is significant, and may be summarized as follows:

Total number of committee posts held by captains	14
Held by "inner circle" (Powell and three others)	9
Held by next five captains	5
Held by remaining seven captains	0

While some captains were certainly better qualified than others, the concentration of power in the hands of Powell and a few henchmen was glaringly evident.

By midsummer of 1915 Ruhleben was organized from top to bottom, and the captains occupied the apex of the pyramid. They had not been placed there by popular vote, but they had worked hard and accomplished much. The chaotic misery of eight months earlier had given

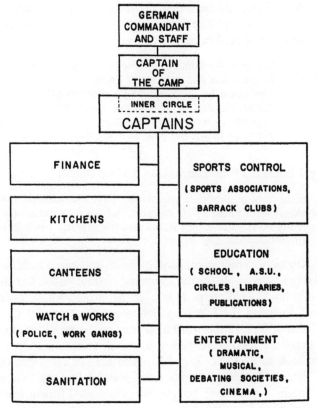

FIGURE 5. Organization of the civil administration of Ruhleben, as established in 1915, showing Captains' Committee and sub-committees.

place to order and relative comfort; the poorest prisoner had money, the canteens were well stocked, the sick were better tended, and the sports field, hot-water house, showers, laundry tubs, and cinder roads were tangible benefits. The captains could claim no direct credit for the games, concerts, plays, and classes that were making interned life meaningful, but they had arranged the necessary funds and space. All told, they must have felt that they deserved the camp's recognition and backing, if not its grateful admiration. What they got, however, was persistent ridicule, widespread mistrust, and a great deal of bitter opposition. It was a genuine shock to them and had permanent effects on their conduct.

The first camp newspaper, the *Ruhleben Camp News*, began the assault in January 1915 by suggesting "Should the captains be hanged?"

as a topic for debate, and from then on almost every published reference was satirical or abusive. "The Seven Ages of a *Kriegsgefangener*" in the first magazine issued read in part:

> Lo, here the Captain, badged and awe-inspiring,
> In discipline and duty never tiring;
> The world he looks upon with scornful pity,
> Alone, unaided by the Camp Committee;
> Superior to men of common clay,
> He gains in self-importance every day.
>
> (*IRC* 1, p. 7)

The July 1 minutes of the Lancastrian Society stated:

Much in the way of profitless speculation might be avoided if the camp were occasionally consulted by its captains, but we must remember that the camp has really no right to expect it, because the captains assist in its administration without representing it.

And in August a writer complaining about hot-water facilities asked: "Would it not be possible for the Captains, without undue loss of dignity, to look into this?" (*IRC* 6, p. 45). L. R. M. Strachan's "Shakespeare in Ruhleben" included the following quotation: "A Captain! God's light, these villains will make the word as odious as the word 'occupy'; which was an excellent good word before it was ill-sorted; therefore captains had need look to 't" (*IRC* 7, p. 23). And a 1916 catalogue of "Camp Curios" listed: "Letter of thanks from grateful barrack to their much loved Captain (very rare; bought for Pierpont Morgan collection)" (*RCM* 4, p. 4).

Serious criticism was equally common, and much of it centred about finance. The obscurity of the balance sheet published in June 1915 brought more indignant letters than the magazine could publish, and in August an influential group complained directly to the American Ambassador about the handling of camp funds. The protest was apparently fruitless, for soon afterwards a correspondent described the financial conduct of the camp as "degenerating into something approaching a scandal" (*IRC* 6, p. 43), and a 1916 statement evoked the editorial comment: "It is no good asking us to explain the Camp's latest puzzle —the Balance Sheet. We do not know any more about it than the people who drew it up." (*RCM* 2, p. 22.) Some complaint was justified, for camp finances were complex, and the summaries published—like those given later in Powell and Gribble's book—contained puzzling gaps and inconsistencies. But the books were ultimately audited by chartered accountants, they were open to inspection by any prisoner, and after some initial confusion there were no solid grounds for criticism. Much of it originated among some "big" businessmen who had little to do in camp, and who resented its being run by men whom they regarded as inferiors.

As the earlier quotations suggest, the captains were also attacked as high-handed, self-important, aloof, and secretive. Cohen speaks of their "insufferable arrogance" (p. 38), and the magazine editor wrote, in an open letter to them: "The most potent factor in arousing the mistrust with which you are at present regarded by an immense majority of the Camp has been your secrecy. . . . You NEVER take the camp into your confidence" (*IRC* 6, p. 41). The attitudes were undoubtedly characteristic of Powell and one or two others, but they were also precisely what would be expected of a harshly criticized group. Public officials who are unexpectedly, mercilessly, and (in their opinion) unjustly assailed are almost driven into a haughty posture; any other would seem like admission of guilt. And they are not likely to begin taking their opponents into their confidence; instead, they draw apart and become unapproachable. The flood of criticism thus tended to produce the very traits criticized, and was also responsible, at least in part, for the defensive solidarity shown by the whole body of captains, and for their reluctance to submit to free elections.

The most specific dissatisfactions of the 1915 summer were focussed on the Entertainments Committee, which had taken over the properties of the various dramatic societies, appropriated all box-office receipts, and published no accounts. In June two of its appointed members resigned in disgust, the musical society demanded direct representation and was refused, and in July the Ruhleben Dramatic Society sent the captains a unanimous resolution protesting the committee's make-up. No reply was received, either to this or to a subsequent list of complaints, and it transpired that Powell had not troubled to lay either communication before the captains' meeting. The dramatic and musical societies then threatened to cease all public activities, but Powell denounced this as an ultimatum and demanded its withdrawal. On August 16 the captains, while stating that they objected "on principle" to representation, offered to reconstitute the committee and allow the performing societies two representatives, as against two captains and four captains' appointees. This was quite unacceptable; next day all plays and concerts were cancelled and Ruhleben's first official strike began. Its impact was not great, for open-air activities were in full swing and the professional variety artists, who were strongly represented on the committee, went ahead with a "blackleg" performance. Nor is it possible to say when the strike ended, since electrical re-wiring of the hall darkened it until mid-October. In any case, the societies won their point. On the new committee, which functioned satisfactorily for the next three years, they had four direct representatives to balance the four appointed members.

The episode illumines Ruhleben's basic political problem, the existence of two contrasted forms of government in the same society. Government from the top down was autocratic, from the bottom up democratic; the question was where the dividing line would be drawn. The captains had tried to restrict representation to the level of the men's own associations; the strike forced its partial acceptance at the top administrative level. That was all that could be achieved at the time—replacement of the captains by an elected body was still three years away—but from a realistic standpoint it was enough. For the citizen's sense of self-determination depends much more on his government's administrative practices than on his right to vote it out of office; where these practices rest on regular consultation and consent, the ballot box becomes of minor importance. And, in the areas of greatest importance to the prisoners, the principle of consent had now been clearly established.

It was well that it had, for the captains' authority was about to be greatly widened. On September 14 Graf Schwerin told Powell that, if he would take full responsibility for order and the daily count of prisoners, the soldiers would be withdrawn and full internal control entrusted to the civil administration. Each barrack was consulted and approved the change, at the same time giving its captain a somewhat questionable fresh mandate. Powell says flatly, "every captain was re-elected except myself" (p. 67) but he is again interpreting "election" rather freely. Cohen says of the procedure: "The Acting Commandant, attended by the Captain of the Camp, asked the inmates of each barrack in turn whether they were satisfied with their respective captain. The only reply was 'yes,' though not all responded" (p. 170). And the following account comes from Barrack 10, where Powell's new responsibilities made a successor necessary: "Powell came round with the Baron at Appell and said: 'You have to elect a new captain, as I am *Oberobmann* now. I propose Mr. Williams. All those in favour hold up their hands. Mr. Williams is elected!" (L 86)

Most contemporary letters report the concession of Home Rule, but none mentions any re-election of captains. The magazine editor, however, though a persistent critic of the captains, accepted their endorsement at face value—"the Camp as a whole has expressed itself as satisfied" (*IRC* 8, p. 1)—and called for full and unprejudiced support of them. Support, in the sense of acceptance of their authority, was forthcoming, but prejudice, after a short lull, grew in certain quarters into something like hatred. Nor did it subside on release; Cohen's references are consistently bitter, Prichard maintained until his death that Powell was simply a German agent, and in 1933 a gifted British writer, rejecting the questionnaire as "one of the many importations from the U.S.A. that we could do without," added: "The only comment I have to make about Ruhleben is that it was a thousand pities that we were represented in an enemy country by such people as the barrack 'captains' " (L 128).

Why were the captains so hated? The question needs qualifying in two respects. First, by no means all were hated; Powell's arrogance and political intrigues made him many personal enemies, but in most cases it was the role rather than the individual that was disliked—"captaincy" rather than "captains." And secondly, hostility was increasingly confined to certain upper- and middle-class circles, including many of the camp's intellectual leaders. The mass of prisoners, at least after 1916, were politically apathetic, and in 1918 they cheerfully voted Powell back into office. And a further point should be mentioned: some of the intensity of the 1915 attacks on the captains must be put down to the fact that they were a natural target for the aggressions caused by internment. Camp life could be rich and rewarding, but it still involved the deep frustrations of enforced separation from home and inability to help in the war. The captains were the only symbols of authority who could be publicly reviled, and they suffered for this as all governments suffer for ills they cannot remedy.

There were more specific causes for resentment, however, and especially for its long continuance. These were the personalities and methods of Powell and one or two others, the social backgrounds of most of the ruling clique, and two important and closely related issues: Powell's ambiguous relations with the German authorities, and the captains' long resistance to free elections.

Joseph Powell was a forceful administrator who well deserved the O.B.E. he was later awarded. In his relations with the prisoners, however, he conspicuously lacked charm. Clean shaven, with an open face and a shock of curly hair, he was not unattractive physically, but his manner was brusque, his tones harsh, and his speech accompanied by impatient gestures like those of a Prussian non-com. Govett described him with gentle sarcasm in 1915: "Who will ever forget Powell as he stands placidly smiling and hinting at his wishes in his musical voice?" (*IRC* 7, p. 4). Singularly little is known of his background or private life; when he died in Berlin in 1925 his obituary in *The Times* mentioned no wife, relatives, or occupation, and consisted entirely of a summary of Ruhleben's history. His pre-war association with the Eclair Cinema Company is established, but otherwise he might have been taken for the hard-driving manager of a small, non-unionized factory. And, like such petty tyrants, he was utterly ruthless towards those who opposed him. Although Gribble says in his autobiography, *Seen in Passing*, that Powell's death was "mourned by a host of friends" (p. 304), in camp he was definitely a "lone wolf"—a fact that may have contributed to the mysterious breakdown in health which kept him in the sanatorium from October 1917 to May 1918.

In the same tribute to Powell, Gribble credits him with both modesty and tact—and Gribble had worked closely with him on *The History of Ruhleben*. More characteristic in the camp's view, however, were the ornate badge and arm-band that Powell invariably wore, each boldly inscribed: *Captain of the Camp: Oberobmann des Lagers*. The same grandiose titles followed his name on all notices and stationery, and were even printed on each one of the tiny hot-water tickets issued in 1915. The magazine commented: "You need not hesitate about buying hot-water tickets. We understand that Mr. Powell has other 'business' cards." (*IRC* 4, p. 1.) And it was a little less than modest to choose, as frontispiece for *The History of Ruhleben*, a full-page enlargement of the 1918 election results, showing in huge figures Powell's majority of 935 over his only opponent. Errors of taste might be laughed at, but the men were definitely irritated by the tone and content of many of Powell's orders. Cohen speaks of the captains' "instinctive imitation of the autocratic Prussian style" (p. 52) and, while this was not true of most of them, it was certainly a fair description of Powell. And the announcement in 1915 that all notices posted on the boiler house must first be stamped in the captains' office struck the camp as brazenly autocratic, for the boiler house had long been the chief medium of public communication.

A less creditable source of hostility was mere class snobbery. The fact that most of the captains were businessmen, with few pretensions to education or social position, rankled deeply among a certain section of prisoners. Ambassador Gerard writes: "Naturally [Powell] was always subject to opposition from many prisoners, among whom those of aristocratic tendencies objected to being under the control of one not of the highest caste in Great Britain" (p. 178). Powell's lack of education, in particular, was mercilessly held against him; one of his written notices was actually placed on an important English examination, candidates being instructed to correct the grammatical errors. Against underhand attacks of this kind Powell could not defend himself; perhaps they explain his choice of a frontispiece for the *History*. To reprint the unfortunate notice now would be unforgivable, but the fact that two ex-prisoners made a point of sending it to me in 1933 shows the hatred felt for Powell even long after his death.

Hostility towards him and his immediate supporters was deepened by a growing mistrust of their relations with the Germans. In theory they were simple intermediaries, but the intermediary's situation in wartime is a dangerously exposed one. One captain, who loyally supported Powell until 1918, wrote: "You must remember that the position of Captain of the Camp involved acting as a collision-mat between the interned and the enemy military authorities, and it was not a very enviable job. One never knew from hour to hour when the whole works was going to blow up." (L 97.) Powell was undoubtedly British in sentiment, but he had to keep in the good graces of the authorities, and there were those who suspected him of being, like Marshal Pétain in the Second World War, a mere German tool. Their suspicions, however, were wide of the mark; the fact is that Powell's hold over the Germans was almost as strong as his grip on the camp.

To understand this it must be realized that the senior officers at Ruhleben were also in an exposed position. They were very minor cogs in the military machine, Graf Schwerin being only a major, Baron von Taube an *Oberleutnant*. They were also immediately under the eye of the War Office in Berlin, and neither had any experience in running a prison camp. It was not a task they would have chosen, and they approached it with some nervousness, having no idea how their four thousand British might behave. When the prisoners promptly demonstrated that they could run their own affairs, organizing the whole camp and turning it into a hive of creative activity, the officers were first astonished and then delighted; they grew proud of their resourceful *Engländer*, and reluctant to see them suffer. Admiration of their charges weakened their position, however, for it bred the wish to be liked by them in turn, a wish incompatible with strict discipline.

The Baron was less moved by such feelings than the Graf, but he was equally sensitive to a stronger argument for leniency that arose once the camp was fully organized. Ruhleben quickly became the showplace of the Berlin Command; important neutral visitors were ceremoniously conducted around it, ambassadors and brass hats applauded its plays and concerts from the "Royal Box." And every state visit ended in the same way: with a shower of compliments to Commandant and Baron on the outstanding success of their administration. The two elderly gentlemen found such praise from the highest quarters irresistible; their paramount if unconscious aim became that of keeping Ruhleben running smoothly, and avoiding at all costs any trouble that might come to the ears of their superiors.

This delivered them into Powell's hands, for all the men who kept the camp running—kitchen workers, canteen staffs, fatigue parties, and many more—were now employees of the captains. If the latter should resign and their staffs follow suit, the Germans would be in serious trouble. They might return to the conditions of 1914 and place soldiers in the barracks and a contractor in the kitchens, but they could not begin to man all the other services, and the resulting hardships, they had good reason to know, would make the prisoners almost unmanageable. Ruhleben's high reputation would be destroyed, and their own with it. The Baron chafed under this dependence and often asserted himself in sudden disciplinary explosions; in most cases he cooled down quickly, but if he went too far Powell exerted his power. As early as April 1915 he and his vice-captain were able to prevent the replacement of a British captain by a pro-German; both resigned, only to be promptly reinstated. Several similar incidents took place, as in October 1917, when soldiers appearing late at *Appell* were booed by impatient prisoners. The irate Baron at once placed soldiers back in the barracks and ordered a third *Appell* daily; but after the captains had threatened to give up their responsibilities the Commandant cancelled both punishments.

Powell was thus in the enviable position of being able to control both British and Germans by playing one party off against the other. Over the camp he ruled as an autocrat; towards the senior officers his manner was unctuously ingratiating. In the main, his ability to manipulate them benefited the men, but there is no question that he also used it for his own political advantage. A 1916 order that no prisoner approach Graf Schwerin without first applying to Powell was deeply resented, since it put Powell in control of all information reaching the Commandant. But it was reaffirmed in 1917 with only minor modifications: "The Commander of the Camp makes it known that he is always ready to grant interviews. Those wishing to see him must first see Mr. Powell. It is not necessary to state the nature of the interview, but in such cases the applicant must have good reasons for not doing so" (H). The order may have originated with the Commandant, but it was so obviously aimed at averting criticism of Powell that its paternity was highly suspect. And in July 1916 Chapman recorded an experience that was not infrequent: "Answered call at Censor's office re a remark I had made in a letter to

Nora about Powell." The offending remark was probably deleted, for Powell had become so necessary to the officers that they would brook no undermining of his authority. Whatever his defects, he knew how to manage the Germans.

Powell's equivocal role was particularly disturbing in connection with the central, perennial issue between captains and camp, that of open elections. The German officers flatly opposed them—and with reason, for captains elected by the camp would be responsible to the camp. But how far was Powell behind the opposition? That was what the prisoners wanted to know. The fullest German statement on the subject was made by Graf Schwerin to a meeting on March 28, 1916, and excerpts from the official report will throw some light on a complex political situation. L. G. Beaumont, Vice-Captain of the Camp, had been exchanged, and three captains had had the temerity to write to the Commandant, without Powell's knowledge, suggesting that his successor be *elected* by the camp. Graf Schwerin immediately summoned a meeting of captains and vice-captains and addressed it to the following effect:

He had that morning received a letter signed by three gentlemen regarding the appointment of a new Vice-Captain of the Camp. He felt very surprised to hear that the Captain of the Camp had no previous knowledge of the contents of the document. . . .

He reminded the gentlemen assembled that he had personally recommended the change from Military to Civil administration, and he had done this as a token of appreciation for the good conduct of the interned and for the manner in which the Captain of the Camp and the Captains had assisted him in maintaining order in the camp. . . .

He had, however, on three occasions been asked to alter existing arrangements by giving permission for a system of election to take place in the Camp. This was impossible. Such procedure would only lead to discontent and divisions within the Camp, and it was his duty to see that order and quiet were maintained.

Whatever might be thought as to the theory of elections, it was an error to believe that anyone could represent the views of a whole community; a Vice-Captain in this Camp could only represent the views of a majority, but he would not have the confidence of the minority, and therefore could not be said to have the support of the whole Camp. . . . He was against elections in the interests of peace and content.

He assured the gentlemen present that . . . the best manner in which the question of the Vice Captaincy could be settled was that he himself should appoint someone who would support the Captain of the Camp in his work. . . . He wanted the support of the men in the Camp, and he did not want them to make things hard for him by causing trouble about appointments. They should stand by Mr. Powell and support him. (CC)

Beneath all his Prussian sophistries about elections, it is clear that the

Graf's real objection to them was that they might threaten Powell. He could have been talked round—but only by Powell himself, who was hardly likely to do it. The new vice-captain was appointed, and it is easy to guess who nominated him.

The fact that three captains addressed the Graf on this occasion suggests the growing gap between the inner cabinet and the rest of the committee. It is surprising that the three were allowed to retain office; a captain who questioned Powell's authority a month later was peremptorily dismissed. But agitation for reform was strong at this period, and Powell was unpopular and knew it. A correspondent who had already drafted a tentative camp constitution approached him after the meeting and asked why he did not want to put the civil government on a proper basis. "Powell's reply was that if he were put up for election not one person in the camp would vote for him" (L 24). And he had already burned his fingers by meddling again with elections in his old barrack. When his successor, Mr. Williams, was repatriated with men over fifty-five, Powell tried to repeat his previous tactics of nominating and electing in one breath. "But this time," wrote a Barrack 10 man, "Prichard was ready for him, and moved that we confine ourselves to establishing procedure—date and place of nomination and so on. Much to J.P.'s chagrin a constitutional method was adopted, and Masterman was elected" (L 86). Like Prichard and other "reform" captains, Masterman did not long hold his position. As further vacancies occurred, however, they were filled in the same way, and in time more than half the captains were duly elected representatives. But the fact had little effect on the regime, for Powell, as chosen instrument of the military, held all the trump cards. Only he knew what took place at his conferences with the Commandant; the rest of the captains had to accept what he chose to tell them. And those who opposed him were either forced to resign or, when he felt strong enough, were summarily dismissed "by military order."

Powell's motives in perpetuating his regime were probably those of any self-made businessman of the period: conviction of his own indispensability, enjoyment of power and its fruits, and a basic cynicism about the electoral process. He had made Ruhleben what it was, and was running it efficiently; what more could anyone ask for? A sentence in *The History of Ruhleben* is revealing: "To the success of the policy followed two conditions were, of course, requisite; the acquiescence of the camp authorities, and the cordial backing, based on faith in our capacity, of the American Embassy" (p. 42). Not a word about the acquiescence of the *prisoners*; that did not occur to Powell.[2] In spite of this blind spot, however, he was probably convinced that he was acting in the prisoners' best interests. A captain who regularly supported him (though he was also one of the three who petitioned the Graf) expressed himself as follows:

> I think Powell did his very best in accordance with his lights. He tried damned hard, but diplomacy was perhaps not his long suit. As a result he undoubtedly rubbed a great many members of the thinking community the wrong way. Whatever his qualifications may or may not have been, he undoubtedly possessed the requisite force, and I doubt whether any other member of the camp could have stood the strain as long as he did without collapsing. (L 97)

Not much need be said about the remaining captains. Powell's vice-captains and the camp treasurer always backed him; others, like the one just quoted, felt that in spite of his faults he was the best man for the job. And some were frankly afraid of his violent temper and his power to drive them from office. That they should wish to retain it under the conditions may be surprising, but many of them, especially those properly elected, felt a real responsibility to represent their barracks. There were privileges, too, attached to captaincy: occupation of the soldiers' room with its coveted stove, the right to buy meals and beer at the Casino, and (for Powell and his favourites) frequent outings to Berlin on camp business. One correspondent regarded these perquisites as the decisive factors, saying, "There were plenty of people in the camp who would have given £1,000 a year for such privileges" (L 24). Motives are never so simple, however, and captaincy also involved a great deal of tedious work. A statement by the captain previously quoted, whether typical or not, is undoubtedly sincere:

> I am not politically minded, and the politics of the Camp never interested me. There was a job of work to be done, and I tried to do my share of it, on the principle that none should be for a party and all for the State. I was merely trying to help my fellow-countrymen in adversity. As a public official I naturally expected to have plenty of mud slung at me. . . . There were plenty of office-seekers in the Camp; others of us hung on resolutely to the bridge-rail in a gale, conceiving it to be our duty to bring the ship into port. . . . Lots of us could easily have said, "Oh hell, run the Camp yourselves

---

2. Article 6 of the constitution adopted in October 1918 provides a telling contrast; it begins: "The Council shall be responsible to the Camp, the Netherlands Legation, the British Government, and the Military Authorities for all matters which concern those parties respectively. . . ." "The Camp" heads the list.

if you don't like our efforts on your behalf," but as Englishmen such a course was of course unthinkable. (L 97)

Powell's rise to power over a camp full of able and distinguished Britons is a fascinating story, and one which has only been outlined here. Later his opponents finally succeeded, when Ruhleben was on the verge of dissolution, in reducing his status to that of a constitutional ruler. It was a belated triumph, but not an empty one.

As one looks back on the long struggle, the fundamental defect of Powell and his oligarchy appears to be one that was sensed in the camp but never clearly expressed: that they had no appreciation of the real significance of the men's organized activities. It is true that Powell once said of Ruhleben, "It is the best bit of corporate life I have ever known" (38, p. 14), but given his character he could hardly have meant more than the orderly co-operation that struck every visitor. For sport, education, drama, and music were to him and most of his colleagues mere pastimes—the "circus" elements in the *panem et circenses* that kept the prisoners contented. Only men actively engaged in the cultural institutions, and probably not many of them, were aware of the social miracle that had transformed the prison camp into an arena of eager and purposeful accomplishment.

The captains cannot be blamed for their blindness; they were not imaginative people, and they were busy with administrative detail. But the result was that all the most important activities were under the control of men who had little understanding of their value. This fact rankled with the camp's real leaders; together with their dislike for despotism *per se*, it accounted for much of their undying resentment of Powell's regime. In any case, there would be wide agreement with a correspondent's assertion that the 404 men (out of 1,743) who voted against Powell in the 1918 election were "the men who really ran Ruhleben—I mean the men who provided the concerts, school, theatres, lectures, and ran all the camp activities" (L 24). Powell was re-elected as "Captain of the Camp," but not to his old sovereignty; his powers were strictly limited, he had to face an annual election, and the actual governing body, the Camp Council, included two able representatives of the activities that had made Ruhleben what it was.

16

WITH THE TOTAL ORGANISATION of Ruhleben in the summer of 1915 its social growth was complete; the prisoners were living in a full-grown society, with far-reaching results on their conduct and attitudes. These were most marked in the case of the active men, whose lives were radically altered in character and tempo, but no one was unaffected by the new developments. This chapter, which closes the account of the period of expansion, will try to convey something of the summer's changed atmosphere, and then consider some obvious abnormalities in Ruhleben's social structure. As a concrete starting point, we may glance at the camp itself as it appeared nine months after its establishment, at six o'clock on the morning of Sunday, August 1, 1915.[1]

It is a clear, cool morning after four days of showers and thunderstorms, and the compound, seen from just inside the gate, looks fresh and not unattractive. Rain has laid the troublesome dust; the five trees in front of Barrack 11 are green against the brick stable, and flower beds along its walls are bright with nasturtiums and zinnias. Thousands of footprints in the damp sand suggest how heavily the stableyard is populated, but no prisoners are yet in sight; they are all in their bunks —though some, as Chapman's diary complains, have been wakened since 3.30 A.M. by the crowing of Barrack 12's pet rooster.

The boiler house in Trafalgar Square yields more evidence of a busy community; the traction engine is working on German farms for the summer, but the shed that housed it is covered with a mass of notices. The most conspicuous is an illuminated proclamation in Old English script, headed: "BOROUGH OF RUHLEBEN: PARLIAMENTARY BYE-ELECTION, 1915"; it announces with grandiose formality the mock political contest that will end on Tuesday with a Suffragette victory. At its head is the Ruhleben coat of arms, here making its first public appearance, but soon to adorn hundreds of souvenirs. Like the Ruhleben Song it

1. The date has no special significance; it was chosen as being an ordinary Sunday, within the period desired, and reasonably well documented.

reflects the camp's unchanging conception of itself; the quarterings contain a soup bowl, a black loaf, a German sausage, and a clog, with a rat and a mouse as supporters, and the steadfast if shopworn motto, "*Dum Spiro Spero.*" Next to this grim self-portrait is yesterday's parcel list, with its hundreds of names in alphabetical order; it throws an ironic light on the symbolism of the coat of arms, for almost 25,000 food parcels have been received during July.

On a large board, labelled "OFFICIAL," a set of brusque instructions about laundering in the barracks, picking up paper, and general conduct is signed by Powell and headed by one of his pet phrases, "Play the Game!" (H). Below it the Sports Control Committee announces a Bank Holiday celebration on the field tomorrow; those who plan to operate shows and gambling devices must make written application for space (H). And at the top of the board a small typed notice states that nothing may be posted on the boiler house without being first stamped in the captains' office. A baize-covered board surmounted by a cross lists an elaborate programme of Anglican services on weekdays and Sundays, including Holy Communion this morning at seven. The Debating Society and several circles and associations have their own boards, and a poster high on the shed announces that the Ruhleben Dramatic Society will produce Galsworthy's *The Silver Box* on August 4 and the three following nights.

Miscellaneous advertisements are legion: for clogs and English tennis rackets, obtainable through the canteen; for tailors, a hairdresser, a carpenter, and the Ruhleben "Practicle" Laundry; for the books, music and war maps that Mr. Mussett orders from Berlin; and for the tempting salads, "made by a professor of the culinary art," procurable from I. Boyer & Co. (S). Teachers offer instruction in languages and London matric mathematics, while individuals advertise for lost note-books, fountain pens, and deck chairs, offer to buy text-books and razor blades, and announce meetings of organizations and informal groups. (It is reassuring to see that most of these individual notices have *not* been stamped by the captains.)

Outside Barrack 12 is a strange assortment of fowls and quadrupeds in a chicken-wire enclosure; the miniature zoo is the special pride of the barrack non-com, the amiable Corporal Pyro. Poor Pyro, though he does not know it, has only a fortnight more to spend in the comfort of Ruhleben; on August 17 his well-meant bootlegging activities will get him seventy-two hours' cells and transfer to front line duty.

Beyond Barrack 12 stands the hot-water house with its tall chimney; here are the first prisoners—three yawning seafarers stoking the boilers in preparation for the opening of business at 7.30 A.M. Across Bond Street, between Barracks 11 and 10, flies a banner reading "VOTE FOR BOSS!", and the hot-water house is plastered with boastful and vituperative election posters. The shops are closed and deserted, but they too bear traces of a lively population. Outside the grocery store, beside a list of what is in stock, an illustrated poster reads: "DON'T stand gaping, the notices are only ornamental, take no notice of them please! Come along now, ask questions, push, shove, help to keep customers away, we hate work!" (S). Scurrilous annotations have been added by waiting customers. And at the stall that serves tea and soft drinks a notice in blue pencil makes the double-barrelled appeal: "Will those persons who have absent-mindedly taken away our cups kindly return same as we are awfully short of them. *Why don't you bring that cup back, you cheap thief?*" (S). Employees in Ruhleben's shops and services were not unduly obsequious.

There is no early *Appell* on Sundays, but by half-past six the camp is coming to life. A policeman in striped arm-band unlocks the police station next the outfitters' stores, early risers in pyjamas make their way to the latrines, and from the barracks come sounds of voices and running water. Camp workers in singlets and dungarees head towards the kitchens, where coffee is being brewed; two young men in suits, collars, and ties start for the grandstand to prepare altar and benches for the communion service, and another waits near the gate to meet the clergyman from Berlin.

From seven onwards there is an unbroken succession of public activities. As soon as the forty odd Anglicans vacate the hall it is taken over by Roman Catholics for eight o'clock mass; at eight, too, a party of golf professionals tees off on the field, while on the third grandstand Mr. Brose begins his second lecture on "The Dynamics of a Particle." He is followed at nine by Mr. Ford on *Richard III*, and at ten by Mr. Masterman on "The Development of England"; both draw large audiences. During the Shakespeare lecture sixty men are doing setting-up exercises on the field, and Masterman's listeners need only raise their eyes to see tennis games along the race-track and the start of a Lancashire-Yorkshire cricket match beyond them. This is a special event, and souvenir programmes are on sale for a penny. A second team match and various informal games also start this morning.

The stableyard meanwhile has been given over to domestic activities. The new wash-house is not finished, and the men still wash in the barrack corridor. A large urn of German coffee is placed in the corridor by workers at 7.30 A.M.; prisoners who prefer their own tea line up at the hot-water house. The breakfast tables are plentifully if simply supplied with bread, butter, margarine, dripping, jam, and English sugar and condensed milk for the hot beverages. After the meal the messmate whose turn it is rinses the dishes under the tap, puts them away, and sweeps the box dirt into the corridor, where barrack cleaners are at work with brooms and pails.

Soon after eight Berlin Sunday papers go on sale, and those with no early appointments read them over their coffee. There is little war news today except from the east, where the Germans are close to Warsaw; the front pages are monopolized by the Kaiser's solemn proclamation on the war's first anniversary: "Before God and history my conscience is clear; I never willed this war!" The prisoners comment scornfully, "No, he never willed *this* war; what he wanted was a quick walk-over!" The *Ruhleben Daily News* with its page of English translations will not appear until the fall, and on the benches against the barrack walls men are translating the German papers to small groups of listeners.

By nine o'clock on this fine day almost everyone is out in the sun, and the camp has its typical crowded appearance. The largest numbers are watching the games or walking round and round the field, but there are many at lectures and meetings on the grandstands and the stable-yard is far from empty. Hundreds of men have settled themselves in deck chairs, some merely reclining, but the majority reading, studying, or writing letters with the aid of little tables fastened to the chair arms. At 11.30 the kitchen parades begin and dinner-getting continues until nearly one. Each barrack marches off at an assigned time, which changes from day to day, so men consult the time-table before planning their morning activities. The soup is not exciting, but it is well studded with potatoes, and the little scrap of meat supplied on Sundays draws most of the men to the kitchens. Special arrangements exist for cricketers and others who cannot line up with their own barracks.

Many older men take a nap after dinner, but otherwise the afternoon is spent like the morning, with crowds on the field and tennis courts until they close at five and the rest of the men variously occupied. Nearly three hundred attend the 3.30 evensong, at which Mr. Williams, returning again from Berlin, preaches a carefully non-political sermon. The service is conducted with great formality; each worshipper is handed a prayer-book as he enters, responses are intoned, canticles chanted, and four hymns sung to harmonium accompaniment. Minister and congregation pay no attention to the occasional rounds of applause from the field, and a policeman restrains the irreligious from walking on the steel and concrete overhead. No concert is scheduled for this summer evening, and walks, cards, reading, and study pass the time from supper until *Appell* in the barracks at nine. By ten the men have settled down and another Ruhleben day is over.

What would most strike a visitor is the orderly, regulated nature of the camp's daily life. In contrast to the confusion and turbulence of November 1914, everything now seems to follow a schedule; all public activities are advertised in advance and take place as arranged. And the men's behaviour is correspondingly orderly. There is certainly some pushing and jostling around the parcel lists, and noisy arguments are often heard in the barracks, but the general picture is of a civilized population that has solved most of the social problems of its mixed and congested camp. The men sleep and wake, dress, eat, read, and write in their closely packed boxes with extraordinarily little friction, they appear on time for *Appell* and kitchen parades, and large crowds assemble and disperse several times a day with a minimum of disturbance.

Nor does this orderliness seem due to external discipline. The barrack soldiers and captains do some urging as they herd the men into line, a forgetful prisoner will be sharply told to take his pipe out of his mouth, and late arrivals run anxiously to their places. But they are usually less afraid of the German sergeant than of their barrack-mates, whose annoyance at being kept waiting is expressed in muttered booing. Everything, in fact, suggests that the men are conforming, not to military rules, but to a code of behaviour established by themselves. They never march smartly to the kitchens as the Germans wish, but walk there in ragged fours; when ordered off the field they leave leisurely, without breaking off their conversations; and at night they cease talking only after the guards have several times demanded silence. Occasionally a soldier loses his temper and marches some chosen delinquent to the cells, but in general an accommodation seems to have been reached on terms acceptable to the prisoners.

The Germans of course have nothing to do with the activities that occupy most of each day, and it is in these settings, where the men are entirely on their own, that their self-imposed orderliness is most conspicuous. As soon as the curtain rises or the conductor lifts his baton, silence falls in the grandstand hall; whispered remarks during a lecture bring immediate "shushing" from those around; the chairman's rulings are respected during the hottest debates; and even in bitterly contested games no umpire or referee is ever challenged. Self-restraint and mutual understanding are particularly evident in the long queues that form for theatre tickets or special canteen sales. After the wild race from morning *Appell* to be first in line, each man accepts his place without argument, though watching jealously that no late-comer edges in ahead of him. When all the seats are sold or the stock exhausted the disappointed ones walk quietly away. If the wait is a long one (theatre queues often lasted all morning) there is a tacit understanding that friends may alternate in holding a place, and that a man may absent himself long enough to go to the latrines without penalty. The policeman on duty seldom has anything to do; the accepted code covers most eventualities.

It was probably this spontaneous orderliness that Powell had in mind when he spoke of Ruhleben as "the best bit of corporate life" he had ever seen; it must have made government remarkably easy. And it was certainly this that moved the Commandant to approach the War Office in September and arrange for the removal of German guards; his own eyes had told him they were not needed.

What it meant, of course, was that the prisoners were under pervasive social control, applied when necessary by their fellows, but residing for the most part in the individual as a sense of "ought" or obligation. The control was a direct outcome of the organizing of the camp, which had changed each separate individual into a *member* of his box and barrack, of various associations, and always and above all of "Ruhleben" —an embattled outpost, proudly maintaining British standards in the face of the enemy. This conscious membership entailed sensitivity to the rights of others and binding obligations towards them, often crystallized in recognized codes of conduct. Thus the prisoner, in becoming a part of the camp and of many groups within it, had transcended his egocentric tendencies and become a socialized, civilized being.

This is not to suggest that Ruhleben gave its inhabitants their basic social training; they had acquired that, well or poorly, in early childhood. What the camp did was to tie them together in a great number of ways and so provide a context teeming with effective obligations. The first feeling of many prisoners on being interned had been one of *irresponsibility*, of freedom from social obligations; that it did not demoralize them was due to the prompt appearance of solidarity with its attendant norms of conduct. To this had then been added the community groups, associations, and numerous personal friendships, each involving the participants in further mutual responsibilities, until Ruhleben became for many of its inhabitants, the richest experience of attachments and obligations they were ever to have. As such it was, in actual fact, a school of social relations, broadening the sensitivities of those already well socialized, and supplementing the training of men whose early social experience had been defective.

The most obvious sign of effective social control was the almost complete absence of crime.[2] All sorts of dubious characters, from pimps, pickpockets, and petty swindlers to professional burglars, had been swept up in the interment, but Chapman, a member of the camp police during 1915, records not a single case of theft in his diary, and Mahoney, also a policeman, says flatly:

> Crime was unknown in Ruhleben. . . . More than one of our number had "done time" in England, but here the predatory instinct seemed to have become stifled. Now and again there was a slight outbreak of lawlessness, but these were few and quickly suppressed. Men who infringed the rules come to fear being ostracized by their comrades as much as, if not more than, being penalized by the German authorities. ([3?], p. 156)

Mahoney's statement needs but little qualification, and its emphasis on social pressure is borne out by the temporal relations between offences against property and the growth of camp organization. In the early, chaotic days petty thieving was clearly prevalent; boxes were never left unattended except when everyone was on parade, and the familiar cry, "Stranger in the barrack!" was a necessary alarm signal. Hughes speaks of the early attitude towards property as resembling that in a boarding school: "If you didn't look out, somebody bagged your towel" (p. 668). Mahoney also refers to towels being constantly guarded, and Henley, during his initial weeks in the grandstand, kept his soup bowl under his pillow at night. Solidarity at Ruhleben, as in the army and similar bodies, did not exclude the "adopting" of small but essential articles.

No serious losses are recorded, however, and with the organizing of the camp all types of theft dropped to a negligible level. A notice dated March 11, 1915, reads: "If the person who took the grey dinner can from the end of the corridor will call at Box 16 he may have the lid" (S), but only one other reference can be found before 1918, when the social structure was weakening. This is in Kendall's diary for April 6, 1916, and its content is startling: "Some day last week a man picked from the pocket of another a gold watch and sold it for M 30. He got three days, and will be kept in cells here for the rest of his internment." This drastic punishment (which must surely have been remitted) might suggest that crime was only controlled in Ruhleben by the infliction of savage penalties. Its true significance, however, is quite different. The camp was peculiarly exposed to theft, for only the horse-boxes had doors, and these had no locks. The perpetual vigilance of the first week or so soon became impracticable, and the safeguarding of household

2. Drunkenness and gambling, of course, were "crimes" only in the eyes of the Germans; those recognized by the prisoners were chiefly theft and extreme violence.

goods and personal valuables had to depend on a collective recognition of their inviolability. Such an understanding, tacit but solemn, quickly emerged in response to the common need; it was part of the *mores* of Ruhleben, and so universally respected that when an infraction did occur, as in the case above, it was felt to be a heinous offence, the breaking of a strict taboo. The actual punishments were meted out by the Germans, but on this occasion, perhaps prompted by Powell, they evidently took the same view: the malefactor must be cut off from the camp. Thanks to this rigid code, surplus food in later years was stacked in the open corridors and never interfered with, deck chairs and other property were parked all over the camp, and lost wallets with considerable sums of money were regularly turned in by the finders to the police station.

There were, no doubt, more breaches of the taboo than are recorded, for habitual gamblers were sometimes in desperate straits for money, and some men's pilfering tendencies probably survived Ruhleben's severe moral climate. But to be exposed as a thief in this closely knit community was, as Mahoney implies, something to be dreaded by the most hardened, and the "pickings" available were scarcely worth such a risk.

No murder was committed in Ruhleben, but physical assault was fairly frequent, especially in the sailors' barracks. Chapman's diary contains half a dozen passing references to "fights" he witnessed. They were usually broken up by bystanders, but were not seriously regarded; only excessive violence and the use of weapons were taboo, and cases of these were almost invariably due to liquor or mental instability. Kendall reports several instances:

May 22, 1916. About 12.30 A.M. was awakened by a great row in Barracks 4 and 5. Wild Mac and some others ran amok. It seems they get a can full of wine in which they mix Spiritus to give it a "tang" and this sends them fighting mad. After laying out Cliff and several more they were mastered at 4 o'clock and put in cells. They got sentenced to 3 days dark cells and 28 days birdcage.[3]

Dec. 3, 1916. Man named S. in Barrack 9 went amok today, damaging Alex Hay badly. He was taken to sanatorium.

Nov. 28, 1917. A nigger from 12 slashed Bruce's neck with a razor. Collins, who was standing near, hit the blackie, who lay stunned for 45 minutes and was carried to lazarette.

---

3. The "birdcage" or detention barrack was a section of Barrack 14 with a small wired-in enclosure for exercise. It supplemented the four punishment cells, and was controlled by German guards.

As among schoolboys, a "fair fight" reflected no discredit on the participants, and was sometimes formally conducted. On January 13, 1916,
Chapman was asked to act as second in a fight; next day he met the
other second to arrange details, and on January 15 he wrote:

> At 7.30 A.M. went to Artists' Studio with White. Besides the two principals
> there was Smyllie and myself as seconds, White as referee, and Egremont
> as doorkeeper. Sixteen rounds of 1½ minutes each were fought with no
> damage. They shook hands.

Episodes of violence were inevitable in a camp so mixed, so crowded,
and exposed to so many strains; under the circumstances, the prisoners
kept the peace remarkably well.

The pervasive effects of social control went much further than the
discouragement of crime; by August 1915 conventional pressures were
being felt in many directions. Leaders in camp institutions were being a
little careful about their dress, decent language and manners were being
cultivated in many boxes, strangers were being formally introduced.
Sun-bathing in trunks had been branded as immoral, and the Education
Committee's banning of a debate on the legitimizing of "war-babies,"
though by no means generally supported, brought at least one approving
letter to the magazine. Individuals were also having to remember their
group affiliations; supermen were not seen in the stalls at music-hall
shows, barrack officials were chary of criticizing the civil administration,
and no one prominent in Protestant religious circles would dare to be
seen gambling. (Nor would a recognized "tough" risk his reputation by
appearing at a church service!)

The most unremitting control was exerted on the hundreds of men
who kept Ruhleben running—captains and other unpaid officials, committee members, lecturers and teachers, actors and producers, conductors, orchestra players, and many others. All these men were now busily
occupied with what was beginning to be called "work," held steadily
at it by schedules reaching well into the future, and by a network of
obligations to co-workers, institutions, and the camp as a whole. These
obligations were rarely felt as burdensome in 1915, for organization
was still fairly flexible, the self-chosen tasks were fresh and purposeful,
and they brought many rewards in social stimulation and personal
recognition. Indeed, the active men were the most contented in the
camp. Merton, a senior barrack official, replying to the question, "What
one thing did most to make life bearable or enjoyable?" wrote in 1933:

> The fact that I had some definite duties to perform, the neglect of which
> would react unfavourably upon others. Having accepted the responsibility

for their performance, I was no longer wholly able to decide how I should spend my time. There was also the fact that the work was done in association with others, whose company was definitely entertaining and congenial.

This perceptively sums up the situation; the second sentence, however, is a two-edged one. It is true, as Merton implies, that prescribed duties kept men alert and free from boredom; on the other hand, the freedom to decide how to spend one's time is a boon that few are willing to dispense with indefinitely. In Ruhleben's later years there were clear indications that many active men were hankering for this freedom, and growing restive under the social control they had so gladly accepted.

The camp of 1915 was a very busy place. As the first review of music put it in June: "Function has followed function breathlessly. We have been swirled from concert to play, from play to lecture, from lecture to debate, and thence back again to the concert, to recommence the cycle anew" (*IRC* 1, p. 19). And, in spite of the hundreds of deck chairs to be seen, Sunday, August 1, was anything but a day of rest. All over the camp preparations were on foot for Monday's Bank Holiday celebration, when free beer, costumed performers, sideshows, games of chance, and an open-air concert and prize-giving would bring Hampstead Heath to the racecourse. Officials of the territorial societies were no doubt planning future strategy in the light of last Thursday's antimedal meeting; the big-wigs of the R.D.S. were putting the final touches on a seven-point letter of protest against the Entertainments Committee; both the promenade orchestra and the cast of *The Silver Box* had morning rehearsals; the election candidates and their agents were canvassing for Tuesday's voting; Mr. Eric Swale, who had just organized the Technical Circle, was probably drumming up an audience for its first meeting next Thursday; and large numbers of men had lectures to prepare or homework to do over the weekend.

As the variety of occupations shows, the busy camp was also a highly differentiated one; while some men idly watched the cricket, others worked feverishly at constructing a ring-tossing game and still others sang hymns at the Anglican service. Differentiation had penetrated even to the homes; the early communicants, with their Sunday faces, had to dress silently to avoid waking their unsanctified boxmates, and the close family life of the winter was often disrupted by outside engagements. Denton wrote home on June 11, 1915: "I had a fine birthday yesterday, though the actual party cannot take place until Monday, for 'As you like it' is on every evening at present and the boys are all very busy from four o'clock on." Meetings and rehearsals might be called for almost any hour of the day, and members of the same box often ate at different times and on some occasions scarcely met until bedtime. And individuals who played more than one role were constantly involved in conflicts; a 1915 pencil notice reads: "Owing to dress rehearsal of orchestra Dr. Darbishire is obliged to postpone his second lecture on the manufacture of beet sugar till the following week" (H). The learned doctor was also a cellist.

Differentiation creates divisions, and Ruhleben was this summer a congeries of institutions, societies, and other formal and informal groups. Many of them were hotly competing for members, space, time, and power, and the camp, in spite of its orderly appearance, seethed with quarrels. The Extraordinary General Meeting of the A.S.U. in June was so acrimonious that the magazine issued a special supplement to cover it; on one speaker's suggestion that a certain proposal might cause friction with other bodies the report commented: "As if any Ruhleben Society ever existed without such friction."[4] In July the medal controversy split the camp for a fortnight; in August the entertaining bodies went on strike against the captains, and a long feud between the school and the A.S.U. culminated in their legal divorce. The supermen were a centre of dissension in every organization they belonged to, and Adler's supporters were loudly condemning the high-handedness of the musicians' society.

What had made the comradely Ruhlebenites so suddenly quarrelsome was again the organization of their camp, for in most of these disputes they were acting, not as simple individuals, but as members of groups with which they were strongly identified. Relations between the newly formed bodies were not yet stabilized by accepted conventions; each was in large measure a law unto itself, pursuing its own interests as determinedly as nations in the modern world. Officials were playing their allotted parts in the social drama; however reasonable personally, they behaved like chauvinist politicians when organizational aims were at stake. Ruhleben, however, was more fortunate than the world of nations, for the representatives of all competing bodies spoke the same language and shared an over-riding loyalty to the camp as a whole. Hence, as contacts continued, conflicts were thrashed out, spheres of action delimited, and mutual relations put on a polite and conventional basis. The school and the A.S.U. were still quarrelling in 1916—their fields were too similar for easy harmony—but otherwise there was little more friction except with that uncompromising body, the captains.

Closely akin to these inter-group quarrels was the extraordinary touchiness displayed by individuals in their new social roles. At the

4. *In Ruhleben Camp*, No. 1, Stop Press supplement (mimeographed).

Mock Trial in March 1915 the camp police had been the targets of some witty shafts; to the astonishment of the Debating Society these were hotly resented, and a police strike was only prevented by a formal apology. It was the police, too, who turned in their badges in May when camp officials, after many complaints from private citizens, were deprived of the privilege of getting hot water at the head of the queue. A compromise was hurriedly reached and the police went back to work. Then in August a critical letter to the magazine about hot-water service was thought to reflect on the rectitude of the staff, who promptly "downed tools." A tea famine was averted by a personal apology from the letter-writer, followed by one from the editor in the next issue. The editor was having a rough time, for another item in the August issue got him into trouble with the redoubtable Tom Sullivan, an early pioneer in sports. Sullivan had been the subject of an imaginary interview centring around his predilection for cups and medals; he protested that his honour had been impugned, and did it so vigorously that the September issue carried apologies from the Education Committee, the editor, and the writer of the article.

A September reference to a cricket umpire was also resented by the victim, but this time there was no printed apology, and by October the editor had decided to stand his ground. A football report had criticized the play of two team members—caustically, but no more so than is commonplace in sports write-ups. Two leading sportsmen, however, wrote letters of complaint, and these were printed under the heading, "Should we criticize?", with rebuttals from the writer and the editor. The essence of the complaints was that sharp criticism was out of place "in a camp like this," and the phrase explains much of the first summer's touchiness. For Ruhleben was no longer what it once had been: a simple community in which social contacts were close and direct, relationships personal, and criticism accepted as "all in the family." A new dimension had been added to it, one characterized by formality and social distance, abstract, impersonal relations, and objective standards of judgment.[5] And the development had been so swift that many prisoners (and perhaps particularly sportsmen) had not yet adjusted to it. Though playing roles in the new society, they were still attuned to the old, and they found the remote impersonality of printed criticism deeply wounding, for it evaluated the comrades of the first winter as coldly as though they were strangers.

It was a drastic change, but irreversible, for Ruhleben had grown

5. These distinctions were exhaustively analysed by Ferdinand Tönnies in *Gemeinschaft und Gesellschaft* (5th ed.; Berlin: K. Curtius, 1926).

out of its crowd and community stages; it was now a public, and public life imposed its own conditions. As the editor put it: "It seems to us that if a man makes a public appearance, be it on the sports field, on the stage, or as a camp official he must as a matter of course be prepared to meet criticism" (*IRC* 10, p. 29).

The police and hot-water strikes revealed a sensitivity that extended beyond the individual to the groups to which he belonged. This too was most marked in 1915 when the associations first became dominant; the prisoner was then acutely conscious of his new group identifications, and the groups themselves were young and vulnerable. After 1915, however, injured feelings produced no more strikes and no more protests to the magazine. Criticism in 1916 was as severe as ever, but Ruhleben was a year older, organizations had weathered the storms and were solidly established, and individuals had accepted the new social conventions.

The letters written around August 1 were so dark with forebodings of a second winter that Chapter 9 spoke of the camp as generally depressed. In view of the busy activity since described, how should these gloomy letters be interpreted? There is no doubt of the writers' sincerity, but there is also little doubt that these same men got great enjoyment from the games, theatre, and Bank Holiday revels. The prisoner writing home was for the moment in a different world from Ruhleben, one in which the cruelty of long separation often dominated his mind. He seldom remained there for long, however, but was soon caught up again in the concrete world about him. It is therefore pointless to ask whether the men were "happy" in their new society; all had their periods of elation and of depression, sometimes private, sometimes (as before another winter) widely shared. And during most of the time they were neither happy nor unhappy, but going about their business in a completely matter-of-fact way. For what the creative outburst of the spring had given them was something more vital than happiness; it was the chance to live a full, normal life on the racecourse. Like real life anywhere, it mixed its many satisfactions with plenty of pain, disappointment, and simple boredom; but it was also, as life always is, a source of inexhaustible interest, capturing and holding the attention of all who took part in it. And that was what mattered at Ruhleben.

The degree to which the prisoners were actually absorbed in camp affairs has perhaps been sufficiently indicated, but further light is thrown on it by the issue of *In Ruhleben Camp* that appeared on Sunday, August 1, and was sold out in a few hours. It was a Bank Holiday issue, but its content and tone were entirely typical. From the gaily coloured cover to the canteen advertisement on the back, the magazine is as oblivious of the outside world as its name suggests; Ruhleben is the sole reality. Illustrations make up a third of the content: there are drawings of camp landmarks, prominent cricketers, and theatrical casts and scenes; caricatures of medallists, sun-worshippers, and other notables; and some enticing but improbable views of the hidden glories of the Summer House. Scores of smaller drawings include a sketch of a mechanical man for standing in queues (he is set to move at one mile per year), and a close-up of Powell's refulgent arm-band, inscribed: "Captain of Captains, Lord of Lords, King of Kings, and only ruler of Camp."

The letterpress is similarly camp-centred; only once in the 48 pages is return to England mentioned even half-seriously. Sports are omitted from this number, but there is a chatty account of the Parcels Office, a humorous story of a man who was led to believe his release had been signed, a flippant debates report, and reviews, complimentary or cutting, of three recent plays. There are short notices of poetry and Dickens evenings, the Art Exhibition, and a concert of French music; Mr. Govett's "Phoebe" gets her first introduction to the quaint folkways of the camp, and "Ruhleben according to Otto" translates some of them into the stilted language of French exercises. "Answers to Correspondents" deals facetiously with lice, mosquitoes, and other plagues, while letters to the editor complain of high tennis fees, high theatre prices, and "agonizing sounds" from rehearsal sheds. There is much else, all of the same character.

What hundreds of Ruhlebenites were reading and chuckling about this morning was, then, their own camp, its amenities, celebrities, and shortcomings. But could the magazine have published anything different? Prison camp magazines are hard to come by, but Vischer's brochure (46) gives a partial answer with excerpts from journals got out by German and French prisoners, including the German civilians at Knockaloe. Many of these are painful reading; the tone is introspective, often self-pitying, and the emphasis is on the grinding monotony of camp life, the loathing of others induced by constant propinquity, the paralysing sense of powerlessness and sterility, and (from Knockaloe, be it noted) the utter worthlessness of everything achieved or learned behind barbed wire. It is true that Vischer's examples were selected, and selected to portray the strains of confinement; they may also have reflected literary convention or editorial bias. Typical or not, however, the fact remains that they were published, whereas they could never have been published in Ruhleben. Life there was sufficiently real and absorbing to cast a cloak of oblivion, not only over its trying aspects, but also over everything that lay beyond the barbed wire.

The fact needs no argument, for it was notorious in the camp and often joked about. In a skit in this same August magazine each member of the editorial staff has to write one wish on a piece of paper. All, it turns out, are identical: to have a pass to the Casino. Only the office boy, asked what his wish would have been, answers promptly, "To be released," at which the others exclaim, "Why, we never thought of that!" (*IRC* 4, p. 33). And a subsequent issue describes Hatfield as "the most practical man in Ruhleben"—so immersed in camp affairs that when asked, "Well, what d'ye think of the War?" he responded with a puzzled look, "War? What war?" (*IRC* 9, p. 14).

It is clear that the Ruhleben society "worked"; it performed its vital functions. It was, however, far from being a normal society, and particularly in two obvious respects: it consisted only of males, and it was not self-sustaining economically. Both facts had important effects on its structure and character.

The absence of women meant that it was biologically sterile, incapable of perpetuating itself, and also that it provided no legitimate sex outlets for its members. But the camp's unisexual character had positive aspects as well, and these deserve a moment's consideration. Suppose that British of both sexes had been interned at Ruhleben, with families, bachelors, and single women in different sections, but allowed to mingle during the day. How would the camp have developed? Certainly not as the deeply united body it actually became, but more probably as three separate communities, interacting but never blending, and each possessing its distinctive norms and atmosphere. Even in the opening days the sharing of emotion that gave birth to solidarity would have been impossible; with the women probably clinging to accepted conventions, and the married men playing their roles as husbands and fathers, no tides of common feeling and spontaneous behaviour could have swept through the camp.

And the rough and ready comradeship of Ruhleben would also have been impaired; it was characteristically a male comradeship, like that in the services, and could not have been extended to women. For sexual attraction, with its possessiveness and jealousy, is inimical to purely social relationships; even the potentiality of it raises subtle barriers between man and man. As Freud wrote: "Sexual need does not unite men, it separates them."[6] Molony gives an interesting sidelight on this.

6. *Totem and Taboo*, tr. A. A. Brill (New York: New Republic, Inc., 1931), p. 250.

After his escape from Ruhleben in 1916 he was sent to the "punishment camp" at Havelberg; it contained three hundred Russian women—segregated, of course, but occasionally accessible with a sentry's connivance. Molony sensed a different atmosphere as soon as he arrived there:

> The interest of our future co-prisoners in our plight soon wore off. In a gathering of men alone, many questions would have been asked. Some attempts at comradeship would have been made. . . . It was Bicycle Billy who enlightened us. He explained that there were women, that there were some 'nice little bits' among them, and that later he might require my assistance for sending them messages. (P. 174)

Thus the lack of women in Ruhleben, which some men felt acutely, was at least partly compensated by the warm relationships among the men.

Lacking its original solidarity, and with its general comradeship weakened, a "mixed" Ruhleben would have been very different—so different that there is no point in speculating on its later development. It would certainly have been a more "normal" community, and perhaps a more healthy one to live in, but there would have been no such creative outburst as occurred in 1915. The drive and enthusiasm that built the new city were not specifically sexual, though sexual deprivation no doubt contributed to their strength. But they were generated within a consciously homogeneous body, in interactions unhampered by any differences as basic as those of sex, and untouched by its disturbing and divisive influences. The men were thus able to give themselves unitedly to constructive social pursuits.[7]

7. The creation of Ruhleben's social structure by men alone was of course typical rather than otherwise, for the popular belief that "society is built on the family" needs qualification. The family is actually in the paradoxical position of making wider forms of association possible by the social training of the young, and then contributing no further to them—if, indeed, it does not stand in their way by its demands on the interest and time of the male. These ideas were first developed by the German ethnologist, Heinrich Schurtz, who traced all non-familial associations back to the men's societies found in many primitive tribes, pointing out that most political, religious, legal, and educational institutions even in our own day still reflect their purely male origins (*Altersklassen und Männerbunde*; Berlin: Georg Reimer, 1902). Freud also saw the source of "social organization, moral restrictions and religion" in the revolt of a "band of brothers" against their father (*Totem and Taboo*, pp. 247–8). Whether or not these views are valid, it seems obvious that societies do not represent the mere overflow or extension of familial relationships, but arise from associations uninfluenced by sex. Thus the speed with which Ruhleben was built may have been due, not only to the men's familiarity with social organization, but also to their relative freedom from conflicting family ties.

The most striking of Ruhleben's other abnormalities were economic. The camp was of course a parasitic community, producing nothing itself, but living on the surplus production of the German and British economies. In this it resembled a fashionable resort town, but the resemblance went no further, for it was also a singularly advanced "welfare state," whose inhabitants enjoyed almost complete economic security, whether or not they chose to work. And with security went a large measure of economic equality; nothing that an individual might do could have more than trifling effects on his standard of living.

These utopian conditions were clearly reflected in the fact that Ruhleben's largest institutions were devoted, not to economic ends, but to games and cultural pursuits. They also had marked effects on the mental outlook of the prisoners, and explain in part the nostalgia with which some of them look back on their internment. For concern with earning a living was banished from its central position in consciousness, and replaced by interest in activities that were broadly recreational—pursued, that is, for their own sakes rather than as means to an end. Such pursuits became for many prisoners the real business of life, as important as work in office or on shipboard, and considerably more enjoyable.

There is no question that such a psychological shift took place; it is shown by the intense seriousness of camp activities, and by the fact that Ruhleben's most prominent citizens were scholars, actors, musicians, and sportsmen. And the dethronement of economic interests was also illustrated in ex-prisoners' answers to the question, "What one thing did most to make life there bearable or enjoyable?" Of 119 replies classified, 59 referred to such social values as friendship and comradeship, and 56 to camp activities—education, sport, theatre, and music, in that order. No one mentioned the canteen or other community services, and only four men referred to that indispensable economic item, parcels. One of them wrote argumentatively, "Parcels from home—obviously the only *truthful* answer to this question," and the rest, on consideration, might have had to agree; for if they had been actually starving, there would have been little sport or study. As things stood, however, the other answers were equally truthful; parcels sustained life, certainly, but it was having something to do, and a warm social context in which to do it, that made life worth living.

There is no need to labour the point; every holiday season shows how gladly men throw off their economic harness and give themselves to other pursuits. The inordinate length of the Ruhleben "holiday," however, makes the developments there relevant to some pressing social problems. There is first the paradoxical picture of men devoting four years of steady work to such organizations as the school, the orchestra, and the parcel post, without any economic rewards whatever. Earlier chapters suggested some of the incentives that replaced them: the men had a sense of belonging to a congenial group and enjoying full status within it; they were free to choose their work and determine, in consultation with others, how it should be done; and the work itself, though not always interesting, seemed to them of definite value to the community with which they were identified. The power of such incentives was long ago recognized by students of industrial morale; what Ruhleben does is to show it in high relief.

The economic peculiarities of the camp, however, have other and more controversial implications. Ruhleben was not only a complete welfare state; it was also a foretaste of the conditions to which industrial societies are rapidly moving, in which the time required for economic production and distribution will be so reduced that new employment must be found for the leisure time of millions. The gloomy views expressed in this connection are familiar: men will not work except when driven by fear of want; hence economic security will destroy any urge to accomplishment, and their increased leisure will be spent in watching television and similar occupations. On these shallow generalizations Ruhleben throws a considerable measure of doubt. It suggests rather that economic security and leisure can, under favourable circumstances, release new interests and aspirations, for which men will strive as hard as they do for subsistence, and with much greater satisfaction. "Suggests" is the most that can be said, for the Ruhleben informants were not representative of the population, and a large, relatively idle class existed after the first year or two. Even so, the camp picture is encouraging, for the only real difference between the idle and the active men—apart from age, infirmity, and similar handicaps—was one that a truly imaginative education could obliterate in a generation.

How to provide such an education for more than a tiny minority is of course the problem. We know little about how it is obtained, except that it is almost certainly "caught" rather than taught—which raises the old question, "Where would we find teachers of such a calibre?" An even greater obstacle, however, lies in the character of current Western civilization. Ruhleben's "state socialism" left almost no place for the profit motive—a deprivation that was, incidentally, painless. Hence the motives of its eager band of students, teachers, performers, and organizers were precisely those that an enlightened education would foster: pleasure in the task itself, the satisfaction of accomplishment, stimulation from co-workers, concern for the wider community. We live, however, not in Ruhleben but in a society so dedicated to making and spending money that more social motives have little opportunity to develop. Those who control commercialized sport and entertainment do not ask the individual what he would like to do in his free time; they tell him. And the voice of the advertiser is so all-pervasive that the very existence of any values other than economic might well be questioned. The prospect of a society more in keeping with the full range of man's potentialities seems remote, but the struggle for it will go on, and it is not a hopeless struggle. For if Ruhleben shows anything at all, it is that work and achievement for their own sakes are as natural to the human being as eating or breathing. The desire to learn, strive, build, and create, in free association with others, does not have to be painfully inculcated; except when it has been stifled in childhood by economic need or mechanical education, it is already there, and will appear whenever it is given a chance.[8]

8. Behaviourist psychology, with its original emphasis on "primary," physiological drives, tended to support the view that all human activity must be traced to hunger or sex. Since the middle of this century, however, many studies, both of animal behaviour and of brain function, have confirmed the importance of intellectual and constructive motives. Even monkeys will learn and work for no other reward than the satisfactions of seeing into the world about them or of solving a mechanical puzzle. See, for example, H. F. Harlow, in *Learning Theory, Personality Theory, and Clinical Research: The Kentucky Symposium* (New York: John Wiley & Sons, Inc., 1954) pp. 66–79. The references to Asch and Hebb in footnote 6 of Chapter 5 are also relevant.

PART V | Stability

17

BY RUHLEBEN'S FIRST BIRTHDAY its social structure was complete. It was an *ad hoc* structure, formed at breakneck speed by pressure from the expanding activities, and intended for only a short life. It was forced, however, to function for three more years, and our chief interest now is in how well it stood the strain and met the prisoners' continuing needs. The narrative can accordingly be speeded up, and this chapter will survey the whole "period of stability," from the first anniversary of internment to the end of 1917. It will be a rapid survey, and will be made in terms of "Ruhleben years," which began with the fall opening of activities and ended in the following July.

The winter of 1915–16, anticipated without pleasure, early threatened to be a hard one. Before November ended a spell of bitter cold closed the library for a week; rugby was cancelled, the clubmen were driven from the Summer House, and Chapman wrote feelingly, "Temperature of barracks cruel to live in." An even colder spell before Christmas sent temperatures below zero Fahrenheit, and a coal shortage cut off hot-water supplies three times in December. Conditions were made no easier to bear by the departure for England of a further 150 men, pronounced militarily unfit, on December 6.

Nevertheless, the second winter turned out to be far pleasanter than the first, and November letters are cheerful and philosophic. Irwin wrote on the 26th, "The first year is always the worst. We've got *that* behind us now"; and Abbot wrote two days later, "We are not dreading the winter as we did last year, for we have been able to make our quarters a little more comfortable." Box improvements did not alter the fact that indoor temperatures were often near freezing and living quarters as dark as ever—except in the horse-boxes, where safety candlesticks were now allowed. But at least the food was better; each barrack now had a weekly dinner of "steak" and onions, and parcels were so numerous that both Irwin and Graham complained of being overstocked.

It was not physical comfort, however, that made this winter so different from the preceding one, but its wealth of occupation and entertainment. There were no exchange rumours—a sure sign that the men's minds were more healthily employed. All the camp institutions were bursting with activity; twenty-four football teams competed in the first and second leagues, hockey and rugby were in full swing, and plays, concerts, and classes left little time for brooding. The value of study, in particular, was increasingly recognized, and even a professional footballer, Fred Pentland, paid tribute to it in his December football summary. Noting how aimlessly hundreds of men wandered about whenever the sports ground was closed, he added:

> Fortunately for a great number of those here it is in their nature to take advantage of our present compulsory inactivity in the world's affairs by studying. . . . The events which have placed some of the most brilliant scholars in Europe in this camp and their generous willingness to give those desiring it the benefit of their knowledge creates a unique opening for those who wish to broaden their education. (*IRC* 10, p. 15)

The theatre had a whole series of "smash hits" in the fall of 1915, especially with the mime-drama, *L'Enfant prodigue*, probably the most completely satisfying of all camp productions. "All parts were exhausted," the magazine said, and a large orchestra, under Charles Weber's direction, excelled itself in Wormser's charming music. The season reached its climax at Christmas with *Cinderella*, a traditional British pantomime with spectacular scenic effects; it had a record run of eighteen nights, including a "Command Performance" for the U.S. Ambassador and his party. Kendall described it as "very elaborate but dull wit" and Chapman found it "too vulgar," but the camp ate it up and many men went several times.

Besides the A.S.U.'s musical evenings there was a full dress concert each Sunday, and many of this fall's programmes were outstanding. The magazine commends a number of orchestral, choral, and concerto performances, and praises the "perfection of taste and technique" shown in Professor Keel's singing of folk-songs. With lectures, debates, and circles added, the crowded programme would have done credit to a city ten times Ruhleben's size, and no one needed to find the days tedious. Indeed, Ewing wrote in December, "Since our 'blue' weeks in August the time has passed like a flash."

So much activity strained the camp's physical resources; the school's twenty-three classrooms were used to capacity and every hour in the grandstand hall was booked a week ahead. There was rejoicing, therefore, when in December the International Y.M.C.A. began erecting a large hut in the space between Barracks 2 and 11, and the religious groups, happy at the prospect of more suitable accommodation, gave practical help. Denton's letter of Sunday, December 19, suggests how busy a Ruhlebenite could sometimes be:

The last two weeks have been terrific, preparation for a great carol service on Wednesday and a tremendous lot of work in connection with the new Y.M.C.A. building. To try to have it for Xmas we have enrolled 100 volunteers from the congregation, who are put on in shifts. All have to be notified (by postcard through our own camp P.O.). Thanks to this and splendid work by the camp carpenters we should be able to have at least a short service on Xmas. Tonight I am pretty tired, as I was writing out carol music until 1 A.M. (the only quiet time of the day) and was up again at 7, going with a party of about 40 to a factory a mile away for cinders to ballast the hall. We had three heavy wagons and when they were loaded up they were tremendously hard to move. Add the frozen roads full of deep ruts and you'll understand why it took us 40 minutes tugging and sweating to get here. Then all had to be shovelled into the building; then a much needed bath; breakfast at 9.30, interview with the Entertainments Committee re rehearsals in the hall; more music copying (Xmas anthem), hurried dinner; choir practice 1.30 to 3, then a wash, corrected proofs of carol sheets from Berlin printer, met Mr. Williams, service 3.30 to 5, and finally, after tea, a little rest.

The hall, which was opened on December 24, held about five hundred; during the day it was used for reading, study, and such pastimes as chess —cards and smoking were forbidden. The building also contained a chapel, the reference library, and several badly needed classrooms. The problems of congestion were not all met, however; Chapman wrote in May 1916, "Electricity lecture 9–10 by Jenkins in Y.M.C.A. but couldn't hear much on account of Verdi's requiem being practised next door."

Christmas 1915 was a festive season, especially for the ninety seafarers, over 55 or under 17, who started home on December 21. But the camp they left was far from disconsolate; the Debating Society performed Dickens' *Christmas Carol*, the grandstand hall was packed for Denton's carol service, and Abbot reported the usual singing in his loft. Delicacies were not lacking for Christmas dinner (Ewing's mess of four had received *fourteen* Christmas puddings!) and the single bottle of beer with which the kitchens marked the day was generously supplemented from other sources. Denton, writing home on Christmas night, reported: "We had our first communion service in the new hall at 7.30, it is a glorious change and doesn't feel like Ruhleben at all. Now it is 11.30 P.M., but the camp is still celebrating (regulations being a little lax) and sleep is out of the question." New Year's Eve was similarly honoured: "High doings, dancing etc. in the square" (Chapman); "Pretty rowdy, jolly, and plenty of good things" (Henley).

The frost retreated over the holiday, leaving seas of mud and water; Ewing complained, "The mud is awful; one goes all day long in wet feet." And the rest of the winter was fairly mild. Another 80 invalids, including most of the remaining coloured men, were sent home on January 6, 1916; football reopened on January 9, and on the 14th the camp settled down again with the beginning of a new school term.

Of the busy activities that followed only highlights can be mentioned. Sports continued as usual, Barrack 9 easily winning the football league. The golf club had so many new applicants that it was voted to limit membership to 135—a vain hope, as subsequent seasons showed. A few innovations appeared: informal smoking concerts proved very popular, as did illustrated travelogues arranged by the Y.M.C.A.; morris dancers got fun and exercise in the new hall, and Highland dances and pipe tunes (played by the piper to the Duke of Saxe-Coburg Gotha) brought the house down at the annual "Burns Nicht" concert. Some delightful chamber concerts included quartets by Mozart and Brahms and the *Romance* for viola and piano by Benjamin Dale, one of the prisoners. Professor Keel continued to produce folk-songs and ballads from his inexhaustible store, and Adler gave the last of his ambitious choral productions. Kendall wrote: "Last weekend Adler gave Verdi's Requiem, a really stupendous undertaking, involving re-arranging the whole score to suit men's voices. The rehearsals have been going on for months." It was not an artistic success, but 150 men had been purposefully occupied.

The 1916 theatrical programme was unremarkable until April, when the tercentenary of Shakespeare's death was given a week-long celebration. Fine posters and a beautifully designed advance programme caused a huge line-up for tickets, confirming the programme's assertion that the festival was for all "who reverence the ideals that spring from English soil and live in the English tongue." *Twelfth Night* was played from April 23 to 25; April 26 was devoted to Shakespearean music, with Elizabethan songs and madrigals, April 27 to an historical and literary survey of Shakespeare's England, and April 28 to 30 to *Othello*. This last play, with a young cricketer cast as the hapless Desdemona, suggested that there were limits even to Ruhleben's dramatic range, and Shakespearean tragedy was avoided in future. But *Twelfth Night* was a triumph, and the whole festival "one of Ruhleben's happiest and most successful efforts" (*RCM* 4, p. 33). The subsequent plays were generally of lower quality, but the total of thirty-one productions in ten months was no mean record for the first full season.

Interest in school work continued to grow after Christmas; 302 new students were registered for the spring term as against 211 the term before. And Fred Pentland, conceding in March that study was affecting some players' interest in football, added generously: "From a sensible point of view they are good judges, too. Unless they desire to become professional footballers . . . they can occupy their time in much more useful ways educationally" (*RCM* 1, p. 13). Such an opinion (which would be treason to modern sports promoters) suggests the high esteem that education enjoyed in the camp. A third art exhibit was held in April ("not very exciting," the magazine thought), the A.S.U. and the circles were continuously active, and in May the Historical Circle began a series of twenty-nine public lectures which drew distinguished audiences.[1]

A new institution was founded in February, when the Y.M.C.A. followed up its gift of the hall by establishing a branch in the camp and despatching two American evangelists to get it under way. The "YMCA Week" progressed from lantern lectures to stirring appeals for Christ, and ended with the signing of "decision cards" by some three hundred men. Though the hall was crowded each night, it may be doubted whether revival services were what this active community most needed. However, a committee was set up under the philosopher and footballer, A. H. Bodin, and in 1916 and 1917 it provided, along with prayer meetings and bible classes, much free and informal entertainment for the ordinary prisoner.

The war was rarely mentioned in this winter's diaries; only the long struggle for Verdun got more than passing reference. At the end of May, however, the naval battle off Jutland caused excitement and "much anxiety," and a week later there was general depression over the drowning of Lord Kitchener. The men were far from indifferent to the war, but it had become a seemingly endless struggle, and only "big news" could pierce through their absorption in camp affairs.

They were now well informed, too—so well that war rumours circulated only when the Germans were suspected to be hiding something. Translations of the official reports appeared the same morning in the *Ruhleben Daily News* or "Daily Daily," and within a week or two the men also saw London papers of the same date. English newspapers were on sale in Berlin throughout the war, and Ruhleben's guards, zealous for "freedom of information," were buying them for one mark and selling them to interned entrepreneurs for ten. The latter made their profit by renting them out for an hour to each of a series of boxes, charging one mark on the first day and less thereafter. The traffic was well known to the German authorities—indeed, theatrical producers lost no opportunity of having *The Times* conspicuously displayed on the stage—and in time the officers even joked about it to the prisoners. And Abbot wrote boldly

---

1. "Distinguished" is used advisedly, for the important figures in Ruhleben's intellectual world were now well recognized, and at least one lecturer noted in his diary the names of those he noticed in the audience.

in 1916: "Theo's brother [himself] reads the 'Times' or 'Telegraph' fairly regularly—of course about ten days late—so he is fairly well posted." Exposure to two conflicting versions of the war not only gave the Ruhlebenite a relatively objective view of it; it also taught him that neither government could be trusted to tell the truth in wartime.

Other offences were less lightly regarded than illicit newspaper reading, and in January 1916 the Baron launched a campaign against the smoking, candle-burning, and other breaches of fire regulations that had been prevalent in the lofts since the guards' removal. Barracks were raided, charcoal stoves and candles confiscated, partitions torn down, and relays of smokers sent to the cells. It was fortunately not long before small accumulators became available to relieve the darkness, if not the cold. With spring several further escapes caused extra roll calls and threats to punish the whole camp—"for *not* escaping," as Chapman put it. And a big flare-up occurred in May when an *Unteroffizier* complained that two rank-buttons had been removed from his cap. The prisoners could hardly have been guilty, but they were sentenced to two days' confinement in barracks. Jarvis writes:

May 11, 1916. 48 hours of double imprisonment because some Hun has lost two buttons off his cap. All went up to tea, for boiler house is shut. One solid line from first galley to Captains' office. Competent men calculate that we used the amount of bread and sausage that should last for a month. In any case we used 379 two-pound tins where 50 are usually necessary. It is estimated that this "Straf" has cost them so far more than £60.

Solidarity reappeared immediately, the barracks sang loudly on their long march to the kitchens, and the economic sanctions were so effective that the punishment was cancelled after one day.

Finally in July a sentry fired his rifle—by accident, it was assumed— and excused himself by claiming that stones had been thrown at him from a barrack. This was a grave crime, and Berlin ordered severe penalties. Kendall reports:

July 27, 1916. Today we got for punishment—the sports ground closed, all games of any sort, marbles, cards, chess, draughts, all music, concerts, theatre, gramophones and similar things forbidden for eight days. We are confined to the steaming compound. Graf Schwerin had a most ridiculous notice posted, saying "he would come into and leave the camp during this time with a heavy heart."

The kitchens were again besieged on the first day, but the food was too wretched to make the protest worth continuing. In spite of Kendall, the old Graf was undoubtedly sincere; indeed, some officer must have told the soldiers to "go easy," for Chapman enjoyed his usual game of bridge every evening, and Kendall wrote on July 31: "Despite the fact we are under punishment, about five roulette wheels are going full swing in the open air."

There was also much discontent with the captains, beginning with a February row about Ambassador Gerard's first report on the camp, in which he implied that the prisoners were too lazy to do their own fatigue work. A British paper ran an article headed "Work-Shies at Ruhleben," and when this was posted on the boiler house indignant barrack meetings demanded that the captains send an official reply. Perhaps wisely, they refused, but votes of censure were passed on them, and several letters show that the men's pride in being Ruhlebenites was deeply wounded. Even angrier protests followed the reduction of relief payments from five to four marks in March—at whose instigation is uncertain. Though the cut was justified by the shortage of canteen stocks, it was bitterly resented, for the men now had a vested interest in their pocket-money. Barrack delegates again interviewed Powell, but to no avail, and the weekly receipts were for some time signed only "under protest."

Then came a significant battle in the captains' committee. More than half its members had been elected since Powell's appointment as chairman, and on April 18 one of them, W. F. MacKenzie of Barrack 5, challenged Powell's right to represent the committee to outsiders. Powell at once adjourned the meeting, and he, his vice-captain, and the camp treasurer refused to attend one which the remaining captains called next day. At this meeting six of the fourteen present favoured the substitution of a neutral chairman for Powell, five backed Powell, and three wished to consult their barracks. Powell, however, had moved swiftly, and before the day was over MacKenzie received the following letter (CC)—a sample both of Powell's methods and of his official style:

SIR,
   In view of the fact that you refuse to recognize or acknowledge me as Chairman of the Captains' Committee, I felt that I was unable to continue with the duties to which I had been unanimously elected, and I therefore advised the Military Authorities of a certain course of action which, under the circumstances, I considered it necessary to take. Messrs. Simon and Jones also felt that they were placed in a similar position.
   I have to inform you that the Military Authorities have declined to entertain the possibility of being placed in the position of having to consider the question of resignation on our part, and, on the other hand, have decided to order you to at once lay down your office as Captain of Barrack No. 5.

Yours truly,
J. POWELL, Captain of the Camp

Although Barrack 5 chanted "We want MacKenzie!" all evening, their captain was out for good. Six other captains tendered their resignations, but five withdrew them when Powell consented to the appointment of the camp treasurer as permanent chairman. Powell's own position was still unassailable, but the captains' insistence on publishing the relevant minutes at least made the issues clear.

The spring of 1916 was again fervently welcomed; a few mild days in March brought happy letters from Ewing and Graham, and on the 24th Kendall, a nature lover, saw "thirty wild geese flying high up in the sky, a fine sight." And Denton wrote on April 2, "Some glorious sunny days, everyone has spring fever and there are 21 daffodils up in our barrack garden." Kendall heard the first frogs in the pond on April 10, and on the 23rd he wrote: "The swallows came back today and our old friend the stork flew over." The spring brought one great boon; on April 7 fifty wives and mothers of interned men were at last allowed to visit them for two hours in Barrack 23. There were two visiting days a week thereafter; since no visitor could come more than once a month, several hundred men must have benefited by this belated act of compassion. After eighteen months' separation the first meetings with wives were not easy; Graham was told by two men that "they seemed unable to talk at all for a long while, they felt so strange together." In April the proprietor of the R.X.D., who had been selling stamps profitably to German collectors, was arrested and the service reorganized as the Camp Messenger Service —equally useful, but less glamorous without the attractive stamps. In the same month appeared *La Vie française de Ruhleben*, an illustrated magazine that had 600 advance subscribers and sold around 1,000 copies. Very few French were in the camp, but the school had 369 students taking 54 courses, the French Circle met twice weekly, and French plays drew large audiences. April also saw the second number of the *Ruhleben Camp Magazine*, which had replaced *In Ruhleben Camp*. It was a larger and better journal, and an "automatic" vending machine (with an operator inside it) sold 108 copies. Rising costs of production, however, were threatening the camp periodicals, and total sales were under 2,000.

Bedtime was extended to 10 P.M. on April 1, and on May 1 the prisoners had their first encounter with daylight saving. Denton wrote: "At ten last night Thorpie [barrack captain] announced, 'By military order it is now 11 o'clock,' and amid loud cheers we all set our watches on. It is a good idea and ought to be universal." May also saw the start of a campaign to get rid of the hordes of rats who had disloyally left their German homes for the well-fed enemy camp. Ewing wrote in July: "We have nearly wiped out the rats, I don't know how many hundred they caught, with a ferret and dog and sticks. The camp cats, who are ever increasing, were afraid to go near them, but used to eat what they left." Some were trapped alive and run down by a terrier in the square amid great excitement. A more questionable improvement was the "wine-line," which the Germans established without consulting the captains—presumably to help dispose of cheap wine that had accumulated in war-time. It was poor stuff—Chapman wrote "Tasted the wine here for the first and probably the last time"—but potent when well "spiked." A commercial photographer was also allowed in, and the Ruhlebenites' passion for souvenirs of their internment gave him a roaring trade. Most prisoners were photographed with every group they belonged to, and photos of theatrical casts and camp scenes were bought by the hundred and mailed to England.

One event of this spring had a remarkable impact: the arrival of two Russian "soldiers" aged thirteen and ten respectively. Peter and Stanislas had hidden on troop trains, been adopted and dressed in miniature uniforms by soldiers, gone through the Russian retreat from Galicia, and been captured at the surrender of Novo Georgievsk. At a loss what to do with them, the Germans finally transferred them, to their disgust, from a military camp to Ruhleben. Word of their arrival spread fast and the whole camp turned out to watch the Baron interviewing them, he smiling benignly, they stiffly at attention. They were put in charge of a group of Russian intellectuals who taught them English, broke them of smoking, built them a play house by the Marble Arch, and tended them devotedly. They were soon perfectly at home, and the presence of two real children had startling effects. They were constantly surrounded by smiling prisoners, trying to talk to them and plying them with delicacies, and their realistic war games were watched with fascination. So many men yearned for some contact with them that their guardians had to put a ban on invitations. They were ordinary boys, and the exaggerated res-ponse to them showed that some important needs were not being met in Ruhleben, in spite of all its amenities. Irwin wrote in 1933: "The boys aroused a queer sort of 'emotionality' in our hearts. We in our mess, I know, invited them to meals and tried to fraternize with them, in an effort to fulfil some hidden longing for the spontaneity and freshness of childhood."

After three months of lessons and play the boys were abruptly removed to a camp where a dozen other children had been concentrated, and Abbot, Ewing, Denton, and Graham all wrote feelingly of the gap they left. The Russians, of course, were particularly stricken; in a notice thanking the camp for its kindness to the boys they said:

> Our profound regret and sorrow at their departure are, we feel sure, shared by the numerous friends they had here. We are glad to be able to say that their famous cabin is being kept by us for the present as a sweet souvenir and a kind of relic. All interested are welcome to visit it, especially on Sundays and the key may be obtained at the "Russian box" (15), Barrack 1.[2]

And Denton, who had coached the boys for a triumphant appearance in Russian folk-songs at a Y.M.C.A. concert, wrote:

> Poor Morozoff is quite heart-broken. It is pathetic to see him hovering about their little hut, tending the flowers they planted, picking up paper and raking the ground. He keeps everything inside just as they left it, only putting up one of their pictures in the little window; all the camp do homage as they pass by. . . . I am *so* lonely without them, as are Alick and all the others; we had no idea we were so fond of them.

It was a revealing episode.

A few glimpses of everyday life at this period may be given from Kendall's diary:

> *April 19, 1916.* A man in Melville's box found a dog's claw in his meatball. Kastner [kitchen inspector] tells us they are made from *good* dog-flesh!

> *May 21.* In the camp we now get about two inches square of meat once a week. Today, it being our turn, we went up and the cupboard was bare. It would go very hard with us if the parcels failed.

> *May 25.* Trietschel came round in the evening to explain that he had just been given five days in the birdcage for smoking in his loft and couldn't take the Concrete class on Saturday. Bainton gave an erudite discourse on "Contrapuntalists," and Keel sang a small cantata by J. S. Bach.

> *May 26.* Today the 500,000th parcel was given out to A. Carlton, and a little demonstration was made at the parcel office. Carlton's ticket was signed by all the post staff.

> *June 3.* Went round to see Squires' electric clock which he has made in the camp out of biscuit tins. It is a work of genius and is going to be patented. A secondary clock works from it. Graf Schwerin is taking a big interest in him.

> *June 17.* Had the usual Saturday busy day. At 7.30 played golf with C.A., L., and S., and won; at 9 went to Lockyer Roberts' Electricity class. 10–11 went to German class, 11–12 prepared dinner. At 1.30 Ferro-concrete class, and at 3 to 5 drawing class. Prepared tea and at 6.30 went to see "The

---

2. *La Vie française de Ruhleben*, No. 3, p. 16.

Knight of the Burning Pestle" which was done in really fine style. To finish this frenzied day we had the usual Appell at 9.20 in the rain.

June 23. Today a man from the loft brought a piece of dog's intestine he had found in his soup, containing all the dung. A filthy sight. The food at the galley is simply shocking. Watched a stork flying overhead and timed him seven minutes without a flap of his wings.

June 26. Gerard came into the camp and a demonstration was made, and he was told some home truths about what was thought about his notorious reports to England. He was also given to see that the Camp Captain and Barrack Captains were not elected nor representative.

June 27. Today the food given to us was one fifth of a potato loaf and very weak tea *ersatz* for breakfast, the bread was to last the day. Dinner consisted of cabbage and the water it was boiled in, nothing else, no potatoes (there will be none in the camp for a month) and no meat of any kind. What the deuce will happen to us should parcels from home fail blessed if I know. Ambassador Gerard came in again today, if he didn't see what was the condition of the food, then he is wilfully blind.

It is not everywhere that an engineer must cancel a lecture because he has been seen smoking, and all Kendall's pithy observations suggest the strange contrasts of Ruhleben, with its highly developed intellectual life set against a background of squalor and petty oppression.

On June 28 the Y.M.C.A. invited five hundred camp leaders to hear Dr. John A. Mott at a special service. Denton wrote enthusiastically:

Our hall was packed with the best men in the camp, and I've never heard such singing. I had a good orchestra and choir there as well as our new organ, and we nearly broke the windows. . . . His address made a very great impression.

Kendall, who was present, commented rather differently:

Dr. Mott, the "champion Yankee Christian," addressed a meeting in the Y.M.C.A. It was very amusing, for just as they were singing "God send us men!" about 45 men from the G.E. Railway Co's boat "Brussels" were marched in from Zeebrugge, having had no food for 48 hours.

The summer of 1916 was cool and rainy, but a full season of cricket, golf, and tennis was played, and baseball and lacrosse made their appearance. Promenade concerts began in May, and the new cookhouse opened on June 15; on the 18th it handled 967 fries, bakes, and boils, besides heating 250 tins. A remarkable Arts and Crafts Exhibit showed what the handicraftsmen were accomplishing, and in August there was a *private* show of sketches by C. F. Winzer—a significant innovation. A dozen men escaped this summer, all but two being recaptured, and there were the first instances of "going over the wire"—bribing a sentry, spending a few gay hours in Spandau or Berlin, and then returning, usually to be caught and punished. German rationing was making the guards very receptive to English butter and cigarettes, and such outings increased later. Then, on September 12, Ruhleben said goodbye to the choleric Baron von Taube, transferred to another post. Kendall notes: "The Baron leaves camp. Most of his belongings were packed in tin biscuit boxes and cardboard cases. Looked most undignified for a Baron."

The diaries show a flurry of interest in the Anglo-French offensive on the Somme, which began in July, and one reports "great excitement" over Rumania's joining the Allies, but such references are very rare, and (except in Farwell's diary) they read as though the war were occurring in another world. It was different, however, at the end of July, when Captain Fryatt of the *Brussels* was returned to Belgium, court-martialled, and shot for attempting to ram a German submarine. The judicial murder of a man who had lived in Ruhleben, if only for a month, caused deep shock and anger, and brought the war home to the camp as nothing had done before.

Camp activities ran on unchecked, however, and it was well that they did, for this was an unsettling summer. Rumours of exchange began before the end of June, and were kept at top pitch for six weeks by agitation for exchange in Britain. Mr. Gerard had salvaged his reputation by condemning Ruhleben's accommodation in strong terms, and by forwarding reports from an American nutritionist that showed the rations to be totally insufficient. The reports led to a British press campaign for "all for all" exchange, and boundless hopes were raised in the camp. Kendall wrote on July 9, "Rumour fever intense, worse than ever before," and Farwell felt so certain of release that he asked in his diary, "What regiments do we join?"

The men's excitement ignored the wide gap between editorial opinions and government policy; though actual negotiations began in June, the British Government held stubbornly to the "man for man" formula, which they knew the Germans would not accept. In December, however, they did agree to exchange all men over 45—a proposal that the Germans had made two years earlier—and this was all that was achieved in 1916.[3]

The prisoners, of course, knew only that something was in the wind,

3. See British Foreign Office, *White Papers*, "Miscellaneous" (1916), nos. 21 (Cd. 8262), 25 (Cd. 8296), and 35 (Cd. 8352). The negotiations are summarized in *The Ruhleben Prisoners: The Case for their Release* (42). In the long exchange of notes, it must be said that the German Government showed itself the more humane and flexible.

and their extravagant hopes were partly a reaction against the thought of a third winter. Though the previous one had often been enjoyable, another would mean a full year added to their sentence, and this, set against the summer's rosy visions, seemed intolerable. Denton, Graham, and Ewing wrote respectively during July: "Awful to think of another winter here," "My mind has been rebelling against the thought of [it]," and, "We turn our faces away from [it]." And so, when the last rumour died and nothing at all had happened, gloom again stalked the camp. "All week has been very cold," Denton wrote in September, "a reminder that summer is over, and the mood of the camp is *not* pleasant." And Ewing wrote on October 16: "A terrible wave of depression here now, with days getting darker and no hope in sight. It saps one's vitality; I can do simply nothing but read novels and wait for the post."[4]

Ewing, however, had dropped his school work or he would have felt differently, for it was precisely at this trying period that the full value of organization showed itself. Left to themselves the men were helpless against their emotions; Denton could not even bring himself to call a choir practice until mid-October. But Graham wrote on October 7, "I think the starting of a new language has bucked me up," and his simple observation suggests what was happening. All the chief activities were governed by a fixed time-table; their ordered functioning took no heed of the moods of individuals; and hundreds of men were now obligated to play active roles in them. The bare record is enough: the theatre re-opened on August 30, the A.S.U. programme on September 4, school started on September 11, the Science Circle on the 13th, orchestral concerts on the 17th, the German Circle next day, the Technical Circle on the 21st, the History Circle on the 23rd, golf competitions on October 1, and football one week later. The machine was in full operation again, and a large proportion of the prisoners were regularly, purposefully, and socially occupied. Whatever their initial reluctance, this activity steadied, distracted, and then absorbed them; Graham remarked on October 20, "Another letter, another fortnight gone, time slips away at a great rate." And in the changed atmosphere even Ewing wrote in December: "We have all got over the 'blues' and settled down for the winter."

That the Ruhlebenite should settle down to work whether he felt like it or not would surprise no one—if only he had had an *economic* motive

4. Further unrest had been caused in September by a German proposal to transfer all merchant sailors to Brandenburg. But the Ruhlebenites, though crowded, wanted to stick together, and after some protest meetings only 120 recently captured men were removed.

for doing so. But that, of course, was entirely lacking. The fact has already been discussed, but one comment may be added about the theories, social and psychological, that make hunger or economic need the mainspring of human activity. All are products of modern societies in which rapid change has dislocated the social structure and torn great numbers of people from their traditional social groupings. In a small, intact society, whose members are conscious participants in an ordered collective life, the driving force of social obligations on the one hand, and of work for its own sake on the other, would have been better appreciated. Many such societies have been described by anthropologists, and perhaps Ruhleben deserves to stand beside them.

Though some weakening of the programme of activity might have been expected after the frustrated hopes of the summer, nothing of the sort occurred. On the contrary, the organized life of 1916–17 was more vigorous than ever. The school was still expanding, the A.S.U. ran a full series of Monday evenings, there were 36 theatre productions as against 31, concerts every Sunday, and a sharp increase in attendance at the Technical Circle. The only negative signs were a change from weekly to fortnightly meetings in the M.E.A., and in the Technical Circle at Christmas; in both cases the aim was to secure better papers. As for sport, Pentland's Christmas comment on football ran: "Those who imagined there would be a decrease in the interest of the game in Camp this season have already been proved quite wrong" (*RCM* 5, p. 58). And there was a "gate" of more than 3,000 at the cup final in April 1917.

The year was outstanding, too, for the quality and variety of its programmes. The school enriched its curriculum, and its first six candidates passed the London matriculation. A.S.U. lecture topics ranged from Javanese Puppets, Pond Life, Irrigation in the Sudan, and American Literature (Whitman, Pound, Frost), to Pre-Norman Ireland, Hints on Market Gardening, and the Platonism of Shelley. Its Hugo Wolf evening was described by Benjamin Dale as "one of the bright memories of our Ruhleben existence," and Kendall's account of the annual meeting, "much obstruction and little business done," shows that its traditions were in no wise weakened. The long theatrical season included plays by Shaw, Wilde, Ibsen, and Somerset Maugham, besides *The School for Scandal* and no less than four Gilbert and Sullivan operas, among them a wonderful Christmas *Mikado* that ran three weeks. There were also plays in French and German and the usual variety shows, while the A.S.U. added Maori plays in costume, Aristophanes' *The Frogs*, a moving performance of the old morality play *Everyman*, and Masefield's *Good Friday*, "excellently done by the Duncan-Jones people" (Kendall).

In music, the orchestra improved still further, a pair of timpani was added, and Dale singled out for praise the Schumann piano concerto, a Brandenburg concerto, *Eine Kleine Nachtmusik*, and "much good work" at chamber concerts. And the Octa Orchestra, of clarinet, horn, strings, and piano, began to provide "welcome relief from the well-meant but depressing efforts of the theatre orchestra" (*RCM* 5, p. 49).

To balance all these good things the men had to face the coldest winter on record, under worse conditions than usual. The barracks were not even heated until November 19, when the engines were repaired; "Too cold to sleep in bed," Ewing wrote. Then on January 17 came a month of unprecedented frost, with temperatures well below zero. Pipes burst everywhere, there was no hot water or porridge, sports were abandoned, theatre and school closed, and Denton said in a letter, "There is nothing to write about except the cold." The frost returned in March, and now the coal gave out, and for six near-zero nights the barracks were entirely without heat. No wonder the Ruhleben winters were dreaded! However, the men put up with it good-temperedly—the strongest complaint is "We felt it pretty badly"—and they made full use of the Arctic conditions. Brisk walks around the frozen field kept the blood flowing, and a heavy snowfall brought the wildest snow-balling yet seen; Kendall wrote angrily, "Boys' Barrack going round viciously hitting anybody." Sculptors built snow statues, there was skating and ice-hockey on the pond, and in March men were skating all over the flooded sports ground. After the frost came famine; during a long stoppage of parcels even Kendall's well-heeled mess had to apply to the "Relief in Kind" Office.

Everyday life was full of incident. Daylight saving ended on October 1, and Chapman, always reliable, started growing a beard on November 1 and put on his winter underwear on the 15th. There was a special matinée of *Hindle Wakes* for the Lancastrians, followed by high tea for cast and committee at Mr. Butterworth's invitation. Duncan-Jones mustered a sewing party on *Everyman* costumes—"good fun," Farwell commented. The delays attendant on the switch to standard parcels caused a rash of complaints; Merton wrote, "I suppose the officials know what they are doing, but I should just like five minutes in their office." An old sailor fell from the loft steps, broke his leg, and died of pneumonia; Kendall commented: "The poor fellow, who is 60 odd, was left lying on his stretcher in the cold at the gate, and put into cold sheets at the lazaret." Seven thousand copies of the Christmas magazine were sold, more than half of them being mailed to England, and eighty-eight men attended the Christmas "beano" of the Technical Circle.

The big surprise of the year was the visit of the Rt. Rev. Herbert Bury, Anglican bishop of Northern and Central Europe, whose pre-war German connections enabled him to spend five days at Ruhleben. His arrival on November 22, 1916, was regarded with some suspicion, but after he had greeted the whole camp from a Trafalgar Square stairway, and given messages of sympathy from the King and Queen, his welcome was never in doubt. He lived in the camp, took meals in boxes, kicked off at a football game, went to the theatre, confirmed a dozen men, and spoke seven times in the Y.M.C.A. to enormous crowds, moving easily from war stories and cryptic assurances that things were "all right" at home to simple pleas for God and injunctions against sin. He was a persuasive speaker, who set out to win the men's affection; by playing on all the feelings they had so long repressed he touched off a great emotional catharsis.

He himself recognized the abnormal responsiveness of his audiences: "The atmosphere was quite electric . . . I could hardly get on for cheers. My words were understood almost before they were spoken" (6, p. 14). And he was modest enough to attribute it to the men's highly strung state. Although his extraordinary success was thus rather cheaply earned, the men themselves could not get enough of him. Denton wrote: "On Monday, when it was not even certain that he would speak, the line-up for the 6.30 meeting began before 8 A.M., and we had 1,048 people in a 500 hall!" Even swearing stopped for a day or two after a few tactful words from the bishop, and when he said his goodbye from the barrack steps and called (by German permission) for *God Save the King*, the crowd responded, as Kendall noted, with "the wildest enthusiasm." Every contemporary account is favourable; Graham, not a church-goer, told his wife: "I can hardly give you an idea of the good done by the recent visit of Bishop Bury. . . . It was an immense success, and cheered the whole camp up enormously."

In Graham's next reference to the visit, however, he wrote, "I think our nerves get very shaky here, and I fancy when I see you again only a real good cry will relieve my feelings." And the bishop reported that, of the scores of men who spoke to him privately, few did so without tears. What he had done was to break down the camp's defences— the barriers against emotion set up in the opening days—and this had conflicting results. The men loved him for it at the time, but they felt vaguely ashamed afterwards, for to give way to one's feelings was to betray the code on which Ruhleben had been built. A reaction was inevitable, and fortunately the bishop himself gave a pretext for it by promptly publishing a book, some passages of which left a not unattractive picture of camp life. The response was a foregone conclusion, and in June 1917 the following limerick appeared—a telling contrast to the warmth of November:

> I could really be very sarcastic
> If I spoke of an ecclesiastic
> Whose tales when in here
> Were decidedly queer,
> But when he got home were fantastic.
>
> (*RCM* 6, p. 24)

On the day of the bishop's arrival in camp *The Times* published Sir Timothy Eden's plea for total exchange, which asserted that the Ruhlebenites, if left for another winter, would suffer "more terribly than we can imagine." Similar letters followed, but, though the papers reached the camp before Christmas, no exchange rumours are anywhere recorded. The busy winters, of course, were always inimical to them, and repeated disappointments had bred a lot of scepticism. Abbot wrote in March 1917: "We have given up thinking about going home. . . . That isn't to say we are downhearted (you know us better by now than to think that) but we don't like to indulge in optimism—we've had some!" Nevertheless, it is probable that rumours did circulate this winter, at least among the "addicts"—the residue of bored men to whom camp activities had little appeal. Those who find this world unsatisfying have always had visions of a better one to come, and the men who could not reconcile themselves to Ruhleben cherished their rumours like biblical prophecies, reinterpreting the mystic words whenever a chosen date failed to bring the apocalypse. Most informants, on the other hand, though far from immune to the summer epidemics, did not need, record, or perhaps even hear the "chronic" type of rumour.[5]

Though beer was put on sale legitimately at Christmas 1916, there was also "a lot of hard stuff in the camp" (Chapman), and at New Year's Ruhleben was "almost totally drunk" (Kendall). Chapman got to bed at three after a singsong in a box crammed with twelve men, and shouting, singing, and marching in procession kept the whole camp awake. It was another form of emotional catharsis, but it might have shocked the bishop.

The New Year's jubilation was justified, however, for on December 26 Mr. Gerard had announced that agreement had been reached and

5. The suggestion gains force from the frequent magazine references to rumours in 1916 and 1917, when so few appear in the record. All these references are facetious, however; to the literate prisoners, at least, rumours have become a mere source of amusement. The camp was so stably organized that the taboo was no longer required.

the "forty-fivers" would begin leaving almost immediately. (It was his last appearance in Ruhleben, for in February his government broke off relations with Germany and the prisoners came under the protection of the Dutch.) Over four hundred men were affected by the news, and the whole camp rejoiced with them. Nine duly left on January 9, 1917, sixteen on the 24th, and forty on the 28th. Then something happened and the movement came to a halt, not to be resumed for another twelve months. A minor feature of war, no doubt, but a cruel one, and disturbing to Ruhleben, for all through 1917 it kept some 12 per cent of the population restless and deeply frustrated.

At Christmas the Y.M.C.A. had daringly run a "conference" of bible study, discussions, and addresses. It was entirely conducted by prisoners, and the fact that 180 men registered and attended the five days' sessions suggests that one branch of religion, at least, was showing signs of growth. And the spring and summer of 1917 brought new growth in other directions. In March the school began extensive structural alterations in Barrack 6, now completely vacated; as Graham remarked, "We continue to extend the school, make new roads, and really we may be forgiven for thinking that we are fixed here permanently." Then on April 3 hundreds of men started digging up the unused portion of the race-track enclosure. The Horticultural Society had persuaded the captains to arrange for the land and to make them an advance of £400 for rent, seeds, fertilizer, and a greenhouse. The results were impressive; lettuce and radishes—the first the men had tasted in three years—appeared in the canteen in July, and in spite of a plague of caterpillars the vegetable crop was large enough to pay off all the society's indebtness. Handicrafts, too, were expanding with great rapidity; at a crowded May exhibit orders of M 3,000 were taken, to be applied to the school's building debt.

The Germans found discipline hard to enforce this summer. On June 6, because of night prowling and other offences, morning and evening roll calls were transferred from the barracks to the racecourse, doubling the time required for them. The announcement was greeted with ironic cheering, and everyone in the camp went down for his German bread ration. That evening Powell sent round a rather pathetic notice: "I have been instructed by the Military Authorities to inform the Camp that the Appells now being held on the playing field are not in the nature of a punishment" (H). As Jarvis commented: "So we are not to punish *them*. The bread 'do' acted quickly!"

The school began using its improved accommodation on May 7, on the 13th a new catalogue listed 3,450 titles in the Fiction Library—and on the 15th Chapman donned his summer underwear. No doubt at this signal, promenade concerts began, cricket, baseball, and tennis followed, and July brought a summer Art Exhibit, a Flower Show, and a further innovation—"La Semaine Française," a week of French plays and lectures that opened appropriately on July 14. The first night had to compete, however, not only with another Y.M.C.A. conference, but with the spectacular fire that destroyed a stable, the studios, and the Boys' Barack. The fire horn sounded at 8.15, interrupting a Y.M.C.A. discussion of "Business," and everyone rushed to the west end of camp where the stable was burning fiercely. Prisoners rescued three horses, but two and some cows perished. Low pressure made the police hoses useless, so lines of men poured buckets of water on the barrack roofs while others carried out beds and belongings. The camp guards did nothing, and it was half an hour before the Spandau fire brigade arrived, quenched the remaining flames, and gave themselves enthusiastically to salvage. "Nearly all the food from 20, 21, and 22 was 'lost' to the salvage party," Jarvis noted, "one of the first things they did was to load the motor with food"; the guards meanwhile "stood in the way with their rifles until it got dark enough to go on the food-hunt." The wire fence had been levelled to let the engines in; sentries were doubled at the gap—and double the number of night trips to Spandau followed.

Of the four diaries now being kept, only Farwell's paid any attention to the dramatic war news of 1917. There must have been interest in some circles, for on February 1, when Germany began unrestricted submarine warfare, he wrote: "Will America go to war? Camp opinion—NO!" But the other diarists do not mention even the American declaration of war in April, let alone the stirring events of July—collapse of the Russian front, a socialist regime in St. Petersburg, British attacks in the west, peace agitation in Germany. On the other hand all camp news, down to circle meetings and cricket results, is fully recorded. Either the men's horizons were narrower than ever or the abundance of newspapers had made war jottings seem unneccessary.

Late in June, however, an Anglo-German conference on prisoners opened at the Hague,[6] and this was a different matter; everyone mentioned it and the wave of rumours it set off—chiefly of internment under idyllic conditions in Holland. Informants' letters were sceptical; Denton described the camp as "unjustifiably excited," and Graham wrote: "Only the youngsters take any interest in [it]; we old 45ers are not

6. It was an unusual "conference," for the negotiators never met face to face, but entered the building by different doors, occupied different suites, and communicated by handing chits to Dutch page-boys.

likely to believe any news is good until we see something done." Others were apparently more optimistic, for the rumours flourished until August 5, when the conference agreements were announced: the forty-fivers would definitely go, and 400 others whose health was suffering would be sent to Holland. A week later no fewer than 1,800 prisoners applied under the second category. Medical examinations began at once, the forty-fivers were photographed and given passports—and not a man left Ruhleben for the rest of the year.

Once again the high hopes of summer curdled into sour dejection, the days grew shorter, and Graham spoke for many when he described himself on August 25 as "fed up, nervous, disinclined for anything at all that Ruhleben can offer." How was such a camp to settle down for a fourth winter? Some found it impossible, and there was a flurry of mental breakdowns and a sudden rise in attempts to escape. But then September came with its annual miracle; theatre, lectures, school, and football opened in rapid succession, and in the quickened atmosphere the dread of winter evaporated. As early as September 14 Ewing (now teaching elementary Italian) wrote, "We are all getting into stride for the winter," and Graham remarked in November: "How am I entering upon another winter? Cheerfully enough, thank heaven, with a few minor troubles that do not amount to much."

The machinery was harder to start this year; two circles that had always met in September did not get going until November, and the epidemic of escapes was unsettling. But the institutional activities began exactly on schedule—not automatically, by any means, but because of the devoted men who had been rehearsing plays, preparing concerts, revising curricula, and arranging sports fixtures all through the troubled weeks. Their quiet courage was a real miracle of Ruhleben, and its roots were still the old ones: a sense of obligation to their co-workers and a conviction that what they were doing was important and helpful. The strength of these social motives was tremendous; not only did they impel men to buckle down to work season after season, but they led several to reject release on the ground that they were of greater use in Ruhleben.[7]

Little need be said about the fall months of 1917. On the surface everything ran as usual, with fourteen theatrical productions up to Christmas, including three further Shaw plays—even G.B.S. should have been flattered at such unremitting attention. Standards were apparently still rising; Kendall noted that one leading actor "excelled

7. "Leslie's" reasons for refusal are found on page 7 of *In Ruhleben Camp* (43). Those of others were similar.

himself" in a courtroom drama, and Farwell characterized the revival of a 1915 hit as "very good indeed—two years ago!" The A.S.U. put on an Italian play, Arthur Speed performed the "Emperor" concerto "very finely," and the Y.M.C.A. introduced Saturday "Club Nights," with ping-pong and other amusements for all comers. These did not last long, for on October 30 the captains, without consulting the Y.M.C.A. committee, issued a notice permitting smoking and card-playing in the hall, and, when the committee objected, deprived them of their control of the building. After fruitless negotiation the committee resigned and left the building, followed by about forty members. Their insistence on keeping the hall free from smoke was in part a reflection of puritan prejudice, but their objection to Powell's strong-arm tactics was soundly based. Powell himself disappeared after this fracas, going to the sanatorium with what Kendall calls a "nervous breakdown."

The only other event that requires mention reflected the increasing strain in the camp; the drawing up, by barrack delegates, of a memorandum for submission to the British Government on the third anniversary of internment. The propriety of the move was much debated, and a small majority finally voted against it. In the light of what the Ruhlebenites had suffered, physically and mentally, at the hands of both warring governments, the dignity and restraint of this, their one official protest, are remarkable.[8]

On December 14 Graham told his wife of "persistent rumours" that the forty-fivers were really going and that he might see her soon; though steeling himself against a further disappointment, he added, "Such a thought quite carries me away, and I hardly know what I am doing." The rumours did not alter the steady pulse of Ruhleben life: on December 16 the Italian Circle wound up the term with a concert of Italian music; on the 18th Barrack 9 defeated 7 in a cup tie game by 3 to 1; on the 19th thousands of Christmas cards, designed in the camp, were mailed, and Chapman spent all morning in the ticket line for *The Gondoliers*; on the 20th there was a football concert with presentations to two officials; on the 23rd Duncan-Jones read a paper by Rudolf Steiner to a "select group"—and that day, with temperatures at 10 above zero, the barrack heating again broke down. Then, on Christmas Eve, it was officially announced that 350 forty-fivers would leave on January 2, and excitement seized the camp. The police presented a French clock

8. A more strongly worded resolution was passed at a meeting of 340 Merchant Marine officers in August 1917, urging their transfer to a neutral country and expressing "disapproval of the lack of material sympathy shown to our cause by the government at home." Its despatch was also voted down in January 1918.

to their superintendent, who was going, and on New Year's Eve all the lucky men were tendered a farewell concert, with speeches, cheers, and a hastily composed song that expressed much of Ruhleben's warm spirit. One verse and chorus follow:

> In this Lager we, by the Havel and the Spree,
> Have lived together just like friends and brothers;
>   Good luck! We wish you well,
>   But don't forget to tell
> The dear old folks at home that there are others.
>
>   Say, comrades, say
>   When you are far away,
> Sometimes you'll think of us lads;
>   A time will come some day
>   When we may get away;
> Remember us, and we'll remember you, lads.

At six o'clock on a bitterly cold morning the whole camp climbed on stairways and roofs to give their comrades a final send-off. It was a long goodbye, for the engine could not get the train moving until 9.30, but the hours were filled with songs, cheers, and endless banter. Some darker emotions were hidden under the exuberance; Jarvis wrote later in his diary, "Saying goodbye . . . seemed something like standing on a wreck and saying goodby to those the lifeboats could hold." Ruhleben was not yet a wreck, but the loss of a tenth of its population was a blow that could not be repaired. And when the train had gone, with Prichard, Butterworth, "Graham," and all the others, Jarvis closed his entry with, "So many of the old faces are seen no more."

PART VI | Postscript *Robert B. MacLeod*

Ketchum's manuscript ends with Chapter 17. He had projected several further chapters, to be entitled respectively: Social Strains and Reactions; Ruhleben and the Individual; An Aging Society: 1918; Closing Weeks; and Afterthoughts. Since he left only the scantiest of notes, it would have been quite impossible for me to recreate these chapters as he had planned them. Instead, I have attempted in the Postcript to do two things: (1) to provide a certain amount of closure for the reader by recounting in narrative form a sketch of the events of 1918, including a review of their wartime setting for the benefit of those whose memories of World War I may have grown dim; and (2) to discuss more systematically a few of the theoretical implications of the study which, in my opinion, Ketchum would have wished to stress. The narrative portion leans heavily on Ketchum's diary and on other reliable sources. It is consequently fairly faithful to the facts. The interpretative portion is inevitably coloured by my own views. Since Ketchum's theoretical position is discernible in every page of his narrative, the reader should feel free to discount, or to omit entirely, my own contribution.

R. B. M.

I. The End of the Ruhleben Story

THE STORY could be brought to its end in a very few sentences. At the beginning of 1918 the outcome of the war was still uncertain. Both sides were weary, but not so exhausted as not to be able to launch a major offensive. The German offensive was powerful, and almost succeeded. By midsummer the allied counter-offensive was gaining strength, and by early autumn the German armies were being forced to retreat along the whole front. On November 7 the civilian government requested an armistice, which was signed on the 11th. During these months the prisoners in Ruhleben continued to live much as they had done before. Until almost the very end there were sporting events, classes, entertainments, a major reorganization of the camp's administrative structure. The society was reduced in size through the departure of the 45'ers, and there was a perceptible drop in enthusiasm; but as a society it remained intact, even through the chaotic final days when German controls had collapsed. The prisoners packed their bags, said their farewells, and by November 24 the last of them had left for home.

But this is obviously not enough. The war ended in victory, or so it was believed, and with it there came to an end a remarkable society, built and sustained by the courage and ingenuity of a heterogeneous group of prisoners. Was this a happy or a sad ending? My first impulse was to report the final months as a case study of the disintegration of morale. Certainly the record shows how the vitality of the group was steadily weakening. If morale had collapsed at any time during those months, the wisdom of hindsight might have explained it as having been predictable from the beginning. The more I have thought about Ruhleben, however, the more convinced I have become that the story is one of triumph rather than tragedy. I believe that the men could have stuck it out even longer, and that even if the final verdict for the Allies had been defeat rather than victory the Ruhleben society would not have disintegrated from internal weakness. This, too, is hindsight.

To grasp the full psychological and sociological significance of the

Ruhleben achievement, and particularly to recreate for oneself the thoughts and feelings of the men during the final months, it may be helpful to step temporarily outside the camp and attempt to see Ruhleben in the perspective of the war as a whole. My account will irritate the historian, but it may be of some value to the reader for whom World War I has become merely a chapter in history.

The background of the war. At the beginning of 1918 the prisoner in Ruhleben was probably as well, or as poorly, supplied with information about the course of the war as was the average civilian on either side. A cool assessment at that time of the military, economic, and morale factors might have led to some such estimate as the following.

From a strictly military point of view the Germans clearly held the advantage. The defeat of Russia had released great quantities of troops for use on the western front; the threat from the south was well under control; French and British resources of manpower were approaching exhaustion; reinforcements from the United States seemed likely to arrive too late; at any time a massive break-through in the west, coupled with an intensification of submarine operations, could have resulted in the capture of Paris, the securing of the whole coastline, and the severing of communications between Britain and France. Under such circumstances the Western Alliance might have been shattered. The war might have come to an end with Germany the undisputed master of Continental Europe, Britain in a hopeless position, and the United States safely on the other side of the Atlantic. As late as July, 1918, this was still well within the realm of possibility, and even during the successful Allied offensive in October there were military experts who believed that Germany was still strong enough to avoid military defeat.

An assessment which stressed the economic situation at the beginning of 1918, and the less tangible but all important factors governing morale, would have given an advantage to the Western Alliance. Germany's economy, though strong in resources and in organization, was by 1918 noticeably weakened. Essential manpower was being steadily drained away by the military; the blockade was producing food shortages which threatened to become acute; reports of military success could not compensate for the lengthening lists of dead and wounded; the German people, courageous and disciplined as they were, were showing signs of war weariness. Less evident but perhaps even more sinister were the spreading suspicions, fostered in part by the social revolution in Russia, that the people of Germany were being duped by reckless and ambitious leaders. There was no open talk of revolution, but the seeds of revolt were beginning to germinate. The British and the French were also war weary. Their casualty lists were equally long, and France especially had not only suffered the loss of productive territory but had once again had to accept the bitter fact of foreign conquest. In spite of crippling military reverses, however, and the appalling destructiveness of the German submarines, the British industrial machine was by 1918 operating in high gear, and the promise of massive support from across the Atlantic was becoming a reality. Perhaps even more important was the fact that the sheer determination to survive was strengthened by the growing conviction that out of victory might come a better world. In characteristic fashion it was an American who supplied the slogan, "to make the world safe for democracy," but there is no question that the French and British determination to win drew support from the firm belief that their cause was morally right.

There is no point in fighting the battles of World War I all over again, but a backward glance may serve to freshen our memories. The war began, as have so many others in the past, with a dramatic precipitating cause, an assassination in the Balkans, which served to release tensions that had been building up for many years. The opposing forces lined up quickly in August 1914: on the one side the Central Powers, Germany and Austria-Hungary, to be supported quickly by Turkey and more than a year later by Bulgaria; on the other side the Western Alliance, Russia, France, and Great Britain with her dominions and colonies, to be joined the following May by Italy, in the summer of 1916 by Rumania and in the spring of 1917 by the United States. Japan was on the Allied side from the beginning, but was not deeply involved. Support from Belgium and Serbia was valiant, but of necessity small, and towards the end of the war Greece was induced to throw in its lot with the Allies.

The plan of the Central Powers, worked out in detail long in advance, was to strike quickly and vigorously towards east, west, and south, to overcome all opposition before it could be adequately mobilized, and then, their strategic objectives having been attained, to announce a victorious peace. Their hope was to bring the enemy to his knees in six weeks; and the hope was nearly realized. As it happened, the opposition was tougher than anticipated and the war dragged on for more than four years, leaving more than 3,500,000 known dead, more than 21,000,000 wounded, and uncounted millions homeless and starving. It is estimated that nearly 58 per cent of the participating troops could be listed as casualties, and this includes Japan and the United States, whose losses were comparatively small. There is no way of assessing the losses in shattered lives and in material waste.

On the eastern front the Central Powers were faced by vast but slow moving, poorly organized and worse led Russian armies. During 1914 and early 1915 the Russians were able to hold their own, and even make gains. By the end of 1915, however, under the brilliant generalship of Hindenburg and Ludendorf, the Germans had driven them back to lines deep within their own territory. During the summer and autumn of 1916 the Russians were able to mount an offensive in the southern sector of their line (Volhynia, Galicia, and Bukowina) which was sufficiently successful to encourage Rumania to enter the war on the Allied side. A counter-offensive speedily crushed Rumania. Further military blows, coupled with internal turmoil, reduced Russian resistance to virtually zero. The revolution in the spring of 1917 left the troops without effective command, resistance disintegrated, and the Central Powers were free to move their armies to other fronts.

In the south the armies of Austria-Hungary invaded the Balkans immediately following the outbreak of war. Allied resistance in this southern sector had perforce to be limited to the whittling away of the enemy's initial successes and strength. The war on the southern fronts was thus a war of progressive exhaustion. As Germany's ability to support her allies diminished in 1918, she lost them one by one. Bulgaria capitulated in September, Turkey in October, and Austria-Hungary on the third of November. Without German help they would have collapsed much sooner.

Germany was victorious in the east; it was her allies who collapsed in the south. In retrospect it is clear that the major war was to be won or lost in the west. The German plan in 1914 was to sweep through neutral Belgium to the coast of the Channel, and then by a great wheeling movement through northern France to overwhelm the French armies before British military and naval support could become effective. The plan nearly succeeded. Within a few weeks the Germans were in possession of most of Belgium and nearly one-tenth of France. At their point of deepest penetration they were within a few miles of Paris, only to be frustrated by stiffening French resistance. By the beginning of the winter, however, the war of lightning attack was over, to be succeeded by long, grim dreary years of trench warfare. A wavy line of trenches, extending from the Belgian coast to the borders of Switzerland, represented what proved to be for the most part a war of sheer attrition. For the next three years the shape of the line varied only as one side or the other mounted an offensive. An offensive meant a great building up of supplies, a regrouping of divisions, a pulverizing artillery barrage, and then the forward movement over no man's land of line after line of soldiers with fixed bayonets and hand grenades, most of whom were mown down by machine-gun fire before the enemy trench yielded. A victory might mean the capture of a shattered village or a strategic hilltop, a successful offensive might mean as little as the gaining of a few hundred square miles of territory at the cost of a hundred thousand lives. The significance of the great battles which became household names was to be measured less in the number of miles gained than in the amount of destruction achieved. Final victory was to be won by the side which held out longer than the other.

The outcome of the western war was thus to be determined by the sheer quantity of human and material resources as well as by the skill with which these were exploited. For the greater part of the war Germany had the advantage on both counts, an advantage which she maintained almost to the end. Germany had more and better trained troops, more and better weapons, a more efficient system of military production, and a strong central command. The Allies, by contrast, were unprepared, ill equipped, and lacking in unity. France had to bear the brunt of the initial attack, supported only by a small British expeditionary force and the remnants of the Belgian army, and French losses during the first few months were colossal. The flow of men and munitions across the English Channel slowly mounted, but it cannot be said that Britain was fully geared for a war of troops, machine-guns, and artillery until well on in 1916. The British and French were further handicapped by the lack of skilled and experienced generals, and even the best of these were frequently at odds both with one another and with their respective governments. Both governments suffered from indecisive leadership, and the early history of the Allied effort is marred by needless suspicions and misunderstandings. Finally, at the end of 1916, Lloyd George emerged as leader of a coalition government, and a year later Clemenceau became premier of France. Together they formed a Supreme War Council to co-ordinate plans for the prosecution of the whole war, but is was not until April of 1918 that all the Allied forces on the western front—with the exception of the newly arriving Americans—were placed under the single command of Foch. For the first time Allied armies were able to serve in concerted action under a leader whose genius could match that of Hindenburg and Ludendorf.

Britain's main contribution, it was thought at first, was to be the undisputed power of her navy, but Britain's navy was doomed to four years of frustration. There were to be no Trafalgars in which the great battleships could slug it out with their opposite numbers. Instead, the Navy's task was to be the humbler one of convoying troops and supplies and blockading enemy ports. The wily Germans had anticipated this by building submarines whose attacks on Allied shipping, particularly in 1917 after the campaign of unrestricted submarine warfare had been launched, were frighteningly successful. Effective counter-measures were developed, but the submarines continued until the end to be a major threat. The success of the submarine campaign, far more than the spectacular zeppelin raids, brought the reality of war home to the British people, and the ruthless submarine attacks on unarmed ships proved to be a major factor in the American decision in April 1917 to enter the war on the Allied side. At the beginning of the war civilian life in Britain was relatively unaffected. The British could talk of "business as usual," and outside the battle zones the French could maintain their cheerful way of life. By the end of 1917, however, the pinch of austerity was being felt everywhere; in Germany the relentlessly tightening blockade deprived the people first of luxuries and then of necessities. There was no spectre of actual starvation, but for the Germans, especially the city dwellers, each new day meant merely more hours of dreary queuing for a meagre ration of unappetizing and decreasingly nutritious food. The soldiers at the front, they knew, were better fed, and better clothed; it was increasingly difficult to believe that all this sacrifice was really necessary. By the beginning of 1918 the morale of the home front was becoming a factor of growing importance. In England morale was stiffening; in Germany it was weakening.

The campaign of 1918 opened with a tremendous German offensive reminiscent of the early months of the war. With the armies from the eastern front now massed in the west, Ludendorf was able in successive thrusts to push the Allies back along the whole line from Ypres to Rheims, and in July there was again the threat of a catastrophic breakthrough. This time, however, there was a Foch in command with a well-planned counter-offensive which could utilize in concert the full resources of the Allied armies, and there were now fresh American troops prepared to join the attack. By the end of September most of the lost ground had been regained, and the Allied armies were still moving forward. By the end of October the vaunted "Hindenburg line" had been left behind.

The German retreat was not a disorderly rout, but to all but Ludendorf the situation was hopeless, and Ludendorf was dismissed. The army was losing not only territory but also vast quantities of equipment. Soldiers were surrendering with scarcely a show of resistance, and men on leave at home were not returning to the front. With the capitulation of Germany's last ally there was a further threat of invasion through

Austria. On November 7 the ineffective civilian government, which had been clumsily manoeuvring for acceptable peace terms, requested an armistice. On November 9 the Kaiser abdicated, and on the 11th the armistice was signed. The war was over and the revolution had begun.

The German revolution was not a bloody one. It flared up first as a revolt among the seamen in the northern ports and spread rapidly to Berlin and other major cities. There was confusion, but not chaos. Red flags were waved, officers were disarmed, "soldiers' councils" were organized after the pattern of the Russian "soviets," and there was some rioting in the streets. On the whole, however, the extremists were kept under control, and the transition from a militaristic monarchy to a parliamentary democracy was effected with characteristic German orderliness. An exhausted but relieved German people settled down to repair the damages of war.

Through the barbed wire of Ruhleben the prisoners were able to watch some of the drama of the revolution. The following, written in 1936 by one of the group, is particularly interesting.

Superficially [in early November, 1918] there was no sign of weakening and even after the High Seas fleet had mutinied, and it was apparent that sooner or later Berlin would revolt, discipline remained almost intact. It took nearly a week for the revolution to reach Berlin, and meanwhile one district after another went over.

The position was tense.

Every day we were marched out onto a field for a roll-call, and the German Army had never succeeded in making us form fours to its satisfaction. The first admission of pending events which I detected was during the critical week. One day, as we straggled out to be counted, a N.C.O. shouted "Nun, doch noch ein Bisschen Ordnung."

Then one day a few hundred insurgent sailors in Hamburg boarded an ordinary passenger train for Berlin, along with the usual load of civilians. At a wayside station an officer assembled a few loyal soldiers and some school-boys with machine guns, but they refused to fire on the train with the mixed load. On arrival in Berlin the sailors were interned in barracks, but the seed was sown.

The socialists organized the revolution well and there was little bloodshed. There was sporadic sniping from housetops for some days afterwards, but remarkably few casualties.

On the day of the actual revolution in Berlin (Nov. 9) trains, telephones and other services continued to function throughout. The trains passing Ruhleben to Berlin were crowded with jubilant workers, many riding on roofs, buffers, etc. . . . There was an atmosphere of rejoicing and of holiday like that of November 11 in England. . . .

On the 9th November, in the morning, the Ruhleben soldiers met and elected their Soldiers' Council or Sovjet, which took charge. With the exception of one temporary lieutenant the officers remained loyal. Through a window I watched this lieutenant (an ex-schoolmaster) making up his mind what to do, and eventually he came out into the yard and joined the revolution.

Other passages in the same account tell of the skill with which the revolution was carried through, "a greater triumph of German organizing ability than was the mobilization of 1914," of the warmth of the writer's welcome when he was permitted to go to Berlin, and of the evidence of great hardship which he observed everywhere. His own judgment was that the German civilians had suffered far more than had the civilians in England.

Life within the camp. On Saturday, November 9, 1918, two days after the petition for an armistice and two days before its signing, Denton's diary includes the following notes:

Revolution in Berlin; Kaiser abdicates; Berlin in Socialist hands; fear of mob attacking camp; private view of Art Exhibition by Goodchild and Moloney, paper by Ransom on "Restoration Tragedy."

A week earlier a group of men were taking matriculation examinations, a new "open stack" system was being inaugurated in the prison library, there had been two chamber music concerts, a play was in rehearsal, and the football competition was still in full swing. Perhaps these items illustrate, as well as anything could, the state of mind in Ruhleben during the closing days of the war. The prisoners knew perfectly well that liberty was now assured, yet they continued with the business of living; not, it is true, without a great deal of excitement and a fair amount of confusion, but with no major break in self-discipline. This was not the behaviour to be expected of a group that had lost its morale; but neither did it suggest a group of men who were still vigorous and full of fighting spirit. In 1918 everyone was weary of the war, including the Ruhlebenites.

A simple chronology of the events of 1918 would make for dull reading. For the most part, until the final weeks, life went on very much as it had during the previous two years, with the activities of a fairly well settled society perpetuating themselves with only minor variations. With the exception of a major overhauling of the political structure of the camp, few of the changes that took place were initiated from within. It would consequently seem best to review quickly the factors which contributed most to the maintenance of social stability, and then to look more closely at the conditions and events responsible for Ruhleben's gradual loss of vitality.

That Ruhleben survived as well as it did bears witness to its essential healthiness as a society, for during 1918 it was subjected to greater stress than at any previous period in its history. Part of its strength may be attributed to its leadership, but not necessarily to the official camp representatives. These, as the record shows, did not all win their positions through demonstrated merit, and there is considerable evidence to suggest that their performance was not beyond criticism. In fact, one of the morale-strengthening developments during those difficult months was the growing protest against the existing camp administration, and against Powell in particular. Complaints which had been quietly circulating for some time were openly presented at a meeting of the Constituent Assembly in March. Wrangling continued throughout the spring and summer, with many meetings and numerous warmly debated proposals for a new constitution. At the end of August Powell announced his resignation, and a legal committee was formed to review the old constitution and draft a set of amendments. After nine meetings the committee presented its report on September 22. A vote on the amendments was taken on September 28, and the amendments were rejected. October 14 was set as the date for the election of a new camp commandant. Meetings were held, candidates made speeches, 1,700 ballots were cast, and Powell was re-elected by a thumping majority. Probably some administrative reforms were secured as a result of the agitation, but the impressive fact is that, with the war visibly in its final stages, the men could show such lively concern about the management of the camp. Exactly two weeks after the election, a committee was appointed to supervise the camp's dissolution.

The real leadership of Ruhleben was to be found among the men who initiated and supported its multifarious activities, but one's impression is that by 1918 these leaders had already made their most substantial contribution. Some of the same names keep cropping up in the records, as lecturers, captains of teams, directors of plays, but by this time the major activities of the camp had become to a great extent self-sustaining. This very absence of the need for visible leadership may in fact be the best indicator of Ruhleben's basic stability. Not only had the simple procedures of everyday living been fairly well reduced to routine, but there were now institutionalized ways of engaging in almost any kind of activity. When the season for football had arrived, the officials were ready to take over the job of allocating practice times and scheduling games; for those who wished to go to church, there was an allotted time and place for the service, and someone had arranged for a preacher; concerts were announced in advance, and people knew where to line up for tickets. For every activity there was at least one committee, and when conflicts occured there was an established procedure whereby further committees could be set up to resolve them. As one reads the record one almost wonders if any little corner of life remained for which there were no sound traditions and sensible rules.

Ketchum has described in detail the major activities of the camp: the organized sports, each played in its own season; the theatrical productions; the concerts; the religious services; the publications; the lectures; the school, with its varied curriculum and its examinations. All continued until shortly before the end, interrupted only by a serious influenza epidemic in July which prostrated more than half of the men. Participation in some of the activities dropped off, owing in some cases to diminishing interest, in others to the departure of key individuals; but no major activity was actually discontinued. In fact, the football teams were still competing for the championship on November 2, and between September 15 and the end there were six different theatrical productions, the last, a play named *Romance*, being presented on November 4, just three days before the Germans petitioned for an armistice. Comments on the play ranged from "very well done" to "utter pizzle"; one man had to forego it because, as he complained, he had to finish correcting his English test papers. There was one variation in the pattern of camp activities which Ketchum thought might have some psychological significance. The final year witnessed a noticeable increase of interest in the arts and crafts, and during the summer months more and more of the prisoners were devoting their spare time to the growing of flowers. Was this, Ketchum wondered, symptomatic of a wish to withdraw from the bustling life of the group?

Ruhleben's basic strength lay, it would seem, in the fact that so much of its life had become solidified into routine and tradition. This may or may not be regarded as an admirable state of affairs, and I plead guilty to the charge of over-simplification for the sake of making a point. Life in Ruhleben was certainly not as utterly dull and predictable as my picture might suggest. Nevertheless, had it not been for its firm foundation of accepted and respected ways of doing things, Ruhleben might not have been able to survive the stress of those final months. And the stresses were many and powerful.

The most jarring single blow to morale, Ketchum believed, was the departure of the 45'ers. Since early in the war, it will be recalled, there had been negotiations for the repatriation, or at least the transfer to a neutral country, of invalids and of those too old for combat service. The negotiations had dragged on and on, with recurrent waves of rumour but almost no visible achievement. In January, 1917, there was a token transfer of sixteen men; then no action until August, when it was announced that invalids and 45'ers would go. Applications were filed by 1,880 men, and on December 24 came the announcement that 350 of these would be sent to Holland. As Ketchum describes at the end of Chapter 17, on January 2, 1918, the first contingent left—actually 370, fourteen of them listed as insane. This was the first massive transfer since the shufflings of prisoners which had taken place in the early days of the war. There was a farewell party the night before. Crowds assembled at 6:00 A.M. to see them off, and there was great cheering and waving of hats as the train finally chugged away at 9:30. "Are we downhearted? No!" But it was not a cheerful crowd that trudged back to resume the daily routine.

This transfer was to be followed by an intermittent series of departures, none quite as large as the first, which continued throughout the spring; and even as late as August 23 a group of eighteen was sent to Holland. The departures meant an easing of the congestion, of course, but the positive effect of this was slight in comparison with the psychological disruption which resulted. The prisoners were not only losing old friends, many of whom had played key roles in the activities of the camp and whose skills could not be replaced; they were also being made acutely aware again of their status as prisoners, with all the concomitant reminders of the loved ones at home, of the drab realities of camp life, of the uncertainties of the future. The achievement of a meaningful, absorbing life within the camp, centred about activities and plans shared with one's mates, involved almost of necessity the keeping of the outside world at arm's length; the misery of a constant yearning for the unattainable simply could not be tolerated. The alternative would have been apathy, depression, or insanity. The psychological reality of the community was thus something precious—not to be talked about openly, of course; that would be silly sentimentality—and with each new departure a little more of the feeling of community was lost.

The second great threat to morale in 1918 came from the course of the war itself. I have already mentioned that by this time the flow of information was reasonably adequate, far better than it had been during the early months of the war. German papers were available at all times and English papers were seldom delayed by more than a week or so. A thoughtful reader could piece together the opposing stories and arrive at an informed opinion. Ketchum has described the rumours which flooded the camp from time to time, wild at first and then gradually coming under control as life became more stable. During the long years of virtual stalemate on the western front the news was not such as to give rise to exaggerated rumours of tremendous victories or catastrophic defeats. It cannot be said that the prisoners lost interest in the war. They read the reports avidly, kept their maps up to date, and cheered when the news was good. But the war was becoming a sort of permanent background of living, something to talk about when the day's work was over. It was always in their thoughts, but there was nothing that they as individuals could do about it.

This was not the case in 1918. The war was beginning to thrust itself upon them again, and war-consciousness mounted with each succeeding month. Even in January, before the great German offensive was launched, they knew that it was to be a climactic year, but they had learned through bitter experience how to keep wishful thinking under control. The great German war machine was still operating in high gear, and for people living in the heart of Germany it was difficult to see how it could ever be crushed. The letters of this period were, as always, written with the censor in mind. There is a decrease in the number of references to camp events and more frequent references to the war; but the sample is a small one. The diary sample is even smaller, but the notations are much less inhibited. From these one gains two fairly consistent impressions: first, that the entry of the United States, while welcomed, was considered to be too late to be of any significance; secondly, that the sufferings of the German people were acute and that trouble on the home front was brewing. Few of the Ruhlebenites were fully confident that the summer offensive would be halted, although almost none were openly predicting a German victory; but neither did many of them foresee with any clarity the civilian revolution that was already in the making.

The effect of this increasing awareness of the war is evident in all the records, and it is easy to translate this into terms of individual and group morale. To state it first in the simplest and most superficial way, the war was literally a distracting influence. People were thinking about it more, talking about it more, finding it more difficult to concentrate on their studies. The same sort of thing happens in any community during an election or at the time of a big athletic contest. To probe more deeply, the awareness of the war inevitably forced the individual to think of himself more frequently and more concretely as an individual. Not merely, "Am I going to be killed? or am I going to starve?", although such questions may have been silently asked; but more probably, "When this is all over, what am I going to do? Will there be a job for me? Will home be the same place again?" These are all questions that emphasize the "I," and whenever "I" is substituted for "we" the cohesiveness of the group is to some extent weakened.

The third factor in the general weakening of morale in 1918 had to do with the actual conditions of living, and here it is difficult to differentiate clearly between cause and effect. In the letters, in the diaries, in the camp publications, and in the opinions voiced in later reports, there was a marked increase in general grumbling about conditions. If one were to be quite "objective" one would have to say that there were legitimate causes for complaint, but not enough to justify the very evident disgruntlement of the men. Housing was approximately what it had been for two years, less congested, slightly more worn down, but also in many minor respects improved. Food, the most frequently mentioned item, continued to be unappetizing and lacking in variety, adequate in calories, probably deficient in some of the vitamins. In the eyes of the German civilians, however, the prisoners were living in luxury. During the final months of the war the urban dwellers of Germany were on the verge of starvation. Nutritious foods were reserved for the army, and civilians were condemned to a diet consisting principally of low-quality bread, occasionally potatoes, and turnips, carrots, or beets. The German contribution to the sustenance of the prisoners had become little more than a gesture, a very small ration of almost inedible black bread, a loathsome concoction that passed for soup, *ersatz* coffee, and once in a while some greens or other fresh vegetables. The appearance of a supply of onions or tomatoes or some other delectable would cause a flurry of excitement throughout the camp, and would be duly recorded in the diaries as a noteworthy event. Ruhleben depended for its food on parcels from home, and by 1918 these were sensibly planned and delivered with remarkable regularity.

The regular delivery of parcels sustained the prisoners morally as well as physically. A parcel meant contact with home, and when the interruptions began to occur more frequently, as they did during the summer months, the grumbling became more audible. This was probably not, to any great extent at least, because of an actual fear of starvation. In certain food categories, especially in the larders of the better connected prisoners, there were surpluses which became a cause for concern as the incidence of thievery on the part of German civilians increased; and, it must be admitted, these surpluses were used by some in certain profitable black-market enterprises. In any case, although the tradition of communal sharing established during the early months of the war had been notably weakened by the formation of strongly structured subgroups within the camp, no prisoner was likely to feel that in a real emergency his comrades would permit him to starve. It was probably the moral effect of the non-delivery of parcels as such, rather than anxiety about future shortages, which reflected itself in the *Stimmung* of the camp. Everyone is familiar with the gnawing disappointment experienced when day after day the postman fails to deliver the expected letter. One finds oneself irrationally blaming the postman, annoyed with the person who should have written the letter, irritated about all sorts of inconsequential things. This in intensified form was observable in the camp; there were complaints about the same old bully-beef, about the inefficiency of the Red Cross, about graft in the camp administration, about the stupidity of the home government. The non-delivery of parcels on the expected day was sufficient to start a wave of grumbling about almost anything.

Evidences of demoralization are easy to recognize when one begins to look for them, the easiest being obviously the frequency and audibility of complaints. There were no official records of attendance at church services, lectures, games, and other public events. Ketchum notes that these maintained their appeal quite well, although unevenly, the interest in games being perhaps the most dependable; but there is no way of knowing how many of the men were slipping into a general state of lethargy. Since there was no adequate psychiatric service, it is difficult to interpret such health records as were kept. Apart from the expected seasonal variations in the incidence of colds and other common ailments, plus several outbreaks of dysentery and the serious epidemic of influenza, there was no marked deterioration of general health; but the gradual decline in physical health seems to have been accelerated in 1918. How many of the cases might have been diagnosed as psychosomatic cannot be determined, but the number diagnosed as psychotic seems to have been on the increase, as was the number of suicides. The psychiatric evidence, however, is really too slender to warrant a generalization. As I mentioned above, Ketchum was tempted to see significance in an increasing preoccupation with the individual arts and crafts, as compared with group or team activities, and with the cultivation of flower gardens. This, he felt, was symptomatic of a growing individuation of behaviour, but he did not regard it as in any sense pathological.

Perhaps the most dramatic of all the symptoms of demoralization was the increasing number of escapes. "So-and-so went over the wire last night" occurs more and more frequently as a diary jotting during the spring and summer of 1918. This symptom again is difficult to interpret. Escapes had been attempted from time to time throughout the war, most of the escapees being recaptured very quickly. The guards were alert and the punishment was severe. By 1918 the prison guards were a much less formidable group, many of them old or for other reasons incapable of front-line duty, and not a few of them easily bribed. An escape was consequently not difficult to accomplish, and the chances of working one's way through to the Dutch border were better than at any earlier time. I have found no record of the actual number of attempts, but they were so common that, on August 3 for instance, an audience assembled to listen to a lecture, only to learn that the lecturer had gone "over the wire." As it happened, he was caught the next day, punished, and then returned to the camp. Even if escape was becoming more feasible, however, an increase in the prevalence of the idea of escape, in the figurative as well as in the literal sense, may be regarded as one more symptom of group disintegration.

Taking into account all the stresses to which Ruhleben was exposed during the months of 1918, my own judgment, to repeat, is that the prisoners were able to maintain the stability of their society in truly impressive fashion. This is, of course, an essentially evaluative judgment. When we review the events of those months coolly and objectively, as the social scientist should, we cannot fail to recognize the symptoms of social decay; and it is perhaps these which the sociologist and psychologist will find most instructive. The symptoms are readily apparent; one's identification of the underlying causes hinges upon one's basic theory of man and his relation to society. Ketchum planned to present his social psychological interpretation of Ruhleben in the final chapters. Since these were never written, or even outlined, the best I can do is emphasize a few of the theoretical issues which I know were uppermost in his thinking. A complete theory would have to be my own, and this I have no right to include in Ketchum's book.

But, first, a very few words about the end of the story.

The last weeks. These, roughly the period from the end of September until the last week of November, deserve a chapter to themselves, one that would parallel in detail and vividness Ketchum's account of the first weeks in Ruhleben. This cannot be written, for it would have to be based on the memories of someone who had himself lived through what must have been a period of great confusion and of varied emotions. "Denton's" jottings for September 30 include references to the war news, a note about the recent vote on the constitutional amendments, the titles of two lectures, and mention of a golf competition. Wedged among these is: "We have won the war!" A reconstruction of those days can be little more than sheer phantasy. The prisoners were obviously trying hard to keep the machinery of living going, trying to keep their emotions under control; there had been too many disappointments during those long years. Yet this time they knew, really knew, that it was almost all over.

If there had been radios, the prisoners would have been glued to them. As it was, they lined up for newspapers as they had never done before, listened eagerly for scraps of word-of-mouth information from Berlin, studied their maps again, and speculated endlessly as to what would happen next. Almost every day brought another cheering item of news. During the weeks of October the old familiar names reappeared—St. Quentin, Armentières, Cambrai, Le Cateau, Lille, Douai, Ostende—as one by one they were reoccupied by the Allies, to be replaced by less familiar names as the German armies were pushed back into territory that had been their own from the beginning. The same weeks witnessed the final collapse of resistance in the south, with Turkey, Bulgaria, and Austria-Hungary laying down their arms. And all the while the Berlin papers reported anxiously on the protracted exchanges of notes with Woodrow Wilson, Wilson remaining firm as, point by point, the German government yielded to his conditions.

The Ruhlebenites were able, too, to see behind the official news something of the unrest that was about to explode into a revolution. It was evident to some extent in increasing laxity of discipline among the guards, who failed to turn up on time for roll call and who were unable or unwilling to cope with the outbreak of petty thievery; then there were the rumours from Berlin that soldiers on leave were refusing to return to duty, that red flags were beginning to appear, that groups were organizing to overthrow the government; and, finally, there were the murmurings against the Kaiser himself which grew towards the end of October into highly vocal demands that he abdicate. The revolution itself moved with remarkable rapidity and relatively little bloodshed from the seamen's revolt to the establishment of a new government in Berlin.

Within the camp the prisoners prepared methodically against all contingencies. The committee to supervise the breaking-up of camp was formed on October 28, and evidently it did its job quite well. As the discipline of the guards began to crumble the prisoners took virtual charge of the running of the camp and eventually of its protection against possible marauders. Postal service was, of course, disrupted, and at one point the supply of hot water disappeared, but at no time were there any signs of panic or threats of serious disorder. After November 11 the Ruhlebenites were officially prisoners no longer, and were consequently free to move in and out of the camp at will. Since Berlin was still in a state of unrest, an attempt was made to limit the visits to Berlin by means of a system of passes. So many lined up at once for passes, however, and so many escaped to Berlin without passes, that the system broke down completely. On Sunday the 17th, Ketchum reports, half the camp were in Berlin, and many did not show up the next day for roll call.

Until November 23 Ruhleben continued to be headquarters for most of the prisoners. Bags were packed, the library dismantled, mementos of all sorts carefully tucked away. Those who had formerly lived in Berlin paid visits to old friends and acquaintances, frequently sharing with them their carefully hoarded food; others simply wandered about enjoying the feeling of being free, and occasionally taking peculiar delight in invading those areas of the camp which for four years had been *Verboten*. There were a few informal gatherings during the final days, but no formal meetings, no lectures, no organized games; just restless waiting, day after day, for the signal to leave. For some of the Ruhlebenites this may have been the first experience of genuine boredom since 1914.

At long last, on Wednesday, November 20, the heavy luggage was piled up for later shipment. On Thursday a thrill ran through the camp as passports were handed out. On Friday the first contingent lined up at 8:00 A.M., to be slowly loaded into dilapidated third- and fourth-class carriages, which finally rumbled out at 1:00 P.M. On Saturday, as the remaining group wandered about the camp to bid it a final farewell, a contingent of Russian prisoners moved in. Early on Sunday the last train left, carrying the last of the Ruhlebenites. The story of Ruhleben ended undramatically.

II. Implications: Sociological and Psychological

KETCHUM'S ACCOUNT OF RUHLEBEN is of primary interest, of course, to the sociologist and the psychologist, but it may also make a modest contribution to the history of World War I. Since I am not a historian, my comment on this third topic must be brief.

Civilian internment in World War I. In the perspective of history and against the background of a colossal military upheaval the fate of a handful of civilian internees may seem to be of little significance. Certainly, it was of no military consequence, and a complete exchange of enemy aliens would probably have had no perceptible effect on the course or the outcome of the war. As it happened, however, there are two reasons why Ruhleben cannot be overlooked. In the first place, the warring governments found themselves in a somewhat ludicrous position in which each side tried, honestly one thinks, to abide by a set of rules, designed with earlier wars in mind, which now proved to be utterly inadequate. The fate of the few became hopelessly enmeshed in a tangle of legalities which only a W. S. Gilbert could have described with justice. There was similar bungling, of course, in the military effort, but even the generals were forced finally to concede that they had a serious war on their hands. The story of the civilians in World War I yields a grim inkling of the fate of civilians in future wars. In the second place, information and misinformation about the state of affairs in Ruhleben received considerable attention in press and parliament and consequently played its part as a determinant of morale on the home front. For both reasons an assessment of the situation from the point of view of the insider deserves the historian's attention.

When the Ruhlebenites were originally rounded up for internment there were probably few who even dreamed that their incarceration would last for more than a few weeks: repatriation would surely be arranged promptly. It is consequently intelligible that, even after they had accepted the probability of a protracted war, there were recurring complaints that the people at home were doing nothing to secure their release. They had no way of knowing that the home government was very busy with the problem but that the problem was proving to be unexpectedly complex.

The simple fact is that at the First Hague Conference in 1899 conventions providing for the treatment of prisoners had been drafted, but no one had envisaged a war of the dimensions of World War I in which literally millions of prisoners had to be cared for. Neither side in its military planning had made adequate provisions for such large numbers, and the amazing thing is that the treatment of prisoners by both sides conformed as well as it did to the accepted code. The German record had some very black spots on it, and the food became progressively worse as the years passed, but the atrocity stories which spread so rapidly and which were so widely believed had little basis in fact. Without the International Red Cross, however, the condition of the prisoners in Germany would have been very bad indeed.

The international code provided for the internment of enemy nationals whose freedom of movement might interfere with the prosecution of the war. The purpose was, of course, to guard against espionage and sabotage and to deny to the enemy any potentially serviceable manpower. On both sides "enemy aliens," a category not easy to define, were at once officially registered but not interned. In England there were approximately 50,000 German subjects and 8,000 Germans who had been naturalized. In Germany the aliens designated as British totalled approximately 5,000. In retrospect it seems a little ridiculous that a complete exchange was not effected immediately, for with such small numbers the disparity could not have given Germany any significant advantage. Nevertheless this disparity loomed large before the legal minds of England, and this plus the troublesome problems of property rights led to a protracted exchange of notes which served to accomplish virtually nothing. A few civilians were repatriated during the first few days, particularly from England to Germany, but popular resentment was mounting on both sides and by the end of two months most of the aliens presumed to be capable of military service had been placed under severe restriction or had been sent to internment camps. In Germany the camp for British aliens was Ruhleben. In January, 1917, both sides finally agreed to release all men over 45. That month a small group were allowed to leave Ruhleben, but the "45'ers" were not released in substantial numbers until a year or more later. The final total was officially reported as 700.

Periodic inspection of the prison camps, including those for civilians, was conducted by representatives of neutral countries, a task which became increasingly burdensome as the war progressed and the number of camps increased. The worst conditions were in camps which housed prisoners from the eastern front: British and French prisoners were reasonably well housed. Ruhleben, however, was singled out for special condemnation because of the serious overcrowding and the utterly inadequate medical, sanitary, and other facilities. United States Ambassador Gerard protested to the German authorities repeatedly but unsuccessfully. As we see from Ketchum's account, conditions in the camp improved, but almost entirely as a result of the efforts of the prisoners themselves.

From the beginning the food provided the Ruhlebenites was unsatisfactory, and it grew steadily worse. The German claims that prisoners were fed as well as were their own troops were manifestly false, for the food ration did not contain enough calories to sustain life. That there was no actual starvation was due to the efficiency with which the Red Cross maintained the delivery of food packages. Deliveries were occasionally interrupted, but at no time were the prisoners denied an adequate, if monotonous, diet. In fact, by 1918 the Germans were making little more than a token contribution to the sustenance of the camp, and the prisoners were beginning to find it necessary to guard their stores of food from German thieves.

Whether or not Ruhleben has taught us any lessons about the treatment of civilians in wartime will have to be decided by the future historian. At any rate, one little bit of history has been recorded and is there to study.

Ruhleben as a society. The sociologist who studies the history of Ruhleben has before him the record of an initially disorganized aggregate of men who became organized into a viable society, a society which underwent interesting changes and which finally ceased to exist. He will ask how the transformation took place, what resources were used and what discarded, how social needs found their expression in social institutions, what maintained and what threatened the cohesiveness of the group. As a cautious scientist he will not seek in this miniature society for a prototype of all societies everywhere, for he will know that different people under different circumstances might have organized themselves in radically different ways. Ketchum has not yielded to the temptation to generalize, but a few of the more salient observations deserve re-emphasis.

One's first general observation would seem to be obvious. The society that came into being at Ruhleben did not begin as a *tabula rasa*, nor is it conceivable that any society ever has or ever will begin as a random array of unrelated and interchangeable individual units. Each individual brought with him to the camp his own past and his own anticipated future; he brought his abilities, his skills, his personal habits, his idiosyncrasies of appearance and expression; in short, he already possessed identity as an individual. Also, whether he realized it or not, he was already a member of a variety of groups; he was a Britisher, he was a seaman or a musician or a businessman, possibly he could speak German, and so forth; some of these group memberships were to become focal and some were to fade out of the picture. Furthermore, he found himself in a situation which was already structured; there were fences, guards, commands, and all the unformulated rules of living in a European culture which even the actuality of war did not suspend. Which of these "inherited" structuring factors proved to have force, which dropped out as inconsequential, and which continued to operate as silent and unrecognized organizers of the society? Only a few of these can be mentioned.

Most obvious is the fact that the group was self-consciously, and at first even blatantly, British. One might register this as merely an initial least-common-denominator basis for group identification. And, indeed, "we're British" as a unifying slogan might in a different setting have been paralleled equally effectively by "we're Irish" or "we're Muslims" or "we're members of the Women's Christian Temperance Union." A label can nearly always create a temporary feeling of unity in the group. Whether the label continues to be significant depends on either or both of two conditions: (1) The label may grow in meaning as the members of the group discover more and more bases of unity to which the label can appropriately be attached. (2) There may actually be a solid, even if unrecognized, basis for the label in the common culture of the group members.

It is evident that both of these conditions were present at Ruhleben. Certainly, for some of the men at least, "being British" was almost a new experience. They had always accepted the label, of course; they were not Frenchmen or Hottentots, and in their secret souls they knew that Britishers are somehow or other superior to all other people; but here, for the first time, "being British" became something to live up to, a code of conduct as well as a form of allegiance. Call this a stereotype if you will, and discount liberally the loudly vocal expressions of the first weeks, it was nevertheless a stereotype which became powerfully meaningful. "Are we downhearted? No!" No true Britisher will ever let those unprintable so-and-so's catch him admitting defeat; a Britisher always plays fair; there are some things no decent Britisher would stoop to;

and so on. There were probably some silent cynics, and there were certainly backsliders who broke the code and had to be punished, but there is no question that, even after the slogan had all but disappeared, "being British" continued to function as a powerful unifier and regulator of the group.

Even more interesting than the role of the stereotype, however, but even more difficult to tease out, is the structuring influence of the different elements in British culture. In a time of social upheaval behaviour patterns of all sorts may be disrupted, some of these deliberately, as in the dropping of the formal modes of address in the Russian revolution, some quite casually, as in the neglecting of the niceties of dress during a fire-alarm. Then, as life settles down again, some of the patterns begin to reappear; but which, and in what order, and why, are not always predictable. One wishes that Ketchum had been able to give us a fuller analysis of the re-emergence of a characteristically British mode of living. The first reaction evidently included the discarding of a good many social conventions which seem to be inherent in the picture of the Englishman: the reserve in the company of strangers, the class consciousness, the unwillingness to show emotion; in fact, for some of the prisoners the disappearance of social constraints produced an almost exhilarating feeling of freedom, an inconsequential example being the obvious enjoyment by some of the freedom not to shave. Yet, one by one, the ingrained habits reasserted themselves: the ritual of tea-drinking, the coat and necktie for the church service, the formality of the letter to the editor, and although the lines of class were at first almost blotted out they became more and more recognizable as the years passed. The society which survived bore the unmistakable stamp of England. One would like to think that in a freshly born society the worthless elements of tradition would be discarded and the essentials preserved. But who is to judge which are the essential elements? The Ruhlebenites were certainly forced to question the sanctity of the traditions of social class, and even as class membership regained some of its old significance there were probably few who had not gained a deeper sympathy and respect for individuals regardless of class membership. This, we would all assert, was a good thing; Englishmen had rid themselves to some extent of one of their less admirable traits. Yet class consciousness was still there at the end. Does this mean that some sort of class structure is necessary for the survival of a society? One might be tempted to think so were it not that certain other traditions, which today would be judged as trivial, maintained themselves with equal tenacity. Why, for instance, did the Englishman who could adjust himself almost cheerfully to a straw mattress on the floor continue to be shocked by the partial exposure of the human body to sunlight? Blame it on Queen Victoria? Possibly, but not a fully satisfying answer; Queen Victoria would have been even more deeply shocked by the Ruhlebenites' language. One is left with an intense curiosity as to why one tradition survives and another dies, but with no really solid facts.

Granted that Ruhleben took shape as a distinctively British society and that people with another tradition might have organized themselves in quite a different way, the fact remains that organization did take place and along lines which suggest that there may after all be something fundamental about the laws of social grouping and social action. Just as a society cannot begin as a *tabula rasa*, so the organization of a society cannot take place in a completely haphazard way. Certain forms of organization seem to be, if not inherently necessary, at least almost inevitable. If the Germans had imposed the iron hand of authority as was the case in the Nazi concentration camps, with the individual forced to cower before the threat of torture and extermination, there would have been little room for spontaneous social organization, although it should be noted parenthetically that even in the most brutal of the Nazi camps the impulse to organize was never completely suppressed. In Ruhleben the iron hand was always there as a potential threat, and one may speculate as to the extent to which it stiffened the authoritarian political structure of the camp, but for the most part the German authorities were clearly relieved to find the prisoners willing to set and enforce their own rules. The picture is consequently that of a group permitted a high degree of freedom of action within some rigidly defined limits, something like the freedom accorded the player of a game who understands and accepts its rules. Within these limits Ruhleben provides an extraordinary example of social creativity.

To extend this observation would be merely to list again, with Ruhleben's vivid illustrative material, the familiar topics discussed in any book on sociology or social psychology. From the very beginning groups began to form themselves, some of these created by the accident of the bedding arrangements, others by the discovery of a common interest, still others through active recruitment; some were small and intimate, others large and formal; some were transitory, others endured through the years of the imprisonment. Any large group such as this would presumably have gone through analogous processes of structuring, substructuring and restructuring, with leadership emerging, rules of behaviour becoming formalized, and individuals gradually being shuffled into categories which concealed more and more of their individuality. Ruhleben invites special attention, however, for two reasons: first, it was a society composed solely of men; and, secondly, it was a society with no predictable termination. The second of these is more interesting than the first.

Complete or almost complete sexual segregation is not an unusual occurrence, and its social consequences have often been studied. In Ruhleben the total absence not only of female companionship but even of its possibility was, if anything, a simplifying factor. If there had been regular visiting hours, as there are in most prisons, or if the prospect of an occasional trip to Berlin had been a reality for every man, the social life of Ruhleben might have been less creative. It would appear that the absence of women was not crippling to the society and that, even if in fact there was more homosexuality than Ketchum reports, the absence of normal sexual outlets did not have pathological consequences. In comparison with other prisons, however, Ruhleben was unusual in that all prisoners were condemned to an indeterminate sentence, with no possibility of early release conditioned upon anything that had to do with individual behaviour. Escape was, of course, always a theoretical possibility which many must have contemplated, but few attempted it and almost none succeeded. For the great mass of the prisoners the requirement was that life be lived with reference to a future which could be neither specified nor controlled. That the end was sure to come was never really doubted; that it might come soon was an ever present possibility which could by the slightest rumour be fanned into a hope; that it might be deferred for a long, long time and should consequently be excluded from present plans was the obviously "realistic" attitude to adopt. And this, in fact, is the attitude which seems for the most part to have prevailed. The prisoners learned to live in a world with an unknown future as though it were going to continue for an indefinite period without substantial change. Even during the crumbling months of 1918 there were sporting events, lectures, and plays, all of which required planning and organization, and as late as October, when the end was surely in sight, one of the burning issues in the camp was the election of new officers.

One might argue that the world we live in is always a world of uncertainty; tomorrow may bring the fatal accident or the windfall of good fortune. True, but we never really accept it; if we did, we could not survive. Life must have its stable anchorage points, and among these the predictability of a future is as essential as is the firmness of the ground we stand on. In the absence of a future we invent one, or else we collapse. The importance of temporal structuring for the understanding of individual motivation is a theme which preoccupied Ketchum and to which I shall return presently. The Ruhleben story shows vividly how crucially important it is for the survival of a society. It has often been said that a people without a history must build one out of their dreams, and the same could be said about the need for a future. Ruhleben did not begin to be a true society until its members began to plan, at first for the next few days, then for the next few weeks or months, eventually for a future which was known to have an inevitable end but which was accepted as indeterminate. From this distance it looks like a great game of make-believe in which the real world was rejected and a world of fiction accepted as reality. In a sense this is a true picture of Ruhleben, but only in the sense that the projects of today and the plans for tomorrow became in themselves intensely real. The war was never absent, but nothing could be done about it; tomorrow's game, or next week's play, or next month's examination were visible goals towards which one could direct one's energy. Thus Ruhleben became a simplified but not a distorted society, a society which defended its integrity by keeping at a distance the concerns which if allowed too much prominence might interfere with concentration on things that were accepted as real and important. Give it a Freudian name if you wish, like repression or rationalization, but it is clear that this "mechanism of defence" had much to do with Ruhleben's social creativity.

But Ruhleben's creativity seems to have involved something more than an efficiently operating mechanism of defence. Whether or not the word "morale" can be given a precise meaning it always carries an accent on the positive rather than on the merely defensive. Ketchum's account of morale at Ruhleben does not pretend to present a new theory, but the analysis he gives is richly suggestive. The morale of the camp had its up and downs. Ketchum did not invent a quantitative index, and could consequently plot no neat little graphs, but his impressionistic judgment was that, although morale undoubtedly responded to the news about the war, the major determinants were to be found within the life of the camp itself. His one attempt at quantification was ingenious but statistically precarious. This rested on a painstaking count of the use in letters and diaries of the personal pronouns "I" and "we." During the periods of high morale, notably between the winter of 1915 and the autumn of 1917, the "we:I" ratio was highest, with "I" steadily replacing "we" as morale began to weaken in 1918. Whatever the indices, however, the *Stimmung* of the camp seems to have been a palpable fact. After the period of initial confusion it mounted rapidly, maintained a high if fluctuating level until late in 1917, and then proceeded to drop. Ketchum has described in detail the conditions which contributed to the rise. These make it somewhat easier for us to speculate about the reasons for the final decline.

Students of group morale always stress the phenomenon of cohesiveness, the mental state in which individuals feel and refer to themselves as "we"; this is perhaps the *sine qua non*. The minimum condition is the recognition that "we" have something in common which differentiates us from "you" or "they," possibly a common location, a common skin colour, a common language. Anything that strengthens the feeling of "we" is capable of raising our morale, anything that fragments us into conflicting subgroups is demoralizing. Students of psychological warfare look for evidences among the troops of confidence in leadership, awareness of the enemy as a threat, belief in the rightness of the cause, absence of anxiety about the people at home, assurance that one's individual contribution is important. The individual soldier will endure limitless hardship and pour out his last ounce of energy if he deeply believes that he and his comrades, "we," are participating meaningfully in a fight against an enemy who is dangerous and evil. Morale is at its peak when the situation has been reduced to its raw elements, when the battle is on, when every man knows what to do, is fully occupied in doing it, and believes it is worth doing. Every good commander knows how to maintain morale during combat, and the breakdowns in combat morale are usually easy to analyse. To maintain morale during periods of inaction is much more difficult, for with the fading of the threat from the enemy and the lack of absorbing and meaningful activity directed towards a common goal the psychological supports for the feeling of "we" begin to weaken. The task of the psychological warfare expert, the propagandist, is to find surrogate supports. These are too well known to need repetition, but they usually involve: (1) emphasis on the enemy as still there, evil, and dangerous; (2) the injection of "meaning" into every little detail of everyday activity; (3) the elimination, so far as possible, of unpredictability. Even the assurance that the war is going to be long and hard is better than the suggestion that it might end anytime. But of these, the awareness of the common threat is by far the most potent unifier.

Ruhleben provided initially the conditions for temporary high morale —the common identity as Britishers, the common enemy (who was distasteful but not yet hateful), the absorption in the business of improvising living arrangements, the challenge to demonstrate that Britishers are never downhearted, the assurance that it could not possibly last very long; for many it was a bit of a lark, something to be talked about afterwards. The test came with the stabilization of the routine of living and the growing uncertainty about the duration of the imprisonment. Morale might have been stimulated by a "hate the enemy" campaign supported by passionate expressions of patriotism, but the energy thus generated could have had no outlet save in rioting. There is no questioning the fact that both "awareness of the enemy" and "pride in being British" continued to function as unifiers throughout the four years. The secret of Ruhleben's high morale, however, lay in the ability of the group to discover positive goals which were both demanding of energy and worth attaining. That all Ruhlebenites were aware of this is to be doubted, but certainly the cooler heads realized clearly that the only way of avoiding chaos was to discover ways of channelling activity in meaningful directions. The first of the activities, the games and some of the little projects, may have had something of the contrived and the make-believe about them; there was certainly a good deal of "whistling in the dark." The impressive thing, however, is that what may have begun in many cases as merely an escape from an uncomfortable present grew into an absorbing and rewarding life. Individuals not only discovered opportunities for the exercise of their skills and talents but even caught glimpses of worlds they had never dreamed of exploring. It would be silly to suggest that all Ruhlebenites were captured by a great common purpose, even that all Ruhlebenites shared the satisfaction of a common achievement; there were complainers, obstructionists, and even a few suicides. It would be equally incorrect, however, to ignore the fact that something like a social miracle was actually taking place, that people were *discovering*, not merely an acceptable way of living together, but a way of actualizing through the life of the group something of great value. That at least something of this feeling of achievement permeated the camp is indubitable. Ruhlebenites felt themselves as Ruhlebenites, were proud of what they had made of the camp, and in some cases were grateful for having had a priceless experience.

The story of Ruhleben raises again, but does not answer, the old question: Is the morale of a group always dependent on the presence of recurrent threats from outside? Must there necessarily be an enemy, even an abstractly conceptualized antagonist, like disease or poverty or ignorance, to unify diverse human elements into a productive and creative human group? Can positive interests and positive goals ever supplant the unifying force of fear and hatred? The ideal of all mankind as a single society would be less fanciful if we had an affirmative answer. The history of social movements provides little ground for optimism; the really vigorous movements have always been *against* as well as *for* something, and success has usually brought with it the first signs of disintegration. Perhaps the enemy, real or imagined, must be there as an ever present threat. This was certainly the case with the Ruhlebenites.

But there is something a little more encouraging that we can learn from Ruhleben. Granted that the firmness of its social structure depended in no small measure on forces from without, symbolized by the enemy, the great outburst of creative activity bore little or no relation to the enemy. Ruhlebenites became creative when, having stabilized the minimal routines of living and consequently eliminated sheer survival as a goal, they found themselves free to pursue goals that were intrinsically challenging and worthwhile. The presence of the enemy, inasmuch as this meant limitation of freedom to choose alternatives, was actually a facilitating factor. The physical cage functioned in a very real sense as a liberator.

Why, then, the decline in morale which became evident early in 1918? It was not, we have seen, because victory was assured; defeat was equally possible. It was not because of deteriorating conditions of living; packages from home were not seriously interrupted until late in the summer. Nor was there any unusual outside interference with the activities of the camp. One obviously important factor was the reduction in numbers. A good many sick prisoners had been sent home, and in January, at long last, the 45'ers began to be shipped out in sizable contingents. My own hunch, however, is that Ketchum's term, "an aging society," is more than a figure of speech. Disregarding the final few weeks when the German army was visibly in retreat and the collapse on the home front was evident, I am sure that if the war had dragged on for another year Ruhleben would have continued as a healthy society, but with steadily diminishing vigour. The institutions were sound, the leadership was competent, and there was a wealth of human resources. There might conceivably have been another great flare-up of creativity, possibly a social revolution; but in 1918 it looked as though the major themes had been played out. This was not a physical exhaustion, but rather an exhaustion of the possibilities of novel action within a restricted field. As more and more of life becomes reduced to routine, the emergence of something new and exciting becomes decreasingly probable. This happens in marriages, in the life of sequestered communities, in games repeatedly played against the same opponent; the unexpected move is seldom made. This is monotony, not boredom. Boredom may lead to an explosion; monotony may be quite comfortable, but it does not favour creativity. In 1918, it seems to me, life in Ruhleben was settling down into relatively fixed, for the most part adequate, routines. The exciting period of construction had come to an end, and the men were proud of their accomplishment. Life was by no means planless, but the stirring innovations of 1915 were now respected traditions, on-going activities which were still interesting and rewarding but were no longer adventures. Ruhleben in 1918 was perhaps a "middle-aged society," but I see no evidence that it was dying of internal disease. It was the end of the war that finally killed it.

Ruhleben and the theory of human nature. Ketchum was a social psychologist, and as such he was impatient with pedantic attempts to separate the study of man from the study of society. He was even more impatient with the psychologies which seek an explanation of man's behaviour in that of animals. Reflecting, as a psychologist, on the Ruhleben story he could never forget that the records he was analysing had to do with the thoughts and feelings of live human beings. What was going on inside them? Why did they behave as they did? One can consequently understand his intense preoccupation with the central problems of human motivation.

What can we learn from the Ruhleben story about the motives of men? Ketchum's first answer might well have been one that was suggested two thousand years ago, namely, that man does not live by bread alone. Certainly the prisoners were hungry and thirsty and sexually deprived, but it would require a great stretch of the imagination to recognize in these the motives behind the achievements of the Ruhleben group. An adequate psychology of motivation needs something more; at least, so Ketchum obviously believed.

Modern psychological theories of human motivation and of the nature of social man, as contrasted with the theories rooted in traditional religion, begin possibly with Thomas Hobbes. For Hobbes, man is by nature a creature of brutish impulses, selfish, fearful, at war with every other man, who ensures his own survival by entering into contracts with his fellows to keep the peace. Rousseau's somewhat nobler conception of man makes a similar distinction between man's original nature and the acquired patterns of social behaviour; and even the logically minded Utilitarians grounded their simplified theory of motivation in "enlightened self-interest." Thus when Darwin proposed his doctrine there was already respectable support for the conception of man as basically a simple, selfish individualist. Darwin's great gift to the psychologists was the assurance that basic human nature is in fact an extension of basic animal nature, that if we are to understand either man's intellect or his motives and emotions we must trace them back to their animal origins.

The Darwinian conception of man is that of an organism adjusting itself to its environment. To explain man's behaviour we must look first for evolutionary origins, secondly for the elementary structures and functions of the body which have survived, and finally for the ways in which these become modified through contact with the environment. During the first flurry of Darwinian excitement the search was for instincts. McDougall was the champion, with a long list of carefully described human instincts which could be identified with the instincts of animals. Freud, with less precision, also traced human motives back to instinctive origins. For both men the instincts were basically irrational, but inherently purposive. They could be modified almost beyond recognition, but the purpose remained the same. For McDougall this was a cardinal point.

The behaviourists reacted against the instincts, not because of their irrationality but because of their purposive character. Purposes, they claimed, cannot be inherited. All we have to begin with are elementary reflexes, drives, and needs, capable of being conditioned in limitless ways to form the complex superstructure of behaviour, including the behaviour which has the deceptive appearance of purposiveness. For the behaviourists the only laws that truly explain are the laws of physiology, which account for original nature, and the laws of learning. If we disregard for the moment the question of teleology, the essential quarrel between the behaviourists and the instinctivists centres about the relative weights to be assigned to heredity and environment as determiners of behaviour. It is an age-old question, which many of us today believe to be spurious and consequently unanswerable. In both camps, however, there is agreement that the springs of human conduct are to be found in primitive, irrational impulse.

To do justice both to Freud and McDougall and to the behaviourists, it must be conceded that all Darwinians recognize the importance of man's capacity for modification. Man is the most adaptive of all animals, and man's social patterns, grounded though they may be in instinct, reflex, or physiological need, may develop a potency and stability which almost assures them the status of autonomous systems. Almost, but not quite. McDougall thinks of the human sentiments, such as love or hate or the master-sentiment of self-regard, any one of which may derive its energy from a number of different instincts, as the effective directors and regulators of human conduct. For Freud the ego, which has grown from almost undifferentiated instinct and been battered into shape by continuous conflict, becomes a structure with its own individuality and its own strength, clothed in its own armour of defence. The behaviourist, too, has invented names for learned patterns of behaviour which have acquired independence and resilience. But these are all secondary and acquired. Scratch the surface of social man, put him under stress, frustrate him, starve him, torture him, as the Nazis did, and the façade of conditioned defences begins to crumble. Real human nature is revealed in its raw and primitive state; it is the hungry, thirsty, sexy, frightened beast that Hobbes described.

This was not the man whom Ketchum found in Ruhleben. True, he was frightened and aggressive, and there were times when his physiological needs were so insistent that they could not be resisted. But Ruhleben man was much more typically the man who in times of shortage shared his food with his boxmate, who cheered for his team on the playing field, who sweated over the grammatical constructions of a new language, who sacrificed hours of sleep to transcribe musical scores for the next concert. The daily routine included eating, drinking, sleeping, and going to the latrine, but these were merely incidental to the really important activities about which Ruhleben life was centred. To build a theory of human motivation about the so-called "primary" needs of man, Ketchum believed, and I agree with him, is to look at man through a medium which filters out all that is distinctively human. The alternative is to look first at man in all his puzzling and entrancing complexity, and then to build a theory that will fit all the facts.

One of the immediate effects of Darwin's cautious but revolutionary theory was to release a flood of fascinating but unreliable reports of the impressive intellectual achievements of animals, all designed to show how narrow the gap is between man and his animal cousins. The excesses of the "anecdotalists" became such a threat to the sober progress of science that the great English biologist, C. Lloyd Morgan, was led to caution his colleagues sternly against the danger of anthropomorphism, the tendency to read human qualities and abilities into the behaviour of animals. So far as possible, urged Morgan, let us abide by the Law of Parsimony. Let us postulate no "high" mental process where a "lower" one will suffice for an explanation. Generations of psychologists since then, faithfully recording the movements of hungry cats in puzzle-boxes, hungry pigeons pecking at bright discs, and especially hungry rats in mazes, have elevated Lloyd Morgan's Canon to the status of Holy Writ. The only truly scientific laws of behaviour, they believe, are those revealed by the hungry rat. The threat to psychological theory lies not in anthropomorphism but, to borrow a similar word from the Greeks, in *musomorphism* (there being no word for "rat" in classical Greek), the tendency to restrict one's interpretation of man to what is known of the behaviour of rats.

This is not to disparage Darwin or the Darwinians. Man is indeed an organism, adjusting itself to an environment and surviving only when the adjustment is adequate. But it would be disloyal to the spirit of Darwin if we were not to look closely at the environment to which man is adjusting, at the machinery of adjustment, and at the effects which the adjustment itself exerts on the environment. When we do this we find the musomorphic approach decreasingly satisfactory.

I happen to find the Darwinian framework a little constricting, as did Ketchum, but it is possible to work within it. In Darwinian language, then, motivation might be regarded as the process or processes whereby behaviour is initiated, sustained, regulated, and directed. For the initiating states we have a wealth of terms, such as instinct, drive, and need. Let us settle for the simplest, i.e., need. Two classes of need have been recognized: a need may be either a simple deficiency of some organic substance, e.g., water, calcium, or Vitamin A, which is necessary for maintenance of the organism in its optimum condition, or a deficiency which has somehow or other signalled itself as a "need for" something. The two are regularly confused. A water deficiency quickly signals itself through well-known mechanisms and becomes in motivation a "need for" water (thirst), but there are many organic deficiencies, e.g., Vitamin A, which either do not signal themselves at all or do so in a way which is not yet understood. When we speak of elementary physiological needs we usually refer to those which are signalled in familiar ways, such as thirst and the various hungers, and which have readily observable consequence in behaviour. Only a moment's thought, however, makes it clear that the concept of need is more complex than it might at first appear to be.

Motivated behaviour is generally conceded to have some sort of direction, and again the terminology is rich: intentions, purposes, end-states, goals. Let us settle for "goal," recognizing at once that goals may vary in specificity, strength, clarity, persistence, and possibly in still other ways. Once more we must make a distinction, one that is not always easy to explain and is frequently difficult to maintain, namely, the distinction between goals that are logically implied outcomes of behaviour and those that are psychologically contained within behaviour. Thus, reproduction may be the predictable consequence of mating behaviour and consequently listed as its goal; yet humans seldom, and animals never, mate for the explicit purpose of reproducing their kind.

Similarly with equilibrium, security, happiness, and the host of other culminating states which may fit the Aristotelian category of "final cause" but which are seldom present concretely as that which the individual is actually trying to do or achieve. If the concept of need is confusing, the concept of goal becomes quite bewildering when we begin to distinguish specific from abstract goals, immediate from remote goals, apparent from real goals, and so forth. We know what we are doing when we open the encyclopaedia to verify a date; but what is our goal when we find ourselves reading the whole article, and then turning to another, and still another, before we return an hour later to the preparation of tomorrow's lecture? We learned some interesting facts; we enjoyed ourselves; we escaped from a tedious task; we brought the dinner hour that much closer. Can we say that one of these reveals the true goal, to the exclusion of all the others? Obviously not; but we are perfectly sure that from moment to moment our behaviour was meaningfully directed towards some goal or other, and this was not some remote or abstract state, such as security, or equilibrium, or the *summum bonum*. A final *reductio ad absurdum* of any strictly logical theory of motivation might be the assertion that death, as the one and only inevitable consequence of all behaviour, must for this reason be our ultimate goal. Freud has played from time to time with the Death Instinct, but in his wisdom he has refused to universalize it.

Given the concepts of need and goal, however loosely defined, and we have the skeleton of a motivational paradigm which may be as appropriate to the men of Ruhleben as it is to the hungry rat. In all motivated behaviour we have a need or needs directed towards a goal or goals. The other two terms in my original definition, sustenance and regulation, are equally important but are subordinate to needs and goals. Directed behaviour may be sustained by anything from the injection of a hormone to the applause of a crowd, and it may be regulated through the machinery of homeostasis or by the dictates of an ethical code, but neither process can be studied outside the context of the relevant needs and goals. Broadly speaking, the psychological theories of motivation have tended to slip into one or the other of two categories: those which stress the importance of primary needs, and those which interpret motivation in teleological or quasi-teleological terms. I shall not try to reconcile the two approaches, but I think there is a more fruitful way of formulating the problem, one with which I feel sure Ketchum would be in substantial agreement.

The need-oriented approach is the one most commonly found in the text-books of psychology. For this we are indebted in part to the laboratory rat, whom we motivate to run by making him hungry or thirsty, in part to our long-standing scientific prejudice in favour of beginning with the simplest things. Hunger, thirst, and other physiological needs, are simple, dependable, almost universal; they make their appearance early in life; and when matched against other motives, the need for oxygen against the desire for a new hat, for instance, they are extremely powerful. Furthermore, as Pavlov showed with his dogs, previously neutral stimuli and responses may be linked up with them through conditioning. If we accept the physiological needs as primary motives we may lump all other motives together as secondary or derived. Few text-books state the position as crudely as this, but the essential point is that what we recognize as the goals of life can be traced back through successive stages of conditioning to the elementary needs, and thereby, explained. In the last analysis, the need generates the goal.

In the goal-oriented theories we commonly encounter some teleological language, even though the theorists themselves may insist that they are not teleologists, and this language may also include the word "need." Thus it may be asserted that all behaviour is governed by a need for security, or approval, or self-actualization, or domination. Some psychologists might prefer to classify such superordinate needs as values rather than as goals, but the point is that the explanation of motivation is sought in that towards which behaviour is directed rather than in that which originally initiates it. Among the many goal-oriented theories, McDougall's probably provides the best example, because he tried to encompass within his theory the facts of physiological need. McDougall was an enthusiastic Darwinian but, unlike Darwin, a convinced teleologist. McDougall saw the whole evolutionary process as the expression of purpose, the successive stages representing the progressive differentiation of an original *élan vital* (borrowed from Bergson) into more and more specific goal-directed dispositions (instincts), each instinct guiding the selection and specialization of its own appropriate structures. Thus the eye is literally something to see with and the teeth something to bite with; and both serve the purpose of selecting and eating food, and thereby of satisfying hunger and surviving. Purpose, according to McDougall, is not an interpretation imposed on behaviour but an observable property of behaviour, something which enters into the chain of causation. In the context of evolution it is function which determines the structure; in the context of motivation the goal is prior to the need.

This is not the place for a revival of the battle between mechanism and teleology, but I think that by looking at our facts a little more closely we may resolve the apparent conflict between the need-oriented and the goal-oriented approaches. If one were forced to take sides I should probably be cheering for McDougall, but fortunately this is not necessary. Remember that the concepts of need and goal begin to blur under scrutiny; and remember, too, that our need-oriented theorists tend to draw their inspiration from rats and pigeons. Instead of talking of need-oriented theories, let us now take a look at need-oriented behaviour. It is easy to see how for a hungry rat the goal can be the food at the end of the maze. A deficiency in the body signals itself, arouses the animal to activity which persists until the consumption of food corrects the deficiency and reduces the need. Only a few repetitions are necessary to establish a directedness of the animal's behaviour towards the food, at which time we may legitimately say that the food has become a goal for the animal. But, and this is the important point, the food is a goal for the animal only under the appropriate conditions of need. Remove the need, and it may remain a perceptual object but it ceases to be a goal. This is an example of need-oriented behaviour. Goals come into existence for the rat in response to emerging needs and endure only as long as the need is present.

This may be a little unfair to the rat, but I am over-simplifying for the sake of emphasis. So far as we know, the rat has very little imagination and is consequently incapable of envisaging remote goals. His most loyal champion, Edward Tolman, has insisted that in his modest way the rat is able to develop "cognitive maps," the reference points of which have meanings which are independent of transitory needs, but even Tolman would not argue that the rat is able to direct his behaviour according to a plan towards goals which can be attained only in the very remote future. The capacity for planning depends on the ability to divorce the goal from the immediate need, to hold it before the mind in imagination as something desirable and attainable even in the absence of need. This capacity we find in man but not, or at least only in rudimentary form, in the rat.

Let us concede for purposes of argument that purely need-oriented behaviour can exist, although McDougall would deny us even this point, that on the simpler levels of life the need literally sets and regulates the direction of the organisms; it may be characteristic of very early infancy in humans; and something like it may be observed, although very seldom, in adult humans. The fact remains that the whole story of evolution, and of individual development, is the story of the progressive emancipation of the individual from control by his needs. Just as the structures of the organism become differentiated and specialized, so the world as the individual apprehends it and responds to it becomes articulated as an enormously complex system of things, events, and persons, related to one another in an infinite number of ways. The needs of the organism do not create this world; if anything they are shaped, perhaps even created, by it. Although the adult human is always influenced by his needs, his behaviour is characteristically oriented towards goals.

The statement that man's behaviour is essentially and predominantly goal-oriented is nothing but a descriptive statement of fact. It is a teleological statement in that it involves the recognition of goal-directedness as an observable phenomenon, co-ordinate with the other phenomena of nature. It may, or may not, lead to a belief in a transcendent or an immanent purpose in the universe; but such a conclusion should not be allowed to interfere with the discipline of scientific observation. It is an irresistible fact of observation, it seems to me, that the whole pattern of man's behaviour is a pattern of directedness towards goals—immediate goals, remote goals, and still more remote goals. There is, of course, a limiting and regulating harness of habit, which James called "the enormous fly-wheel of society," but the habits themselves are for the most part useful residua of earlier goal-directedness. Habit can indeed act as a check-rein on creativity, as it may have acted in Ruhleben during the decline of 1918, but when the simpler procedures of living have been reduced to routine man becomes free to plan for the future. This is certainly what happened during the creative years of 1915–17.

Even if we recognize the goal rather than the need as the key to the understanding of man's most distinctively human behaviour, the need-theorist might still argue that needs are both ontogenetically and phylogenetically prior to goals and are therefore fundamental to an explanation of motivation. There are two ways of answering the argument. The first is by challenging the sanctity of genetic explanations, and thereby risking the wrath of the unreconstructed Darwinians and Freudians. This is not nearly as heretical today as it was only a few years ago. The second is by looking again at the needs of man, but this time within the context of specifically human motivation. One's first observation is that in everyday human activity the goal may actually create the need. We are trying to communicate an idea and we "need" just the right expression; we need a coin of the right dimensions to make the telephone call; the soup needs a little more salt. In each case something initially neutral becomes instrumental with reference to a goal. Needs of this sort keep coming into existence at every moment of waking life, and in almost every case the need derives its meaning from the prevailing directions of behaviour.

But in using the word "need" in this way have we not subtly changed its meaning? Are not the physiological needs somehow or other different and more basic? The answer is no, if we continue to accept the distinction between an organismic deficiency and an active need. The "need for" water comes into existence only as a result of a water deficiency. In a hypothetical environment which automatically provided a constant temperature and a constant supply of water, calcium, phosphorous, and all the other constituents of the body, there is no reason to believe that physiological needs would ever develop. Some such environment may be there for the embryo, but it does not last long. At birth the environment suddenly and dramatically creates deficiencies which generate needs; and a different environment might generate quite a different set of needs. But after all, one might ask, cannot we say that the organism really needs some substances, and not others; calcium, for instance and not helium? Only, we answer, if to the word "need" we add "for adequate growth," "for optimum functioning," "for survival," or for the attainment of some other presumably desirable goal; and this would indeed open the door to a teleology. Let me repeat that there is nothing inherently reprehensible in teleological explanations. If we wish, however, to keep our science as dispassionately descriptive as possible, the simplest procedure, it seems to me, is to give up the notion that human motivation can be explained away as a flimsy superstructure of secondary goals piled on an insecure foundation of primary needs, and to think of need and goal instead as essential characteristics of every motivated act. Needs, or their synonyms, may be the more useful terms when we talk about rats in mazes or babies in cribs, but when we attempt to understand the motives of men as they confront the problems of living in a complex world it is the goals towards which they are striving which make their behaviour meaningful. This is not the whole story, of course, but without a hint as to what it is a person is really trying to accomplish his behaviour remains a mystery. The study of rats does not yield much insight into the patterning of human motives. It is a good thing that once in a while we find a psychologist who is willing to look at and wonder about the motives of people.

I have dwelt at length on the problem of motivational theory because Ketchum was impatient to the point of exasperation with what he considered to be the over-simplifications of the behaviourists. For him the men of Ruhleben were a living refutation of any psychology that would explain away human beings as though they were slightly more complicated but less disciplined laboratory rats. He did not give us a theory of his own. He was undoubtedly influenced by Freud, but found the basic

Freudian concepts confused and the jargon cumbersome. He felt a good deal of kinship with Asch and with Sherif, and his general approach was close to that of some of the more recent writers on psychological phenomenology. Perhaps this is why we always found it so easy to communicate. At any rate, his more or less phenomenological approach to the analysis of motivation can be extended to his treatment of two or three other themes which keep recurring in his account of Ruhleben society. These have to do principally with the psychological structuring of the individual's world, particularly in its temporal dimension, and with the meaning of individuality as such. Since he has expressed his ideas quite clearly in the context of the specific topics he has discussed, I need do nothing more than attempt a brief reformulation.

When we emphasize the importance of goal-orientation in the theory of motivation we are by implication recognizing the importance of the temporal structuring of behaviour. This would seem so obvious as to need no further comment; in every study of behaviour, whether of animals or of humans, we use time as one of our co-ordinates. But this is not what Ketchum is concerned about. It was time as a set of reference points within the stream of day-to-day living which became so vitally important for the Ruhlebenites, time which has a structured past and which thrusts itself forward, as it were, in search of a structured future. Most of our psychological studies of the perceptual world have dealt with the qualities and configurations of objects in space, partly perhaps because vision is the most highly developed and the most accessible of the senses, and because most of the objects we deal with are presented visually, partly because psychological time is so difficult to study under conditions of experimental control. The familiar phenomena of "object constancy," whereby perceived objects tend to retain the same apparent size, shape, colour, and position in spite of fluctuating conditions of stimulation, are nearly always visual objects in visual space; and, although visual percepts have temporal properties, these are seldom their salient characteristics.

The temporal analogue of the perceived object is the perceived event, and the principles of perceptual organization ought to apply as truly to the structuring of events as they do to the structuring of objects. Students of the psychology of perception are now paying more attention to the structuring of psychological time than they have in the past, and this is leading to what may possibly prove to be a fruitful reformulation of the whole problem of perception. The most challenging contributions to the study of perception have undoubtedly been those of the Gestaltists. Their preoccupation with visual phenomena, however, tended to give us a somewhat flat, diagrammatic picture of the perceptual world, and even Lewin's conception of life-space leaves us with the impression of life as a series of successive cross-sections of static relations. This was not intended, of course, and those of the Gestalt principles which have stood the test can be readily adapted to a psychology which takes the temporal dimension more fully into account. This, however, is likely to be a psychology in which the traditional categories of perception, memory, and imagination will have lost their distinctiveness and will have become integrated with the processes which have traditionally been listed under the separate heading of motivation.

But to pursue this line of speculation farther would lead us away from Ruhleben. Ketchum's emphasis on the importance of temporal structuring, on what was almost a compulsion in some of the men to order their lives with reference to some sort of future, is another reminder that in Ruhleben we are dealing with humans and not with animals. The simpler the animal, the more closely his behaviour is bound to the immediately here and now; and this, one might remark parenthetically, is also true of simple men. Man's great evolutionary achievement has been the ability to transcend the immediately here and now, and this does not mean merely the ability to respond to more and different stimuli in the physical environment, or even the ability to manipulate the physical environment, both of which are of prime importance. It means the ability to live in what in old-fashioned language we have called a world of ideas, and this is a world that extends far in space and in time, and may vary from person to person in entrancing ways. John Locke once wrote, "Each man's mind has some peculiarity as well as his face that distinguishes him from all others." Animals too show their individual idiosyncrasies, but far more than in his face a man's uniqueness is to be found in the world he has come to live in.

The Darwinians speak of the adaptation of a species to its environment, and the parallel psychological term is adjustment. We are pleased with the child who is well adjusted in school, and we are amazed by the success with which the Ruhlebenites adjusted themselves. But to speak of adjustment without specifying to what the adjustment is being made and what changes it has involved is to say virtually nothing. The Ruhlebenites were adjusting themselves, fairly efficiently and without a great deal of grumbling, to the food, the housing, and the various restrictions of the camp; but this tells us little of the really interesting adjustments that were taking place. Each man was to some extent learning to live in a new world, and for some it was a larger and more exciting world than he had ever known before. In one sense, the Ruhleben story tells us nothing more about the kind of psychological world a person is living in than we ought to be able to learn from the careful observation of any person under any set of circumstances. In laboratory studies we try to keep as many conditions as possible under control without destroying the phenomenon we are observing. This becomes more and more difficult as we focus on complex social interactions. In this sense, Ruhleben became perforce a sort of social laboratory; not an ideal laboratory, it is true, but one in which under more or less specifiable conditions human beings could be observed playing out their roles as real human beings.

Just a few final words about the conception of individuality suggested by the Ruhleben story. Apart from an occasional thumb-nail sketch, Ketchum avoids the analysis of individual persons. This reflects in part his concern for the preservation of anonymity; he obviously did not regard individuals as interchangeable elements in the group, each endowed with the same basic human nature. One thing that impressed him deeply, however, was the importance in the make-up of the individual of social role and psychological group membership. The concept of social role harks back to the social psychology of G. H. Mead, and it involves more than the picture of a person merely playing a part on a stage. One's role includes one's pattern of goals and values, and these may become so "internalized" that the role becomes an essential part of one's self. Roles may shift, of course, and one may gradually grow into or grow out of a role. In many an instance in Ruhleben an individual found himself forced to accept a new and sometimes distasteful role which with the passage of time finally became a part of himself.

Similarly with psychological group membership. Every prisoner entered the camp as a member of one or more sociologically definable groups—he was a seaman, a musician, a Londoner, a university man, and so on; and these groups could be clustered or sub-classified in many different ways, all of them meaningful. During the first day he was arbitrarily thrust into another group, which might be a box or a barrack, also to be classed as a sociological group. A sociological group becomes a psychological group as the individual begins to feel himself a part of it, the first test being the spontaneous use of the pronoun "we." As in the case of the social role, Ruhleben does not add much to the basic theory of psychological group membership, but the story is richly illustrative. Some of the sociologically defined groups, notably the seamen, were psychological groups from the beginning and continued as such throughout the years of the internment. Within the dwelling units, what were initially heterogeneous collections of individuals sometimes developed the solidarity of families, sometimes remained heterogeneous to the end. There was a steady shuffling and reshuffling, very lively at first, as new bases for grouping were discovered. In many cases what began as a quite casual group, the membership of a barrack, for instance, became powerfully unified by something as incidental as its football team and actually developed a public image of itself. This is not to suggest that all of life at Ruhleben was uniformly and enthusiastically "groupy." Ketchum was a sociable type himself, and probably tended to overlook many individuals who withdrew into solitude; but the crystallization of so many genuinely psychological groups based on such widely different criteria, many of them quite new to the individuals concerned, is still a fascinating story. It emphasizes once again how much of one's individuality is to be recognized in one's unique pattern of psychological group memberships.

The over-riding group membership which was evidently shared by nearly all was Ruhleben itself. The growth of Ruhleben as a society was something of a social and psychological miracle, undoubtedly not unique in history but probably never before recorded with such care and insight. One wonders about the subsequent history of the group, and Ketchum was unable to ferret out the necessary facts. A post-war Ruhleben Society was formed, with annual dinners and a good deal of continuing correspondence, but the membership has dwindled to a mere handful. A man who was 40 in 1914 would now be 90. One cannot help wondering about what happened to the 4,000-odd individuals who fifty years ago were dumped helter-skelter onto a race-track near Berlin and forced to live together for four years. We know now a great deal about their lives during those four years. But what did they carry away with them from Ruhleben? What difference did it all make? We shall never know the full story.

JOHN DAVIDSON KETCHUM
1893-1962
D. O. Hebb

ON APRIL 24, 1962, John Davidson Ketchum was released from a severely crippling illness that he had borne for five months with courage and good humor. He had retired in 1961 from his professorship at the University of Toronto to be able to give full time to his writing and the completion of the book that was his life work, but in the minds of his colleagues and former students he was still very much part of the University, and his death leaves a great gap in psychology at large in Canada.

Dave Ketchum was born at Cobourg, Ontario, son of Judge Jay Ketchum and Margaret (Davidson) Ketchum. After two years at the University of Toronto (Trinity College) he decided to make his career in music, and left in 1912 to study in London and Germany. He was in Germany when war broke out, and was interned in Ruhleben Prison Camp with 4000 others for the four years of the war. The camp did not operate in the same way as some of the German prison camps did in the Second World War, and a good deal of autonomy was permitted the prisoners—but still as prisoners. The reactions of the miniature society thus arbitrarily established, the modes of organization that were generated and the impact on the individuals concerned, caught and held Ketchum's mind. At the time of his death a book was near completion.

On his return to Canada, Ketchum completed his undergraduate work at Toronto, in English and History. For some years he continued to make music his chief interest in life, as teacher and choirmaster, but social psychology and sociology had caught his attention by now, probably because of Ruhleben. He thus undertook advanced work in both fields, at Toronto and later (1932–33) at the University of Chicago. He did not obtain the Ph.D., for the thesis was to have been the book on Ruhleben, and the book went slowly. Back at Toronto he was made Assistant Professor in 1934, and married Dr. Katherine H. Dawson in the same year. They have two children, a son and a daughter.

In 1950 he became full Professor, and was elected President of the

Canadian Psychological Association. Then he gave six years of his professional life (1953–58) to editing the *Canadian Journal of Psychology*. In his own writing he had compulsively high standards that delayed publication of his book, and account for his relatively small output of scholarly papers (some twenty in all). To the editorship he applied similarly high standards, but not merely by rejecting papers. He rewrote many, some almost *in toto*, working long hours to the virtual exclusion of everything but his teaching. In this undertaking he raised the whole status of Canadian psychology, and under his hand the *Journal* developed in literary quality and in scientific significance, to become widely read and consulted throughout the world.

I did not know Ketchum in the role of teacher and lecturer at the University, only as scientist and editor and colleague at meetings, and I have permission to quote from a resolution of Senate, University of Toronto (moved by his colleagues Professors Myers and Bernhardt), that my account may be more complete:

"As a lecturer, he was always stimulating, often brilliant. . . . He presented his material with the artistry of a composer and the dramatic skill of an accomplished actor. He was meticulous in assessing the efforts of his students. For thirty-five years, he taught them to be skeptical of the cliche, to question assumptions, to cherish clarity and to write plainly. . . .

"He maintained a dual devotion to both serious music and serious psychology. . . . In moments of relaxation, he enjoyed combining the two in songs of biting satire about psychology and psychologists. The entire history of the Department of Psychology at Toronto is documented by a series of such songs and parodies composed by him and rendered to his own accompaniment, and in his own dramatic style, before successive audiences of delighted colleagues and students."

To this I must add, what may not have been appropriate for a Senate resolution, reference to his widely known and virulant social commentary of the depression years, "Hymn to the Glory of Free Enterprise." He was no mere academic but a discerning critic of the society in which he lived, and of which, on many counts, he heartily disapproved; but he was an academic too, and an equally discerning critic of the false, the pretentious, and the obtuse in present-day psychology.

INDEX OF SUBJECTS

INDEX OF NAMES